MAN/child

MAN/child

*An Insight into Child Sexual Abuse
by a Convicted Molester,
with a Comprehensive Resource Guide*

by

Howard Hunter

McFarland & Company, Inc., Publishers
Jefferson, North Carolina, and London

British Library Cataloguing-in-Publication data are available

Library of Congress Cataloguing-in-Publication Data

Hunter, Howard, 1930–
    Man/child : an insight into child sexual abuse by a convicted
molester, with a comprehensive resource guide / Howard Hunter.
        p.   cm.
    Includes bibliographical references and index.
    ISBN 0-89950-528-7 (lib. bdg. : 50# alk. paper) ∞
    1. Child molesting—United States.   I. Title.
HQ72.U53H84   1991
362.7′6—dc20   90-52509
                                                                    CIP

Manufactured in the United States of America

McFarland & Company, Inc., Publishers
  Box 611, Jefferson, North Carolina 28640

This book is dedicated to my son, Howie III,
who gave me unfaltering support and love and who
must continue to suffer the sins of his father
throughout his life.

To Margo V., whose encouragement helped to make
this project a reality and who truly defines
the word "friend."

To "Bud," whose opportune and sincere guidance and
research abilities enhanced *MAN/child*.

A note of thanks to "Chuck," a very special person
and one to whom I entrusted the responsibility
of the rough draft typing of this book.

There is an old printers' saying, "Follow the copy
though it fly out of the window."
Mistakes, faults, omissions . . . they are mine. There would be
more except for the editorial abilities of
Virginia Hege Tobiassen. Thank you.

My heartfelt gratitude to those fellow inmates
who responded to my questions, initially with anger,
indignation or cautious anxiety,
and who then greatly helped in the development
of my ideas and thoughts.

Contents

"Once we perceive, question and challenge the existence of the sexual abuse of children, we have taken the first crucial step toward the elimination of the degradation, humiliation and corrosion of our most valuable human resource—our young." Florence Rush, 1980

Introduction:
Why This Study?

Once the initial shock of my arrest for child molestation had abated somewhat, I started thinking of what I had done and what caused this obvious malfunction of normal human behavior. It took several weeks before I even admitted to anyone that I was guilty. I then figured I had best do some studying to try and determine why I walked this road to self-destruction. In my research I found that scores of books and pamphlets for children and their parents were just not complete enough to really help prevent child sexual abuse. I hope that *MAN/child,* almost four years in preparing, will fill the need for parents and other interested parties to understand the insidiousness and the motivations of child molesters.

The sexual abuse of children is an unspeakable subject, but in recent years people have realized the need to speak about it. Glaring publicity, sensationalism and long-term prison sentences for offenders are now the norm. The wide variance in suspects and their diversified socio-economic backgrounds have awakened some parents and some professionals to how the danger cuts across class lines to put all children at risk.

It is my hope that *MAN/child,* as a source of information for parents and others, will disclose some of the more insidious aspects of nonviolent child sexual abuse. My goal, of course, is to save one child from this potential trauma. If I am able to warn and stop a suspect from continuing his activities, that will also further my goal. According to one report I read, stopping one suspect may save a minimum of 14 children from abuse. Another report gave a figure of 380 victims.

Please realize that not all crimes of child sexual abuse can be prevented. I wish *MAN/child* could give you all the answers and magically protect all children. It can't and I can't. While you, as a parent or guardian, have a responsibility for protection, anyone who would tell you that you hold the supreme power to protect your children from sexual abuse would be irresponsible as well as inaccurate. But your main weapon is information. With correct information we can decrease the chances of potential abuse.

In *MAN/child* you can examine and perhaps better understand the crime

1

of child sexual abuse. You will gain an insight into the motivations of suspects involved in this heinous crime; learn some possible indicators of offenders; become acquainted with hundreds of books, reports, papers and studies that have been or are currently being written; and have access to resources and areas of further assistance, as well as an extensive bibliography that includes incest and child abuse references. Once you have this information you may have a better idea of how to present this subject to your children.

A note here about incest. The sexual activities are essentially the same, but because of the special circumstances and the relationship with the suspect, many professionals treat incest as a completely different subject. Certainly I do not dispute that incest can have a profound effect and lead to serious difficulties in the child's development—but *any* sexual activity with *any* adult or significantly older person will have a traumatic effect. For this reason I have had some difficulty in clearly separating intrafamilial and extrafamilial sexual abuse.

In preparing for this study I found that most of the authors delved heavily into statistics following their interviews with victims and offenders. My contacts with fellow inmates were on a one-on-one basis and the only bottom-line statistic I can come up with is that all suspects received sexual gratification of one degree or another. Officials say that the recidivism rate of convicted sex offenders is very high, approximately 80 percent, and I certainly must agree. It is frighteningly clear when I listen to offenders that some are not about to change in their desire for sex with children. "Next time I won't get caught!" They blame the judge, the D.A., the state, the arresting officer, the victims, and their own mothers, but most refuse *just to stop!* Many offenders have spent hundreds of hours and considerable sums of money in therapy or counseling and continue their nefarious activities before and after the sessions. In one case a thirteen-year-old male victim waited in the car until the suspect completed his weekly "therapy." In another instance, an offender became friendly with another man undergoing therapy and they engaged in a foursome of sexual activity, swapping their young victims. One man admitted he used the county medical center to pick up teenage youngsters who were themselves undergoing treatment for sexual or other abuse. Remember, the molester is a con-man and has a great abundance of love and attention that he can offer a youth who needs them. A potential victim who receives no caring at home or anywhere else is easy prey for a skilled suspect.

There is certainly an abundance of victims who, for one reason or another, could be classified as "willing" victims. There are many reasons why they do not report their sexual activity with an older person, and thus the suspect can continue molesting for many years. I must state that a "willing" victim is still a victim. If he had just said "no!" (to borrow a phrase) the suspect would have gone on to another potential victim.

Any molester reading this book should be perfectly aware that it is just a matter of time until he is reported. With parents advising their children and with children themselves exposed to publicity about child molesters . . . just a matter of time. If a molester stopped right now and entered into therapy with the proper attitude, he could save himself a great deal of trouble and possible incarceration. He could be recognized as a man who realized he had a problem and took action to forestall future activity. A judge could take that action into consideration. But first the offender must be honest with himself. No matter how much you loved your victim(s); no matter how you helped and advised and counseled and how you were such an upstanding citizen, great family man, good church person, all-round Mr. Nice Guy, etc., the fact remains: you are a child molester. You must be realistic and realize the potential emotional damage to your victim and perhaps even the future damage to those he may victimize in turn.

Be aware that the paramount thought in a juror's mind is, "How long can we keep this child molester in prison?" It was not always this way. I remember a case many years ago where a scoutmaster was reported molesting several members of his troop. His reasoning was that he was instructing the boys in the "facts of life." He was warned not to do that anymore and never spent a night in jail or even a moment in custody. Today, in some geographical areas in the United States, he would be sentenced to 100 years in state prison. Also in the past were cases of child molesters who, when convicted, spent a few months in the county jail or at the road camp. Those days are forever gone.

Most states do not have a special "mentally disordered sex offender" program anymore. Some have abbreviated programs for the younger offenders but, in general, you can't get much help in a prison setting. I am told that in some states a person may voluntarily place himself into custody for a period of up to two years under a mentally abnormal sex offender program. I am not certain which states still retain this type of program.

One of the inmates I listened to went into this type of program several years ago when he was 21. He was deeply depressed, worried and uneasy with his homosexuality and had attempted suicide on two occasions. He was sent to Atascadero State Hospital in California where he was assigned a good job, had all the male sex he wanted and "graduated" as a "well-adjusted" homosexual. He felt the only thing he learned was to forget about suicide . . . that there would always be another "lover" just down the road or around the corner.

I volunteered for therapy. My psychologist has stated that we may never find out *why* I committed the acts but with continuing therapy and counseling we may be able to answer some peripheral questions. I have found, even after reading all these learned books by learned authors, that I am not as smart as I think I am. Perceptive questions and some really heavy "soul searching" are helping me to better understand my own motivations. I still can't answer why, but I feel better about it.

I mentioned public awareness earlier when I suggested that molesters stop right now. You will be caught as more and more people learn what to look for and children become aware of their rights of personal privacy. And when you are caught, you must take into consideration the hurt and embarrassment and almost irreparable damage to your own family.

As an example of increasing public awareness I can take just one day, October 25, 1988. Michael Jackson on his ABC radio call-in program featured Fay Yeager, founder of Mothers Against Raping Children, speaking from her home in Atlanta, Georgia. Mrs. Yeager stated that her husband sexually abused their four-year-old daughter and that nobody believed her. Calls came in from all over the country with mothers stating they were forced to abduct their own children and flee to another state to escape after judges had not believed their stories of sexual abuse and awarded custody of the victim to the suspect. The program focused on the gross misconduct of social agencies and judges. One caller reported that her "all–American" husband sexually molested both daughters, aged 4 and 3, and the Department of Human Services investigated and found no evidence. The judge felt she was vengefully accusing her husband as a part of their divorce proceeding and awarded the children to her husband. She took the children and set up a new life in another state.

Now, whether or not all of the stories were true, and taking into consideration that Mr. Jackson and other talk show hosts encourage issues of this type, the fact remains that the word does get out and makes people aware of such problems. Frankly, anything that makes people think has some redeeming value.

On this same date Geraldo had an NBC TV special on "Satanic rites." As a portion of this two-hour program child sexual abuse was featured. An eight-year-old Mississippi boy told of being molested by his father during Satanic rites. A five-year-old Orange County, California, girl was the victim of her father and a neighbor during similar Satanic ceremonies. Other reports involved a family minister and a ten-year-old boy and another father and other men having sex with his child in a Satanic cult. Also mentioned was killing of animals and the killing of children as a part of these Satanic rites.

All of these stories seemed too outrageous to be true, too unbelievable to be possible. Yet these same stories were repeated in various towns and cities from coast to coast.

I hope that *MAN/child* contributes to the growing public awareness about child sexual abuse. It is not written as a scholarly text or exclusively for professionals or experts in the field. It is not comprehensive, not a survey and is certainly non-technical. The resource guide and bibliography can offer more detailed information for those of you who wish to delve deeper into this subject. *MAN/child* is a highly personal book, representing my own experiences and views. I certainly cannot attempt to do justice to such a complex and complicated problem, but I hope that through information I may be able to advance the understanding of parents and other interested persons on the subject of sexually abused children and adolescents.

Taking the entire *MAN/child* study into consideration you, as a parent, should be better prepared to translate this information into warnings and danger signs for your children. It takes a psychological strength far beyond the average child's experience. They must be given this strength by you, supplemented by schools and awareness programs.

Why this study? Because I wish to redeem myself in the hearts of my victims. It is an almost impossible task. But I'm going to try.

I. Questions and Answers

Here's the first question:

Why are children molested?

The answer is: I don't know. And the answer to the last question is the same.

That's a helluva way to start and end a question-and-answer section, isn't it? But I must make it very clear that while we can answer some questions almost exactly, there are others we cannot possibly answer. I'm quite certain a psychiatrist, psychologist or self-labeled "professional" would give a firm "I know it all" response. I wish there really was an answer so that a percentage of our children and their parents would not have to face the reality of child sexual abuse.

What does child sexual abuse mean?

Child sexual abuse should not be confused with physical contacts between an adult and a child that are fond or playful expressions of love. Responsible adults automatically limit their physical exchanges with a child, thereby respecting the child and at the same time maintaining a warm, healthy, affectionate relationship.

Child sexual abuse is quite different. The child is used for the sexual gratification of an adult or significantly older person. Under most state laws a child is defined as anyone under 18 years of age.

Is sexual abuse against the law?

Yes. All 50 states and the District of Columbia identify such abuse as criminal behavior. (See the section on Definitions, Laws and Legal Aspects for more detail.)

What are the types of sexual offenses that are committed against children?

Children may be the victims of every kind of sexual mistreatment. Gary May, M.D., a child psychiatrist, places possible offenses under two general categories: nontouching and touching sexual offenses.

Under nontouching offenses, May includes verbal sexual stimulation, such as speaking about sexual acts in a way meant to arouse or shock the child; obscene telephone calls; exhibitionism; voyeurism; and deliberately making it possible (or even unavoidable) for the child to watch or hear an act of sexual intercourse.

Dr. May cites the following as touching offenses: fondling; vaginal, oral, or anal intercourse or attempted intercourse; touching of the genitals; incest; prostitution; and rape.

Most state child abuse and neglect statutes do not include all the offenses listed here.

How many children in the United States are actually abused sexually?

An exact figure for sexual victimization experiences is difficult to come by. Estimates vary considerably. The American Association for Protecting Children, a division of the American Humane Association in Denver, Colorado, using official reports of state child protective agencies, states that there were 100,000 cases in 1984 (American Association for Protecting Children, *Highlights of Official Child Neglect and Abuse Reporting,* 1984).

Studies of the incidence of sexual victimization in the general population, however, have suggested that the problem is far more widespread. One such study was conducted in 1979 by D. Finkelhor, using a sample of 769 college undergraduates. Of that sample, 20 percent of the females and 9 percent of the males reported that they had been sexually abused before their eighteenth birthday (D. Finkelhor, *Sexually Victimized Children*). Another study, conducted by D. Russell, surveyed a random sample of 900 households in San Francisco. Russell found that 16 percent of the women had been sexually abused by a family member and 31 percent had by a nonfamily member before their eighteenth birthday. Overall, 28 percent of the women had had sexual victimization experiences before reaching their fourteenth birthday (D. Russell, *The Incidence and Prevalence of Intra-Familial and Extra-Familial Sexual Abuse of Female Children*).

Despite the variance in figures, one can draw some conclusions from the studies that have been conducted so far:

• Sexual abuse of children occurs frequently, affecting large numbers of children. Perhaps even if accurate figures could be assembled, they would be so high that people would have a hard time believing them.

• Although more and more cases are being reported throughout the country, the rate of reporting still comes nowhere close to a figure that would match the incidence indicated in surveys of adults. We must conclude that far too many cases are still unreported.

• Even adult surveys may not give a fair estimate of occurrence; it is possible that some adults have repressed or denied abusive experiences they suffered as children.

Are most sexual offenses against children committed by strangers?

No. The people most likely to sexually abuse children are their own family members, friends of the family, neighbors, and acquaintances. (See "Is the suspect usually known to the victim?" p. 47.)

Does sexual abuse occur more frequently inside or outside the family?

It occurs more frequently inside the family.

What is incest?

Incest is sexual intercourse between family members. The entire spectrum of parent-child sexuality, however, may range from a mother's sleeping with her son but not engaging in sexual relations, to taking pictures of children posed for or engaged in activities to arouse sexual desire and interest, to group sexual activities with children, to torture.

How many victims of incest are there?

Dr. Kempe says that the lowest estimates based on official reports suggest that at least 1 of every 100 women has been the victim of incest. Kempe feels the number should be 2 percent or higher. But please realize these figures are very low because most cases of sexual victimization are never reported to anyone.

Father-daughter and stepfather-daughter cases account for about 75 percent of all reported incest, usually nonviolent.

Is it true that incest occurs mostly among rural, isolated, and uneducated poor families?

No. Incest occurs among all groups of the population — both rural and urban and all socioeconomic and educational levels. It may seem, just from statistics, that incest is more common in poor families because more of those cases tend to be heard in court. Probably all this statistic means is that middle- and upper-class suspects are more adept at staying out of court. Finkelhor and Baron state that sexual abuse does not seem to be the curse of any one particular class; rather it is common to all.

Are sexual offenses against children usually committed by "dirty old men"?

No. A study conducted by Vincent DeFrancis, past executive director of the American Humane Association, showed the average age of the sex offender as 31 years, with 20 percent of that group under 20 years of age. The National Crime Survey (*National Crime Survey Report,* Washington DC: Government Printing Office, 1981) states that males between the ages of 13 and 18 committed 21 percent of the forcible rapes in the United States in 1979. Other sex crimes show an equally alarming incidence in the adolescent male population. One study (S. Ageton, *Sexual Assault Among Adolescents*) suggests that physical sexual assaults (including any forced sexual contact) may be committed by as many as 5,000 to 16,000 per 100,000 adolescent males.

Are child molesters sick?

Certainly their behavior is extremely disturbed — and disturbing — but most people who molest appear perfectly normal in other ways. As in other forms of child abuse, less than 10 percent have a specific mental illness, and most do not benefit from the usual types of psychiatric care. Sexual abuse is most often a symptom of severe problems in marriage, family, and life adjustment. Effective treatment requires resocialization, emotional support, changing or controlling sexual interest or behavior, strengthening every member of the family and at the same time demanding responsibility from the parents and their protection for the children as well as alleviating the psychosocial effects of abuse on the victim. (But see "Can a molester be cured?" p. 10.)

Can a molester be cured?

The Sexual Assault Center of Harborview Medical Center in Seattle says that "most sexual offenders can be successfully treated." I have a great deal of trouble believing that. I feel we must have a strong motivation from the suspect first and his real and determined effort not to commit additional offenses. How do we get that? A couple or four years in prison ought to gain his attention. Remember, he has already had warnings of one kind or another and he still has not stopped molesting. Even more distressing, the majority of inmates I have spoken with and listened to state they will not stop molesting. This is consistent with the findings of many researchers who state that certain types of offenders, such as those who abuse boys, those who are exclusively pedophilic, and those who have an "ideological" commitment to offending, show great propensity to reoffend (G. Abel, et al., *The Treatment of Child Molesters;* N. Groth and A. Burgess, *Sexual Trauma in the Life Histories of Rapists and Child Molesters;* V.L. Quinsey, *Men Who Have Sex with Children*). One prisoner told me that he now hates children and will have nothing to do with them, ever. Very unrealistic—and it sounds to me as though he is still blaming the children for his actions.

Obviously the treatment of the sexual offender depends upon the type of problem a particular suspect presents. A small percentage are mentally ill, psychotic (out of touch with reality), schizophrenic, or senile and may respond to various psychiatric interventions or medication. Another group includes the sadistic offender who must physically harm the child during the offense. These suspects have a general pattern of violence and criminality and are usually unresponsive to treatment; in most cases they must be incarcerated. A percentage of offenders are teenagers who are not only committing sexual offenses but are struggling with the normal conflicts of adolescence and require individual and family intervention. There are pedophiles that have no adult sexual preference at all and are very difficult to reorient toward normal adult sexuality. The remaining group of offenders are those most responsive to specialized treatment, since with these men the sexually deviant arousal is a secondary sexual preference and the suspects also have normal outlets with adult partners.

Some offenders are so compulsive and unable to control their behavior in the community that they must be treated in an inpatient facility. Others are so untreatable, in terms of accepting responsibility for their behavior, that they must be in an environment which is totally structured to effect a complete resocialization process. Western State Hospital, a Washington state mental hospital, has sex offender programs designed for this type of offender and those with other contributing problems such as chronic alcoholism. The offender may be sentenced there for a 90-day evaluation. If it is then recommended that he be treated in the program he can be sentenced there for a minimum of 24 months. Those who are not amenable to treatment will be sent to prison to protect the community.

All offenders should be evaluated by trained professionals who can determine the meaning of the suspect's behavior, determine the risk of repetition and then recommend the type of treatment plan that should be conducted. This treatment should attempt to eliminate any deviant arousal pattern, confront and correct the morally wrong ideas and attitudes of the suspect, and direct him to appropriate and responsible behavior.

Not so many years ago, so-called treatment centers (usually a room in a prison hospital) used a blast of electricity to a suspect when he displayed incorrect arousal patterns. Fortunately, that method has given way to more sophisticated treatment modalities.

A. Nicholas Groth, William F. Hobson and Thomas S. Gray, writing in *Social Work and Child Sexual Abuse/Journal of Social Work and Human Sexuality* (Jan.-Feb., 1982), suggest that "treatment" may be defined as any type of intervention designed to reduce, prevent, or eliminate the risk of a child molester again committing an offense. Change is necessary, either in the "internal psychological predisposition of the suspect; in his external living environment; or in both." The goal of any treatment should be control—either self-control by the offender, enabling him to overcome his pedophilic urges, or control by an external source. Groth, Hobson, and Gray offer four basic treatment modalities aimed at developing controls over pedophilic urges:

1) Chemotherapy. Various antiandrogen hormones, such as Depo-Provera, have been shown to have a moderating effect on sexual aggressiveness and enhance self-regulation of sexual behavior. Although the use of Depo-Provera in the treatment of sexual offenders is still in the experimental stages, it does offer promise as a chemical control of antisocial sexual behaviors such as pedophilia. 2) Behavior Modification. Another approach in working with child offenders is to address the specific behaviors associated with the offense and, through a series of conditioning exercises based on learning principles, to diminish sexual arousal to children and enhance sexual responsiveness to adults. Progress is monitored by physiological measurements of erection responses to relevant stimuli. This modality attempts to change the clients' sexual preferences by making aversive those sexual behaviors which are outlawed and by replacing them with more socially acceptable sexual behaviors. 3) Psychotherapy. This modality encompasses a wide range of approaches based on interpersonal interaction and views the offending sexual behavior as symptomatic of internal emotional conflicts which can be resolved through achieving awareness and better understanding of the underlying issues. Through such introspection the offender is expected to arrive at better controls over his sexually inappropriate behavior. 4) Psychosocial education. The modality views sexual offenses to be the products of defects in human development and attempts to remedy such defects through a combination of re-education, resocialization, and counseling. The aim is to alert the offender to the life issues that stress him, to either find ways of avoiding such stresses or develop life management skills

to better cope with such demands; and to self-observe and recognize character-
istic early behavior or warning signals that indicate he is moving towards a
repetition of his offense.

Dr. Groth and his group have stated that "no single method of treatment
of a type of therapeutic intervention has proved to be a totally effective
remedy. Treatment has to be tailored to the specific needs and abilities of the
individual client." They also state that, in a minimum, three major issues (aggression, sexuality and interpersonal relations) must be addressed in any program of treatment or rehabilitation. They feel there are two basic options in
regard to disposition of child molestation cases: 1) incarceration, or 2) treatment in an outpatient program. I certainly agree with their view that in any
outpatient program, probation or parole should always be stipulated as a condition.

All of the treatment programs as well as groups and individual therapy
can only work if the suspect really wants to change. To my mind, a very good
reason to change is the threat of returning to prison.

Should all child molesters go to prison?

The Drs. Kempe state that first-time borderline offenders should not
necessarily be criminally prosecuted when prompt disruption of the contact is
made. They feel that the self-punishment of the suspect is great and the loss
of esteem and employment are in themselves punishment of great magnitude.
They go on to say that child molesters are brutally assaulted in prison and I
can certainly attest to that. (I can also add that there seem to be various
"classes" of molesters in prison society: the baby killers and rapers are the
lowest of the low, with the violent and seemingly unrepentant molesters next
up, followed by the nonviolent grouping.)

However, I find it hard to believe that without jail time, a suspect who
has molested several children over a period of years really will suddenly cease
all activities and change his environment, perhaps change jobs and in general
start all over again to be a good, lawful citizen. The suspect has already received
several warnings of one kind or another. He should, first of all, be aware that
what he is doing is against the law. And every time he sees or hears a radio or
TV spot telling children what to do if they are "uncomfortable" with a touch,
or reads a newspaper article about a man arrested for molesting, he should take
this warning. He most likely has had close calls with children who have learned
to respect improper advances. He may even have been questioned by parents
or well-meaning friends. He has ignored these alarms; the sinking feeling in
his stomach when a police car parks next door; and other ominous signs only
a molester will recognize.

This man should go to jail, for it is only while incarcerated that the real truth of one's inner being can surface. I am still undergoing analysis because I must find out why I did the things I did. Why? Why should I jeopardize a fine standing in the community — a reputation as someone who is there to help in almost any situation, active in so many charitable and worthwhile organizations? Why? I don't know. I do know that it took jail to make me stop. I do know that I will never again molest a child. It took jail, not warnings, to make me realize what I was doing was wrong no matter how I justified (in my own mind) the actions I practiced.

Now, the Kempes say "first-time borderline offenders." One objection I have to this phrase is that it's so hard to tell if an offender has really committed his first offense, or simply *been caught* for the first time. The latter is more likely, especially when you consider a study by Dr. Gene Abel which found that of 571 sex offenders against children, suspects over 18 years of age had an *average* of 380 victims. (Cited by Kenneth Lanning in *Child Molesters: A Behavioral Analysis.*)

Also, what the hell do they mean by "borderline"? Presumably, that the suspect has never sexually touched a child before and that he *really* did not mean anything perverted by his actions. A complete and thorough investigation should disclose whether this is the case, but too often the pressures of the situation will not allow that type of investigation. Thus the suspect has everything going for him. Those trying to convict him must prove sexual intent; and what is a sexual act? Hugging a child? Kissing a child? Taking pictures; changing clothes in front of a child? The victim is the most valuable source of information concerning the intent of the suspect because the victim can feel the difference between a "good touch" or a "bad touch." But the accusations are still difficult to prove in court.

I have stated that I feel jail is necessary for a molester, but of course every case must be judged on the evidence presented.

Are all molesters pedophiles?

No. The terms child molester and pedophile are not necessarily interchangeable and are not synonymous. A pedophile has a sexual preference for children. Although he may engage in sexual relations with adults, the preference is for children. A child molester may or may not be a pedophile. For example, a psychopath may be involved in all forms of antisocial behavior, including child molestation. These people operate under a philosophy: "If it feels good, do it."

This distinction between pedophiles and child molesters is especially important in terms of treatment and should be taken into account when developing treatment programs.

In 1985, S. Araji and D. Finkelhor reviewed the experimental research conducted up until that time regarding pedophilia. Diane DePanfilis summarizes their review as follows:

> [The review] identified four causal theories of pedophilia: 1) emotional congruence—why the adult has an emotional need to relate to a child; 2) sexual arousal—why the adult could become sexually aroused by a child; 3) block-age—why alternative sources of sexual and emotional gratification are not available; or 4) disinhibition—why the adult is not deterred from such an interest by normal prohibitions. This review also suggests that: 1) the best experimental research has focused on pedophiles' unusual pattern of sexual arousal toward children, however, no evidence exists identifying why this pattern occurs; 2) a number of studies have agreed that with pedophiles, social and heterosexual relationships are blocked; 3) many studies report that the use of alcohol is a disinhibiting factor and it plays a significant role in many pedophile offenses; 4) at least one study supports the "emotional congruence" theory that children, because of their lack of dominance, have special meaning for pedophiles; and 5) there is evidence that many pedophiles were themselves victims of pedophile behavior when they were children.

Speaking for pedophiles, Tom O'Carroll, "Paedophilia—A Response" (London: *Gay Left Magazine*, Summer 1979), offers this gem:

> What we are talking about as the activity of most paedophiles, then is touching and licking—the kind of sexual pleasuring that children do among themselves (given a chance) and which is accepted as legitimate for parents in many cultures to do with their children. I have slowly come to believe that PIE's (Paedophile Information Exchange) proposals for abolishing the age of consent (these proposals were formulated in 1975) do not take sufficient account of this fact, and I believe a great deal of legitimate concern could be obviated if the issues of full penetrative sex on the one hand and "sex play" on the other could be distinguished and considered separately. For my own part—PIE has yet to deliberate formally on this—I feel it may be both theoretically and practically acceptable to endorse a minimum age for penetrative sex, while allowing other forms of consensual sex at any age.

Here's another quote, this one from the Gay Commission of the International Marxist Group, 1979:

> ...we should see the involvement of children in the social life of the wider society and the development of relationships with adults as entirely positive ... the involvement of children in adult society will mean that, while children cannot have the same experience as adults, they need not be systematically deprived of an understanding of adults, as at present. This means that relationships of adults to children, including sexual ones, can be on a much more equal basis.... [A] widening of the scope of relations between adults and children will inevitably mean an increase in the incidence of paedophile relationships as being an integral part of the liberation of children and of women.

Paedophile relationships are not only allowable, they are to a large degree inevitable in a socialist society.

Edward Brongersma (Netherlands Doctor of Law), in his article "Aggression Against Pedophiles" (*International Journal of Law and Psychiatry,* 1984), continues in this vein. This author states, "There's no proof whatever that children who have consensual sexual relations with adults suffer any lasting damage from the sexual experience itself." He offered references of Professor Schorsch and Professor Kerscher in West Germany; Doctor Hauptmann in Austria; Professor Giaven in Switzerland; and the Government Committee, presided over by Judge Kjellin in Sweden. Mr. Brongersma goes on: "If there is any damage that these children suffer, it is always secondary, caused by the reactions of upset parents on discovery of the facts, or caused by police examinations."

Brongersma (certainly a friend of any non-violent molester) adds:

> it seems evident from these facts, that there is only one reasonable solution to the problem: to divide sexual behavior of adults towards children into three categories. Category one: The child is subjected to violence, threats, or abuse of authority. Against such aggression it should be protected with the full force of the law. Category two: The child is put into a position which it more or less strongly dislikes, which gives it the creeps or which it thinks odd, funny, queer. The child runs away, shuddering with disgust or sniggering. Of course society should try to prevent such things from happening. If they have happened nevertheless, parents or others should take care of the child and see to its problems, if any, just as if it had witnessed a nasty road accident or other unpleasant spectacle. But it is not in the interest of the child to make a tragedy out of it, to ram the events into its mind, to render things which otherwise are quickly passing by so frightfully important and unforgettable by using it as a witness in a criminal procedure. Criminal proceedings, therefore, should be avoided. Category three: The child likes the adult and the sexual relationship. Penal law, with its blunt weapons, should abstain completely. Civil law should empower parents to stop the relationship effectively if they're convinced that the adult in question is morally or psychologically a bad influence on their son or daughter. The judge, of course, should pay utmost importance to the opinion of the child itself. This—as I have said—would be a reasonable solution.

I think we can all agree with category one, but there our agreement should end. Category two saves the molester from jail or treatment or both so that he may go on to the next victim. Category three is against the law. Most experts agree that all such relationships have "morally or psychologically a bad influence."

Dr. Roland Summit *(The Child Sexual Abuse Accommodation Syndrome)* states that the male victim of sexual abuse "may cling so tenaciously to an idealized relationship with the adult that he remains fixed at a preadolescent level of sexual object choice, as if trying to keep love alive with an unending succession of young boys." Dr. David Finkelhor *(Sexually Victimized Children)* said that "sexual preoccupation with children resulted from an unusually pleasurable childhood sexual experience—response to that stimulus." He also points out that a negative sexual experience could have a similar effect.

What should I do if I suspect that a child is being sexually abused?

Report it. Every state has child abuse and neglect laws that require certain persons or groups of persons to report suspected child abuse (see "Who must report cases of child sexual abuse?" on p. 17) and every state has at least one statewide agency mandated to receive and investigate those reports. Anyone, however, who suspects that a child is being abused in any way should report his or her suspicions to that mandated agency, which is usually called the Department of Social Services, Department of Protective Services, or Department of Children and Family Services. If in doubt, call your local police department.

Do I have legal protection when I report a suspected case of child abuse?

Yes. Persons who report in good faith are granted immunity from civil and criminal court action even if the report proves to be mistaken.

What is good faith?

It is an honest belief that a child is being abused.

How sure must I be before I report?

There is no rule. If there is serious doubt, resolve that doubt in favor of the child, and report.

What happens if I report?

The agency to whom you report will investigate to determine whether sexual abuse has indeed taken place. In some cases, the agency may file a petition in court. In these cases the court makes final resolution. A court may take certain actions; for example, removing the child from the home, ordering mandatory participation of the family in a treatment program, or bringing criminal charges against the offender.

Who must report cases of child sexual abuse?

Any child care custodian, medical practitioner, nonmedical practitioner, employee of a child protective agency, commercial film and photographic print processor, law enforcement agency. "Child care custodian" covers a wide area; for complete details see the Definitions, Laws and Legal Aspects section.

Can a victim be removed from the home?

Yes. A child under 18 may be taken into temporary protective custody without a warrant. (See Definitions, Laws and Legal Aspects section.)

Will the victim be legally represented?

The law requires that the court shall appoint an attorney or the district attorney to represent the child. I go into great detail on this question in the Definitions, Laws and Legal Aspects section.

Are sexual offenders usually prosecuted and convicted?

No. The majority of sexual offenses committed against children are not even reported, let alone prosecuted. And if an individual is brought to trial, conviction is unlikely because these cases are very difficult to prove. Reforms in the legal system and departments of social services are occurring, however.

Sexual abuse of a child occurs in the home, behind closed doors, and there are usually no witnesses to corroborate the child's testimony. If one of the child's parents does not support the child's allegations, the child is usually intimidated into retracting his or her story. Further, there are some emotionally estranged children who may accept inappropriate sexual advances because, to them, such attentions are better than nothing. For these tragic, emotionally starved children there is at least some closeness and touching.

Physical evidence is often scant or nonexistent. Medical evidence could prove, for example, that a five-year-old girl has a perforated hymen. But it is impossible to prove that it was perforated as a result of sexual intercourse unless the child is taken to the hospital immediately after it happens. In cases of oral molestation, there is no physical evidence — no bruises, no perforated hymen, nothing to prove that the child was assaulted.

Finally, sexual abuse cases are usually tried in criminal court, where defense counsel tactics include postponements and cross-examination techniques designed to confuse and discredit the child.

In practical terms, sexual offenses against children go unreported, unprosecuted, unconvicted; offenders and children go untreated; society goes unprotected.

What factors contribute to sexually abusive behavior?

There are two general characteristics common to those who sexually abuse children: one is a lack of impulse control, and the other is a confusion of roles, where the child becomes an object for the needs of the adult without the adult's recognizing the inappropriateness or inability of the child to meet these needs. These two dynamics — lack of impulse control and confusion of roles — are common not only to instances of sexual abuse but also to child abuse cases in general. Additionally, the practice of incest is frequently passed on from one generation to the next.

Other factors to consider are:
• Prolonged or habitual absence of either the mother or the father from home.
• Assignment of a "mother" role to a daughter; for example, caring for other children, cooking, looking after father.
• Stepparent or live-in boyfriend.
• Loss of the wife by divorce, separation, or death.
• History of child abuse in the background of one or both parents.
• Conditions of overcrowding, alcoholism, drug addiction, or intellectual limitation of parents or child.
• Inability to establish normal social and emotional contacts outside the family because of eccentric belief systems, extreme poverty, or remoteness of the area in which the family lives.

Are teenagers more frequently the victims of sexual abuse than younger children?

No. Four studies reporting on the age distribution of sexually molested children indicate that the average ages are 8.5, 10.7, 11.0, and 13.0 years.

Are girls sexually abused more often than boys?

Statistics indicate that girls are more frequently the victims of sexual abuse, but the number of boy victims appears to be on the increase. Estimates suggest that male abuse is less than 20 to 25 percent of child victims. According to the Clearinghouse on Child Abuse and Neglect, March 1986, "the incidence rate for sexual abuse is highest among adolescent females vs. males, but half the female victims of sexual abuse are under 11 years of age."

Why are there more girl victims?

It is important to remember that statistics must be based on *reported* cases. Thus it is difficult to get a true account of the age and sex of the majority of victims. It is clear that, at any rate, girls are *reported* at a much higher rate than boys. For instance, one agency specializing in the treatment of child sexual abuse — the Child Protection Center of Children's Hospital National Medical Center — offers statistics for 1978–1981 showing that only 25 percent of their cases involved male victims (Rogers and Thomas). A February 1985 report by Finkelhor and Baron sets forth similar evidence that girls are at higher risk than boys.

I am sorry to argue with Dr. Finkelhor as his writings certainly reflect a great knowledge of this subject and he seems deeply concerned over the overall problem, but I really feel that his estimate — that one in every seven or eight boys will be sexually molested before the age of 18 — is low. I feel that as time goes on and we become more educated and open regarding sexual victimization, the ratio will increase to one in every four or five boys. (See below, "Why don't more boys tell of molestation?")

A study by Pierce and Pierce, "The Sexually Abused Child: A Comparison of Male and Female Victims," compared female and male victims and found several differences in the variables surrounding their cases. Diane DePanfilis, writing in *Literature Review of Sexual Abuse,* summarizes the findings of this study: "Males were less likely than females to reside in a home with a father figure, were more likely to be abused by stepfathers than female victims, and were more likely to have a nonperpetrating parent who was emotionally or physically ill. Finally, the suspects who abused males were less likely to be alcoholics and more likely to use force and threats."

Why don't more boys tell of molestation?

There has been quite a bit written on this question but I think I can boil it down to a short answer: many boys feel that if they told anyone about being molested (including an actual rape) they would be criticized for a failure to fight off an attack. No boy wishes to be known as a coward, but he may feel that he acted like one. He has fear that his friends will find out and call him a queer or homo. The victim may feel that he participated in an unmanly and dirty activity. He may feel ashamed. There may be a fear of retaliation. He may also like the experience.

Kempe says that the sexual assault of male children occurs more frequently than is reported. Studies have shown that 12 to 15 percent of all rape victims are male.

Dr. Roland Summit, in "The Child Sexual Abuse Accommodation Syndrome," 1983, says that

> because of the extreme reluctance of males to admit to sexual victimization experiences and . . . the greater probability that a boy will be molested by someone outside the nuclear family, less is known about possible variations in accommodation mechanisms of sexually abused males. Various aspects of secrecy, helplessness, and self-alienation seem to apply as does an even greater isolation from validation and endorsement by incredulous parents and other adults. There is almost universal assumption that a man who molests a boy must be homosexual. Since the habitual molester of boys is rarely attracted to adult males [Groth and Birnbaum: "Adult Sexual Orientation and Attraction to Underage Persons," 1978], he finds ready exoneration in clinical examination and character endorsements. While there is some public capacity to believe that girls may be helpless victims of sexual abuse, there is almost universal repudiation of the boy victim.

Diane DePanfilis, in *Literature Review of Sexual Abuse,* writes:

> More information about sexual abuse of boys has been gathered. For example, a review of the records of 81 sexually abused boys treated at a major hospital revealed that boys of all ages were subject to sexual maltreatment. The sexual abuse took many forms, for example: coercion which varied from rewards and bribes to threats of serious bodily harm; and anal intercourse and oral and genital contact, occurred with boys of all ages. Only three percent of the abusers were female. Perpetrator was most frequently a teenager known to the boy.

If a girl is the victim of incest, is she likely to report it to the authorities?

No. The "courtship" of a child usually begins when she is very young and culminates in intercourse when she nears or reaches adolescence. In many middle-class families the man is "getting even" with his wife for failure to create a happy marriage. Over the child's "courtship years" the entire relationship with the father is shrouded in secrecy, which includes the father's convincing the child that she alone is responsible for maintaining the family as a unit because only her ready availability to him keeps him there. His line may also include how special his "family love" is; if she resists, the courtship may include bribes, threats, or violence.

Even if the approach is brutal or humiliating, fear, loyalty to the family, and the nearly total dependency of the child tend to ensure secrecy. If the child discusses it at all, it is when she is older, and then she is most likely to tell a friend or a favorite teacher.

A mother surely must know if her husband or boyfriend is sexually abusing her daughter. Isn't she the one most likely to report?

Most mothers do report abuse as soon as they are aware of it. The problem is that sexual abuse of a child is often difficult to detect. Children often tell their parents in indirect ways or don't tell at all. Mothers often can't imagine that the male they care about would do such things to a child. A few mothers or other responsible adults may not detect abuse because of some psychological problem of their own.

For example, some mothers who were themselves abused as children appear to be especially unaware of the signs and signals of sexual abuse. A few other mothers may allow the sexual abuse to take place. (See page 59, "What are the family dynamics surrounding incest?") All available data suggest that most mothers take action to protect their child as soon as they are aware that their child has been abused.

How common is mother-son or father-son incest?

Mother-son incest patterns are relatively uncommon although more cases have been reported in the past few years. Father-son cases are also being reported more frequently as adults talk about their childhood. They are also considered somewhat rare, but we must understand the reluctance of the victim to report.

How can I tell whether a child is being sexually abused?

Symptoms of sexual abuse may include physical and behavioral signs as well as indirect comments made by the child. There are several clues to look for when considering the possibility of child sexual abuse. One sign alone may not be a positive indication; if a number are present, it is wise to consider the possibility of abuse.

Physical signs may include:
- Hematomas (localized swelling filled with blood)
- Lacerations
- Irritation, pain, or injury to the genital area
- Vaginal or penile discharge
- Abdominal discomfort
- Difficulty with urination
- Blood in anal or vaginal area
- Pregnancy
- Venereal disease in a young child
- Nightmares

Behavioral signs may include:
- One child's being treated by a parent in a significantly different way from the other children in the family
- Arriving early at school and leaving late
- Nervous, aggressive, hostile, or disruptive behavior toward adults, especially toward the parents
- An aversion to certain places or particular people
- Running away
- Use of alcohol or drugs
- Sexual self-consciousness, provocativeness, vulnerability to sexual approaches
- Sexual promiscuity that is "the talk of the town"
- Withdrawal from social relationships
- An appearance of mental retardation
- Regressive behavior such as acting childishly, crying excessively, sucking the thumb, withdrawing into fantasy worlds
- Changes in toilet training
- Acting out of aggressions, sometimes including petty thefts, giving trinkets to other children to form friendships, stealing merchandise or money
- Formerly outgoing child becomes clingy
- Poor peer relationships
- Inability to make friends

Comments may include:
- He fooled around with me.
- My mother's boyfriend does things to me when she's not there.
- I don't like to be alone with my father.
- I'm afraid to go home tonight.
- Will you help me go live with my aunt?

See also the Indicators and Guidelines section for additional signs and more detail—pages 103–117.

When incest happens, whose fault is it?

The parents bear the entire responsibility. It is not the child's! Even if a child is provocative or doesn't object, the law wisely states that incest is the fault of the adult. Where father-daughter incest occurs, the father is the key to the disturbed dynamics and is responsible for choosing a sexual relationship with the daughter. (See page 59, "What are the family dynamics surrounding incest?") Whatever else is said in sympathy with his motivations, and regardless of the wife's and daughter's contributions, the father's responsibility must be emphasized and must be identified in any therapeutic encounter.

What proof is there that incestuous offenders can be helped to change their behavior?

Several programs working with incestuous families have noted promising results with the perpetrator, the victim, and the family. Henry Giaretto, director of the Child Sexual Abuse Treatment Program in San Jose, California, reports successful rehabilitation in more than 90 percent of the incestuous families treated (H. Giaretto, *The Treatment of Father-Daughter Incest: A Psychological Approach*). Similarly an evaluation of 19 federally funded demonstration programs targeting services to specific subpopulations of maltreatment noted more positive outcomes for families involved in sexual abuse than for those involved in chronic neglect or severe physical abuse (D. Daro, *Confronting Child Abuse: Theory, Policy and Program*).

Considerable controversy exists, however, with respect to the long-term effects of services. To date, only limited follow-up studies have been done on incestuous families, and those follow-up studies that have been conducted suggest reincidence rates of more than 20 percent. (See also page 61, "What are the effects of incest?")

How much harm does a child suffer from sexual abuse?

In all instances of child sexual abuse, one must consider both physical and mental harm to the child. The degree of harm depends upon the nature of the act, the age of the child, and the child's general environment. Physical harm may include cuts, disfigurement, deformity, and pregnancy. Mental harm may elicit feelings of pain, panic, devastation, betrayal, shame, fear, guilt, vulnerability; these may persist throughout the victim's life.

Child sexual abuse may not always lead to permanent injury. There are some researchers who go so far as to say there is no evidence of lasting damage to victims; among these are Rasmussen, 1934; Landis, 1956; Lempp, 1968; Bernard, 1972; Corstjens, 1975; and Tindall, 1978. However, it is in the best interests of the child to assume that all sexual abuse experiences are potentially harmful. Research is greatly needed in this area. The implications of harm are now based only on complaints of people already identified as being harmed. (See also page 55, "What are the effects of sexual abuse on children and families?")

The importance of a child and the parents talking about the incident is often overlooked. A child usually believes that she or he is responsible for the assault, for causing the crisis in the family, and frequently thinks, "I did something bad. I shouldn't have told. I'm causing a lot of trouble." Getting the child's fears and feelings out in the open and dealing with them could do a great deal to reduce the possible harm the incident may have on the child.

Parents should keep in mind, however, that the child's feelings and needs may be completely different from their own. The child, for example, may be afraid that the offender will be very angry because the child told. A parent, on the other hand, may be concerned about how the experience may affect the child's adult sexual life. Parents should try to concentrate on the child's needs first by reassuring the child, repeatedly if necessary, that they know it's not the child's fault; that telling was the right thing to do; and that the fault lies with the offender.

What is the greatest obstacle both to preventing and to treating child sexual abuse?

Society. The sexual abuse of children is something most people neither talk about nor believe. A top priority should be a national public awareness and education campaign about sexual abuse. People do not do anything about a problem until they know the problem exists. Also, with more education and treatment programs, more individuals would seek help for themselves.

Equally problematic is society's reluctance to deal with sexuality in a realistic and open way. Certainly one's sexual behavior is a most personal side of one's life, but the attitude that it is dirty or must be whispered about prevents children and many adults from acquiring basic biological knowledge and from experiencing mature and joyful adult relationships.

It is encouraging to note, however, that many schools are implementing child safety courses. While not a perfect or sole solution, the courses do address some basic barriers and have resulted in some children disclosing their own sexual abuse, thereby getting help for themselves and for their families.

What's wrong with sex between adults and children?

There are several organizations and groups that advocate sex between adults and children.

The North American Man-Boy Love Association (NAMBLA) was founded in Boston in 1978. This organization, with many members in several states, says it is a lobbying group with a "libertarian, humanistic outlook on sexuality." NAMBLA argues that adult society has no right to limit a child's right to a sexual partner.

> NAMBLA condemns sexual abuse and all forms of coercion. But we insist there is a distinction between coercive and consensual sex. Laws that focus only on the age of the participants fail to capture that distinction, for they ignore the quality of the relationship. Differences in age do not preclude mutual, loving interaction between persons any more than differences in race or class.
>
> NAMBLA calls for the empowerment of youth in all areas, not for just the sexual. We are against arbitrary constraints on the rights and freedom of all, young and old. We support greater economic, political, and social opportunities for young people and denounce the rampant ageism that segregates and isolates them in fear and mistrust.

The René Guyon Society, a Los Angeles–based group, has as its motto, "Sex by eight or it's too late."

The British Pedophilia (or Paedophile) Information Exchange (PIE) wants to lower the age of consent to as low as age four.

The Child Sensuality Circle (promotes child/child love as well as adult/child), The Pedo-Alert Network (PAN) and the Lewis Carroll Collector's Guild all openly advocate adult-child sex and changing the laws that make it a crime. These groups and organizations claim to oppose forced sex with children and suggest only "consenting" sexual activity with children.

I have talked with members of NAMBLA and it's almost like a political or religious discussion. No matter how right you think you are, the NAMBLA member is quite certain that he is righter. These people are simply not to be confused with facts. Nevertheless they might benefit from reading a paper by Dr. David Finkelhor entitled "What's Wrong with Sex Between Adults and Children? Ethics and the Problem of Sexual Abuse" (*American Journal of Orthopsychiatry*, October 1979).

Dr. Finkelhor writes that laws prohibiting sexual relations between adults and children need to be backed by a strong ethical position against such relations, a position "less dependent on an empirical presumption that is not firmly established" (i.e., that sex with adults inevitably causes harm to children). Finkelhor cites "inadequate arguments" generally used against adult-child sexual relations and suggests that "a sounder line of reasoning in support of such a prohibition" is necessary. The "inadequate" (or "intuitive") arguments are:

1. That such relations are "intrinsically wrong" because they are "un-natural from a biological and psychological point of view." The strong taboos of nearly all societies against such relations are cited as evidence of the "intrinsic wrong." However, Dr. Finkelhor calls this approach "too categorical," pointing out that "many assertions of 'intrinsic wrong' made about other sexual taboos, such as homosexuality, have been called into question in recent times."

2. That adult-child sex is wrong "because it entails a premature sexualiza-tion of the child." This argument is generally based on the belief that "childhood should be a time of relative immunity from sex." But as Dr. Finkelhor points out, "Children are sexual; the asexuality of childhood is a myth. Most children are curious about sex. They explore sexuality with one another. In fact, when adults shield children from sex, it probably does more harm than good."

3. Finally, Finkelhor cites the "very common argument . . . that sexual encounters with adults are clearly damaging to children. Children are frightened and disturbed by them. They are the source of sexual problems in later life." While Finkelhor acknowledges the existence of clinical evidence tending to support this assumption, he sees the argument as weak for more than one reason. First, he points out that

> it is based on an empirical, not a moral, foundation, and an empirical founda-tion that is far from absolutely established. It is indisputable that some children are harmed by their childhood sexual encounters with adults, some severely so. But what percentage? From clinical reports, we cannot tell. The number of cases that do not come to clinical attention is very large, and it is possible that a majority of these children are not harmed.

Finkelhor goes on:

> Further, the idea that an experience causes harm is not sufficient in itself to earn condemnation. Compulsory education, divorce, even going to the doctor cause harm and trauma to an important number of children. If sex between children and adults is wrong, and if it merits serious condemnation in our moral hierarchy, then some additional criteria need to be introduced into the argument beside the possibility that it can cause harm.

Rest assured, however, that as a strong opponent of adult-child sex, Dr. Finkelhor does not leave us with no argument against it. Recall that his purpose in writing this paper was to provide "a sounder line of reasoning," less able to be refuted by organizations such as NAMBLA and others defending child sexual abusers. The argument Finkelhor suggests turns on the issue of whether a child is capable of giving "true consent" to sex with an adult. Finkelhor writes:

> As a society, we are moving toward a sexual ethic that holds that sex of all sorts between consenting persons should be permitted, but that in situations

where a person does not consent, sex should be considered illegal and taboo. Rape, for example, is an act that is clearly criminal because it is done without the consent of one of the parties.

But don't many children "consent" to sexual acts with adults? Sex between adults and children may often seem much less coercive than rape, because many children appear to consent passively or even to cooperate. If we say that sex is permissible where consent is present, doesn't this legitimize much adult-child sex?

The key argument here is that children, by their nature, are incapable of truly consenting to sex with adults. Because they are children, they cannot consent; they can never consent. For this reason, sex between an adult and a child cannot be sanctioned under our moral standard that requires that consent be present. . . .

For true consent to occur, two conditions must prevail. A person must know what it is that he or she is consenting to, and a person must be free to say yes or no. . . .

. . . Can children give informed consent to sex with adults? It is fairly evident that they cannot. For one thing, children lack the information that is necessary to make an "informed" decision about the matter. They are ignorant about sex and sexual relationships. It is not only that they may be unfamiliar with the mechanics of sex and reproduction. More importantly, they are generally unaware of the social meanings of sexuality. For example, they are unlikely to be aware of the rules and regulations surrounding sexual intimacy, and what it is supposed to signify. They are probably uninformed and inexperienced about what criteria to use in judging the acceptability of a sexual partner. They probably do not know much about the "natural history" of sexual relationships, what course they will take. And, finally, they have little way of knowing how other people are likely to react to the experience they are about to undertake, what likely consequences it will have for them in the future.

They may know that they like the adult, that the physical sensations feel good, and on this basis may make a choice. But they lack the knowledge the adult has about sex and about what they are undertaking. This is something that stems from the very fact of being a child and being inexperienced. In this sense, a child cannot give informed consent to sex with an adult.

Further, a child does not have the freedom to say yes or no. This is true in a legal sense and also in a psychological sense. In a legal sense, a child is under the authority of an adult and has no free will. But in a more important psychological sense, children have a hard time saying no to adults. Adults control all kinds of resources that are essential to them—food, money, freedom, etc. . . . The child has no freedom in which to consider the choice.

This is especially true when the adult propositioning the child (assuming the adult even asks the child's consent, which rarely happens) is a parent, a relative, or another important figure in the child's life, as is so often the case.

Dr. Finkelhor admits that "some objections might be raised" even to this argument, strong as it is compared to those previously cited. He points out that even many adults may not be entirely capable of giving truly informed consent to sex, as "a very imperfect awareness of the consequences" seems to exist among the general population. He also acknowledges that not all adults are truly free to say no; wives, secretaries and prostitutes have all been coerced more than once by their circumstances into unwanted sexual relations. Finally, he observes that some people might consider this argument "a condemnation of all child sexuality." Finkelhor himself approves of "sexual experimentation among adolescents" as well as "sex play among prepubescent children."

To all these objections, Finkelhor responds:

> The crucial difference in adult-child sex is the combination of children's lack of knowledge and lack of power. Children in relationships with adults are both uninformed and unable freely to say no. By contrast, in relationships with peers, children are uninformed, but at least there is no inherent power differential. While relationships between adults often involve subtle coercion, adults have great knowledge about the social meanings of sexuality, or at least they have accessibility to that knowledge.
>
> Thus, peer experiences among children and among adults are not morally suspect because participants' level of awareness is relatively mutual. It is where the ability to understand the situation is inherently unequal, and is compounded by a serious difference in power, that we draw the line.

Are three-, four-, or five-year-olds sexually attractive?

Certainly. I, personally, have a preference for the older youth; someone just beginning to develop sexually. But I am aware that a very young child can be very attractive sexually to pedophiles and others, and it is important for you to realize that fact. Some suspects are attracted specifically to the fact that the child is *not* sexually developed.

The most child sexual abuse referrals to health agencies, according to one source, are children under five. We have to look at this situation and face the fact that tiny children are victimized. Worse, they are even more vulnerable because they cannot verbalize and most parents wouldn't recognize this plea for help anyway.

Is there a pattern of disclosure for victims that have been repeatedly abused?

Dr. Roland Summit says yes. He calls it "the window of disclosure." If we are able to communicate properly, the child will open the window just a little bit. The child must have your trust and your willingness to believe what he is saying. You have to show that you are not afraid or angry with what you see in that first disclosure. As soon as you get anxious, the child will get anxious. Dr. Summit says there is an order of disclosure. Having been alerted by something your child said, you ask: "What happened?"

"Nothing happened!"

Press on. The next disclosure will likely be, "Well, something happened . . . but it didn't happen to me!" Thus the self will be protected. Now the child will describe in great detail everything that happened to "all the other kids" before ever acknowledging that he was personally involved. There could be a sequence of disclosure based on how embarrassing or outrageous the activities are.

Generally the child will describe being sexually touched before he can describe sexually touching others. He will describe being a passive victim before acknowledging being an active victim. The child will describe any approach to the genitals before talking about any approach to his rear or into the anus. There is an assaultive quality about being attacked from behind, since the victim can't see what happened; he is left feeling even more weak and helpless and more ashamed.

What is the final stage of disclosure in a large group of children that have been abused over a period of time?

I think we have all read about some of the day care center cases involving several children. Researchers feel that in the worst cases, where the most outrageous acts have been involved, the last thing to come out are the areas of greatest cruelty, where animals may have been killed and especially where the victims have participated in blood rituals, harm to animals or sexual activity on each other.

Once again, we are going to react with skepticism when we hear of such sordid and almost unbelievable stories. Remember that the suspects are aware of your disbelief and these rituals are also used to scare or terrorize the victim.

Is it unusual in this type of case for the suspect to defecate or urinate on the victim?

No. Apparently, that kind of deliberate perversity is part of the dynamics of someone who is so regressed as to be sexually involved with children in the first place.

When the suspect urinates or defecates on the child or kills animals to show what could happen to the victim if he tells, it could be his perverted way of building an alibi. There is an advantage for the suspect when he perpetrates such an outrage: Nobody would believe it!

Furthermore, sexual gratification is only one aspect of child abuse; another is the molester's desire for power. Besides raping someone, there is no better way to demonstrate power than to force excrement into the mouth of the victim.

Are many women identified as child molesters?

There just aren't many studies that reflect women as suspects. In some day care center cases women have been involved along with men but I believe it is rare for women to be involved in a one-on-one basis.

I have read that a woman who has been punished, ordered or forced by a man to engage in sexual activity with children, could become an enthusiastic molester herself. Well, any woman who is enslaved and dominated to that point of submission could be capable of anything. And I think that situation could relate to anyone.

A fellow inmate handed me a note one day with his recall of a 1965 article in "Penthouse Forum." He had written that "67.9 percent of all physical and sexual child abuse is committed by custodial mothers." The inmate stated the author was Sidney Siller and the article was titled "Men's Rights." Mr. Siller allegedly wrote, "I am a lawyer practicing family law. I've handled custody cases in more than 20 states in all regions of the country. Dozens of these cases involved charges of sexual abuse of children. The current rage is for a woman to accuse her former spouse of sexual molestation." The inmate who gave me this note is in prison because his ex-wife accused him of molesting their children. He says he is innocent. I don't have the slightest idea where attorney Siller obtained his statistics. Perhaps he took *child abuse* figures and added the word *sexual*. Nothing I have read could possibly substantiate those figures.

I know another inmate who was charged by his wife of molesting their two girls. Both children had a venereal disease when examined. So did a teenage nephew. The father did not. This fact was not allowed as evidence for some reason, and the nephew could not be located anyway, allegedly spirited out of town by the mother-in-law. I'm certain that there are men in prison falsely accused of this crime. It certainly is one way a wife can create trouble for her husband as the police usually arrest first and investigate second. We seldom read about a man being released for lack of evidence. It seems only the arrest makes news.

I could mention here that Dr. Kempe wrote that "biological mothers were thought to be accessories to their daughter's involvement of incest in 43 percent of reported cases—at least to the extent they knew about the incest and allowed it to continue, often for many years." This was from earlier studies, but I believe there is a large percentage of mothers today that fit into the "accessory" category.

What is the historical background on child sexual abuse?

The sexual abuse of children is certainly not new. Let us consider just a few historical examples:

Anal intercourse of young boys by adult males (often within the family) and by teachers was routinely accepted in Greece and Rome. I think we are all familiar with the countless books, fiction or nonfiction, that tell of the love between soldiers and their youthful lovers and that explain the formal "courtship" and procedures used in those ancient times.

The Keraki tribe in New Guinea had (or possibly still has), as a part of an initiation into manhood, the ritual of anal intercourse of the youth by one of the tribe's older men. According to Ford and Beach, 1951, in some societies sexual contact takes place on a regularly sanctioned basis between adults and children. (Margaret Mead, 1968, says that sexual victimization of children is not universal.) According to Tom O'Carroll writing in London's *Gay Left* magazine, summer 1979, the Lepcha adults of Sikkim perform sexual acts with children, including full coitus with girls of eight or nine. A male Aranda aborigine of Central Australia who is fully initiated but not yet married, commonly takes a boy of 10 or 12 to live with him as his wife until the older man marries.

There are many books on oriental sexual beliefs and traditions. In 1926 Lady Murasaki (Murasaki-Shikibo) wrote *The Tale of Genji*. Young prince Genji (978 to 1031 AD) had many romantic escapades, including the sodomization of a 12- or 13-year-old boy, and he adopted a 10-year-old girl who became his second wife.

Early child sexual abuse studies disclose that an actual penetration had to be made with the victim significantly traumatized or injured before the suspect would be arrested. Simple molestation, attempted sexual contact, exhibitionism and pedophilia were not considered, as physical proof was need that a crime had been committed.

It is interesting to note that in 1970 Florida reported an overall incidence of 17 cases of child sexual abuse. In 1971, following the passage of a reporting law and a public education program, 19,120 reports were made.

In the not-too-distant past it was reported that child molestation happened only in poor, isolated, remote rural areas of our country, such as Appalachia. (See *Pissing in the Snow and Other Ozark Folk Tales* by V. Randolph, 1976.) In a Williams and Hall study about 55 years ago it was reported that a large percentage of all child molesters had low or subnormal intelligence and that of their girl victims in the 8 to 14 age range, 30 percent were mentally retarded.

I think we are aware of the social origins of child sexual abuse with the man holding wives, slaves and children as his property. An uncontrollable child could be taken to the city gates and stoned to death. Girls, the handicapped or the sickly would be killed or sold into slavery. The selling of children into prostitution was widespread.

In early Jewish civil law a girl had to be three years and one day old for her father to give permission for betrothal and sexual intercourse. The Jews stopped infanticide, and the Bible condemns the practice of sacrificing children. There was also a taboo against anal sex. In the sixteenth century the Talmud recommended a daughter be given in marriage between 12 and 12½ years, but a father could marry her off before that.

Actually, according to Florence Rush in *The Best Kept Secret,* the father was not required to give his daughter in marriage. He could keep the money paid for her, keep the daughter as well, and hire her out again and again. Some would consider this child prostitution, but remember, the child was the father's property.

In those days it was believed any female under three was too immature to have sexual validity and had no virginity to lose, and any male child under the age of nine was not a sexual person.

Early Christian societies proscribed marriage under 12 for a bride, 14 for the groom. In the thirteenth century, statutory rape with a child under age 12 was a misdemeanor, and in the sixteenth century, 10 was the legal age at which a female child could consent to sexual intercourse.

There were reform movements and Pope Gregory IX established convents. During the Inquisition, children as young as six were believed to have entered into pacts with the devil through sexual intercourse.

In Colonial America the Puritans had their own strict code, steeped in Biblical tradition, but rape and child molestation were apparently ignored. However, sodomy between consenting adults meant death to all involved.

Child marriage in India had age limits of 10 for girls and 14 for boys, but in 1955 it was determined that the legal marital age would be 15 and 18 respectively. The Penal Code of the Philippines, 1977 edition, shows the age of consent for all sexual activities as 12.

S. Janus in 1981 said that social (sexual) revolutions upset traditional values so that children have been abused as a result. M. de Young says that Janus fails to recognize that children have been sexually abused since the beginning of time.

How can you identify a child molester?

You can't. Nobody can. There are many reasons why a specific man might molest a child, but the motives of molesters as a group are impossible to identify. Later in *MAN/child* I set out some "Indicators and Guidelines" of possibly what to look for or be aware of, but I count them as only possible mannerisms, backgrounds or activities. There is no sure way to spot a covert child molester.

Even the molester himself may not be aware he is one until he takes that first overt action against a child. (I have quite a bit more to say about this in the Indicators and Guidelines section.)

How can I protect my child?

We don't want to be suspicious of everybody — but do be suspicious. We don't want our children to be mistrustful of everybody, but they must be aware of the possibilities of child sexual abuse.

We can monitor adults and older children that have contact with our children. We can back up our child's right to say no. Now, we all realize that relatives can be a problem, and we can provide some comfort by letting the child know that we are aware of his discomfort when Auntie Jane slobbers all over him. This shows that his feelings are not being ignored. We can notice when children are being bullied, pushed around, or taken advantage of by friends or older brothers or sisters. Talking to all involved can help in figuring out a way to stop it. We can provide protection by demonstrating that we take seriously what our children say about the way people treat them. They need to know that we won't automatically assume the people in charge (youth leader, coach, teacher, etc.) are always right and the children are wrong. We can refuse to leave our children in the company of adults, relatives or friends we do not trust. We can take that second look at someone who is in a position to take advantage of our children.

How many types of child sexual abuse are there?

What are the limits of a child molester's imagination? From "just looking" to a sadistic death. The main thing I have found is that in the majority of the nonviolent assaults the feelings of the child victim are seldom in the mind of the suspect.

Taking the least offensive act first, a type of abuse may be simply voyeurism: looking, without touching. This can progress to touching and fondling — vaginally, even with babies, or anally if possible, or orally. The suspect may like to be fondled by the victim; the abuse may include several children involved in doing to each other what the suspect has taught them to do. In its more violent forms, abuse may be intentionally causing the child pain, forcing intercourse despite the victim's size, or simply beating or whipping the victim and enjoying the screams.

An abuse pattern may start out quite innocuously; the abuser may simply be helping a child with her bath, for example. If there exists any motivation to molest then this "cute" situation, such as a shared bath or shower, can progress as sexual appetites are aroused. The cuteness becomes abuse.

Sexual intercourse is rare; some assaults involve no physical contact. The most common forms of child sexual abuse are handling and fondling — feeling the child's genitals — and exhibitionism. A child may be forced to look at the genitals of an older child or adult or the child may be asked to undress or otherwise expose herself. When there is contact, it is sometimes oral; sometimes it includes attempts at penetration of the vagina or anus.

Abuse can also be defined as exploitation with money as the main gratification for the molester. This type of abuse includes child pornography; seducing a child into prostitution; or "renting" the victim to a friend.

Because the person who approaches a child in order to gain a sexual contact is usually known and trusted, the onset is usually gradual. There are opportunities to prevent an approach from turning into an assault. Many potential sexual assaults can be prevented, according to Adams and Fay, "not by superhuman children who respond heroically — but by children who have learned something about sexual assault and are not caught by surprise, trapped by shame or immobilized by confusion."

This is where you come in. A child needs caring parents to protect him. For children to protect themselves from adults, they need the help of another adult. As parents we often forget the power that adults have over children. Children are taught to obey adults. You must make the right to say *no* understandable.

The various nature and degrees of the abuse and the motives of the suspect are of considerable importance to the prosecutors of the crimes involved. Consideration is taken in incest cases whether to punish or rehabilitate. All considerations must be included by therapists and others working with the victim and his family on trying to explain what happened and why and what steps can be taken to prevent a recurrence. Researchers need this information about rehabilitation and punishment and possible prevention so they might recognize early indications of potential sexual abuse.

What are the chances that a child will be sexually assaulted?

Chances are that we all know someone who has been a victim, even if we are not aware of it. In *No More Secrets* by Caren Adams and Jennifer Fay, the following 1981 statistics are used: (1) In the United States at least one in four females is assaulted before reaching age 13 (a possible source: A. Kinsey, *Sexual Behavior of the Human Female*). (2) Ten percent of victims reporting are boys (Sexual Assault Center, Harborview Medical Center, Seattle WA). (3) At least 10 percent of children who are assaulted are under age 5 (Children's Hospital National Medical Center, Washington DC). (4) There are more children between ages 8 and 12 reporting sexual assault than teenagers (National Committee for Prevention of Child Abuse). (5) From 30 to 46 percent of all children are sexually assaulted in some way before the age of 18 (Child Sexual Abuse Prevention Project, Hennepin County Attorney's Office, Minneapolis MN).

Are some children more vulnerable than others?

Information indicates that *all* children must be considered vulnerable to sexual assault—simply because they are children.

What about babysitters?

These people play an important part in the life of any parent. Not everybody has a mother or close relative available to watch over a child. But parents should carefully screen this vital person. We should also do more than tell our children, "Now mind the babysitter and do what he/she tells you." Some tips: Explain to the babysitter that our children don't keep secrets and will tell us if something is wrong. We might say that our child has permission to say "no" if he or she doesn't understand a request. We can make a statement like, "My child has already had her bath, she always puts on her pajamas by herself, and she knows she is to be in bed by eight o'clock and is not to stay up later than that for any reason." We can follow up with our child and the sitter and find out how each one feels about their time together. If there is a change of feeling, take a second look.

Is it unusual for a child that is a victim of sexual abuse to later retract his allegation?

No. This seems to be a more or less predictable pattern. (See discussion of the Child Sexual Abuse Accommodation Syndrome under the question, "What is the background regarding treatment of victims and families?" p. 65.) The victim most probably has not told anyone for a long period of time; even had he been asked if anything was happening he would have denied it. Remember, he was locked into a mode of secrecy—so, in a way, any acknowledgment of being molested is a turnabout of all the prior denials.

What factors may cause the victim to retract allegations of sexual abuse?

If the parents fail to respond correctly, with much support and love, the victim feels he or she must reassure the parents that it really didn't happen. One of the ways children survive being molested is to make believe that it didn't happen. This is for their own protection and to make them feel better about the whole situation. There is always a tremendous amount of guilt present. The victim may try to convince grown-ups not to worry, and act as if nothing has happened.

If a child denies that he was abused should we automatically conclude that he was in fact a victim?

We cannot deny that sometimes children say they were abused when they weren't or distort the proportions of the abuse. Everyone involved must be alert to determine whether the child is trustworthy and accurate. That is where investigation plays such an important role. People who say "children don't lie" have never been parents. Proper questioning by trained professionals will determine the facts of the case. Remember, parents sometimes have difficulty really hearing things that they do not want to hear.

Suppose that a child, in making a statement about sexual abuse, says something that doesn't make any sense or seems impossible. Should we necessarily discount everything that the child said?

Obviously, most parents are not aware of the dynamics of a covert child molester. Child molesters do things that we don't want to believe anyone would do. Children can give in or participate in various activities that we just don't want to believe that a child would do. We cannot fathom that our child would readily submit to these sexual actions, or that a suspect would even suggest them. Remember, people really wish to believe the best about someone.

Why do we want to believe the best?

When you think about it, there is absolutely nothing to be gained by believing a child is molested. Our sense of outrage at such actions destroys our trust in our own society. We all just want to believe that our children will be safe when we leave them in the care and control of someone who seems normal in every way. Furthermore, suppose the person implicated is a male, and I think he is guilty, and he is known as a "normal" person—then I might be concerned that others would believe that *I* did it or, at least, that I am as capable of doing something like that as anyone else. The whole thing is outrageous to one's personal sense of comfort. If you are a mother, you feel that you have failed if someone has molested your child.

Many of us were victimized in various ways when we were children. We have forgotten it. We have denied it. And to come face to face with this situation again is something that is internally painful and almost impossible to contemplate. Former victims of sexual abuse are often totally incapable of taking action when a child has been molested. To believe that the abuse has occurred is to be obligated to take action. You have to challenge somebody you have trusted. Someone your child has been trusted with. You have to convince other people. You are aware you could be blamed by others who are certain that anybody else would have protected the child. Finally, if you succeed in gaining attention outside your family, and then have to go to court . . . you are likely to feel punished and lose your dignity and freedom by being exposed in the process of being a witness and being attacked on cross-examination. It is a strong parent that can stand up to this multitude of obstacles and persevere.

Why would intelligent people simply not notice that their children are crying out for help?

It is normal for adults to wish not to be involved in this "dirty" subject. We have created our own mythology. We believe that no one would molest a child except someone who is visibly disturbed. The grimy bum in the park; the carnival worker; any stranger . . . all of these are stereotypes of possible molesters.

But let's take a neighbor as an example. (See the Scenarios section for a further look.) Here is a person who is likeable, easygoing, and friendly— someone who really gives the impression that he likes children. You can see that your child likes this man and you are delighted when he takes him off for a movie, ball game or day in the park. It is beyond our willingness to accept that a person that nice will take our children and molest them under this position of trust. It is also beyond our ordinary ability to believe that, if it happens, the child wouldn't tell us about it when he came home. It is hard for us to understand why, of all the people in the world that the child could tell, the mother or father would be the last to know, but such is often the case. The child "protects" his parents from the information for fear of destroying the family.

It seems to me that our greatest index of suspicion should be directed toward those whom we trust the most. Isn't that a frightening thing to say?

Can a child initiate acts of sexual aggression?

Many suspects have used the defense that they were lured or overcome by children making positive sexual advances toward them.

First, let's remember that in early childhood there is a strong interest in one's own body; a healthy curiosity; perhaps jealousy of the intimacy shared by parents from which the child is excluded; a little boy's ability and pleasure in manipulating his penis; a little girl's envy of little boys because she doesn't have one; strong physical sensations in general; and the constant adjustment to what an adult wishes, with a child's readiness to respond to adult commands.

With these sketchy characteristics in mind, let me add that children tend to be cute, cuddly and affectionate. They can easily awaken sexual desire in an adult if that adult has had or is having a poor sex life with his spouse, or has already had strong sexual desires toward children, or was himself violated as a child. Rationalization comes easily to a pedophilic or to a potential child molester.

Do child sexual abusers manipulate the self-concept of the child victim?

Linda Sanford, in her 1980 book for parents entitled *The Silent Children,* says they do. She explains:

> Self-concept means the child feels good about herself. The molester's entice-ment of *really* liking her if she lets him put his hands down her pants is not effective with her. She likes herself, so it's nice if he likes her, but ok if he doesn't. And certainly she doesn't have to *perform* in any way to get people to like her.

She goes on to say that parents who have a history of abuse or alcoholism have a poor concept of themselves. "How can a child be taught if the parent is a stranger to that feeling?" The child has no point of reference and no positive action to imitate.

What can you do to improve your child's self-concept?

Author Linda Sanford says that a balance between praise and criticism is crucial to the child's positive self-concept, and that praise or positive reinforcement is not permissiveness. Praise should be specific rather than general. Sanford gives the following examples:

> *Situation:* After much coaxing on your part, your child voluntarily cleans his room before visitors come.
> *General Praise:* You are a good boy.
> *Specific:* I really like it when you see what needs to be done, then you go ahead and do it. It makes me trust you more. You're really growing up.
>
> *Situation:* You feel sick and stay in bed one morning. Your child fixes you breakfast in bed.
> *General:* Oh, thanks, dear.
> *Specific:* You are so special because you are sensitive to other people and are willing to give something of yourself. I feel better already.

General praise is not bad and certainly better than no praise at all; however, specific praise bolsters the child's self-concept.

Sanford also says that criticism needs to be specific, and that in criticizing a child one should never apply general labels such as "lazy" or "stupid."

> *Situation:* Child's room always messy and she refuses to clean it.
> *Labeling:* You are the biggest pig I have ever seen.
> *Specific:* I am really tired of walking in here and seeing this mess. You have a choice: Clean it up, or stay in here for the rest of the day.
>
> *Situation:* You catch your child in a lie about spending allowance money on candy.
> *Labeling:* You are a liar.
> *Specific:* It makes me very uncomfortable when you lie like this. I want to trust you but right now it is difficult.
>
> *Situation:* Your child accepts a ride home from a stranger because it was raining.
> *Labeling:* You get what you deserve when you do that!
> *Specific:* That upsets me. I want very much for you to be safe, and that was dangerous. Let's talk about it.

A child receiving those labeling messages will conclude he is a stupid, deaf, lying pig destined to be murdered in a stranger's car. He builds his self-concept on praise and also takes on criticism as a part of the same building process.

Some children are vulnerable to labels and feel "different." These children can become victims because of the "special friendship" child molesters offer.

If a child believes he is lovable and worthwhile, that feeling can be translated into a response to a molester's approach: "I don't have to trade access to my body to gain friendship or affection."

Are parents automatically "all-knowing"?

Linda Sanford, in her fine book for parents about the prevention of child sexual abuse, *The Silent Children,* stated that it is a difficult job we have as parents. We receive no grades, there is no tabulating system and we won't even make the honor roll. It's on-the-job training — we learn as we go along. But she did lay out an excellent bottom line: "Treat the child as the parent would like to be treated if he were in the child's shoes." Among the suggestions she listed for parents:

• Be consistent in enforcement of agreed-upon rules.

• Avoid exploiting the inevitable size difference by physically abusing the child.

• Point out child's mistakes with ways to correct them rather than humiliating, punishing, hitting or shaming the child because he failed.

• Point out successes and positive aspects of the child just as quickly and forcefully as we point out the mistakes.

• Teach the child the value of privacy by respecting your child's needs for privacy.

• Acknowledge the presence of fear, uncertainty, failure, and frustration in life, rather than denying their existence or punishing the child for having these feelings. If the child understands that these feelings are normal, he will learn to manage them better. Acknowledge behavior connected to these feelings, such as crying when we are sad.

• Avoid domination by parental authority and help guide the child to her own sense of self-authority.

• Exercise fair and constructive limits so the child can imitate with healthy self-imposed limits.

• Allow each child to move at his individual pace.

• Encourage the child to make decisions or expand territory but be available for nurturance and redirection if the child fails.

• Do not question the child's right to say "no" to matters of personal preference that do not endanger the child's safety or unduly disrupt other family members.

• Stress the importance of friendships outside the family and realize that good family relationships are the beginnings of good relationships *outside* the family.

• Understand that there are many levels of "wrong" or misbehavior and try not to react to every misdeed as if it was the *worst* of all possible fates.

- Assume the child is telling the truth, unless or until the parent knows for a fact that she is lying.
- Allow the child to have time and things all to himself free from sharing.
- Intercede with unconditional love (not recrimination) to set limits when the child is over tired or over extended and unable to cope on her own.

Author Sanford also explored the "feeling" state of the child and gave several examples of what a four-year-old child may be thinking after her mother is called away from home and leaves her with a neighbor's husband. The husband wants to play a "secret" game. The child may think that although the game is unpleasant for her, it is rude to say "no," especially to an adult. Her parents have probably told her to "do what he says." Even if she has doubts about the situation, she may feel that she is "never right about anything" or prone to "mess things up," in which case the adult's authority will carry even more weight. If the child has a poor self-concept, she may feel that this person is the only one who likes her, and she will do what he says to keep his friendship or avoid hurting his feelings.

Ideally, careful parenting will help a child avoid these thought patterns. Instead, one hopes, she will say to herself: "This is wrong—I'm not going to do it. Then I'm going to tell someone what he asked me to do." To the would-be molester she says: "No, I don't want to play that game. I'm going to play with my dolls."

Sanford also talks about the "voice from within" that she says is learned at home over a period of years. To guide the parent in developing that voice, she asks several questions:

- Is the child taught to put other people's rights and needs before her own?
- Is she taught that adults are more important than children?
- Is she taught that she must obey *any* adult?
- Are rules about what she *should* do in a given situation so rigid that they totally ignore the child's feelings?
- Can the child say "no" to *anything* or is absolute compliance demanded at all times?
- Where could the child go with questions about confusing situations?
- If she tells someone about the neighbor, is she confident they will take her seriously?
- Is the child encouraged to follow her own "intuition" about the rightness of situations or are her feelings discounted?
- Do *other* people always know what's best for the child?
- Does the child have any doubts that she is lovable . . . [making her] vulnerable to the flattery of others?

• Does she feel justified, based on her own worthiness, to remove herself from a situation that might cause her harm?

According to *The Silent Children* parents come up with surprising answers to some of these questions—answers the parents do not particularly like. Perhaps a few changes here and there might enhance a child's safety.

What can be done to prevent child sexual abuse?

Any parent, professional, student of psychology, educator, or other interested person who takes the time to read just a portion of the books and studies listed in the bibliography has gained some insight into the problem. However, one should bear in mind that the explosion of activity focusing on the prevention of child sexual abuse began only in the early 1980s. The studies listed are all just really getting started, and there have been few programs that have undertaken to evaluate and determine the effects or quality of these efforts.

For parents I particularly suggest you read the Indicators and Guidelines section of *MAN/child* for some thoughts on possible prevention activities.

Of course, the people I really wish to contact are those who will not read *MAN/child* or any other publication. These parents prefer to leave the teaching of their children up to the schools and maybe a radio or TV spot or two. School programs are many and varied, but the actual prevention of sexual abuse must start in the home.

I am reminded of a report by Dr. Finkelhor concerning his Boston study of parents of children ages 6 to 14. His report stated that there is a great need for more parent education regarding sexual abuse. Parents, Finkelhor states, need to be aware of the signs of possible sexual abuse. They need to know how to respond if their children report abuse (it is especially important that they be prepared to *believe* their children). They need to know how to get professional help, including an evaluation of the victim's condition, from community resources and to understand the importance of such help. Rogers and Thomas offer further support in their study of 402 cases of child sexual abuse treated at Children's Hospital National Medical Center, stating, as DePanfilis summarizes, "that prevention should focus on teaching children to avoid situations which place them at risk. They should be taught specific strategies for handling the method used by offenders to gain compliance."

DePanfilis rightly points out that "even when parents provide basic sex education to their children, they may be reluctant to discuss sexual abuse." However, children *need* to understand the nature of sexual abuse. MacFarlane, Jenstrom and Jones emphasize that a concept of appropriate physical interaction between adults and children is a necessary tool by which a child might avoid being victimized.

The "What If" game described by several authors is certainly full of merit. You are teaching your child, communicating with her, and . . . it's fun! Don't get too heavy, and feel free to throw in a few zingers: "What if an elephant wants to sleep on your bed?" (Answer: "Say goodnight and sleep on the floor!") "What if a man from Mars wants you to fly home with him?" (Answer: "I'll have to ask my mother first.")

Citing an NCCAN guide to prevention resources, DePanfilis states that recent public prevention activities "have primarily included general public awareness efforts, dissemination of printed materials for parents to teach their children about sexual abuse, education for professionals who come into contact with children, and prevention education for children of all ages." (See also page 64, "What has the government accomplished in preventing child sexual abuse?") TV and movie stars have been a big help, I am sure, in their TV spot announcements making children aware of "funny touches" and what to do about them. It's too bad that these well-produced prevention spots are not seen in prime time, but frankly, any time the networks and local TV stations allow is a plus factor. Ideally, the entire family would view a spot and then turn off the TV and engage in an in-depth family discussion, but in most homes this is probably unlikely. Nevertheless, television has an important influence.

The television movie "Something About Amelia," which dealt with the problem of incest and its effect on one (fictional) family, was telecast in January 1984. The telecast resulted in widespread media attention to the subject of incest, and according to A.H. Cohn, who testified on behalf of the National Committee for the Prevention of Child Abuse, in three months' time the NCPCA "received over 3,000 letters from individuals poignantly and personally touched by the problem of child sexual abuse."

Another nationwide effort in prevention has been the publishing and distribution of a "Spider-Man and Power Pack" special comic book teaching children about ways to protect themselves from sexual abuse.

Program effectiveness is usually evaluated by pre- and post-testing. That is, before introducing materials to a target group, researchers will administer a test to check that group's knowledge and attitudes about the subject to be discussed in the materials. After the group has worked with the materials or completed whatever program is involved, another test determines whether there have been changes in knowledge and attitudes. A control group also takes the tests so that the answers of people who worked with the materials can be compared with the answers of people who didn't.

So far, evaluation of various programs has come up with mixed results. For example, Swan et al. report on a play called "Bubbylonian Encounter" designed to teach children about sexual assault. The play emphasizes how to tell "good" and "bad" touches and attempts to raise a general awareness of what sexual abuse is (including the fact that friends or family members — not just strangers — can be the abusers). The play also stresses that children should report abuse to a trusted adult. Pre- and post-testing of this play, conducted with 44 elementary school children, asked children to distinguish between sexual and nonsexual touching in five video vignettes shown before and after the play. Pre- and post-test results were the same (72 percent correct responses for the nonsexual touch vignettes, 92 percent for the sexual assault vignette), which showed that the play apparently hadn't helped the children recognize these touches any better. However, other test questions did suggest that children had become more aware that they should report abuse and that it could happen within the family.

DePanfilis summarizes another evaluation, this one of a "Personal Safety Project" in Vancouver, as follows:

> [P]re-test and post-test questionnaires were used with a quasi-experimental design to evaluate the effectiveness of three Personal Safety Project workshops on child sexual abuse—a teacher's workshop, a parents' workshop, and a personal safety awareness workshop for children. Evaluation results indicated that the workshops significantly improved the participants' appropriate behavior in most studied areas. Comparison of pre-workshop and post-workshop scores indicated that teachers' knowledge of how to respond to a child's complaint of sexual abuse had improved. Parents' post-workshop scores indicated that they would be more likely to believe a child's complaint of sexual abuse; however, parents' post-workshop results showed that they were no better prepared to obtain help for a sexually abused child. Intermediate students reported improved body evaluation and self-esteem, as well as increased knowledge of potentially dangerous situations. Finally, in contrast to a control group not in the program, grade five students were more likely to successfully terminate an uncomfortable touch (a continuous hand shake), while in the control group of primary students only 1 out of 10 were able to successfully terminate the continuous hand shake despite their discomfort.

Evaluation of a third program, reported by Wolfe et al. in *Child Abuse and Neglect*, offered some suggestions for developing other prevention programs. The suggestions included:

- providing programs appropriate for young children
- conducting programs over several occasions—children seem to learn better this way than they do from a single session
- giving children a chance to increase their knowledge about how to respond when actually confronted by a potential abuser—for example, a program could include role-playing in which children could rehearse appropriate actions.

According to Finkelhor and Araji:

> Many educators in the field emphasize the need for an integrated approach to prevention, reaching audiences of children, parents and professionals. But sometimes choices need to be made about which audiences deserve priority. Some prevention educators clearly believe that working with children holds the

greatest potential for impact on the problem. Others raise questions about this priority. Unlikely as it seems, it is within the realm of possibility that children have relatively little control over whether they are abused or not. Greater knowledge about rights or advance warning about the nature of molestation, although soothing to adults who want to protect children, may in reality be of little use to most children when confronted by actual molesters. Or we may find out that, even with the best instruction, children retain little of what they are taught.

Crici et al. recommend the following steps in organizing effective community prevention programs: first, organize a task force within the community. Second, go to the public; raise their awareness of the problem of child sexual abuse. Third, go to teachers and parents; enlist their help in developing a program and getting it going. Finally, go to the children; work with them according to the program you have developed.

DePanfilis addresses the role of professionals in prevention efforts, pointing out that "professionals who have contact with children, including teachers, pediatricians, school counselors, day care workers, clergy, and police, are critical providers of prevention education for children." She summarizes the recommendations of Finkelhor and Araji for educating professionals:

(1) They must understand the nature and dynamics of the sexual abuse and be able to discuss it in terms that children can comprehend. To be able to do this, professionals need to role play or practice so that they can feel comfortable discussing such topics.

(2) They must know how to identify children who are at high risk for sexual abuse and possible signs of abuse. They must be reminded to maintain high levels of suspicion.

(3) They must know how to question a child sensitively about the possibility of abuse. This also requires role playing or practice so that professionals can feel comfortable asking such questions.

(4) They must know how to react when a child confides that he or she has been victimized. Professionals should be aware of responses that would harm the child, such as blaming the victim or showing exaggerated sense of alarm.

(5) They must be familiar with resources for referring children who have been victimized.

(6) They must be able to communicate basic concepts of prevention to the children.

A 1979 guide published by the Department of Health, Education, and Welfare (written by James Jenkins, Marsha Salus and Gretchen Schultze) includes some guidelines for professionals working with child sexual abuse victims. Like the rest of this document, the guidelines are noteworthy if somewhat oversimplified. One hopes that the HEW guide will not be the only thing a worker reads before becoming involved in a case. Nevertheless, for a professional with thorough training from other sources, the following guidelines are likely to be useful.

When Talking with the Child DO:

Build trust in the child.
Conduct the interview in private.
Sit next to the child, not across a table or desk.
Explain to the child how the information they have given will be used.
Conduct the interview in language the child understands.
Ask the child to clarify words/terms which are not understood.
Explain the necessity of seeing the child's injury in a nonthreatening, comforting way.
Tell the child if any future action will be required.

DON'T:

Allow the child to feel "in trouble" or "at fault."
Disparage or criticize the child's choice of words or language.
Suggest answers to the child.
Probe or press for answers the child is unwilling to give.
Display horror, shock, or disapproval of parents, child, or the situation.
Force the child to remove clothing.
Conduct the interview with a group of interviewers.

When Talking with the Parents DO:

Inform the parents of their legal right in regard to the investigation.
Conduct the interview in private.
Tell the parent(s) why the interview is taking place.
Be direct, honest and professional.
Be sympathetic and understanding.

DON'T:

Try to "prove" abuse or neglect by accusations or demands.
Display horror, anger, or disapproval of parent(s), child or situation.
Pry into family matters unrelated to the specific situation.
Place blame or make judgments about the parent(s) or child.
Reveal the source of report.

Finkelhor and Araji have identified common themes of child abuse prevention programs, as cited by DePanfilis:

(1) All the efforts have tried to educate children about what sexual abuse is.

(2) All the efforts have attempted to broaden children's awareness about potential sexual abuse offenders. In contrast to educational programs of earlier generations which warned exclusively about strangers, almost all current

prevention programs teach children that potential offenders include people whom they may know and like.

(3) All the efforts have attempted to teach children specific actions they can use if someone tries to sexually abuse them. They all encourage children to tell someone, especially someone they trust, and to keep telling until they are believed.

Both parents and professionals would do well to include each of these elements in their own prevention efforts.

Is the suspect usually known to the victim?

"My mommy told me never to talk to strangers." Your mommy (and daddy too) had better tell you more than that if you wish to escape being a victim of sexual abuse. Studies have shown that a high percentage of sexual abuse cases involve parents or other people the child knows.

In her *Literature Review of Sexual Abuse* Diane DePanfilis cites several of these studies to give us the following statistics:

• Study by Conte and Berliner, 1981: In 583 cases, 15 percent of offenders were the natural fathers of the abused children; only 8 percent were strangers.

• Study by Finkelhor, 1979: 76 percent of offenders were known to the child; 43 percent were family members.

• Study by Scherzer and Lala, 1980: In 73 cases, 82.5 percent of the assailants were known to their victims.

• Study by DeJong, 1982: Of 142 subjects (all boys), 78 percent knew their assailants.

Just what happens in an episode of sexual abuse often depends on the offender's relationship to the victim. Luther and Price have pointed out that many cases of abuse by strangers involve exhibitionism or fondling rather than penetration. According to Groth, an episode with a stranger is usually a one-time occurrence (for that particular child), most likely to happen in the warm weather months and in a public place.

Sexual abuse within the family or by an acquaintance—again according to Groth—is more likely to happen in the home of the child or the offender, and may be repeated over and over. Justice and Justice note that violent sexual offenses such as rape or sadism are rare (though not unheard of) within the family.

In his paper "Four Preconditions: A Model," Finkelhor lists four conditions that research suggests must exist in order for sexual abuse to occur. First, a potential offender must be motivated—his psychological makeup must make him want to commit this crime. (See "Are child molesters sick?" and "Are all molesters pedophiles?" on pages 9 and 13 for more on this.) Second, the potential offender must overcome any internal inhibitions that keep him from acting on his desire. Third, he must overcome external impediments to committing the sexual abuse. Finally, he must undermine or overcome a child's resistance to the sexual abuse. These last two conditions are obviously easier to achieve when the potential offender knows his victim. It is much easier to find a place and opportunity to abuse a child who has been placed in his care. As for undermining a child's resistance, that's easier, too, when the child has been told by his parents to "do whatever Uncle Johnny says." You get the idea.

Can we believe everything we read or hear about child molestation?

I have a box full of newspaper and magazine clippings that report men arrested for child molestation. You, most probably, have read these same stories. We do not read or hear much about those suspects released for lack of evidence or because the alleged victim admits he or she was lying. One case, July 1988: School teacher accused by 15-year-old girl. He denies all charges in a home video and then commits suicide. Shortly before his death, and unknown to him, the girl admitted she was not telling the truth.

That's a frightening situation but fortunately very rare. With one exception the convicted felons I have spoken with admit their guilt, or almost admit it. I actually find very few people in prison who still adamantly deny guilt. The one exception, whom I believe, is a young man who was accused of sexually molesting his 9- and 11-year-old daughters. I read portions of his transcript and saw evidence not presented at his trial that should have exonerated him. He is working with VOCAL (Victims of Child Abuse Law; see Resource Guide) and is continuing to fight his case.

Although I personally feel that parents must educate and inform their children, we must be careful not to excite or mislead children into rash actions. A case in point occurred in California in October 1987 (*The Orange County Register,* May 23, 1988). Eight fifth grade girls reported a teacher to a trusted adult, their principal. The teacher, charged with misdemeanor molestation, was cleared when the court testimony revealed that he had placed a hand or two on the children's shoulders for a few seconds as he praised their efforts while making his way around a classroom full of students. I don't know if he got his job back or where he got the $50,000 to defend himself, but the case had parents and teachers concerned about the state-funded Child Abuse Prevention Program. They criticized a skit about a lecherous uncle and his niece that might confuse children and cause them to falsely brand relatives or teachers as child molesters. The skit shows the uncle fondling his niece while watching television. The uncle places his hand and touches her on the upper thigh. This scenario is repeated with the girl telling her uncle not to touch her and that she intends to tell her mother. Now, I can imagine over-reactions, but the script does give a detailed explanation saying that a molester may try to touch children's genitals or take nude photos of them. You really can't expect the actor in the skit actually to touch a child on her private parts.

Since 1985 thousands of California children have seen the material and few complaints have been received. Incidentally, following presentations at a school, three or four formal reports are usually received by the Child Abuse Registry telling of physical and emotional abuse and neglect as well as molestation.

Sometimes false accusations may occur, but if the investigators will take the time and effort to build evidence prior to an arrest or any publicity regarding the alleged case, then they may be able to forestall tragedy to an innocent person.

I will suggest that most molesters have more than one victim—that they have been engaged in this activity for a period of time. If the investigation were very thorough, additional charges, including upgrading from misdemeanor to felony, could occur. These are the covert, insidious child molesters that should go to state prison. These could be the men who, after exhausting their abnormal but nonviolent sex drive on children, fantasize into actual sexual intercourse with tiny babies and additional perverted activities which could lead to the serious injury or death of the victim. These particular suspects could kill to save themselves from arrest.

It is my opinion that all molesters should be incarcerated and depending upon the severity of the attack(s), remorse notwithstanding, should be given commensurate time in prison. (See page 12, "Should all child molesters go to prison?")

Of course, we must all guard against overreaction. (See "What about witch-hunts?" on page 86.) That includes investigators, social workers, and prosecutors as well as parents and victims. California's McMartin Preschool case may be an example.

Are all homosexuals molesters?

I can't speak knowledgeably about the homosexual scene or sex drive or why they are what they are. All I can do is listen and read and form my own opinions. The gay community would certainly have you believe that they would never attack a child. I believe that most homosexuals would not go out of their way to have sex with a child under 12 or so, but I have listened to many homosexuals speak of their activities and they most all include sex acts with teenage boys. Now, remember that a teenager below the age of 18 is still a child in the eyes of the law. It is still a violation to have sex with a person that age, even if the victim is willing as many youngsters are.

I cannot be convinced that a boy of 15 or even 17 really knows his own mind or knows what is really happening when he gets involved with an older man. Some of the homosexuals I have listened to state that they knew their sexual desires even before they turned 15 or 16. One acknowledged homosexual, a married man with four children, stated he found out his nine-year-old son had been "turning tricks" with older men. After severely beating the boy (later admitting he was jealous), he then became sexually involved with his own son. At the time he had a 12-year-old lover, a street boy whom he had picked up at the beach. He brought the boy home (with the acquiescence of his wife) and had taken over as a lover-father image to the former homeless boy. This man and others tell of their early experiences with older men, and some admit that they were "turned on" to homosexuality by these men, some of whom were not homosexual. This may be; but the truth is that literally thousands of studies (I am told by Dr. Kempe) have reported on developmental traits and we still do not know why an adolescent develops a sexual preference, whether heterosexual, homosexual, bisexual, or asexual.

For further information see Gebhard, et al., 1965, which breaks down the sexual case histories of more than 1,500 men convicted for a variety of sex offenses. Mary de Young (*Sexual Victimization of Children*, 1982) has statistics on father-son relationships as do other authors writing on incest.

I saw an ad in the national gay newsmagazine *The Advocate*, August 2, 1988, that showed the small hands of a child tying a man's shoe in which he had placed his foot. His left leg sported a Band-aid, and he was wearing typical "small kid" socks. The ad said, "Big enough to fill your shoes and your fantasies," and gave an address in Hermosa Beach, California. If I was a pedophile I think I would write or call that "retail entertainment business." Another ad in this same issue featured an "Insider Video Club" ad that contained, among other erotic verbiage, promises of "cheerful, black-eyed Arab boys who reveal themselves before the cameras with a beguiling innocence and a total lack of self-consciousness." There was a picture of a nude young man in his early twenties (private parts darkened out) holding the hand of what appeared to be a "cheerful, black-eyed Arab boy" of 12 or 13 wearing loose-fitting Arab garb. The 130-minute video, in color, was titled "Arabian Nights."

However, the most important thing to remember is what Florence Rush wrote in *The Best Kept Secret* (1980): "A child molester is neither heterosexual nor homosexual . . . he is a *child* molester!"

Can you give some general child sexual abuse statistics?

Remember, statistics change constantly. Quote these only as approximate figures. These are figures compiled by the American Association for Protecting Children, a division of the American Humane Association.

• In 1985 an estimated 113,000 children were reported with sexual maltreatments.

• Experts estimate that 1 in 3 girls and 1 in 8 boys under the age of 18 will be involved in some form of forced sexual experience with an adult.

• In all reports of child abuse the perpetrator was male in 41 percent; in specifically sexual abuse reports, the perpetrator is male 77 percent of the time.

• In all reports of child abuse, the perpetrator was white in 56 percent of the cases; in cases involving sexual abuse the perpetrator is white 63 percent of the time.

• 70 percent of runaways are running away from an abusive environment.

• 80 percent of prison inmates have been abused as children.

• More than 80 percent of all prostitutes and hustlers were sexually abused as children.

• Most cases go unreported.

How widespread is the problem of child sexual abuse?

As I stated in the previous question, statistics should be regarded only as approximations, liable to change as more research is done. I do not feel we will ever be able to come up with truly accurate figures on the incidence of child sexual abuse in the United States, because so much about the problem will always be concealed.

According to the United States Department of Health and Human Services, there have been 19 studies using volunteer, college student, or random community samples. These studies have shown significant variance in the prevalence rates, ranging from 6 percent to 62 percent incidence of abuse among females and from 3 to 31 percent among males.

I will skip over most of the studies previous to 1982, when they guesstimated 22,918 sexual abuse cases in the United States. This research was compiled by the American Humane Association, which collects statistics from all 50 states. This figure is over 10 times larger than the 1,975 cases reported in 1976, the first year of the AHA's collection effect. In that year concerned people realized the figures were low and a National Incidence Study was commissioned by the National Center on Child Abuse and Neglect (NCCAN). Twenty-six counties in ten states were chosen to be representative of the whole country. By using confidential questionnaires and a toll-free number the survey estimated that 44,700 cases of child sexual abuse were reported in the year beginning April 1979.

Dr. David Finkelhor, associate director of the Family Violence Research Program, University of New Hampshire, has written that "although 44,700 cases of sexual abuse in a single year is a serious problem, even this figure is still considered a gross underestimate." It is likely, he points out, that cases never reported to any agency or professional—and thus unavailable for statistical compilation—may actually outnumber reported cases.

Dr. Finkelhor explains that it is difficult for researchers to question children about abuse for statistical purposes. Problems occur when questions are asked of children who are currently victims. Parents would be unlikely to allow interviews, and the victims themselves might place themselves in a dangerous situation if they did tell.

Research today, then, often consists of questioning adults about any sexual abuse that may have occurred to them as children.

In *Sexually Victimized Children,* Finkelhor studied 796 students at six New England colleges and universities. He defined sexual victimization as a sexual experience between a child 12 or under and a partner at least five years older, or between a child 13 to 16 and a partner at least 10 years older. By this definition, 19 percent of the women (approximately one in five) and 9 percent of the men (about one in 11) had been sexually victimized. About 20 percent of the experiences were with exhibitionists. Like the famous earlier study by Alfred Kinsey showing that one in four women are sexually abused, Finkelhor's research did not use samples that were representative; but there have been three other studies of the prevalence of sexual abuse that used more systematic samples.

In 1980, Glenn Kerdher, a researcher at Sam Houston State University, mailed questionnaires to 2,000 people randomly selected from those who possessed Texas drivers' licenses. In reply to one question, "Have you ever been a victim of sexual abuse as a child?" 12 percent of the females and 3 percent of the males—of a total of 1,054 respondents—admitted they had been sexually abused.

Dr. Finkelhor conducted another study, a household survey of a representative sample of 521 adults in the Boston metropolitan area, all of whom were the parents of children between the ages of six and 14. The adults were asked about sexual experiences they had had when they were children, prior to age 16, with a person at least five years older, which they themselves considered to have been abuse. Under this definition of sexual abuse, 15 percent of the women and 5 percent of the men had been sexually abused.

In the third study, one that found the highest rate of sexual abuse, sociologist Diana Russell, "The Incidence and Prevalence of Intrafamilial and Extrafamilial Sexual Abuse of Female Children," interviewed a random sample of 932 adult women in San Francisco in 1978 about a wide variety of sexual assault experiences. She found that 38 percent of these women had had a sexual abuse experience involving physical contact before they were 18. If noncontact experiences—such as encounters with exhibitionists and unwanted advances—were included, the figure rose to 54 percent.

Dr. Finkelhor analyzed Russell's figures and said the reason they were so much higher was in part due to the thoroughness of her questionnaire. Where other studies asked adults a single question about sexual abuse, Russell asked 14 separate questions about sexually exploitative experiences, any one of which may have reminded people about some sexual abuse that occurred in their childhood. She also included abusive experiences at the hands of peers in her definition of sexual abuse.

Margaret Hyde, in her 1984 book *Sexual Abuse: Let's Talk About It,* said that one of every five children in the United States is sexually abused before the age of 18, and 75 percent of the suspects are known to the child. Dr. E.H. Forsyth, a child psychiatrist, says one girl in four and one boy in six will be victims. Jennifer Aho and John Petras in *Learning About Sexual Abuse* (1985) report that Dr. Vincent Fontana, Chairman of the Mayor's Task Force on Child Abuse, New York City, relates that one of every three girls and one of eight boys have experienced some form of sexual exploitation. Joy Berry, in *Alerting Kids to the Danger of Sexual Abuse* (1984), cites one of four girls and one of 10 boys, with 90 percent of suspects being known to the victims. Colao and Hosansky, 1983, say that one in four girls is sexually abused and boys may be of equal risk.

Obviously these studies have added greatly to the general knowledge of child sexual abuse and have shown that an alarming number of children, both boys and girls, have been molested. They have also shown that most victims have never told anyone before, which confirms the assumption that reported cases are only a small percentage of actual experiences.

Remember that these studies cannot be generalized to the country as a whole and that they are reports from adults who were children many years ago. Times have certainly changed as we all know, and with the current attitude toward sex in general and the overall permissiveness of so-called "liberated parents" and "free thinkers" it's a wonder our children survive. The abnormal and perverse seem to be predominant factors in our present society.

More and more former victims, now adults, admit they were sexually molested as children. These people are helping to prevent future offenses by revealing their childhood experiences. I personally feel that more boys have been and are being molested than the average estimate of one in seven or eight because most cases are not reported to the police and do not come to the attention of any child welfare agency or professional. (See page 19, "Why don't more boys tell of molestation?") Also, all of the studies have not included child victims of pornography or prostitution, many of whom are male.

In 1984, the most recent year for which statistics are available, approximately 13 percent of the cases of maltreatment reported were identified as sexual abuse. Figuring from the above, the AHA estimated that 110,878 children were reported as victims of sexual maltreatment in 1984. These figures represent an increase of 54 percent between 1983 and 1984 or over 200 percent from

1976. Most experts consider the rise of incidence statistics to be the result of increasing awareness, and professional attention to the problem.

Does the victim seduce the suspect?

What do you think? Does a child wake up in the morning and wonder who he or she is going to seduce that day? A child molester does, and that includes adolescent child molesters, too.

If you think about it you have heard, "Well, she brought it on herself wearing those sexy clothes!" or, "She practically grabbed his cock in front of all of us!" or, "That child is really asking for it bending over like that!" But you cannot convince me that a child not previously engaged in sexual activity is "asking for it."

In past years many researchers have written about the role of the victim in sexual abuse. DeJong ("Sexual Abuse of Children," 1982) says the writers erroneously identified the child as the seducer. DeJong suggests that such theories are a narrow view of a very complex problem. David Finkelhor stated in his book *Sexually Victimized Children* that new understanding of the nature of rape, brought about largely by consciousness-raising efforts of the women's movement, has resulted in less blame toward the child victim. We should all be grateful for that.

See also the question, "Can a child initiate acts of sexual aggression?" on page 38.

Is there violence in child sexual abuse?

I am what the authorities call a nonviolent offender. This means, I guess, that I did not use force to seduce my victims. I did not beat or hit or torture or threaten. I just violated their minds as well as their bodies. I think my attack on a child, nonviolent or not, is still an attack and that "I just touched the child for a second" is a lame excuse for a suspect. We do not know what the short-term or even long-term trauma could be. We do not know how each individual victim will negatively respond. Molesters who "just touch" could cause a great deal of harm to a specific individual. (See "What are the effects of sexual abuse on children and families?" page 55.)

Diane DePanfilis, in *Literature Review of Sexual Abuse,* cites the work of K. MacFarlane in "Sexual Abuse of Children," which developed the following conclusions:

> In cases where the perpetrator is a family member or friend, physical force is rarely necessary to engage a child in sexual activity because of the child's

trusting, dependent relationship with the perpetrator. The child's cooperation is often facilitated by the adult's position of control/dominance. For example, the perpetrator may offer material goods, threaten physical violence, or misrepresent moral standards. In complying with the adult's wishes, the child may also be attempting to fulfill needs that normally are met in other ways. For example, a child may cooperate for love, affection, attention, or from a sense of loyalty to the adult. Conversely, a child's need to defy a parental figure, express anger about a chaotic home life, or act out sexual conflicts may increase a child's vulnerability to sexual abuse and exploitation.

DePanfilis goes on to discuss studies suggesting that violence in child sexual abuse may be on the increase. She cites the study by Burgess et al., "Child Sexual Abuse by a Family Member," which covered 44 cases of attempted and completed child sexual assault by a family member. This study differentiated between "sex-pressure" and "sex-force" assaults, which DePanfilis explains as follows:

> In the sex-pressure assault, the offender is an authority figure and pressures the child, who may not know that sexual activity is part of the offer. In this type of assault, sexual approaches are often presented to the child as instructional. Sex-force assaults, on the other hand, involve the threat of harm or physical force, rather than engaging the child emotionally. Intimidation and exploitation are used to gain power. In some cases the assault may be sadistic, for example the child may be beaten, choked or tortured. In these situations, the intent of the perpetrator is to hurt, punish or destroy the victim.

Burgess's study showed 39 percent of the cases as sex-pressure assaults and 61 percent as sex-force assaults.

Despite the kind of violence that has been shown to exist, some suspects will still insist that they *loved* the child — that they would never hurt or injure anyone in any way. That's exactly what I said: "I would never hurt that little girl!" And I really meant it! But now, after years of study and research, I realize that I did hurt that little girl, and all the boys and young men too.

What are the effects of sexual abuse on children and families?

We now get into an area where I really can't pin anyone down. There are so many variables. Some of the studies I have read just flat state, "A child will forever be damaged," and others say, "They forget about it in a few weeks." In truth, it seems that children are affected by sexual abuse in many different ways. A victim's reaction depends on several factors surrounding the abuse, both as it occurs and after it ends.

In her *Literature Review of Sexual Abuse,* Diane DePanfilis summarizes the findings of several who have studied sexual abuse to determine what these factors might be. MacFarlane suggests that they "include the child's age and development status, the relationship of the abuser to the child, the amount of force or violence used by the abuser, the degree of shame or guilt evoked in the child for his/her participation, and perhaps most importantly, the reactions of the child's parents and the professionals who intervene in the child's life." Another study, "Sexually Exploited Children: Service and Research Project" (from the New England Medical Center in 1984), gives other factors identified as contributory to emotional distress of sexually abused children: "maternal reactions to the abuse, the presence of physical injury, and the child's removal from the home." DeJong in 1983 "indicated that depression and depressive symptoms were significantly more common in cases that involved: intercourse; victims older than age six; delayed reporting; or multiple episodes of the sexual abuse."

C. Bagley reviewed a great deal of research on child sexual abuse from 1978 to 1982 and identified studies which found similar conditions in adolescents and adults who were victims of sexual abuse. DePanfilis summarizes them as follows:

> 1) suicidal gestures and attempts; 2) long-term personality problems, including guilt, anxiety, fears, depression and permanent impairment of self-image; 3) serious personality dysfunction, including chronic psychosis, self-mutilation, induced obesity, anorexia nervosa, hysterical seizures, and a chronically self-punitive lifestyle which is a response to feelings of guilt and self-disgust; 4) running away from home, or removal by judicial and child welfare authorities unaware of, or indifferent to, the sexual abuse; 5) prostitution or sexually dominated or explicit lifestyle; 6) withdrawal, coldness, frigidity or lack of trust in psychosexual relationships; 7) aggression, aggressive personality disorders, and chronic delinquency; and 8) substance abuse leading to chronic addiction and health impairment.

In all of my reading the researchers do agree that a child may experience less trauma and fewer long-term effects when the abuse is committed by a stranger rather than a close acquaintance. The main reason given is that parents will support the victim when a stranger is involved. Their reaction may be a bit hysterical, but it is the offender who receives the brunt of their anger. The child will be protected, his well-being the concern of family and friends. But if the abuse has been committed by a family member, the child may not receive this support. His report of the abuse may be disbelieved or suppressed; he may even be blamed for "causing" it to happen.

Not all stranger episodes are without their trauma, of course. If violence or physical force is involved, if rape or other physical harm has taken place, serious short- and long-term effects may result.

In incest cases, according to K. Meiselman, it is impossible to determine the effects of the sexual abuse alone, since the problems caused by the sexual acts cannot be separated from the problems of living in a disrupted and disturbed family. Depression, anxiety, lack of sexual identity, confusion, fear of sex, and traumatic neurosis have all been noted by various researchers, in addition to "more behavioral problems and general signs of harm than peers in the general population" (DePanfilis, citing Gomes-Schwartz et al.). Running away, described by Reich and Gutierres as "escape behavior," and self-injury are possibilities. Sadly, the victim of incest may also be in danger of further victimization by other offenders, even while the original abuse is ongoing. Finally, DePanfilis summarizes some of the short-term physical effects of sexual abuse as follows: "Eating and sleeping problems, vomiting, restlessness, and a failure-to-thrive syndrome;... genital irritation, stomachaches, painful discharge of urine, altered sleeping patterns, enuresis, encopresia, and hyperactivity;... and venereal disease...."

DePanfilis also summarizes the findings of Browne and Finkelhor in their study of the effects of child sexual abuse. Their research concerned only the initial effects, those manifested within two years of the termination of the abuse. They reported

> [effects on] emotional reactions and self-perception; physical and somatic complaints; effects on interpersonal interaction; effects on sexuality; and effects on social functioning. Based on this analysis, the authors report that the empirical literature confirms the existence — in a percentage of the victim population — of almost all the initial effects reported in the clinical literature including: fear, anxiety, depression and self-destructive behavior, anger, aggression, guilt and shame, impaired ability to trust, revictimization, sexually inappropriate behavior, school problems, truancy, running away, and delinquency. However, no effect was found to be universal.

Researchers differ significantly in their assessments of the long-term effects of sexual abuse, but deYoung suggests the following: family disturbances; psychological disturbances; sexual problems; sexual victimization; lesbianism; and prostitution. Vander May and Neff note in deYoung's "Sexual Victimization of Children" the following long-term effects: promiscuity; inability to assume a mother-wife role; alcoholism and drug abuse; prostitution; sexual dysfunctioning; delinquency; depression; and suicide. Greenberg (1982) and Wilbur (1984) both add that multiple personality disorders have been seen in some victims.

Dr. Brandt F. Steele, "Notes on the Lasting Effects of Early Child Abuse Throughout the Life Cycle" (1986), has the following to say regarding sexual abuse victims:

> Children, both boys and girls, who have felt inadequately cared for and protected by their mothers and have also been sexually maltreated by other family

members seem to have an especially difficult time as they grow up and try to be part of society. They have an especially low sense of self-esteem and a poor sense of identity which is particularly evident in the sphere of sexual identity. They continue to feel exploited and have some tendency to exploit others. Males tend to feel much more ashamed, embarrassed and denigrated by their past experience. Girls seem to feel more degraded and dirty or despoiled. Both carry a deep, lasting, although often unconscious sense of fear, anger and hatred toward authorities and against those . . . they feel have exploited them in the past and will do so again in the future. A significant number of such youngsters of either sex eventually get into prostitution . . . but most have other types of sexual problems. True intimacy seems unattainable. They may develop a significant or even a complete aversion to sexual activity and maintain celibate, rather lonely anhedonic lives without ever developing significant relationships with the opposite gender. Such experiences may also contribute in many cases to the development of homosexual orientations and alternative life styles. A great many, possibly the majority, maintain a superficial, more normal pattern. They marry, although they may decide not to have children. Yet even in a superficially normal marriage they often remain vaguely, bewilderingly unhappy, unsatisfied, unable to describe what is really wrong except that they are unhappy and cannot relate to the opposite sex in a comfortable, pleasurable way.

Results of two studies indicate that between 50 and 75 percent of minors involved in pornography had been sexually abused within the family. In James and Meyerding, "Early Sexual Experience and Prostitution," it is reported that incestuous abuse makes a child (especially a runaway) more vulnerable to sexual victimization by others.

Many victims of incest have revealed their sexual histories while undergoing therapy for other reasons. In a May 1983 study, Husain and Chapel report that out of 437 adolescent girls admitted to a psychiatric hospital for emotional problems, 13.9 percent reported incestuous relationships in their backgrounds. A study by Emslie and Rosenfeld, involving 65 children and adolescents hospitalized for severe psychiatric problems, showed incest reports among 37.5 percent of the nonpsychotic girls, 10 percent of the psychotic girls, and about 8 percent of all the boys. These studies support the statement of J. Spencer ("Father-Daughter Incest") that victims of incest often become involved with courts, social workers, or other agencies of intervention, not because they have reported themselves as victims of incest, but because their sexual history has resulted in antisocial behavior. Many victims may go all the way through the various interventions without ever reporting the incest. Perhaps they are never asked; perhaps even if they are asked they may not give a correct answer. So much depends upon those initial contacts. That's why we need specially trained counselors in juvenile facilities, as well as training for others who may represent the first adult authority to confront the child — a nurse, doctor, welfare worker, policeman or the undergraduate student who works the night shift at the juvenile detention facility.

As I said at the beginning of this question, the many variables involved make it difficult to state with certainty the effects of sexual abuse. The 1985 work of Browne and Finkelhor is, however, useful to quote: "Empirical studies with adults confirm the presence of many of the hypothesized long-term effects of sexual abuse mentioned in the clinical literature: suicidal tendencies, fears, isolation and stigma, lowered self-esteem, distrust, revictimization, substance abuse, and sexual problems such as sexual dysphoria, sexual dysfunction and promiscuity." Also useful is the framework proposed by Browne and Finkelhor for understanding the effects of child sexual abuse. This framework identifies four areas of trauma from which the psychological injury springs. As summarized by DePanfilis, they are

> traumatic sexualization, betrayal, stigmatization and powerlessness. "Traumatic sexualization" refers to a process in which a child's sexuality is shaped in a developmentally inappropriate and interpersonally dysfunctional fashion as a result of sexual abuse. "Betrayal" refers to the process through which children discover that someone on whom they were dependent has caused them harm. "Powerlessness" refers to the way in which the child's will, desires and sense of efficacy are continually contravened. "Stigmatization" refers to the negative connotations — e.g., badness, shame, and guilt — that are communicated to the child during the abuse. These statements are incorporated into the child's self-image.

Has research on long-term effects been valid? It's hard to judge. Finkelhor, in a 1984 paper *(Designing Studies on the Impact and Treatment of Child Sexual Abuse),* points out that samples used for this research have not necessarily been representative of the population as a whole. This is certainly true, since these samples have often been drawn from prisons, psychiatric hospitals, drug and alcohol treatment programs, etc. People in these populations have serious problems and are often only too happy to tell you what they think you want to hear. Every con has his own "con"; convicts and alcoholics can be very glib and run off at the mouth like a water faucet on any subject. Better sampling and research design are needed.

What are the family dynamics surrounding incest?

The most commonly reported forms of incest are father-daughter or father-figure and daughter. (Incest is defined as sexual abuse among members of the same family, and in most states the definition of "family" includes members not related by blood, such as stepfathers.) Incest involving the father abusing the son or the mother abusing either child is much less common, at least in the reports.

One type of incest that is showing up in the literature and evidently deserves further attention is stepfather-daughter abuse. DePanfilis cites a study by Diana Russell:

Russell attempted to analyze the differences between the prevalence and seriousness of incest between children and stepfathers and children and biological fathers. She interviewed a random sample of 930 adult women in San Francisco . . . and concluded that 17 percent, or approximately one out of every six women, for whom a stepfather was the principal father figure in childhood, were sexually abused by him. The comparable figures for biological fathers were two percent, or one out of approximately 40 women. In addition, when a distinction was made between "very serious sexual abuse" and other less serious forms, 47 percent of the cases of sexual abuse by stepfathers were defined as "very serious," compared with 26 percent by biological fathers. At least three other studies have found that a stepfather as the principal father figure increased a girl's risk for all types of sexual abuse.

In most research on incest, the samples studied have been too small (that is, not enough cases have been studied) for the researchers to draw firm conclusions about the causes of incest. But in the research that has been done, some very similar findings are showing up, which suggests that researchers are on the right track. Diane DePanfilis summarizes some of these in her *Literature Review of Sexual Abuse*. She first cites the work of Lustig et al., in "Incest: A Family Group Survival Pattern," who note that the following conditions are often present in families where father-daughter incest occurs:

1) The emergence of the daughter as the central female figure of the household, in some respects taking over the role of the mother; 2) the relative sexual incompatibility of the parents; 3) the unwillingness of the father to seek a partner outside the nuclear family; 4) pervasive fears of abandonment and family disintegration; and 5) unconscious sanction of the incest by the mother, who condones or promotes the daughter's sexual role with her father.

From K.C. Meiselman, *Incest: A Psychological Study of Causes and Effects with Treatment Recommendations,* DePanfilis draws descriptions of three different types of incestuous fathers: "1) fathers for whom the incest is part of a pattern of 'indiscriminate promiscuity'; 2) fathers with an intense craving for young children (pedophilia); and 3) fathers who, in the absence of a satisfying relationship with their wives, choose a daughter as a sexual partner because they do not wish to cultivate sexual contacts outside their own families."

Some researchers, DePanfilis notes, have described incestuous fathers as "passive, ineffective, and introverted," while others have found them "strong, authoritarian, and extremely controlling." Though these descriptions seem to conflict, perhaps they can be explained by what other researchers have described as a dual role played by the father, who "uses his position of authority to control the daughter's behavior, obtain her developing sexuality for himself, or protect her from rival boyfriends, while at the same time playing the awkward adolescent lover" (DePanfilis).

Finkelhor, in *Sexually Victimized Children,* refers to the social isolation many researchers have noted in incestuous families, and points out that the incestuous relationship usually increases the isolation.

DePanfilis cites several studies suggesting a connection between alcohol abuse and incest.

Finally, J. Spencer, in his article "Father-Daughter Incest: A Clinical View from the Corrections Field," notes that other family members may actually be aware of the incest and ignore it, deny it, or even actively attempt to keep it a secret from those outside the family. People who react this way are really protecting themselves. After all, what happens to the family if someone finds out? The suspect could go to prison; the family could lose its source of income; the community might turn against them; family members might even turn against each other.

What are the effects of incest?

Everyone in an incestuous family suffers. Society's rules about what a family should be are turned upside down, and confusion and conflict result. In a father-daughter incestuous relationship, perhaps the greatest confusion and anxiety are borne by the daughter, especially if she is an adolescent. After all, adolescent girls have enough to deal with growing up in normal homes. They need reassurance and guidance to adjust to their developing sexuality. Imagine the additional strain placed on a girl involved in a sexual relationship with her father. Because family roles are distorted, she doesn't understand her place in the family—how she should relate to parents and siblings.

We can see the suffering in these young victims when we look at the behavior of adolescents being treated for incest. Truancy, drug use, and promiscuity are common. These are self-punishing behaviors, and they are also seen in women who were sexually abused as children but never reported the abuse until adulthood.

In *Incest: The Ultimate Sexual Taboo,* Masters and Johnson report:

> The [incest] victim suffers from the experience itself, which occasionally causes physical damage and frequently results in psychological damage; and she (or he) also eventually suffers the loss of her sense of security and of her own personal worth. In fact, a long-continued, guilt-ridden repression of the feelings generated by incest may eventually affect every aspect of her life.

The psychological damage resulting from incest often leads to sexual problems by the time victims reach adulthood. These problems can range from frigidity to nymphomania. An inability to develop intimate relationships or enjoy sex of any sort is common. M.J. Baisden in *The World of Roseaphrenia* reports that of 160 women he treated for sexual problems, 90 percent had been molested as children. Of that group, 22.5 percent had been abused by fathers or stepfathers.

Other family members also suffer the effects of incest. If the case is made public, the community often reacts harshly, and the legal intervention is punishing. The stress on everyone in the family is tremendous. The marriage often ends in divorce, and family members are driven even further apart.

I've heard that the "cure" of intervention in child sexual abuse cases can be worse than the abuse itself. How can this be?

This is a painful subject. I wish I could say that everyone involved in assisting the victim was on the same train.

What is the proper approach to handling sexual abuse? Why is there such great disagreement even within small communities? You can imagine the debates in a large medical center. Why does a "helping hand" often slap the victim down? Is there a strategy that can solve everything?

Since I have added several questions to the original, let's try and get some answers from a body of people who have taken time and effort to expound their thinking on the subject of proper intervention.

Diane DePanfilis states that "the reactions of parents, members of the community, and interviewing professionals to the sexual abuse of a child are crucial in determining the psychological effects on the child." L.G. Schultz asserts that "the greatest potential damage to the child's personality is caused by society and the victim's parents, as a result of 1) the need to use the victim to prosecute the suspect (to whom the victim may be deeply attached, as in the case of an incestuous parent), and 2) the need of parents to prove that the victim did not participate voluntarily and that they were not failures as parents." V. DeFrancis adds that some parents seem more concerned about how the report disrupts their own lives than they are about the child's trauma. This kind of response crops up most where incest is involved.

It would be nice to know that when the parents don't respond right, we can rely on people who've been trained to handle child sexual abuse cases. Unfortunately, this is not always so.

One problem with intervention is that it must happen at a time when a family is in crisis. They are afraid, angry, confused, and vulnerable. It can't be easy at any time to have a lot of police, lawyers, social workers, doctors, etc., poking around asking a lot of personal questions. Imagine how much harder it must be at such a sensitive time. Making it worse is the lack of coordination between intervening agencies. The family may have to submit to the same interrogations over and over. Or their case may never be reported to the proper authorities because somebody in one agency disagrees with the way another agency handles such cases and so decides not to mention it. (Finkelhor found that this does happen; a survey he conducted of 790 Boston-area professionals showed that 64 percent of the sexual abuse cases were not being reported to the proper agencies by certain professionals because of disagreement as to how the cases should be handled.) Families can be caught in the middle as various agencies squabble over how to handle the cases. As DePanfilis puts it, "The police and prosecutors may want to prosecute the offender; child protective services may want to remove the child; and mental health personnel may want to involve the entire family in treatment. Very few communities have been able to achieve true cooperation and coordination of services." And that doesn't even include the "good advice" and suggestions the family and police will receive from other family members, in-laws, crusading organizations, church groups, and busybodies. All pressures on the victim and family at the worst possible time. In cases of incest, the pressures can be even worse as the family is often separated and may lose their source of income (if the father is jailed or loses his job). No wonder families often feel that the "cure" is, indeed, worse than the original problem. And researchers have found this feeling to be well-grounded. DeFrancis, Giaretto, Miner, and McKerrow have all agreed that "the emotional damage resulting from the intervention of 'helping agents' in our society may equal, or far exceed, the harm caused by the abusive incident" (DePanfilis).

Surely the most important goal of intervention is to protect the child victim. Maybe if agencies would keep this goal in mind, they could cooperate better. Cooperation is vital because no agency by itself can protect all those children and meet all their needs. Also, no one type of intervention can take care of every case of sexual abuse. There are too many cases and the cases are too different. After all, each case involves a unique group of individuals. It is important that every family be comprehensively (and *sensitively*) assessed to determine the most effective intervention and treatment for that case.

Sometimes it is also necessary that the victim undergo a medical examination. This, too, should be handled with extreme sensitivity. (For cautions, see page 82, "Will a doctor's examination show that a child has been molested?") It is recommended that the examination include a test for venereal disease and for gonorrheal infections of the throat and rectum, as well as documentation of any evidence that foreign objects have been inserted into an orifice.

Research by Veltkamp, et al., and by Stember strongly suggests that the suspect undergo a psychological evaluation. Ideally this evaluation will help the intervening agency to develop a treatment approach that has some hope of success.

These all seem like common-sense suggestions. So why do the various agencies seem to have so much trouble figuring out what to do in child sexual abuse cases? There are many reasons. For example, DePanfilis summarizes the findings of J. Goodwin ("Helping the Child Who Reports Incest") in identifying reasons for professional unresponsiveness:

1) lack of experience with incest cases, 2) fear of being fooled by an incest hoax, 3) the difficulty of working with the family without joining the family's system of blaming and recrimination, 4) failure to remember the health and interpersonal problems in the child and in the family that preceed [sic] the accusation of incest.

The Newbergers report that society tends to respond in one of three ways to child sexual abuse. DePanfilis lists these responses:

1) an egocentric orientation, in which child sexual victimization is avoided, denied, or responded to out of individual need; 2) a conventional orientation, in which the response is organized around rules of correct behavior; and 3) an individualistic orientation, in which the response focuses on examining the particular circumstances in individual cases, considering the child's needs for protection, the perpetrator's need for corrective intervention, the family's need to maintain intimate relationships, and our institution's needs to do their jobs.

Obviously, the third response is what we'd all like to aim for.

Finally, DePanfilis lists the following recommendations for successful intervention, from the research of Friedman et al.:

Successful intervention: 1) protects the child and stops the abuse; 2) minimizes trauma; 3) accurately and completely establishes facts; 4) controls the family situation; 5) accurately assesses needed services; and 6) rapidly implements treatment and/or a treatment plan.

It certainly sounds good on paper, doesn't it? If every community and the various agencies involved would strive toward these six goals, a lot of problems would not occur and victims wouldn't be revictimized or assaulted over and over.

As you read *MAN/child* you must sense the frustration I feel when I am forced, time and again, to recognize the validity of the arguments for the use of trained professionals in this area, and then have to qualify statements knowing that people are just people, degrees or not. Some profess to know what they are doing, when in reality they are causing a great deal of additional harm to the victim.

What has the government accomplished in preventing child sexual abuse?

Between fiscal 1980 and 1982, the National Center on Child Abuse and Neglect, with federal funding, launched six projects for the purpose of developing educational materials that would teach children to avoid sexual abuse. Five of the projects concentrated on developing full-scale educational programs, including curricula and materials, for children from preschool through high school. The sixth project developed a film on child sexual abuse to be used with 8- to 12-year-olds. The final report on these six projects indicated that the programs were well accepted by the school systems and other organizations who helped in the testing of the materials.

State governments, too, have been working to develop education and prevention activities. S.L. Kleven and the Coalition for Child Advocacy report that a project in the state of Washington was field-tested in 25 preschool or day care programs, with pre- and post-tests used to check its effectiveness. This sort of testing helped the researchers identify criteria for evaluating such projects.

The Attorney General's Task Force on Family Violence, like most researchers, has stressed the importance of continued development of prevention programs. Among several recommendations developed by the Task Force was the suggestion that "the public at large ... be aware of the magnitude and urgency of the problems represented by family violence and the costs to society if prevention is not given high priority, for many of today's abused children will be tomorrow's abusers, runaways, and delinquents" (*Final Report,* September 1984, p. 64).

What is the background regarding treatment of victims and their families in child sexual abuse cases?

I hate to start on a negative note (as I have had to do quite often in this book), but so far there has not been nearly enough research on the effectiveness of different treatment approaches. Everybody seems to have a different way of handling child sexual abuse cases, including casework counseling (probably the most common), placement of the victim in foster care, crisis services, and long-term mental health services or day care assistance. But no one has done a nationwide study on the outcome of these approaches, or even how they are used in specific cases.

DePanfilis states:

> A variety of treatment models have been developed which explore new approaches for helping sexually abusive families to function in healthier ways. MacFarlane and Bulkley have categorized the major program models as follows: 1) the victim advocacy model, is characterized by a victim-centered orientation and by the belief that child sexual abuse is a crime which requires visible condemnation by society in the form of strong legal sanctions and the active involvement of the criminal justice system; 2) the improvement model, uses the criminal justice system, but also uses multidisciplinary approaches for improving and humanizing the investigation and prosecution of child sexual abuse cases; 3) the service modification model, focuses on modifying systems in order

to reduce the impact and trauma of the legal process upon the child and family, but uses the criminal justice system as a motivator for rehabilitation; 4) the independent model, operates without a stand for or against criminal or juvenile court involvement and provides a variety of treatment services which function independently from the legal system; and 5) the system alternative model, operates from a philosophical position against the deliberate use of criminal or juvenile court and maintains a treatment orientation which does not use the legal system and focuses on the family as a unit.

Various treatment programs have been springing up around the United States in the last 15 years or so, and most of them fall somewhere in between the categories MacFarlane and Bulkley list, using some of this approach and some of that. More programs dealing with child sexual abuse can be expected to develop, what with all the attention the problem is getting in the media these days. Even Congress has opened its eyes enough to authorize special funding for sexual abuse research (Public Law 98-457, an amendment to the Child Abuse Prevention and Treatment Act).

One of the first treatment programs was developed in 1971 and became a model for others that followed. Developed by the Juvenile Probation Department of Santa Clara County, California, it is now called the Child Sexual Abuse Treatment Program (CSATP). H. Giaretto tells us that the program makes use of three different (but coordinated) types of help to achieve its goal of resocializing families. The three helping efforts come from professional staff from several different agencies; volunteers; and self-help groups (Parents United and Daughters and Sons United). Giaretto reports that CSATP has had an average increase in referrals of about 40 percent every year since 1974, so it must be getting the word out and doing something right.

The National Center on Child Abuse and Neglect (NCCAN) has funded a number of projects over the years. Four programs in 1978 provided a variety of services (such as crisis intervention, 24-hour hotline counseling, legal assistance, and much more), working through public and private facilities in Albuquerque, Chicago, Knoxville TN, and Edina MN. In 1980, NCCAN funded the following five institutes for sexual abuse treatment and training: the Joseph J. Peters Institute, Philadelphia; the Knoxville Institute for Sexual Abuse Treatment, Knoxville TN; the Child Abuse Unit for Studies, Education and Services (CAUSES), Chicago; the Sexual Assault Center, Harborview Medical Center, Seattle; and the Institute for the Community as Extended Family (ICEF), San Jose CA. That same year, NCCAN also backed 14 projects to demonstrate how services for victims and families could be improved. These latter projects were carried out by various community agencies such as a mental health center, a children's hospital, and a police department, among others. Kendrick reports that in all but one of the 14 cases, project directors were able to obtain additional funding from other sources beyond the NCCAN-backed demonstration period, which suggests that the results were good enough — or at least the approaches proved valid enough — to get attention. (In the one case where funding was not obtained, other arrangements were made so that service to the families could continue.)

Recently, as Kendrick points out, researchers have begun to question the validity of any cut-and-dried approach that assumes all families behave in the same way. Spencer suggests that *what* treatment is chosen is probably less important than how it is tailored to meet the needs of the individuals involved. And many researchers have stressed that whatever treatment is used, it should be regarded as a long-term effort, not something that can be accomplished in a session or two.

Dr. Roland Summit has identified and described what he calls the Child Sexual Abuse Accommodation Syndrome, a sequence of five conditions or events common to child victims of sexual abuse. In a 1983 paper, Summit proposed this syndrome as "a simple and logical model for use by clinicians to improve understanding and acceptance of the child's position in the complex and controversial dynamics of sexual victimization." The syndrome is caused by children's vulnerability and the rejection children often meet when attempting "to reconcile their private experiences with the realities of the outer world." Dr. Summit notes that a child's mechanisms for coping with the trauma of sexual abuse contradict an adult's expectations of "normal" behavior for a victim, expectations which are inappropriate where children are concerned. The result of this contradiction is often that the child is branded as a liar or manipulator. Summit says that "such abandonment by the very adults most crucial to the child's protection and recovery drives the child deeper into self-blame, self-hate, alienation and revictimization." The options open to the child at this point are, sadly, the very behaviors certain to destroy any credibility his accusations may initially have had. These options make up the last three of the five categories comprising the accommodation syndrome, which Summit lists as "(1) secrecy, (2) helplessness, (3) entrapment and accommodation, (4) delayed, unconvincing disclosure, and (5) retraction." He goes on to discuss each of these categories in detail, demonstrating how each represents reality for the child even as it contradicts adult assumptions about victim behavior.

From the secrecy surrounding sexual abuse, the child victim perceives the message that what is happening is bad and dangerous. The victim believes the molester's threats of a fearful outcome if the secret is revealed. The few victims who take the chance and try to report the abuse to another adult are met with disbelief, even told not to say such things again. Retrospective surveys of adults who were sexually abused in childhood confirm these patterns: Most were prevented by fear from telling anyone, and those who did tell generally received negative and suppressive responses from parents. Yet as Dr. Summit points out, adults *expect* victims to report abuse; if a child delays and then complains, his credibility is even further diminished ("Why didn't you tell me this before, if it was so bad?").

The helplessness and dependency of children are not given proper consideration by adults, who expect self-protection and prompt disclosure by victims. Children who are taught to say "no" to strangers are still expected to "behave" and comply with the requests of a trusted adult, and studies have amply demonstrated that abuse is far more likely to come from a known adult figure than from a stranger. Yet despite the obviously unequal power between a frightened, compliant child and an adult that child recognizes as an authority figure, other adults on hearing of abuse will find it impossible to empathize fully with the child's helplessness. Unless the abuse involved overwhelming force, adults will tend to believe that the child was a willing party to the affair. This belief reinforces the child's self-blame.

Accommodation is the child's natural and necessary response to the realization of his or her entrapment. Particularly in cases of incest, the abuse is seldom a one-time occurrence, and the child who did not seek or did not receive immediate help has no option but to accept the situation. Acceptance requires accommodation, which involves a complex and ultimately destructive "vertical split in reality testing." In this split, the bad, abusive parent must be seen as good, else the child must admit to herself that she is left without support or safety. If the parent is "good," then the child assumes herself to be bad because she has somehow caused this pain to be brought on herself. So she must learn to be "good" also, which the abusive parent defines for her as complying uncomplainingly with his demands. Failure to do so, he warns, will destroy the family. Thus the child is given responsibility for the fate of the family. Now, Dr. Summit says, "There is an inevitable splitting of conventional moral values. Maintaining a lie to keep the secret is the ultimate virtue, while telling the truth would be the greatest sin. A child thus victimized will appear to accept or to seek sexual contact without complaint."

Although most sexual abuse is never disclosed, delayed, unconvincing reports sometimes result from an overwhelming conflict in a family where sexual abuse has been accommodated for years. An incest victim who has been silent throughout her childhood may challenge her parents' authority in adolescence and try to break free from the abuse. Unfortunately for the victim, her psychological adjustment to the abuse may have led to a pattern of delinquency and rebelliousness that hurts her credibility when anger against her father finally compels her to disclose the secret. It is much easier for adults to identify with a father trying to "control" this rebellious child.

Alternatively, some children's psychological adjustment results in an overachieving, eager-to-please personality. These children may grow up to be honor students or football team captains. If one of these model teenagers tries to disclose a history of abuse, adults will be all the more disbelieving, or they will assume the abuse was not harmful to the child. Thus, whatever behavior and circumstances surround the disclosure, adults are likely to be unconvinced that there is any cause for complaint.

Meeting at all levels with such discouraging reactions from adults, the child moves naturally to the fifth level of the accommodation syndrome by retracting his accusations. Sadly, the lie of retraction is much easier for adults to believe than any truthful disclosure, and the cycle of the accommodation syndrome is perpetuated as children learn to keep quiet and adults learn not to listen.

Dr. Summit states that "recognition of sexual molestation in a child is entirely dependent upon the individual's inherent willingness to entertain the possibility that the condition may exist." He also says that, unfortunately, the professionals with the most advanced training often seem the least willing to accept such a possibility. Summit urges that professionals at all levels and in all fields be more aware of child sexual abuse and the accommodation syndrome. He further suggests that no one agency is in itself sufficient to address the needs of child sexual abuse victims and that agencies must learn to work as a team to insure the best outcome for victim, offender, and family.

A. Mayer has proposed several treatment goals for incest victims. They are listed by DePanfilis as follows:

1. Stabilize the environment.

2. Provide a trustworthy, nurturing and consistent role model via the therapeutic relationship.

3. Diminish guilt/blame/sense of responsibility via role plays and bibliotherapy.

4. Help the victim understand inappropriate family dynamics (role reversal, betrayal of trust) via supportive information sharing.

5. Enhance self-esteem by assertiveness training and environmental manipulation.

6. Teach assertiveness training and environmental manipulation.

7. Help rechannel acting out and self-destructive behaviors by enhancing self-esteem, and teaching self-control and social skills.

8. Encourage catharsis/ventilation of repressed affect (anger, fear) followed by correct labeling of affective states.

9. Diminish compulsive sexual behaviors and the tendency to sexualize all relationships and promote a healthy sexual orientation through behavioral change and sex education.

10. Alleviate fear/anxiety/alienation by providing support, nurturing, empathy and understanding.

11. Provide dyad sessions with offender to enhance communication and provide offender with opportunity to accept/acknowledge feelings of victim and assume full responsibility for molestation.

12. Provide dyad sessions with the mother to enhance bonding, allow for

victim to ventilate and provide the mother with the opportunity to assume full
responsibility for not protecting victim and for not being aware of the molestation.
13. Provide triad (and/or total family) sessions to solidify gains in dyad sessions, improve communication skills and formulate family goals/plans.

Two other researchers, S.M. Sgroi and N.T. Dana, suggest treatment
issues for mothers of incest victims. As summarized by DePanfilis, they are:
"establishing trust, sharing past history of abuse, dealing with denial, identifying unreasonable expectations, practicing limit setting, dealing with anger,
improving communication, assertiveness training, improving social skills,
assisting with concrete services, improving body awareness, and support
through legal justice system involvement."

Other researchers cited by DePanfilis have noted the need for more attention in the following areas: "treatment needs of the victim's siblings, . . . the
special considerations involved with stepfamilies, . . . [and] the increasing
number of reports of sibling abuse in incestuous families."

K. MacFarlane, in "Program Considerations in the Treatment of Incest
Offenders," suggests general treatment goals for families in cases of incest.
These include lessening the atmosphere of crisis in the family; giving the family some kind of framework within which they can function rationally and thus
cope with their situation; teaching family members to use some acceptable
channels or outlets for their anger; helping them get past the denial instinct
so that they can accept their treatment; and lessening their need to isolate
themselves as a family.

For further research and study on this specific treatment area see the
following authors (all listed in the Bibliography): Kroth, A.J., "Family
Therapy Impact on Intrafamilial Child Sexual Abuse"; Mrazek, P., "Special
Problems in the Treatment of Child Sexual Abuse"; Russell, A., and Trainor,
C., *Trends in Child Abuse and Neglect: A National Perspective;* MacFarlane,
K., and Bulkley, J., "Treating Child Sexual Abuse: An Overview of Current
Program Models"; Brecker E., *Treatment Programs for Sex Offenders;* Gia-
retto, H., *Integrated Treatment of Child Sexual Abuse* and "A Comprehensive
Child Sexual Abuse Treatment Program"; Berkeley Planning Associates and
Urban and Rural Systems Associates, *Historical Case Studies: Evaluation of the
Clinical Demonstration of Child Abuse and Neglect;* Whitcomb, D., *Assisting
Child Victims of Sexual Abuse: How Two Communities Developed Programs
for the Special Needs of Child Victims;* Kendrick, M., *What We've Learned
from Community Responses to Intrafamily Child Sexual Abuse;* Spencer, J.,
Father-Daughter Incest; Zaphiris, A., "Father-Daughter Incest" and *Methods
and Skills for a Differential Assessment and Treatment in Incest, Sexual Abuse
and Sexual Exploitation of Children;* Summit, R., "Sexual Child Abuse, the
Psychotherapist, and the Team Concept"; Gottlieb, B., *The Co-Therapy*

Relationship in Group Treatment of Sexually Mistreated Adolescent Girls; Mayer, A., *Sexual Abuse Causes, Consequences, and Treatment of Incestuous and Pedophilia Acts;* Sgroi, S., and Dana, N., *Individual and Group Treatment of Mothers of Incest Victims;* Costell, R., *The Nature and Treatment of Male Sex Offenders;* Yaffe, M., "The Assessment and Treatment of Paedophilia"; Groth, A., and Birnham, H., "Adult Sexual Orientation and Attraction to Underage Persons"; Groth, A., "Patterns of Sexual Assault Against Children and Adolescents"; Groth, A., et al., "The Child Molester: Clinical Observations"; Renshaw, D., *Incest Understanding and Treatment;* Thomas, J., and Rogers, C., *A Treatment Program for Intrafamily Juvenile Sexual Offenders;* and Herman, J., "Recognition and Treatment of Incestuous Families."

What is the legal response to child sexual abuse?

(Before we start on this question let me direct you to the Definitions, Laws and Legal Aspects section of *MAN/child.* References are listed at the end of that section that pertain to this answer.)

It is difficult to determine the "correct" role for the legal system, especially the criminal justice system, in child sexual abuse cases. The attempt to do so has led to many battles in legislatures and courts, and the laws are constantly changing.

Naturally, every state has laws regarding child sexual abuse, but they vary widely in approaches and even definitions. For example, who is a "child" victim? Kocen and Bulkley, in "Analysis of Incest Statutes," report that the upper age limit established by the various states ranges from 11 to 17 years. And what is "abuse"? In Massachusetts (just for example), the sexual victimization of a child may be filed under 25 different statutes. No wonder we have trouble determining how widespread the problem of abuse is. It travels under so many assumed names.

Fortunately, legislators around the nation are working to improve child sexual laws. DePanfilis reports that

> New child sexual abuse criminal legislation has improved upon previous laws for statutory rape and child molestation. In general, these new statutes specifically define the prohibited acts, establish a tiered structure of offenses with graduated penalties based on the age of the victim and/or perpetrator, and protect children from abuse by family members or others in a position of authority over the child.

All states have reporting laws; that is, all states require certain individuals to report any instance where they suspect child sexual abuse. As with everything else in this legislative stew, there are variances in who must report, whom they must report to, and what action is taken upon reports once they are made. Doctors, teachers, and others who work closely with children are generally included in the "who must report" column. Depending on the state, some need report initially only to a child protective services agency; others may choose child services or a law enforcement agency; and some report only to law enforcement. In a state where reports are made to child services, most laws leave it up to that agency to decide whether to pass the reports on to police.

Results of reports may include criminal prosecution of the offender; juvenile court action to protect the child, if a family member is involved; or a combination of juvenile and criminal court proceedings.

Incest presents special legal problems. It is specifically prohibited in all states except New Jersey, but most states define the criminal act as sexual intercourse only. Thus when any other type of intrafamilial sexual abuse, such as fondling or even oral or anal intercourse, is involved, the offender usually must be prosecuted under some combination of criminal child sexual abuse laws.

DePanfilis cites Kocen and Bulkley's "Analysis of Incest Statutes" in summarizing recent incest law reform:

> On the one hand, some incest statutes are moving toward greater protection of the minor child. Others, however, are decriminalizing all incestuous sexual activity between relatives, which would include minors. One State decriminalized incest only where it involves minors. At least half of the States seem to have expanded the purpose of their incest laws to include step-parents and adoptive parents.

Charges involving child sexual abuse in the family may also be filed (again, depending on the state) under family violence laws. Such laws are generally designed to aid battered spouses, but they often provide for court action that can be beneficial to the sexually abused child as well: For instance, the offender can be ordered to vacate the home, to have no contact with the victim, to undergo counseling, or to pay support (Lerman, "State Legislation on Domestic Violence").

In other cases, sexual psychopath laws are sometimes involved. Under these laws, some sex offenders may be committed to mental health facilities rather than sentenced to prison terms (Bulkley, "Other Relevant Child Sexual Abuse Statutes").

Finally, DePanfilis reports that

> laws dealing with sexual exploitation have been enacted in all States.... In 1978, Congress broadened the definition of sexual abuse in the Federal Child Abuse Prevention and Treatment Act to include sexual exploitation. This required States to make their laws consistent with the Federal Act in order to be eligible for Federal assistance.... Further, in 1984, Congress amended the Federal Protection of Children Against Sexual Exploitation Act of 1977, which

addresses the sexual exploitation of children through prostitution and pornography. These amendments have increased the fines for offenses and changed the definition to include prosecution of individuals who *trade* pornographic materials, as well as those who *sell* them.... While the majority of children affected by these laws are exploited by persons not responsible for their care, there is some relationship between sexual exploitation and sexual abuse....

Here is a sub-question: What is the legal intervention in sexual abuse cases?

Here's where the controversy about "correct" use of the legal system really becomes heated. When you consider what is usually involved in traditional legal intervention — rigorous and repeated interrogation by a variety of questioners from law enforcement, medical, and social service agencies; unpleasant medical examinations; polygraph tests; and testimony and cross-examination in the presence of the suspect — it is not surprising that many experts consider such intervention severely traumatic to the victim and family.

The problem is that many of the procedures that may prove traumatic to the child are designed to protect the suspect's constitutional rights. It is not easy to change the laws in a way that protects both victim and suspect.

Consider the need for a child to testify in open court, in the presence of the suspect. Surely that is traumatic for some if not most child victims. Some experts suggest that a child may not testify accurately or may, out of fear, retract his statement when confronted by the person who has threatened and hurt him. Yet the Sixth Amendment to the United States Constitution guarantees that suspect the right to confront his accuser. What's the answer? The American Bar Association in 1982 recommended that testimony by children in open court be avoided whenever possible. The United States Attorney General's Task Force on Family Violence in 1984 recommended allowing hearsay evidence at preliminary hearings and videotaped testimony by the child during trial. But laws attempting to institute such changes have been challenged all the way to the Supreme Court, and the verdicts are still unclear. (See the sub-question "What legislative changes have been made?" below.)

DePanfilis summarizes the other recommendations of the Attorney General's Task Force and the American Bar Association as follows:

> [The Task Force's recommendations] include: ... specialization among prosecutors and institution of vertical prosecution (same prosecutor through all stages of the court process) whenever possible; ... use of anatomically correct dolls and drawings to describe abuse; ... appointment of a special volunteer advocate for children, when appropriate; ... a presumption that children are competent to testify; ... flexible courtroom settings and procedures; ... carefully managed press coverage; ... and ... limiting continuances to an absolute minimum.
> ...[T]he recommendations [of the American Bar Association] include: promoting innovative and interdisciplinary procedures; implementing

coordinated court proceedings; establishing procedures which reduce trauma
to the child; providing an advocate for the victim; implementing procedures
to prevent duplicate interviews; instituting vertical prosecution; . . . training
and specialization of professionals who deal with intrafamily child sexual abuse
cases; adding amendments to improve State legislation; and implementing
specialized procedures for handling juvenile offenders.

Another sub-question: What legislative changes have been made?

One of the most controversial issues surrounding the reform of child abuse
laws is the problem discussed above: How can the courts meet the needs of
both the child victim, who may be further traumatized by testifying in the
presence of the accused, and the suspect, who has the constitutionally
guaranteed right to confront his accuser?

Most states have by now attempted to enact laws that prevent children
from having to confront their alleged molesters in open court, through the use
of videotaped testimony, "hearsay" evidence, closed-circuit television
testimony, and other such methods. But the constitutionality of these laws is
still in question.

In 1988, the United States Supreme Court (Coy vs. Iowa) voted 6–2 to
overturn the sexual assault conviction of an Iowa man whose two 13-year-old
accusers had testified from behind a screen, shielded from his view. The opinion, written by Justice Antonin Scalia, cited the Sixth Amendment right to a
"face-to-face confrontation" as "absolute." However, only four of the justices
signed the full opinion. Sandra Day O'Connor and Byron White, although
voting with the majority, stated their belief that the right to confrontation is
"not absolute."

Scalia's opinion has been cited by courts in several states which since then
have overturned convictions of child molesters. In January 1990, the Supreme
Court agreed to hear appeals of two such cases in another attempt to determine
the scope of the Sixth Amendment. One case, Maryland vs. Craig, involved
the use of closed-circuit TV testimony against a preschool owner convicted of
sexually abusing four children. The second, Idaho vs. Wright, concerned the
use of evidence that under other circumstances might have been thrown out
as hearsay: A pediatrician found evidence of abuse in a 2½-year-old and
testified that the child told him "daddy" caused the injuries. The parents had
been convicted.

These cases were heard by the Court in April 1990. On June 27, the opinion was handed down: abusers need *not* be allowed to confront their victims.
This design will doubtless have a major impact on child sexual abuse cases
across the United States.

As reported by DePanfilis, other legislative changes concerning child sexual abuse have been made in recent years; some have met with considerably
less controversy than the provisions just discussed. Among the reforms
DePanfilis lists are changes in competency provisions (allowing more children

to testify as competent witnesses) and exclusions of spectators from the courtroom during a child's testimony. DePanfilis also summarizes some non-legislative changes that attempt to reduce the trauma for child victims. These include "modifying the physical environment" — making the court situation less intimidating by such practices as having the judge sit at the same level as the child or wear business clothes instead of a robe — and "preparing child victims for a courtroom appearance" by allowing them to meet the judge, tour the courtroom, etc.

State laws must change rapidly to keep up with the legal opinions. For the latest information on your state's laws, I suggest you contact the American Bar Association's National Resource Center on Child Advocacy and Protection, 11800 M Street NW, Washington DC 20036, (202) 331-2250.

What part does child pornography play in the life of a molester?

First, let's define pornography as material that is sexually explicit and intended for the purpose of sexual arousal. Now, let's go a bit further and say that this material is sexually explicit to the extreme and has no apparent purpose other than sexual arousal. But what is arousing to one person may not be to another. Many pedophiles are initially content with masturbating while looking at pictures of children modeling underwear in the Sears catalogue, while the most perverted of child molesters gets his sexual climax viewing a picture of a nude dead child. Dr. James Dobson relates a horror story in an interview following his 14-month tenure as a member of the U.S. Attorney General's Commission on Pornography. He was asked, "What aspect of what you saw was most troubling to you, personally"? And he answered, "I will never forget a particular set of photographs shown to us at our first hearing in Washington, D.C. These pictures were taken of a cute, nine-year-old boy who had fallen into the hands of a molester. In the first photo, the blond lad was fully clothed and smiling at the camera. But in the second, he was nude, dead and had a butcher knife protruding from his chest."

I have not spoken to one inmate who has not been stimulated to one degree or another by viewing pictures of naked children. More specifically, convicted molesters seem to prefer pictures of children and youth engaged in playing with themselves, mutual masturbation, actual acts of intercourse, fellatio, and sodomy with other youngsters, male and female, or various lurid sexual acts with adults.

Pedophiles are almost always collectors of child pornography. They don't necessarily produce it, but they don't just look at it: They save it. They save all sorts of things; pictures, video and audio tapes, toys, games, drawings, clothing, etc. — but all relating to children. Professor Ann Burgess has identified four kinds of pedophilia collectors: "closet," "isolated," "cottage," and "commercial." The "closet collector" keeps his collection a secret and is usually not active in molesting children. The "isolated collector" is usually an active molester as well as a collector, but only he and his victims know of his activities. He may take his own pictures as well as obtaining them from other sources. The "cottage collector" shares his collection and sexual activity with other pedophiles; this is done primarily to validate his behavior, rather than for profit. Video tapes and photographs are often swapped with other molesters. The "commercial collector" is in business to make money; he makes duplicates to sell to other collectors. The commercial collector is usually an active molester as well.

A subquestion: Why do pedophiles and others collect child pornography and erotica? Nobody really knows but it obviously helps the suspect satisfy his compulsive sexual fantasies about children. Professor Burgess mentions validation, and FBI special agent Kenneth Lanning says that "pedophiles swap pornographic photographs the way boys swap baseball cards."

Another, more insidious use of pornography is to lower the inhibitions of a potential victim. When shown pictures of other children "having fun" while engaged in sexual activity a child can be led to believe that the activity is acceptable because other children are involved. Children have a tendency to believe what they read in books and see in pictures. I have used porno magazines to arouse and stimulate youthful victims and it is very effective.

Molesters can also use pictures they have taken of their victim as blackmail. "We must keep this secret because you wouldn't want your parents or friends to see these pictures."

I remember a novel titled *Strega* by Andrew Vachss. The author, apparently very knowledgeable of such matters, plotted the story around a day care school student who had pictures taken while engaged in a sex act with an adult. The author was very heavy on the trauma the young boy was suffering and spent a great deal of time discussing psychotherapy, pedophilia, "anatomically correct" dolls, pornography and distaste for the suspects involved. Incidentally the protagonist was an ex-con.

I feel that the active pedophile is very dangerous as he could easily slip from the "looking" or "touching" phase into desiring to re-create scenes from pornographic pictures or video tapes (much like a drug abuser or an alcoholic who no longer gets the same kick from his regular dose).

According to Dr. Jerry Kirk, president, National Coalition Against Pornography, 77 percent of molesters of boys and 87 percent of molesters of girls admitted trying out sexual behavior seen in pornography. (This probably was the testimony before the Senate Judiciary Committee of Charles Keating, founder of Citizens for Decency Through Law.) Dr. Kirk also reports that Arthur Gary Bishop, a 32-year-old accountant convicted in 1984 of sexually abusing and killing five young boys, admitted that pornography was a determining factor in his criminal actions.

I think the main thing to be aware of is that the child pornographer must have a victim. A child must be sexually exploited in order to produce the picture. And because child pornography emphasizes the deviant as well as the erotic—often portraying bestiality, weird pseudo-religious rituals, sadomasochistic and other abnormal and violent situations—the exploitation may involve truly horrifying acts.

Naturally, a child pornographer must get his victim alone or away from watchful eyes to engage in his activities, so again the child is in a one-on-one situation with no one to protect him. Parents must train their children to promptly report any "picture taking" by a stranger or friend; with luck, this reporting will prevent serious exploitation from taking place.

In child pornography, the facts are clear. There is only one way to make child pornography, and that is to sexually molest a child. It is a picture of a crime being committed before your eyes.

What part does child pornography play in the life of a molester? Answer: Any part sufficient to satisfy the lustful desires of the abuser. Child pornography exists primarily for pedophiles and child molesters. As Kenneth Lanning puts it, "The child in a photograph or videotape is young forever."

Are pornography and child prostitution linked?

There is a very close relationship, of course, and several references in the Bibliography are excellent resources. See *For Love or Money* by R. Lloyd; "Adolescent Prostitution" by Michael Baizerman et al.; "Preying on Playgrounds: The Sexploitation of Children in Pornography and Prostitution" by C. Baker; *Research on the Use of Children in Pornography* by A. Burgess; *Child Pornography and Sex Rings* edited by A. Burgess; "Child Sex Initiation Rings" by A. Burgess and M. McCausland; and *Child Sexual Exploitation Background and Legal Analysis* by H.A. Davidson.

Now, we are talking big money when it comes to child prostitution, whether male or female. The doctors Kempe report in *The Common Secret* that testimony at one congressional hearing revealed that in Los Angeles a 12-year-old boy can earn as much as $1,000 a day in prostitution. One inmate told me that he "ran" a 13-year-old boy on the Hollywood Strip and made enough in three months to buy a new car. He added that "professional pimps" ran him off after stealing his boy. The youth in question was a runaway from Idaho who had been sexually molested over a period of years by his uncle.

Some children are involved in prostitution while still living at home. "Sex rings" are established with several other friends, organized by men who meet with them offering gifts and money. (See "What are sex rings?" on page 83.) Family friends and youth leaders are suspects, as are fathers and stepfathers, who benefit financially. Heavy peer group pressure, threats and the victims' own fears mainly keep these activities secret. There is a sense of belonging and being wanted, and the suspects offer support and add security. These children hunger for affection and approval and have little self-esteem and no skills. Sex is the only commodity they can trade on as they look for an easier and more rewarding life.

Children involved in prostitution find it difficult to resist entering into pornography, and the reverse is also true. In either case the dangers are great. Just for example, consider the 18-year-old boy who ran away from Kansas City, Missouri, and came to California to be a movie star. He wound up working as a prostitute and was eventually killed by a 58-year-old college professor who had led a double life cruising the homosexual haunts of Hollywood. (The professor, whom acquaintances described as "nerdy" and "a sissy," is facing 25 years to life in prison.)

A parent should always be aware that children and adolescents hired as fashion models, child stars, etc., could be lured into dangerous activities by promises of big money.

Where does this pornography come from?

According to what I have read, Holland, Denmark and the United States produce the majority of pornographic commercial magazine and book photographs, movies and video tapes.

According to the Attorney General's Commission on Pornography, "80% of all pornography sold in the U.S. is produced in Los Angeles county." The report goes on to say that "85% of this multi-billion-dollar industry is controlled by organized crime (the Mafia)." It is also believed that children most often "starring" in porno films are runaways or throwaways, abducted children and those coerced by parents and other adults.

Worldwide customers are mainly in West Germany and the United States. You must remember that because of strict federal and state laws child porn is not openly sold in the United States. There are some magazines that feature young-looking models. This is simulated child pornography geared especially for pedophiles and hebephiles but is not illegal because the young men and women are over 18.

For a small investment—about $1,600 or $1,800—a pedophile can set up shop with his own video camera and video recorders. With this minimal equipment he can produce and even duplicate his own child pornography.

Because California, specifically the Greater Los Angeles area, is a major creative and distribution center for child pornography I am adding the following notes from the *Child Abuse Prevention Handbook* published by the California Office of the Attorney General:

Although it is impossible to make an exact assessment of the number of California children who have been the victims of pornographic exploitation, it is clear that by even the most conservative estimate, the number is alarmingly high.

The difficulty in assessing the number of children involved in pornography is compounded by a number of factors. First, the evidence indicates that in the vast majority of cases, this kind of sexual exploitation goes unknown to even the parents of the children. Additionally, the ever-increasing number of juvenile runaways who have migrated to California in recent years, together with the associated and growing problem of child prostitution, contribute to the difficulty in making this assessment. The runaway juvenile, alone and without support in a strange city, is a particularly attractive target for pornography or prostitution. Finally, some parents use their own children to produce pornographic material. Therefore, the only reasonable conclusion which can be drawn is that the number of children involved is substantial. Moreover, the number appears to be growing.

In recent years, police have been able to increase the number of arrests in California of persons suspected of producing and disseminating child pornography. These arrests have resulted in literally thousands of films, magazines and still photographs being seized which depict children (some as young as four years old) involved in sexual activity. However, the problem still outweighs the arrests by a large margin.

I'd like to interject here the story of one man who did get caught with his videotape showing. He was a 56-year-old educator, married 33 years, with 30 years as a respected elementary-school teacher. As reported in the Fresno, CA, *Bee,* June, 1988, he entered a no contest (guilty) plea to 11 felony and 17 misdemeanor counts of video taping young girls in various stages of undress and touching the genitals, buttocks and breasts of some of them. He was never accused of engaging in sexual intercourse with any of the elementary-school girls. He faces a maximum of 16 years in prison. In the Orange County, CA, Register on June 8, 1988, was a story of a former California Highway Patrol Officer who pleaded guilty to pimping and other sex-related charges. He pleaded after he was told that an additional 30 counts were going to be added to his 29 sex and drug charges. One of the counts involved a 14-year-old runaway girl who was staying in his apartment and who was the victim in a child-pornography case a year earlier. Police confiscated 152 video tapes, cameras and other video equipment. The judge indicated he might sentence the former 14-year Highway Patrol Officer to eight years in state prison.

As the California Attorney General's booklet goes on to say:

> The production and distribution of pornographic material has been limited, in part, due to amendments to [California] Penal Code sections 311.2, 311.3, 311.4 and Labor Code sections 1309.5–1309.6, which now provide essentially:
> • that anyone convicted of producing, distributing, or exhibiting pornographic materials depicting a minor is guilty of a felony and punishable by imprisonment in the state prison for two, three, or four years or

by a maximum fine up to $50,000 or by both fine and imprisonment (Pen. Code, §311.2);

• that anyone convicted of developing, duplicating or exchanging any film, photograph, videotape, negative or slide depicting a child under 14 years of age engaged in defined sexual conduct is guilty of a misdemeanor punishable by imprisonment in the county jail for not more than one year or by a fine of up to $2,000 or by both fine and imprisonment (Pen. Code, §311.3);

• that anyone convicted of promoting, employing, using or coercing a minor under age 17 to perform a sexual act in a film or photograph is guilty of a felony and punishable by imprisonment in the state prison for three, six or eight years (Pen. Code, §311.4); and

• that wholesale distributors of films depicting minors engaged in defined sexual conduct must keep records indicating names and addresses of those from whom the material is obtained (producer). Failure to keep such records for the specified time period is a misdemeanor offense which is punishable by a maximum $5,000 fine for each violation (Lab. Code, §§1309.5–1309.6).

All mandated reporters are required to report suspected sexual exploitation, which is defined to include Penal Code sections 311.2, 311.3 and 311.4. . . . In addition, 1982 legislation amended the Child Abuse Reporting Law (Pen. Code §§11165, subd. [1], and 11166, subd. [c]) to include, as mandated reporters, "any commercial film and photographic print processor who has knowledge of or observes, within the scope of his or her professional capacity or employment, any film, photograph, videotape, negative or slide depicting a child under the age of 14 years engaged in an act of sexual conduct. . . ."

(For further details on these laws and related Penal Code section see the Definitions, Laws and Legal Aspects section of *MAN/child.*)

Other states currently (1989) outlawing possession of child pornography include Alabama, Arizona, Colorado, Florida, Illinois, Massachusetts, Minnesota, Nebraska, Nevada, Ohio, Oklahoma, Pennsylvania, Texas, Utah and Washington.

Efforts are also being made on the federal level to stop use of children in pornographic films and magazines, but it seems to me our lawmakers are going about it in an incorrect manner. Instead of making a concerned and concentrated effort to prosecute the people who produce and distribute this material, so far our representatives seem to be giving only "lip service" for political purposes.

Here's an example. I read the following story in the September 29, 1988, issue of the *L.A. Times* (page 25):

SENATE BACKS SWEEPING CURBS ON "KIDDIEPORN"

The U.S. Senate voted 97 to 0 to outlaw the use of children in pornographic films or magazines and to impose a broad ban on the distribution of obscene material for profit.

The measure, sometimes known as the "Kiddieporn Bill," would also forbid transmission of pornographic programs on cable television and bar possession of pornographic materials on virtually all Federal Territory, including U.S. Government Buildings.

Violators would be subject to criminal penalties ranging from two years to life in prison and fines up to $250,000, with provisions for forfeiture of property used to sell or distribute obscene material.

The term "kiddieporn" to me really seems to make light of a very serious matter, but that's another windmill.

This bill was actually an amendment to a bill that would require large businesses to grant 10 weeks of unpaid leave to parents with a newborn infant, a newly adopted child, or a child with a serious illness. It wasn't even a bill by itself. It was just tacked on to another bill that was later defeated.

Had this amendment been made law, the ACLU and all of the varied anti-censorship groups could really have jumped on it because it would, in addition to prosecuting child pornographers, allow officers to arrest a soldier on an army post or even a camper at a national park who had a pornographic magazine in his possession. No wonder the ACLU called it "the most sweeping censorship law in decades." That's a little far out . . . but what else is new.

I learned, as a three county chairman of the CLEAN campaign (an early '60s California grass roots effort to get "dirty" magazines off of newsstands) that people just don't want to be told what they can read or possess in the way of what they call "adult" magazines. In retrospect I feel the same way but I also feel that our lawmakers go about things so stupidly (or maybe so carefully) that they invite opposition and ultimate defeat. That way they can still say, in all honesty, that they voted against child pornography!

I think by now you have a pretty good background regarding this special horror of child sexual abuse. For additional study see the Bibliography: Baker, C., "Preying on Playgrounds: The Sexploitation of Children in Pornography and Prostitution," 1978. Burgess, A.W. (ed.), *Child Pornography and Sex Rings,* 1984, and Burgess, A.W., *Research on the Use of Children in Pornography,* 1982. Dillingham, J., and Melmed, E., *Child Pornography: A Study of the Social Sexual Abuse of Children,* 1982. Kempe, R.S., and Kempe, C.H., *The Common Secret,* 1984. Kronhausen, E., and Kronhausen, P., "The Psychology of Pornography," 1961. Kutchinsky, B., "The Effect of Easy Availability of Pornography on the Incidence of Sex Crimes: The Danish Experience," 1973. Lanning, K., *Child Molesters: A Behavioral Analysis,* 1987. McLawhorn, Richard, *Summary of the Final Report of the Attorney General's Commission on Pornography,* 1986. Nash, D., "Legal Issues Related to Child Pornography," 1981. O'Brien, S., *Child Pornography,* 1983. Pierce, R.L., *Child Pornography: A Hidden Dimension of Child Abuse,* 1984. Steinem, Gloria, "Pornography—Not Sex but the Obscene Use of Pornography," 1977. Walters, R., *Child Pornography,* 1986. Wilson, J., "Violence, Pornography and Social Science," 1971.

Will a doctor's examination show that a child has been molested?

It is a common belief that a psychiatrist or a physician can detect a molested child. I believe that doctors are as naive as anyone. Most child molestations do not involve actions that are physically scarring. If you, as a parent, need some sort of reassurance or have the feeling that you must do something . . . I would certainly think twice about subjecting your child to another attack on his body, especially when it may not prove at all helpful. Studies have shown that medical doctors often have explanations for everything: Symptoms in the genitals of young children are attributed to allergy or underpants or masturbation. Rectal problems are written off to constipation. Like anyone else not specifically trained in child abuse, doctors are not instructed that sexual molestation could be a problem. They are not taught and find it hard to comprehend that very young children could be victims.

Despite the unpleasantness of the exam, if parents have any reason to suspect that the child has been infected with a venereal disease (not uncommon) they should certainly seek medical attention.

If an examination is to be performed, remember that the experience will be very frightening and upsetting for the victim, who will feel she is being violated yet again. Ask the doctor and nurse to explain what is going to happen and why. Let the victim ask questions. Insure that the doctor spends some time with the child prior to the examination.

Medical schools really don't give much attention to adequately preparing pediatricians and gynecologists for giving examinations to sexually abused children. Some material I have read states that only in the last few years have medical students been trained to do pelvic exams on real people rather than watch films or practice on mannequins.

Pelvic and anal exams are very uncomfortable under the best of circumstances, and following a sexual assault I would think they would be almost unbearable.

The victim does not need another assault, and doctors must be made aware that rushed, insensitive exams would be, in the mind of the victim, an additional violation. Little things, like warming the speculum and using the smallest size when examining a child, are important.

A doctor in the course of a regular medical examination, might observe an enlarged vagina or tears; these should be questioned. Certainly a doctor should ask questions when infections typical of sexual activity are discovered.

It all boils down to common sense. The doctor is just another person, perhaps the parent of children, and probably has about the same knowledge of child sexual abuse as you.

What are sex rings?

Any group of victims manipulated by an adult or adults for a variety of sexual reasons. (My definition.) For example, the "Revere Ring" was a homosexual child sex group active in Boston for many years. Seventeen prominent Boston area men were involved as well as more than 60 young boys aged 8 to 13 (Geiser, 1979).

A.W. Burgess, editor of *Child Pornography and Sex Rings,* conducted exploratory research and gathered significant data from 55 sex rings. DePanfilis summarizes the findings:

> An analysis of the first 40 cases suggests that the majority of victims were male children, ranging in age from less than one year to seventeen. Approximately half of the suspects used their occupation to gain access to child victims. These suspects included teachers (nursery school, grammar, and junior high levels), a city health physician, an engineer, a school bus driver, a camp counselor, a photographer, a gas station owner, and scout leaders. Although the number of victims actively involved in a ring at a specific time ranged from 3 to 11, cases involving hundreds of children could be reported if the number of victims were counted consecutively over the life of the sex ring.

There has been much in the news about day care center abuses and satanic cults. These can also be considered as sex rings.

For details see Burgess, A.W., ed., *Child Pornography and Sex Rings.* Burgess also joined with FBI Special Agent Kenneth Lanning in a similar article for an FBI *Law Enforcement Bulletin* article.

What do you know about sibling sexual abuse?

Not much. The Kempe group say that sibling sex play is very frequent and innocent in very young children. It includes such activities as playing doctor, frequent exposure of the body, mutual exploration, genital touching, and bathing and sleeping together. There is more opportunity for acts if the children are close in age. As the children get older increased social awareness makes sexual activity more guilt-provoking.

Sibling *abuse* is altogether different, and probably more common than most people realize. In a Human Development Services booklet, *Perspectives on Child Maltreatment in the Mid '80s,* author Martha M. Kendrick, in her "What We've Learned from Community Responses to Intra Family Child Sexual Abuse" states:

> One of the most startling findings is the degree of sibling abuse in incestuous families. Even in families where there is no sibling abuse, sibling relationships

play an important role in treatment for the victim. However, many agencies are hamstrung in their inability to protect these children. Since many state laws are totally inadequate regarding the special needs of siblings, community agencies are often unable to help unless they can establish parental neglect. To do this, agencies often face the difficult task of establishing lack of supervision or failure to report.

Virtually every program had to grapple with substantial increases in reports of male juvenile sex offenders. Most programs now identify the needs of these offenders — who often fall through the cracks in terms of treatment as well as legal handling of cases — as critical. Several programs were surprised to learn that when they began treating adult perpetrators, more often than not they discovered patterns of abuse that began during the adolescent years, usually by victimizing younger children. This finding concurs with other research in the field, which suggests that the adolescent sexual abuser of today, if untreated, is likely to become the adult sexual offender of tomorrow.

Several projects also noted the special needs of parents and siblings (particularly siblings who were victims) of adolescent offenders. They report that the dynamics of adolescent sex abuse seem different from adult patterns. This, too is perceived as another area requiring legislative attention in several states. Finally, these projects also consistently point out that abuse of males is far more prevalent than previously thought; a significant proportion of the male offenders were themselves victimized as children or teenagers.

I am aware the author did not necessarily mean that all these boys were the victims of older brothers or sisters and that they could have been victimized by other adolescent offenders; however, her thinking parallels mine with her belief that adolescent sex abusers need treatment and that the sexual abuse of boys is much higher than we think.

Statistics on the incidence of sibling abuse are nil and studies are the same, but with the increasing reporting of sibling incest I'm certain we will find a much higher incidence than is currently suspected.

I am reminded that Virginia Woolf was "used" for years (until age 11) by her half-brother George, and if I recall correctly she was also molested by another half-brother, Gerald, when she was six.

There's a poignant little story in *Discovery Digest,* issue 109 (December 1988), where a young woman writes, "He made me promise God." She relates that when she was in the fifth grade her brother talked her into having intercourse. He made her promise God that she would never tell. Senior Editor David C. Egner replied to her letter saying, "It is never good to keep a bad promise" (see Numbers 30:3–5) and went on to quote additional assistance: Psalm 33:20, 46:1, Isaiah 41:10; Deut. 31:6 and Heb. 13:5.

Why won't a child seek help when she or he is suffering abuse?

In *Your Child Should Know* by Colao and Hosansky several reasons are listed: (1) The child is physically, financially, or emotionally dependent on the abuser. (2) The suspect has threatened the victim's safety or that of the family (If you tell, I'll kill your mother). (3) The victim blames himself for what happened. (4) The child has been taught that the good are rewarded and the bad are punished and therefore assumes responsibility for the assault (This happened to me because I went out when I wasn't supposed to). (5) The victim fears that no one will believe her, either because the suspect is a known and trusted adult (How can you say such a thing about your grandfather) or because they have no proof (What do you mean he hurt you, there's nothing wrong with you!). (6) The victim has been given the message that sexual issues are never discussed. (7) The victim does not have the words to explain what happened (Uncle Joe is always bothering me) and the adults in the child's environment aren't able to pick up on what the child means. (8) The victim totally blocks the incident from his or her memory, due to the trauma of the assault. See the discussion of the Child Sexual Abuse Accommodation Syndrome, under the question "What is the background regarding treatment of victims and families in child sex abuse cases?" (pages 65–71), for further analysis of these thought patterns and their results.

What part does alcohol play in child molestation?

According to Mary de Young, *The Sexual Victimization of Children* (1982), 14 percent of her studied cases gave as a primary reason for their actions that their emotional state and control were weakened by alcohol. Other studies have shown that alcoholism was infrequently reported by incestuous fathers: Kroth, 1979, found 12 percent; Lukianowicz, 1972, 15 percent; Justice and Justice, 1979, 10 to 15 percent; Cavallin, 1966, found that 33 percent of his sample were "drinkers." Dr. Finkelhor, 1979, says that there is a consistent connection, but alcohol is not the *cause,* nor does it inspire a sexual interest in children. It may instead be a way activity is excused or rationalized by the suspect.

Vander May and Neff note that an effect of sexual abuse is alcoholism along with promiscuity, drug abuse, prostitution, sexual dysfunctioning, delinquency, depression and suicide.

The doctors Kempe report that alcohol merely acts as a trigger-reducing inhibition against impulses which are present but which might not be indulged so readily without alcohol. Alcohol does not "cause" rape; it makes its commission easier.

I think we can all agree that alcohol plays a role in child molestation as it does lower weak inhibitions against impulses which might otherwise be resisted. Deliberate use of alcohol when temptation is mounting is a self-deceptive way of denying responsibility.

One of the first questions I was asked by a psychiatrist was, "Do you feel that heavy drinking caused you to molest children?" My answer, of course, was no. This seemed to please the doctor.

References include: Sullivan, Jeanne, *Catapulting Abusive Alcoholics to Successful Recovery*. In many families child abuse can be prevented only after alcohol or drug abuse is controlled. This pamphlet from The National Committee for the Prevention of Child Abuse defines alcoholism and co-alcoholism; it discusses confrontation techniques, stresses the importance of treatment for the entire family, and outlines preparatory steps for appropriate intervention. Also see the following references in the Bibliography: R. Rada, "Alcoholism and the Child Molester"; Browning, H., and Boatman, B., "Incest: Children at Risk"; Virkkunen, M., "Incest Offences and Alcoholism"; Barnard, C., "Alcoholism and Incest"; Silbert, M.H., Pines, A.M., Lynch, T., "Substance Abuse and Prostitution."

Can we predict sexual abuse of children?

Studies on incest cases show that this offense has continued through generations in the same family. And we know that the huge percentage of molesters have themselves been abused as children. We know that neglect and physical abuse continue from generation to generation. Yet to predict sexual abuse of children is just not possible. It is a mostly unstudied field with several current attempts in progress.

We are aware that children learn very early that rewards go with sexual activity. Check out the research on prostitutes who were victims of incest or heavy molestation, James and Meyerding, 1977. Children in need of those rewards—whether in the form of parental approval or large amounts of money—may be at additional risk for abuse.

An interesting point, I think, is that women who have themselves been molested should be in a good position to be certain their children are not sexually abused. Yet studies have shown that, too often, this is not the case.

What about witch-hunts?

Every so often we hear of a man being released from prison after several years of serving time for a crime he did not commit. This happens. I don't know what the statistics are, but I suspect the odds against such an incident are great. Yet, I hear fantastic tales of "witch-hunts" and injustices. Certainly mistakes have been and are being made constantly, especially when it comes to child molestation . . . a highly volatile and extremely involved and sensitive subject. There certainly are many cases where unskilled and untrained police and social workers have done almost irreparable harm to the victim and to those innocent of any knowing crime. But we should try to take everything in perspective. Consider the size and sensitive nature of the problem. It is easy to make mistakes, and perhaps we learn from them as we go along.

Those who write against our continued and, one hopes, increased vigilance may strongly believe that the government, by enactment of stronger laws, will take away parental rights. I firmly support the right of every parent to raise his or her child as long as the current laws of the land are obeyed. I only wish more parents would take the time to do a better job of parenting. But we are thrust into the job and must develop skills to handle it.

I read an article called "Family Abuse" in *Reason* Magazine, May 1986. Author Allan C. Carlson cited columnist Nat Hentoff's report (according to Mr. Carlson) on a man that was convicted in 1984 of "creating pornography" by taking photos of his romping daughter, age six, in the buff following her bath. He was turned in by a drug store clerk who saw the negatives. Unfortunately, there are wild and disturbing injustices of this sort that happen.

Carlson describes arrest and investigation for child sexual abuse in dramatic terms:

> The police often strike at night. Your children are seized and taken to a secret location. They are placed in the hands of state doctors who strip them down and give them thorough examination, focusing attention on their genitalia. Meanwhile, you are hauled into court to face an inquisitorial hearing into your character. Your accusers enjoy complete anonymity and full legal protection. Your guilt is essentially assumed. Many standard rules of evidence are tossed out, including the hearsay prohibition. Also unavailable to you are ancient privileges such as husband-wife and patient-doctor confidentialities. Even among those who, against all odds, manage to prove their innocence and recover their children, many escape only by agreeing to state-directed psychological counseling, where therapists work to restructure one's mind and values.
>
> This is modern American justice styled for those parents accused of child abuse, particularly sexual abuse. Over the last twenty years, legitimate concern over the complex social problem of violence within the family has been translated into a witch-hunt, with devastating consequences for the Constitution and for thousands of innocent families who have had their lives shattered by the minions of the therapeutic state.

As an "archetypal" witch-hunt, Carlson cites the case of the small town of Jordan, Minnesota:

> In late 1983, a trash collector and babysitter named James Rud was arrested for allegedly molesting two children. In custody, he cut a bargain with the prosecutor and, in a trade for a short jail term, described his participation in a child sex ring composed of Jordan parents. With virtually no further investigation, the police arrested the newly accused and seized the children.

The children, now in the care of welfare authorities, were forcibly examined and repeatedly interrogated, but for weeks they stoutly denied any abuse had taken place. Eventually it was suggested to some that if they told "the truth" they might go home. The children responded by "confessing." Yet no corroborating evidence to these "confessions" could ever be found. As the weakness of the cases became apparent, the prosecutor offered plea bargains (tantamount to bribery in one case that included offers of relocation, a new identity, and money) in return for testimony against the others. All the defendants rejected all offers and insisted on being tried. The first couple tried was acquitted by the jury. Before the other trials took place, Rud admitted in a radio interview that he had lied about the sex ring—yet the prosecutor still insisted that the defendants were guilty. Carlson writes that "only the intervention of the Minnesota Attorney General's Office finally brought this reign-of-terror in a small town in America to an end."

This is a terrible story, and I could add others like it from around the country. Yet they should be kept in perspective. They are still quite few in number compared with the documented cases of abuse that ended with conviction of the offenders. I have met some of those offenders in prison and they freely admit their guilt (as well as their plans to continue their activities when they are released). Child sexual abuse does happen and should be fought. Our best weapon in the war, and at the same time our best hope for avoiding witch-hunts, is correct information. Children, parents, and professionals all need to be taught what to look for and how to handle any situation that arises in connection with potential child sexual abuse.

Two organizations are in existence to assist parents and others who feel they are being unjustly accused. VOCAL (Victims of Child Abuse Laws) is very active with chapters in many states. An acquaintance of mine who is in prison because his ex-wife stated he molested their daughters professes his innocence and VOCAL is working with him. Another group, the Family Rights Coalition headquartered in Crystal Lake, Illinois, serves as a clearing house for information on "cases of unjust aggression" by government agencies against families.

How can we be sure day care centers are safe?

The U.S. Department of Health and Human Services conducted a national program inspection to examine child sexual abuse prevention in day care and to develop recommendations for assertive prevention efforts. (Report submitted in January, 1983.) Interviews were conducted with 300 individuals in 49 states, including social and child protective services staff, licensing officials, physicians, day care providers, and parents. While nearly everyone agreed that screening day care employees was a good idea, there wasn't much agreement on how to do so effectively or without violating the rights of applicants.

Techniques suggested for screening generally proved impractical or unreliable. The problem is that you just can't identify every potential molester by comparing him to a predictive model or set of guidelines.

The interviewed experts unanimously agreed that education of parents, teachers, children and day care providers is the most effective child sexual abuse prevention method.

It is no surprise that parents are concerned about day care centers. The most explosive child molestation arrests to hit American sensibilities were those in the McMartin Preschool case (Manhattan Beach, California), which actually started in August 1983.

On January 18, 1990, after 33 months in court, the nation's longest and costliest criminal trial ended with not guilty verdicts for Raymond Buckey, 31, and his mother, Peggy McMartin Buckey, 63. They were acquitted of 52 counts of child molestation. (Mistrials were declared on 13 additional counts.) Buckey, his mother and five other teachers—charged with 321 counts of child molestation—were arrested after some 500 families came forward with allegations their children had been molested at the day care center. Before trial, 222 of the charges were dropped and five defendants were released. During the trial, more charges were dropped.

Raymond Buckey was jailed for five years before he raised $1.5 million in bail. Mrs. Buckey spent almost two years in jail, and was freed on $295,000 bail. She admitted that as a girl she had been molested by a neighbor. The son admitted he had kept pornography for sexual gratification.

Seven of the jurors indicated they felt that children had been molested, but they weren't certain the Buckeys were to blame.

It was encouraging for me to read the words of law professor John Banzhaf, George Washington University, who stated that this case and other high profile child molestation cases are finally forcing the legal community to look at how to handle the need for children to testify in court. (See "What is the legal response to child sexual abuse?" page 71.) Jill Hiatt, a former child abuse prosecutor in California now with the National Center for the Prosecution of Child Abuse, states that investigators and interviewers must be extremely well trained in working with child victims.

Are all missing or abducted children the victims of child abusers?

Linda Meyer in her 1984 book *Safety Zone* reports that each year over 1.8 million children are reported missing. About 90 percent run away of their own volition and return home a few days later. But many others are the involuntary victims of kidnapping. About 100,000 children are abducted in parental custody fights, while for 50,000 children there is no clue—they simply disappear.

Does "shock rock" aid and abet sex crimes?

I'll just offer a few words on this as I have not researched this area. In a July 1988 *Reader's Digest* article, "How Shock Rock Harms Our Kids," *Digest* staff writer Peggy Mann states that our children are being "bombarded by obscenity, violence and perversion." In the article she says that the average teen-ager listens to rock music four hours a day according to "studies." According to the author, the rock star "Prince" in his "Dirty Mind" album has a song titled "Sister," which informs listeners that "my sister never made love to anyone but me/ Incest is everything it's said to be." I don't think we need this kind of thing. I'm not saying that a kid is going to listen to the song and then rape his sister but who knows what could be implanted in a mind? For further information on this and related subjects, contact the Parents' Music Resource Center and Morality in Media. (Address listed in Bibliography.)

I also read in *The Forbidden Apple* by Ross and Marlowe, 1985, that school administrators feel popular music lyrics are a good barometer for educators to heed. They use as an example "Don't Stand So Close to Me" presented by the rock group "Police." The lyrics tell of a school girl wanting her teacher ... and getting him. They also mention Olivia Newton-John's "Let's Get Physical" and the Beatles' "Lucy in the Sky with Diamonds."

In an excellent book for teens, *No Is Not Enough*, 1984, authors Caren Adams, Jennifer Fay and Jan Loreen-Martin relate that there is a frequent linking of sex and violence in the media and that rock videos frequently feature women who are tied down, physically threatened and even beaten.

Is AIDS a danger in child sexual abuse?

AIDS is a sexually transmitted disease. A young victim almost never could give his molester AIDS but the reverse certainly is true. This is another piece of information we can give our children that might help us fight a potential suspect.

I am reminded of a story told me by a young inmate. He and his male lover were engaged in sexual activity one afternoon when a thirteen-year-old neighbor boy walked in on them. The sexually naive but precocious youth joined in the activity. Both men were aware of the danger potential in the situation but the boy persisted in coming over and participating and even initiating sex acts. This went on for several months until the boy asked his father if he could get AIDS from homosexual actions. The alert father listened and got to the bottom of the question. The men went to jail.

*   *   *

You have read in *MAN/child* how the sexual abuse statistics keep going up and up every year. One major reason is because more adults are talking about what happened to them as youngsters. Forcing themselves to remember what they don't want to remember. Think for a moment. Have you hidden away a memory or two? Bring it out and discuss it with someone you trust, someone who will understand. You may have unconsciously been repressing those secret experiences for many years and it may be affecting your current thinking or actions. If you have a hang-up—hang it out. You don't have to carry a burden alone. You can see that there are many others who have shared similar experiences. You might have been yesterday's sexually abused child but by helping to inform others, you may help to spare some other child tomorrow's pain and anguish.

I wish there would be no more sexually abused children of tomorrow. Realistically, we know there will be, but I guess we just can't give up hope that our world could someday become a safe place to be a child.

Which leads us to our last question.

Will the reader of this question ever molest a child?

I don't know.

II. Scenarios

A child cannot be molested unless the suspect gets the victim into a situation that makes molestation possible. That is a one-on-one situation, with variations. In such a situation the child has no one to protect him but himself. He will be better equipped to do so if he knows in advance what to watch out for. This section is offered to help parents understand how a molester might work, so that they can warn their children.

The dictionary says a scenario is an outline for any planned series of events, real or imagined. In this section I will list a few scenarios to further acquaint you with the mind of a pedophile or hebephile (lover of youth). These outlines of possible courses of action are based upon personal experiences, interviews and case studies and are real. They are limited only by imagination, and there is no lack of imagination when it comes to a practicing molester. Ordinary adults working or associating with youth would never think twice about similar situations, but the mind of the suspect is constantly developing methods to gain his perverted goals. Even if the suspect does not plan to attack (my word, not his) a particular child at that time he still cannot keep from setting up a potential situation and, at least, getting a glimpse of the possible target. A suspect's mind is constantly, even unconsciously working toward another conquest.

"Now you be good and do everything Howie tells you to do!" What an invitation to any child molester. Remember, a molester weaves his web slowly and builds a psychological confidence in the child. (A child is no match for the intelligence of an older person.) "Your mother is right" — building upon what the child knows and really believes. "Your mother said to do everything I say. Raise your right arm — raise your left leg — raise your right leg — now raise both legs." (Much laughter and hugging — falling around, etc.)

It is all a psychological building toward the ultimate goal of a conquest. Suspects have different methods to gain the trust, love and obedience of a potential victim and often are helped by parents who seemingly just don't care about the child. Parents who just don't care or are too busy to listen to what their child is saying or trying to say. Parents who will not take the time to pass on information that may save their child a grievous hurt, or even take the time to gain the knowledge themselves.

One of the main objectives a suspect tries to accomplish is to view the child naked. This involves some manipulation as children often are inherently shy about displaying their bodies.

Some families, not necessarily nudists, bring up their children so that the wearing of clothing is not mandatory around the house. I think this is fine as long as the children are aware that not all other people subscribe to this practice and that they should be circumspect when away from the family environment.

The Pool

A perfectly natural setting is a swimming pool area. The suspect is aided by signs that say "Shower before entering pool" ("Let me hold your suit while you shower!") and, of course, by normal and natural horseplay in the pool. In horseplay the suspect will "accidentally" touch private areas whenever possible. In this situation, it is easy to have accidental touching, which allows an excuse if the victim responds negatively. Suspects can quickly drop or alter a plan if the potential victim recognizes a bad touch and immediately takes action to see it is not repeated. But most children, without proper prior guidance and instruction, will write it off as an unintended touch or grab. In the exuberance of the situation they will not pay much attention. They might even touch back in a playful manner. Suspects don't need any stimulation, but a child in all innocence may give the suspect the impression that she or he wishes it to happen again ... and it will. The mind of the suspect often does not remember (or refuses to admit) that he is dealing with a person with limited sexual experiences and desires. The suspect has regressed into the age level of the victim and, with the strong possibility that alcohol is breaking down what few inhibitions he may have, will increase his attack on this seemingly willing individual.

The rubbing of suntan lotion on the body allows for more intimacy, with the victim getting used to the touch of the suspect.

Following the swimming party every child knows that a shower is necessary to wash off any oils and chlorine, another perfect time for a suspect. "You go first, I'll wring out your suit." "Let me know when you're almost ready to get out and I'll hop in." Or, if the suspect is ready to make a move, "I'll go first and you be ready to hop in to save the hot water." The suspect will then wait for the victim to finish and will have a towel ready. The suspect is usually naked himself, having been "too busy" wringing out the victim's suit, cleaning up, preparing soft drink, etc. "Let me dry your back and you can dry mine!"

The suspect will display his body to the victim subtly with the "you've seen mine" unspoken attitude.

The suspect may allow his private parts to briefly come into contact with the child's buttock or leg and will most probably receive no reaction during the rough toweling. When the victim is drying hair or legs the suspect may spend excessive time drying his private parts — often gaining a partial erection — and allows his victim every opportunity to watch while not apparently being seen by the suspect. Children are curious, and the suspect will take advantage of this while displaying the attitude of a normal situation. The suspect may even playfully splash water on an already dried victim to keep him from too quickly getting into street clothes. The suspect will often look for scars, marks, hairs or moles on the victim's body and relate with touching and guiding the victim's fingers to a similar feature on his own.

The Outing

I would be remiss if somewhere in this book I implied that parents should not allow and that youngsters should not join youth clubs and organizations. The preponderance of youth leaders are straight and have an intense desire to help and guide our future citizens. One must remember, however, that molesters are drawn to such groups. With the devious mind, extreme patience, and intelligence factor each suspect has it is difficult to pinpoint a potential suspect even by trained leaders and observers.

An important rule of thumb is that anytime a one-on-one situation develops with your child — that is, anytime a leader proposes "special" activities involving only himself and your child — you should make inquiries. However, I am aware that suspects can seduce two or more victims at the same time. An example would be an observation of two young friends engaging in mutual masturbation. This is certainly a normal occurrence with youth, but the suspect will exploit the situation. For example, while checking the perimeter of the campsite the suspect will listen for betraying sounds of sexual activity. He will be aware of any youngster already demonstrating sexual knowledge verbally or otherwise. He knows that adolescent sexual curiosity can lead to "jack-off" parties with two or even several youngsters participating. Because the development into male puberty is so varied, youngsters are acutely aware of the advancement or development of others and may try to compensate by increased or bizarre sexual activity.

A child with little male adult companionship may reach out and practically (and unknowingly) force himself into the suspect's arms. One suspect told me that a child pretended an injury to his ankle in order to be given special attention. Because of this injury he was left behind with the suspect when the others went on a hike. Another suspect said a child was afraid of wild animals and was allowed to sleep in the suspect's tent. I certainly don't feel that the victims were trying to be seduced, but in their eagerness for attention (and the suspect has plenty of attention to give) they made the task easier.

Skinny dipping is a wholesome American pastime but is a suspect's dream. Not only can he observe potential targets but he can watch for overt actions of older youths who may have their own desires for another boy. In that particular circumstance both will probably become victims.

I can almost hear a reader or two scratch out a note to argue about this youth-on-youth seduction factor, but it has been mentioned in some of the boy prostitution literature and I recall it from my own youth. Several members of my study group have also agreed that it is a factor in molestation.

For further information see W. Breer, *The Adolescent Molester*, 1987; and F. Knopp, *The Youthful Sex Offender*, 1985. A packet of information on the detection, assessment, and treatment of adolescents who are molesting younger children or committing other sexual offenses may be obtained from the National Center for the Prevention and Treatment of Child Abuse and Neglect, 1205 Oneida Street, Denver CO 80220.

Geraldo on his ABC television program (July 25, 1988) featured three youthful offenders who told a national audience of their child molesting experiences. All were undergoing group therapy and all agreed they were attracted by youngsters. The trio spoke of molesting young sisters and brothers. An interesting note came from a young man in the audience who stated (apparently for the first time) that he had been raped at age 15 by his uncle whom he sees every day. He asked the offenders if they felt guilty or disgusted about their own actions. Dr. Ed Scheckowitz, Miami, Florida, said that as few as 14 percent of his patients felt any guilt. Two of the three had been molested themselves, and a 15-year-old offender stated that he started out peeping into windows and even going into occupied bedrooms where he would masturbate.

One of the suspects said an older female cousin had molested him, and it was mentioned that more women were molesters than was generally acknowledged.

Once on a downtown street corner I was approached by a 15- or 16-year-old who asked if I had any work to do around the house. This is a suspicious offer, a ploy that burglars sometimes use. I sized up the situation and offered him a job. I was careful to determine that he was alone and really needed pocket money before I made any moves on him. As it turned out he knew exactly what he wanted and how to get it. I still don't know who seduced whom. But he was a victim, aggressively willing or not. I violated the law.

The evidence clearly suggests that a youngster who has been a victim will, in turn, seek a willing companion to share his knowledge and possibly his unconscious torment.

The Substitute Teacher

One suspect, a school teacher, stated that he refused any permanent assignment to a school as he preferred substituting at junior highs in order to add to his list of 12- and 13-year-old victims.

His method of operation was that he, with the use of double meanings and attitude, would gain the support and attention of his class and by using carefully chosen words and body language would soon ascertain a potential victim. He looked for a youngster who was obviously more knowledgeable in sexual matters and who left little doubt that he had already had more experience with sex than his peers. This victim would be given a bit more attention; a touch on the shoulder or arm; a wink, and a knowing look or glance at an appropriate moment. This would lead to a brief meeting after class and if the victim was willing (although he probably didn't know what he was getting into), a meeting after school.

This suspect likened his conquests to those of a straight man who, at a party or some such situation, would set out to get a date with that pretty girl in the green dress.

Homosexuals have told me that they can spot a willing partner seconds after walking into an occupied room of strangers.

The Neighbor

The helpful, friendly neighbor is certainly an asset, but familiarity can have unhappy results. Years of living next door or down the street do not negate the fact that your neighbor may be a molester.

The suspect may have recently suffered a traumatic experience and could in a very short time deviate from normality, or he may have been engaging in undetected nefarious child molesting activities for some time.

The neighbor who asks a youngster to do some work around the house is usually very successful. (A kid will break his back for a friend or neighbor but "forgets" to take out the garbage at home.) The promise of money to a victim who doesn't have any is very enticing.

I remember one time I was sitting on my porch when a youth of about 14 or 15 came walking by. I yelled, "OK, you've got the job!" He asked what I was talking about and I said I needed the lawn mowed and would pay $4.00 for it. Less than an hour later the lawn was mowed and the kid was in my shower.

In one case a suspect asked a victim to crawl under his house to retrieve a ball (placed earlier by the suspect). The victim got his pants dusty and was encouraged to take them off so the suspect could clean them up. The youth complied and thus helped the suspect gain his first step in his seduction plan.

In this particular case the suspect noticed the victim had his undershorts on inside out and mentioned it. The suspect then declared he wanted to see what it was like to wear his shorts that way. He proceeded to take off his pants and his shorts and turn his own shorts inside out — with the victim observing, of course. He then suggested they both wear the shorts the regular way, and within a short space of time he had the victim naked. This particular suspect seduced the boy on his third visit, the second being a short, straight work project. Patience, as I have explained, is a main factor in a molester's operation, and even though the opportunity was there on the first visit with an obviously willing (if naïve) victim, the suspect took the time to gain more trust and to allow for any reaction from the victim or his parents regarding the pants-off situation.

The "neighborly" approach may be months or even years in the making, and the suspect may have developed a close personal relationship with the victim's family. This is the true insidious aspect of child molesting: the suspect gaining the complete confidence and trust of the victim and his parents.

Parents who do become suspicious and make inquiries must remember that a molester can con you into thinking that today is tomorrow and that the day after yesterday never happened.

A case in point: A 37-year-old inmate, whom we called "the judge," was serving time on a molestation charge. The tall, strikingly good looking man spoke and conducted himself in an imposing manner. This former life insurance salesman related that he "fell in love" with a 13-year-old neighbor boy and that a mutually satisfactory sexual relationship ensued almost immediately. The boy was spending so much time at his house that the youth's mother became suspicious and confronted the unmarried suspect.

He convinced her that he had only the purest motives in assisting her fatherless son. It was over three years before another of the boy's relatives asked a friend, a private investigator, to look into the situation.

The "judge" is serving a six-year sentence.

I mention this particular case to point out the lengths to which you, as a parent, may have to go to verify your suspicions.

Don't expect your child to confess. Don't expect the suspect to own up to his involvement. If you can afford it you might consider hiring a private investigator.

The Coach

A fellow inmate discussed at length his activities with boys while working as a high school coach. He had little job supervision and was excellent in performing his duties; he was well-liked by his charges and peers and was active in school functions.

His conquests were gained over a period of years and involved more than 50 children. He could not give an accurate count.

Of course, the shower room was a focal point. He had the shop department build a towel room near the entrance, and from this vantage point he could watch the shower area. Per his instructions each youth would have to leave the shower and approach his room to pick up a towel. Also, he had a view of most of the lockers in the area.

He would pick out a likely target and give special attention to him. He found it difficult to define his choice of victims and could not specifically say what drew a particular victim to him but said he just knew there was a strong possibility of a potential and willing subject. Perhaps a youth would observe him watching and indicate his interest (knowingly or not). If a potential victim expressed disgust (in any number of ways) or disinterest at any preliminary advance, the coach would move on to the next possible victim.

The power and authority of his position would override weak objections by an uninformed and naïve victim and, of course, this is exactly why the suspect was so successful in his endeavors.

Another effort to engage in touching was the "let me adjust that jock strap" ploy (explaining that injury could be caused by improper wearing, etc.). Or, "I'll show you a new wrestling hold," etc.

Often a victim would be asked to stay after school to perform various tasks around the gym, locker room and office.

The Job

Several child molesters have told me that they were seduced in their early teens by an employer or supervisor. And almost every research study I have read includes statistics supporting this fact.

The situations vary but you should be aware that most assaults occur when there is an alleged inventory, special clean-up jobs, preparation for a sale, late or early work, or any number of opportunities for a suspect to get a victim alone. I will also point out that none of the victims in the studies I have read reported the molestations, which included everything from simple touching to mutual sex. The contacts lasted from several weeks to over two years. There are many reasons for compliance and silence on the part of the victim (see "Why won't a child seek help when he or she is suffering abuse?" in the Question and Answer section, page 84), but one reason in an employment situation is that income derived from a job and, of course, the gifts and extra money given to the victim by the suspect play an important part in a teen's life.

One suspect told me that a 14-year-old, with parental permission, invited him to his home for dinner and engaged in various social activities with him, almost cutting out the family unit altogether. Such a victim can be very defensive of his boss, and parents will not interfere for fear of alienating their son.

I believe that work-area seduction is very much under-reported. Parents need to look carefully at any after-school or weekend employment.

One prominent example of an employer who molested: John W. Gacy, Jr., who killed 33 young men in Chicago. He offered jobs to male teenagers. He is presently on death row.

I don't know if this is the right place to mention my being seduced by a boss. But it's my book. I was 14 or 15 and I had always had a part-time job somewhere. Sweeping out a neighborhood grocery; stocking in a large department store and a shoe store; running a hospital elevator; delivering items for a hardware store; working in a gas station; I even helped fix cigarette lighters for a while. Anyway, I don't remember how I got this job stocking and sweeping for a small variety store, but I do remember my boss touching my crotch one day commenting on my tight Levis. I did not rebuff his advances, and we entered into a sexual situation. I was never into any sort of anal action but was a willing participant in mutual fellatio. The affair lasted only a short time. My psychotherapist posed an interesting question: "Do you think that your interest in young boys may relate to *your* seduction as a young boy?" Interesting, isn't it? I have already repeatedly stated that victims create other victims. Perhaps my memories of that time led me to attempt to relive the past. I'm still working with this and other personal questions in my attempt to discover "why."

One inmate, a homosexual, told me that he was sodomized by an 11-year-old cousin when he was 7. He liked it. By the time he was in his teens, growing up in a very strict family setting that allowed no dating prior to senior high school, he was not interested in dating as he had established a large circle of male friends including several relatives. This same man said that he was working in Los Angeles as a paramedic and on several occasions used his profession to seduce young boys. He stated that he would give classes in first aid and through them meet youngsters. He would ask a promising victim to stay after class for additional training. This "training" consisted of showing, for example, the various pressure points on the body, which of course would be much easier to demonstrate if the clothing were removed. And so forth.

Hitchhiking

Much has been written about the danger of accepting a ride from a stranger. One fellow prisoner (who received the same sentence as I did) was convicted of raping a 15-year-old hitchhiker, hacking off her forearms and throwing her by the side of the road to die. (She lived, and testified against him.)

Another suspect said that he, following one of his frequent fights with his wife, would get into his car and just drive around looking for young boys to pick up. Under the driver's seat he kept four pictures of sex activity between a man and a woman (showing intercourse with heavy emphasis on the man's penis inserted into the vagina) and six pictures of a youth performing fellatio upon another youth. When he found a youngster needing a ride he would feel the potential victim out by asking questions and listening very carefully to answers. It is very difficult to report exactly what questions were asked as each situation was different, and it is equally hard to state what answers would trigger a positive response. However, when the suspect felt (and this, again, is something only a suspect feels) that he had a possible victim he would whip out the pictures and watch carefully for reactions from the victim. If he still received no negative response, he would park the car in a secluded area and look at the pictures himself, overtly touching his erection and then reaching over to touch the victim's erection.

Another inmate related that he always obtained his victims by picking up hitchhikers, citing an 80 to 90 percent success rate. He would drive by the potential victim (he preferred teenage boys) and check him out. He then would turn around and pick him up. This particular suspect was direct and to the point. He would ask if the youth spent a lot of time hitchhiking and say, "I'll bet you get propositioned by a lot of homosexuals." If the answer was "I hate those fucking faggots," or something like that . . . he would be let out at the next corner. This inmate said that he only had a knife pulled on him one time following his direct proposition, and he stopped the car and the youth walked away. (This inmate was careful never to pick up anyone larger or appearing stronger than himself, so that confrontations of this sort were not risky to him.)

Another inmate, and a part-time homosexual, stated that he never feared any retaliation as he carried his Pasadena policeman lovers' .38 caliber snub nose revolver when out picking up hitchhikers. When I asked him if he would use it if threatened he said, "Sure, and I'd just kick the body out and drive away. Another unsolved crime against hitchhikers." I believed him.

The Church

I spoke with one felon who holds degrees in theology and had been an active pastor for over 40 years. He is a non-violent pedophile who enjoyed the loving context of the "church family" and would hug and fondle children especially in the 5-to-9 or -10 age group. He would show some of the older boys his "special" collection of religious pictures. These photographs of actual paintings showed graphic views of the male and female genitalia. (His line: "I'll bet yours looks just like that one.")

Another man was a youth leader in a Jewish temple. He called himself a lay-rabbi or a chaplain and told me of scheduled meetings with youngsters of 13 and older where they would watch pornographic films. He stated that his victims would be so aroused that it was easy to engage in mutual masturbation or fellatio. He did state that it was usually just a one-time-only affair but that a few of his victims engaged in further sexual activities with him.

Radio newscaster Paul Harvey reported on October 12, 1988, that three Pentecostal ministers had admitted having sex with boys. One suspect said he had seduced over 100 boys in the southern and eastern United States.

Medical Personnel

A young man with a strong professional background in nursing told me that he obtained sexual gratification in bathing young male and female patients. He even admitted he performed acts of fellatio on sedated youngsters. He was one of the rare persons who was an admitted homosexual and mostly led his private life along strict adult homosexual lines. He considered his job-related sexual activity as a "bonus."

The doctors Kempe report that a 53-year-old medical doctor was accused of fondling the genitals of his pre-adolescent boy patients. A hearing confirmed he regularly measured the penis, much as he would record their weight. His defense was that this was part of his comprehensive care. The board held the procedure was not routine. He voluntarily resigned his license to practice but refused offers of help.

I feel I really don't have to go into areas like preschools, public restrooms, playgrounds, babysitters, carnivals, etc. There are so many opportunities, and so many "lures" that are effective with the uninformed child. Kenneth Wooden, in his 1986 book *Child Lures Family Guide,* cites examples like the assistance lure (asking for help or directions—teach your child that an adult should ask other adults for assistance); the authority lure (suspect dresses like a police officer, clergyman or firefighter); the bribery lure (candy, toys and money are offered); the emergency lure ("Your mom is sick"); the fun and games lure (activities allow for intimate body contact); magic and rituals lure (children are enticed into physical and psychological rituals); pornography lure (suspect uses pornography to arouse victim); heroes lure (suspect poses as Big Bird or Santa Claus, for example); job lures (victim will not want to offend employer); and the affection/love lure (used by suspect whom the child knows, loves or trusts).

You, as a parent, must be constantly aware that your child is vulnerable. Give him the tools of information that will help him fight against possible molestation.

As you have read, the child is no match for the experienced and motivated suspect. Although the preceding scenarios tend to deal with older children you can imagine similar situations for a younger child.

Anytime a child is in a non-parent area or is entrusted to the care and control of a non-related adult, the situation could be dangerous and extra caution should be taken. Too often parents feel that they are interfering in their child's activities—but who else is there to watch out for their children?

Remember, a suspect needs access to a child. Without this access he is just another abnormal citizen.

III. Indicators and Guidelines

This section contains some suggested guidelines in three different areas. First we will discuss research on child molestation and suggest some *possible* indicators of a child molester. Next we will look at some signs that *may* indicate a child is being sexually abused. Finally, I will quote some guidelines from various agencies on how to talk to your child about sexual abuse, including how to deal with a child you think may already have been abused. All the material in this section is based on research, personal knowledge and common sense. Some of the material is taken from several books written especially for children or their parents; some comes from published suggestions by the federal government and other organizations.

Regarding our first topic, please remember that these are only suggestions and possibilities. You may feel that some of the suggestions contradict each other. It is just not possible to write down a list and say, "These are the things that positively identify a child molester." There are too many variables. However, if a suspect fits several of the categories there may be cause for concern, and at the very least, discreet inquiry or examination of the situation should be made by the parent. I positively feel that the suspect, when confronted by a concerned parent, will disengage himself from further activities concerning the victim or potential victim. However, realizing that the suspect probably feels he will never be caught, especially if the child is very cooperative, continuing vigilance by a parent is a must.

First, let's take a moment to refresh our memories of a child's world from a child's perspective. Obviously a child is smaller and weaker, almost powerless. It is easy for a child to believe in the incredible because the immense power wielded by adults seems to be magical. Adults decide when and what a child eats; when and where a child sleeps; what a child wears; and where a child attends school. Adults define what is good and what is bad.

Children do not realize that even as adults we, too, often feel vulnerable and helpless in our world.

We must examine our communication level with children if we are to be effective. Children are smaller and haven't been around for a long period of time but they are people and should be treated with consideration, respect and the knowledge and belief that someday they will grow up and be parents too.

Okay. Let's see what to look for in a possible or potential victim: short or tall; healthy or sick; athletic or physically disabled; very intelligent or mentally retarded; well cared for or neglected and unsupervised. No stereotype there.

How about the suspect? All different classes, backgrounds, races, religions and ethnic groups; the president of a bank or a vagrant; a trusted leader in the community known to everyone, or someone lonely and isolated; a married person in an apparently stable long-term relationship or a young "swinging" bachelor. No stereotype here.

I'm sure you get the idea.

In my reading there is no clearcut profile of how a man becomes a child molester, although there is general knowledge of some patterns of deviant behavior. Most molesters actually develop "leanings" in their teenage years. A large percentage were victims of abuse themselves. As an adolescent a molester may have observed a father or uncle molesting his sisters, or some other type of abuse.

It is believed that a molester develops an inappropriate arousal pattern, that the suspect can be sexually aroused by, or is sexually attracted to a child. Obviously this is abnormal to adult men. A couple of examples: A man may be masturbating and just happen to think of a child attractive to him, or a father may be simply holding his daughter on his lap and get an erection. If this arousal pattern is repeatedly linked to a child or children in general, the sexual attraction is learned. This process is called conditioning, a learning process which maintains behaviors through reinforcing experiences. I don't want to get too technical, but unless a suspect becomes aware of his deviant behavior, his fantasies mold into a pattern that he might not be able to control. Now we have what the psychiatrists call a compulsion. The suspect goes through certain psychological processes which allow him to commit the sexual acts. He knows what he is doing is wrong and against the law, but he justifies his behavior by rationalizing that he is doing it for the sex education of the child or some other excuse that will keep him from facing his real problem.

The suspect will molest a particular child once or twice or many times, or many children once or twice, mainly on a one-to-one basis. He may molest one daughter for many years and then go on to the younger sister. He may molest only children within his family unit, or only children outside his family, or both. He may molest only girls, only boys, or both.

We must realize that most of the men who commit sexual offenses against children are not criminal or anti-social in their regular everyday lives. Generally these men are well liked by peers but really have very few close friends. Most appear to be somewhat socially inadequate and seldom form close relationships. They often are bossy and controlling and prefer to dominate their wives and children. Some studies show offenders to be self-centered, and although they appear normal they feel ashamed about themselves and cover up insecurity and dependence by acting tough or domineering.

Sexual Assault of Children and Adolescents by Ann Burgess, et al., states that offenders tend to be young. Virtually all men studied had committed their first offense by age 40 and 80 percent by age 30. This book described the molester as handicapped by poor impulse control, poor ability to tolerate frustration or to delay immediate gratification of his needs, and low self-esteem. He is concerned with his own needs and feelings and has relative insensitivity to the needs and feelings of others. He has little insight into or understanding of his own behavior. In essence—and this strikes me as very close to home—he is a psychological child in the physical guise of an adult.

Dr. A. Nicholas Groth, noted prison psychologist, says that a suspect feels a sense of isolation or alienation from others; ineptitude in interpersonal relationships; deep-seated feelings of inadequacy; and a tendency to experience himself as the helpless victim of an overpowering environment.

Please remember, as we go along, that each opinion I report is based on a particular study sample, and that some of the earlier studies were in very controlled situations such as a prison setting. One study showed that two-thirds of the crimes against children were committed between noon and eight P.M. All I am doing in this section of *MAN/child* is passing along information I have obtained and, I hope, adding a thought or two. I am not judging what the various studies have shown ... after I was judged, I stopped judging others.

In the Burgess book *The Silent Children,* some descriptions of various offenders were given:

Adolescent offender: a teen who, for example, molests while babysitting (I recall that a guest on a nationwide TV program stated he would never hire a male babysitter. I feel that's a bit strong but it is a place to start). Things to watch in a teenage boy: helping out in Sunday school; coaching a sports team; volunteering to take neighborhood children places parents don't have time to take them. Watch for lack of contact with others of his own age.

Fixated offender: an early attraction to young people; marriage is no deterrent; 80 percent were married at time of offense; recidivism rate is high; and the suspect is usually 27 to 29 years of age at first offense.

Regressed offender: shows little sexual interest in children until time of first offense, usually 32 to 36 years of age; 75 percent married. The suspect has faced a crisis, has great stress such as family problems, trouble on the job, or physical illness. In later life the stress may include fear of getting old; retirement; death of wife and friends; decreased normal sexual functioning; poor health. I would place myself in this latter category.

Aggressive offender: violent, sadistic, premeditated. These suspects are more likely to choose strangers as their victims. In a small minority, misuse of alcohol plays an important part. (See "What part does alcohol play in child molestation?" in the Question and Answer section, page 85.)

I feel this observation of types is very important to help you understand

that not all child molesters are alike and that there are various patterns of
pedophilic and other behavior to be aware of. I'll quote from Dr. Nicholas
Groth and his associates in "A Study of Child Molesters: Myths and Realities":

> *Fixated Child Molester:* For one type of offender his sexual attraction to
> children constitutes an arrestment of his sociosexual maturation resulting from
> unresolved formative issues which undermined his subsequent development
> and persist in his personality functioning. Such an offender exhibits a com-
> pulsive attraction to and sexual fixation on children. From the onset of his
> adolescence children have been the primary or exclusive object of his sexual in-
> terests and any sexual contact with age mates that occurs is usually situational
> in nature, initiated by the other individual involved, and never replaces his
> preference for and chronic sexual involvement with children.
>
> *Regressed Child Molester:* For another type of offender his sexual involve-
> ment with a child constitutes a temporary or permanent departure from his
> more characteristic attraction to age mates. Such a regressed offender did not
> previously exhibit any predominant sexual interest in significantly younger per-
> sons (during his formative years) but when he entered adulthood and ex-
> perienced the attendant responsibilities and life-demands as overwhelming
> and/or when his adult relationships became conflictual and emotionally un-
> fulfilling a sexual attraction to children emerged. Such cross-generational sex-
> ual activity is typically activated by some precipitating stress and may wax and
> wane in response to the amount of stress the offender experiences in coping
> with adult life demands.
>
> *Clinical Example of a Regressed Offender:* Brad is a 37 year old, white, mar-
> ried male of average intelligence. He reports a fairly unremarkable life history.
> He had no difficulty in school and feels he grew up in a basically stable home.
> His sexual development does not appear unconventional. As a child he en-
> gaged in sexual play and experimentation with his siblings. He began mastur-
> bating at age 15 and experienced intercourse at age 19 with a girlfriend he
> ultimately married. He reports no extra-marital affairs, but became sexually in-
> volved with his 11 year old daughter when he lost his job and discovered that
> his wife had a terminal illness. Under the pressure of mounting medical bills
> and other responsibilities Brad began drinking heavily. He states "I loved my
> wife and children and still and always will. I don't know how this happened.
> There were times I would get into a deep depression and one day I came home
> and my daughter was asleep on my bed. That's how it began. At first I just
> touched her but later I started having intercourse with her." Brad's sexual activ-
> ity continued for two years during which time he did not engage in sexual ac-
> tivities with persons his own age. (See *Typology of Child Molesters,* page 107.)

Sexual Assault of Children and Adolescents (Burgess et al.) also gave some
advice from offenders. First, parents should be comfortable in their relationship with their child. They should make sure they are acquainted with any
adults or older children with whom their child is in frequent contact, especially
any authority figures. If any adult or older child seems unusually or excessively
interested in the child, parents should examine the relationship carefully. They
should also be alert to anyone the child tries to avoid. Watch out for overnights
at the home of a "big brother"; special field trips or campouts without most

Typology of Child Molesters

Source: Groth et al., "A Study of Child Molesters: Myths and Realities," Table 1.

Fixated Type	*Regressed Type*
1. Primary sexual orientation is to children.	1. Primary sexual orientation is to agemates.
2. Pedophilic interests begin at adolescence.	2. Pedophilic interests emerge in adulthood.
3. No precipitating stress/no subjective distress.	3. Precipitating stress usually evident.
4. Persistent interest and compulsive behavior.	4. Involvements may be more episodic and may wax and wane with stress.
5. Premeditated, pre-planned offenses.	5. Initial offense may be impulsive and not premeditated.
6. IDENTIFICATION: Offender identifies closely with the victim and equalizes his behavior to the level of the child and/or may adopt a pseudo-parental role to the victim.	6. SUBSTITUTION: Offender replaces conflictual adult relationship with involvement with a child; victim is a pseudoadult substitute and in incest situations the offender abandons his parental role.
7. Male victims are primary targets.	7. Female victims are primary targets.
8. Little or no sexual contact initiated with agemates; offender is usually single or in a marriage of convenience.	8. Sexual contact with a child coexists with sexual contact with agemates; offender is usually married or common-law.
9. Usually no history of alcohol or drug abuse and offense is not alcohol related.	9. Offense is often alcohol related.
10. Characterological immaturity; poor sociosexual peer relationships.	10. More traditional lifestyle but under-developed peer relationships.
11. Offense = maladaptive resolution of life development (maturation) issues.	11. Offense = maladaptive attempt to cope with specific life stresses.

members of a scout troop; or vacation invitations or a trip alone with a single adult. In your child, look for behavior changes; physical complaints; signs of stress; money unaccounted for; toys, candy or other gifts.

The offenders who offered these suggestions agreed on one other point: Parents must be sexually informed.

Gerald Arenberg, ex-director of the National Association of Chiefs of Police, wrote *Preventing Missing Children: A Parental Guide to Child Security.* In this excellent 1984 book he notes, as others have, that there are no reliable statistics on the loathsome crime of child molesting. He goes on to relate that 90 percent of the molesters are men, and they are usually young, with only 10 percent over 50 years of age and 31 years as the median. In 75 percent of the reported cases, the suspect is a family member, relative, friend, neighbor or acquaintance. Arenberg also mentions a heavy involvement of ministry and teaching professionals in child molestation. Arenberg talks about fixated and regressive categories and agrees that most (about 80 percent) suspects were abused as children. He states that most molesters are sincere, though immature, in their love for children and mean no physical harm; in fact, the sexual aspect of their relationship with children is usually relatively unimportant when compared to the value the molester places on the child's friendship and companionship. I certainly agree with that statement from my own experience and emphasize that sex plays a small part, but in most cases the relationship is meaningless to a molester without it. I also agree that molesters will not attempt sexual advances with every child they meet—but remember that every child has a brother or a friend and the suspect has patience.

Mr. Arenberg also quotes Dr. Groth and William Hobson and points out they have developed guidelines that may or may not indicate that a person is a molester. I'll list them for you: (1) single and past 25; (2) not playing competitive sports; (3) having an absence of appropriate peer relationships, confining his circle of friends to significantly young people; (4) having been abused, neglected or sexually victimized as a child; (5) exhibiting character immaturity, being shy, passive or non-assertive; (6) having a history of being treated by mental health clinics or psychiatric units of hospitals; (7) functioning well in a non–decision making job without interest in advancement; (8) having a police or FBI record. Remember, though, that these should all be considered *together,* in the overall context of a person's behavior. No one is suggesting that every unmarried 25-year-old male is a molester.

No More Secrets by Caren Adams and Jennifer Fay (1981) is a fine book for parents, and the knowledgeable authors offer some personal characteristics which many sexual offenders share (although no single item is an absolute signal): (1) Rigid and authoritarian background—military, religious or from a punitive family; (2) heavy alcohol use (at least one-third of sexual assaults appear to involve the use of alcohol by offenders); (3) background of abuse in own childhood; (4) wife-battering; (5) social isolation, difficulty relating to people of the same age; and (6) previous sexual offenses.

To give you a bit of a background on how professionals in the past analyzed the various types of sex offenders I am including the following notes drawn from Gebhard, et al., *Sex Offenders: An Analysis of Types,* 1965.

The authors, all from the Kinsey Institute of Sex Research, Inc., spent years in study and analysis of the sexual case histories of over 1500 men convicted for a wide variety of sex offenses. The men were inmates of Indiana and California prisons and were interviewed *before* the researchers examined their records. The research time span was from 1941 to 1949; 1953 to 1955; and 1959 and 1960. Bibliographies of 135 books, reports, studies, papers, journals, etc., and control groups were used for comparison. The researchers delved into each suspect's early life; masturbation; sex dreams; petting; premarital coitus; age of partner; animal contacts; criminality; other factors such as alcoholism and pornography; circumstances of the offense; and the varieties of offenders: hebephilic (sex with boys from puberty to middle teens), violent, showing mental pathology, and pedophilic (sexual interest in children). The studies also included "peepers," exhibitionists, obscene communication offenders, masqueraders (transvestites), and fetish theft offenders.

The purpose of the involved study was to determine if and how persons who have been convicted of various types of sex offenses differ from those who have not, and how they differ from one another. Here is a breakdown of their findings, taking into account both offenders against children (victims under 12 years of age) and offenders against minors (victims age 12 to 15):

Heterosexual offenders and aggressors against children: older men; some mental deficiency; turning to children rather than working out adult relationships; high masturbation by married men; use of prostitutes; and a large ratio of child victims who were strangers. In general: moralistic and conservative. Had normal sex life previously; now guilt ridden; some alcohol; said children encouraged the acts; no force; no penetration; no signs of aggression. No big problems with parents.

The more aggressive offender was more likely to be the youngest child; 75 percent married (some several times) but 40 percent divorced or separated; some misuse of alcohol; some parental friction and broken homes; heavy use of prostitutes; and used force or violence to effect penetration on victims; criminal activities.

Heterosexual offenders and aggressors against minors: excellent relationship with parents; late puberty; little homosexual activity; intellectually dull; first conviction; no violence; friends or relatives of victim reported offense; some gambling background. The aggressor: primarily amoral; delinquency; poor family relationships; unstable home life; irresponsible; aggressive; active sexually at an early age; considerable sexual experience with other males and animals; hasty, brief marriages; pornography.

Incest offenders against children: strongly heterosexual; few juvenile offenders; heavy alcohol; poor adjustment with parents; preoccupation with sex.

Incest offenders against minors: seldom only child; heavy drinking; sex not important; no criminal record. The researchers found this category difficult to summarize.

Homosexual offenders against children: worst parental relationships; early homosexual activity; some serious juvenile records; average age 30; few married; comfortable with boys; broken homes; sex with adult males when child.

Homosexual offenders against minors: most sexually oriented toward males; early sex contacts; average age 32½; few married; easy to dominate; poor relationships with parents.

Peepers: rank high in homosexual activity; average age 19; masturbating while peeping; mental deficiencies; some alcohol; fear of rejection; only or youngest child; criminal records and juvenile delinquents.

Exhibitionists: average family life; moderate arrest record; average age 30; three varieties: repeater, drunk, and mentally deficient; awkward; bashful; desire to frighten and shock with exposure of genitals or buttocks; numbers decline after age 40; normal intelligence; good work history; appear socially intact, but shy and immature; usually married and may have one or two children. The suspect finds reassurance about his masculinity from surprise, shock and fear on faces of victims. Some masturbate, but no contact. Rare cases included molesting, rape or murder.

Obscene communications: sexual arousal; crude and explicit; masturbation; little alcohol or drugs; use of telephone or pictures.

Masqueraders: desire sexual gratification; distorted and confused, often early in life; not necessarily homosexual.

Fetish theft: sexual arousal from clothing designed for genitals or breasts; many homosexuals; wearing female clothing in private; underdeveloped heterosexual life; bad marriages; antisocial tendencies.

Obviously, times and research have changed. Be grateful.

An Associated Press article in late 1989 published in a San Luis Obispo (California) newspaper was headlined: "Sex Offenders Tend to Be Passive." The article quotes Margretta Dwyer, coordinator of sex offender treatment at the University of Minnesota, who says that the typical male sex offender is passive, has low self-esteem and looks down on other sex offenders. Ms. Dwyer, after ten years of treating offenders, feels that she has pinpointed 14 common characteristics; she notes that 70 percent of 56 offenders studied had 11 of the traits and 83 percent had eight. According to Dwyer these traits should help in developing treatment. But she emphasized that more research is needed, with control groups made up of those who didn't commit sex offenses.

Dwyer's subjects ranged in age from 20 to 82. Eighty percent were incest offenders or pedophiles. Thirty-four were married. Sex offenders grow up "learning to be passive," Dwyer wrote in an article for the *Journal of Psychology and Human Sexuality.* "Passivity is their way of interacting with life ... encouraged by the overprotective mother and/or wife who makes decisions for them. Offenders tend to attract partners who will mother them."

Other traits: The typical male sex offender is manipulative. He has to be tricky to keep from being discovered. His relationship with his father, if he knew his father, was lousy. He's angry, but he keeps his anger bottled up. Other adults intimidate him. He tries to hold back his sexual thoughts in an effort to keep from committing sex crimes. He often believes someone other than himself is committing the act.

Thirty-six percent recalled being sexually abused as children, and 40 percent had upsetting sexual experiences around age 4. Strict religious codes figured in the offenses of 26 percent.

I agree that more research is needed.

Now let us consider several authors' suggestions of signs that may indicate a child has been sexually abused.

Frances Dayee in *Private Zone* lists the following sexual assault indicators: personality change; changes in toilet training habits; signs of being uncomfortable with someone formerly trusted; child talks about sex acts without prior knowledge; moody, crying excessively; changes in eating, sleeping habits; sudden unfounded fears; child has unusual need for "you're ok" reassurance; child shows unnatural interest in own or others' genitals; social skills change; outgoing child becomes clingy; child withdraws into self; increased activity; behavior problems; and unusual shyness.

In *No More Secrets,* authors Caren Adams and Jennifer Fay stress that parents should pay attention to behavior changes because most often a child will tell of assault not in words, but in behavior. Be alert to comments such as "Don't leave me alone with that person" or "I don't want to go with that person," or a change in play habits — new fear of schoolyard, neighbor's house, church area. Also be aware of the normal stages of sexual curiosity and development so that you will notice any unusual interest your child shows in the genitals of others, or any sexual knowledge beyond his age. Such behavior from a small child can be so startling that most adults do not know what to think. Do not overlook the possibility that the child has been sexually victimized and has learned the behavior from an adult or an older child. Other signals: sleep disturbances (nightmares, bedwetting, trouble falling asleep, demanding a night light); not wanting to be left alone; irritability and crankiness; school difficulties (inability to concentrate); loss or sudden increase in appetite; lots of new fears; need for more reassurance; returning to younger more babyish behavior; any unusual behavior shift; and suddenly turning against one parent. These are just general indicators that the child is troubled, but they do not necessarily mean the child has been involved in sexual abuse. A new baby, family money problems, talk of divorce, etc., may lead to some of these behavioral changes. Nevertheless I urge parents to heed any and all signals and follow up on them. Quickly determine what is wrong and rectify the situation. What is very minor to you might be (and usually is) extremely important to your child.

Francis Ilg and Louise Ames published "Normal Stages of Sex Play" in *Child Behavior:*

> *Age 2½:* Child shows interest in different postures of boys and girls when urinating and [is] interested in physical differences between the sexes.
>
> *Age 3:* Verbally expresses interest in physical differences between sexes and in different postures in urinating. Girls attempt to urinate standing up.
>
> *Age 4:* Extremely conscious of the navel. Under social stress may grasp genitals and may need to urinate. May play the game of "show." Also, verbal play about elimination. Interest in other people's bathrooms, may demand privacy for self but be extremely interested in bathroom activity of others.
>
> *Age 5:* Familiar with, but not too much interested in physical differences between sexes. Less sex play and game of "show." More modest and less exposing [of] self. Less bathroom play and less interest in unfamiliar bathrooms.
>
> *Age 6:* Marked awareness of and interest in differences between sexes in body structure. Questioning. Mutual investigation by both sexes reveals practical answers to questions about sex differences. Mild sex play or exhibitionism in play or in school toilets. Game of "show." May play hospital and take rectal temperature. Giggling, calling names or remarks involving words dealing with elimination functions. Some children are subjected to sex play by older children; or girls are bothered by older men.
>
> *Age 7:* Less interest in sex. Some mutual explorations, experimentation, and sex play, but less than earlier.
>
> *Age 8:* Interest in sex rather high, though sex exploration and play is less common than at six. Interest in peeping, smutty jokes, provocative giggling. Children whisper, write or spell "elimination" or "sex" words.
>
> *Age 9:* May talk about sex information with friends of same sex. Interest in details of own organs and functions, seek[s] out picture books. Sex swearing and sex poems begin.
>
> *Age 10:* Considerable interest in smutty jokes.

CHILDHELP USA has listed some possible sexual abuse indicators in the school setting:

Interaction Between Sexually Abused Child and Classmates:
- Low self-image.

- Few (if any) friends.
- The young child may exhibit precocious sex play.
- Not allowed social activities.
- May have boyfriends at school but no dates.
- Not allowed to spend the night at a friend's house or vice versa.
- Self-destructive behavior—drugs, alcohol, persistent running away.

Classroom Behavior of the Sexually Abused Child:
- Abrupt change in child.
- Severe drop in grades.
- Extreme moodiness.
- Depression, excessive crying.
- Newly acquired bodily complaints, especially stomach aches.
- Lack of self concept, self esteem.
- Afraid to be alone with an adult, especially a male.
- Vacillates between being ultra-adult and ultra-immature.
- Won't undress for P.E.

The Sexually Abused Child (In Classroom) While Discussing Sex:
- Either he becomes restless and agitated or he tries to become invisible (avoids eye contact, sinks down in chair, pulls away from others).
- Midway through discussion complains of headache, dizziness, and/or muscle cramp.
- May ask more questions than normal, or know terminology inappropriate for age.

Interaction of Sexually Abused Child with Parents:
- Blurring of generational boundaries.
- Role reversal of mother and daughter.
- Father is overly protective of daughter.
- Father has close physical contact with daughter while mother is completely left out.
- Father thinks of self as young boyfriend.
- Mother thinks of daughter as a rival.

These guidelines were exactly the same as those compiled by Lynn Batdorf, member, Sexual Abuse Team, Coalition for Child Advocacy, in a paper from the Sexual Assault Center, Harborview Medical Center, Seattle, Washington.

What if your child tells you, or you are otherwise able to determine, that he or she has indeed been abused? The National Center for Missing and Exploited Children (address in Resource Guide) has published the following parental guidelines in case your child might someday be the victim of sexual abuse or exploitation:

DON'T

- Panic or overreact to the information disclosed by the child. With your help and support, you will both make it through these difficult times.
- Criticize the child. The worst thing you can do is express anger at the child having violated previous instructions. Outbursts such as "I told you not to go into anyone's home!" will only hurt your ability to help.

DO

- Respect the child's privacy. Accompany the child to a private place where he or she can relate the story. Be careful not to discuss the incidents in front of people who do not need to know what happened.
- Support the child and the decision to tell the story. It is normal for children to fear telling others—especially parents. Make it clear that telling you what happened was the right thing to do and that you will protect the child from future harm. Remember, often a child molester or exploiter will tell the child that bad things will happen if the child ever tells anyone what has happened. The child is especially fearful of punishment, panic, or the loss of the parents' love.
- Show physical affection, and express your love and confidence with words and gestures. Avoid challenges starting with why, such as "Why didn't you tell me this before?" or "Why did you let it happen?" Give positive messages, such as "I'm proud of you for telling me this," "I'm glad it wasn't worse," or "I know you couldn't help it."
- Explain to the child that he or she has done no wrong. The child may well have feelings of guilt and responsibility and assume that he or she is to blame for what happened. Most children are enticed or tricked into acts of exploitation, and they think they should have been smarter or stronger.
- Remember that children seldom lie about acts of sexual exploitation. It is important that the child feel that you believe what he or she has told you.
- Keep open the lines of communication with the child. In the future, it will be vitally important that the child believe that you are sympathetic, understanding, supportive, and optimistic so that he or she will be comfortable in making additional disclosures and in discussing feelings.

Steps to Take

1. If you think the child has been physically injured, seek out appropriate medical attention. Remember, often we do not realize that a child who has been sexually exploited is also physically injured. Do not guess. Let the professionals make an independent judgment about treatment.
2. You must alert the child protection, youth services, child abuse, or other appropriate social services organizations. The police, sheriff's office, or other law-enforcement agency must also be notified.
3. Consider the need for counseling or therapy for the child. To ignore the incident, to "sweep it under the rug," to act as if it did not happen is not going to help the child deal with the exploitation. In deciding what counselors to use, look for someone who is experienced in cases of sexual victimization. Ask about the number of children they have counseled.

The above suggestions are simplified but certainly accurate if you remember that your reactions are so very important. You can never tell when your child may disclose past acts of molestation or general feelings of fear. How you handle the initial information is vital to the victim as well as yourself and others in the family unit.

Many sources also offer good advice on what to teach children to help prevent sexual abuse from occurring. In *Your Children Should Know,* Colao and Hosansky printed a "Child's Bill of Personal Safety Rights":

1. The right to trust one's instincts and funny feelings.
2. The right to privacy.
3. The right to say no to unwanted touch or affection.
4. The right to question adult authority and say no to adult demands and requests.
5. The right to lie and not answer questions.
6. The right to refuse gifts.
7. The right to be rude or unhelpful.
8. The right to run, scream, and make a scene.
9. The right to bite, hit or kick.
10. The right to ask for help.

The authors explained and gave examples of the above. For instance, a child has the right to lie (Right 5) if a telephone caller asks, "Are your parents home?" and the child has been told never to say he is alone in the house. A child may be unhelpful (Right 7) if a suspect knocks on the door saying he has been in an accident and has to use the phone. The child may offer to call the police or a neighbor for him but still not let him into the house. A child is not under any obligation to assist every adult that asks for his help. Regarding Right 9, the authors explain that children are natural fighters and suggest that if attacked, they focus on vulnerable areas: kicking knees and shins, poking into the throat or biting.

Your Children Should Know also includes a whole chapter on self-defense, along with pictures of a child and an attacker in various attack/defense poses. I should mention that Ms. Colao, MSW, is co-director of SAFE (Safety and Fitness Exchange, Inc.). She is also on the faculty of the Sex Crimes Seminars of the New York City Police Department. Ms. Hosansky is a co-founder of SAFE and holds a black belt in karate. Their book is heavy on self-defense, but I just don't know enough about the value of teaching a child how to kick a suspect in the groin. I assume that there would be reactions from parents like, "My kid is always getting into fights since he learned karate," or "Teaching self-defense gives children false confidence and if they ever tried to use it, the attacker would probably kill them." If the self-defense school also presents a strong background of a state of mind and body that allows one to feel comfortable in relation to one's own safety, then that would be quite beneficial, it seems to me. The authors would like *all* martial-arts schools to offer realistic, effective and sensitive programs for children on personal safety, but I just don't think that's possible without some sort of governmental intervention.

SLAM, Society's League Against Molestation, suggests you teach your children: (1) That no one has the right to touch the private parts of their body or make them feel uncomfortable. *They have the right to say NO!* (2) That they should tell you if anyone asks to take, or has taken, their picture. (3) That adults do not come to children for help; adults ask other adults for help. (4) That they should never go near a car with someone in it and never get into a car without your knowledge. (5) That they should make you aware of any unusual discussions or strange requests. (6) That they should tell you when any adult asks them to keep a "secret." (7) That they should tell you of gifts and money given to them. (8) That they should never go into someone's home without your knowledge. (9) That when away from home, scared or uncomfortable, they have the right to use the telephone without anyone's permission. (10) That they should tell you of any situation where a statement or gesture is made about sex or love. (11) That they should never answer the door alone. (12) That they should never admit to anyone over the telephone that they are alone. (13) That you will always believe them about a molestation and will protect them from further harm. Children usually do not lie about molestation.

For parents, SLAM suggests: (1) Question any money or gifts your children bring home. (2) Ask your children whom they are spending time with and what activities they engage in. (3) Find out who their best friend is, and why. (4) Be watchful of any strong bond that seems to develop between your children and an adult figure in their life (friends, teachers, coaches, clergymen, etc.). (5) Avoid male babysitters and overnight trips alone with an adult. (6) Maintain constant and regular telephone contact with your children whenever one of you is away from home. (7) Never leave your children unattended, day or night. (8) Never leave your children alone in a car. *It only takes a minute.* (9) Be involved in any sports or activities your children participate in. (10) Beware of coaches or leaders who do not have children of their own in the same group. (11) Listen when your children tell you they do not want to be/go with someone. *There may be a reason for their reluctance!* (12) Never make children submit to physical contact (i.e., hugs and kisses, etc.) if they do not want to. They have a right to say no. (13) Remember that no one should want to be with your children more than you. When someone is showing your children too much attention, *ask yourself why.* (14) Be sensitive to any changes in your children's behavior or attitudes. Encourage an open communication. Never belittle any fear or concern your children may express. Never compromise any private or confidential matter your children may share with you.

CHILDHELP USA stresses the following points: Sexual abuse is not the victim's fault. Teach your children that they have the right to say no to any touch that is scary or uncomfortable. Children should be taught whom to tell, including people outside the family; they should also be taught that it is good to tell someone if this is happening to them. Tell the children what will happen after a child tells someone in authority. Identify private parts and define sexual assault. Remember that sexual abuse prevention must have involvement and commitment from school staff and parents.

When you teach your child about sexual abuse, it is good if the discussion also contains the following elements:

- "Touch" presented as a continuum with emphasis on nurturing touch as well as exploitive touch.
- "Touch" should be defined and discussed with children.
- Kids should gain a sense of their own power to protect themselves.
- Take cultural differences into account.

The following items are not desirable in prevention discussions:

- Do not focus on "strangers."
- Do not indicate that the offender is sick, crazy or weird.
- Do not scare kids—use a balance of success stories.
- Do not confuse kids.
- Do not leave the child open to assuming guilt or responsibility for the offense.

Above all, listen to what your child is saying. Imagine this conversation: "What did you do over at Howie's house?" "We watched TV." "That's nice." Well, my TV set was in the bedroom. I had another in the front room but seldom used it. The TV in the bedroom was for my convenience, sure it was. It was also an attractive place to seduce victims.

Don't expect signs of unsavory activities like smoking or drinking to give you clues that your child is involved in a bad situation. I never smoked with my victims (unless the victim also smoked in front of his parents) and certainly never had them drink. Most molesters have strong convictions along some lines and by rigidly adhering to these self-imposed rules, convince themselves that they are upholding the law and have high moral values. I doubt that a molester would even jaywalk or go through a yellow light, so great is his desire to enforce the law—yet he will violate a child.

The molester also believes he is a "great guy" for paying attention to the child who is shunned by destiny or nature. This child may receive no attention from anyone else except when he is abused or yelled at by parents or other authorities, or taunted by peers. The suspect will take advantage of such a situation and congratulate himself for his generous character. Yet that's one thing a child molester doesn't have: depth of character.

Furthermore, it is my firm belief that a previously convicted child molester will kill his victim to stay out of prison. In this situation all the "love" for the child is even more obviously just so much bull. If an ex-con molester is facing solid additional charges, the child victim is unimaginably close to death.

IV. Definitions, Laws and Legal Aspects

One of the difficulties we face is finding two authorities who have the same definition of child sexual abuse.

Child sexual abuse suggests the sexual exploitation of a child by an older, more mature person, and I think that everybody will agree with that, but there is a lot more to it. Various state penal codes differ widely in the legal definitions and in penalties to the suspect. Legal jargon includes "child molestation," "carnal abuse of a child," "lewd and lascivious acts with a child," "impairing the morals of a minor," etc. Nor do the state laws agree about the age of consent or the age difference that makes one partner a victim and the other an offender (MacNamara, D., and Sagarin, E., *Sex, Crime and the Law,* 1977).

There are those who suggest that the term "child sexual abuse" incites excessive alarm and that this is injurious to the victim and the family. Of course, there are also those groups that take the extreme view that children might profit from early sexual indoctrination by "responsible" adults. (These include the René Guyon Society; Paedophilia International Exchange [PIE]; Pedophilia Anonymous Network [PAN]; North American Man/Boy Love Association [NAMBLA]; and the Lewis Carroll Circle. (See "What's wrong with sex between adults and children?" in the Question and Answer section, pages 25–28, for some of the rhetoric from these groups.)

In this section I will make an effort to report on the lack of uniformity in definitions and laws and the wide variance in thinking by professionals, consultants, various organizations, the criminal justice system and the general public. My main concern, however, is not to establish a uniform definition, but to examine how quickly the system (such as it is) is able to provide treatment for a victim.

The Federal Child Abuse Prevention and Treatment Act (Public Law 93-247 as amended and including one child abuse amendment of 1984, Public Law 98-457, October 9, 1984 [42 U.S.C. 5101, note]) incorporates the following definitions for purposes of the act: (1) The term "child abuse and neglect" means the physical or mental injury, sexual abuse or exploitation, negligent treatment, or maltreatment of a child under the age of eighteen, or the age specified by the Child Protection Law of the state in question, by a person (including any employee of a residential facility or any staff person providing out-of-home care who is responsible for the child's welfare under circumstances which indicate that the child's health or welfare is harmed or threatened thereby, as determined in accordance with regulations prescribed by the Secretary); and (2) (A) The term "sexual abuse" includes—(i) the employment, use, persuasion, inducement, enticement, or coercion of any child to engage in, or having a child assist any other person to engage in, any sexually explicit conduct (or any simulation of such conduct) for the purpose of producing any visual depiction of such conduct, or (ii) the rape, molestation, prostitution, or other such form of sexual exploitation of children, or incest with children, under circumstances which indicate that the child's health or welfare is harmed or threatened thereby, as determined in accordance with regulations prescribed by the Secretary; and (B) for the purpose of this clause, the term "child" or "children" means any individual who has not or individuals who have not attained the age of eighteen. (3) The term "withholding of medically indicated treatment" means the failure to respond to the infant's life-threatening conditions by providing treatment (including appropriate nutrition, hydration, and medication) which, in the treating physician's or physicians' reasonable medical judgment, will be most likely to be effective in ameliorating or correcting all such conditions, except that the term does not include the failure to provide treatment (other than appropriate nutrition, hydration, or medication) to an infant when, on the treating physician's or physicians' reasonable medical judgment, (a) the infant is chronically and irreversibly comatose; (b) the provision of such treatment would (i) merely prolong dying, (ii) not be effective in ameliorating or correcting all of the infant's life-threatening conditions, or (iii) otherwise be futile in terms of the survival of the infant; or (C) the provision of such treatment would be virtually futile in terms of the survival of the infant and the treatment itself under such circumstances would be inhumane.

On October 9, 1984, after receiving expert testimony, the United States Congress amended the definition of sexual abuse in the Child Abuse Prevention and Treatment Act of 1974 (the summary above contains the amendments) and for the first time "persons responsible" was legally broadened beyond the family. It is my understanding that this federal law is not used in individual cases; instead, the state civil and criminal laws govern the handling of child sexual abuse. And, according to J. Bulkley (*Child Sexual Abuse and the Law,* 1981) the diversity of laws makes it difficult to arrive at a standard legal definition in any one state. Bulkley in his "analysis of civil child protection statutes dealing with sexual abuse" *(Child Sexual Abuse and the Law)* says that the degree of specificity of sexual abuse definitions varies widely from state to state and that criminal statutory definitions are not uniform; there are wide variations in the penalty structures and in the upper age limit of the child victim. K. MacFarlane, "Sexual Abuse of Children" (in J. Chapman and

M. Gates, *The Victimization of Women*, 1978) relates that the definition of what constitutes sexual abuse of children remains largely a matter of jurisdictional and individual interpretation; and she says that a sexual abuse act committed by a person outside the family may be handled quite differently from the same act committed by someone legally responsible for the child. For example, the penalties for incest range in severity from simple fines to fifty years in prison. Some states specify that the partners must be blood-related for a sex act to be considered incestuous.

Let us look at some of the differences in state laws and some differing definitions by a number of authors and researchers in the field.

New York state laws define degrees in the crime of sexual abuse with different penalties for each crime. For example, an act of sexual abuse is treated differently if the victim is less than 11 years old, if the vicitm is under 14 years, if sexual contact is without the victim's consent, or if the suspect is less than five years older than the victim.

Some states rather ambiguously say that "a person is guilty of sexual abuse when he subjects another person to sexual contact." I am told that many state laws provide little guidance as to the meaning of the words "sexual abuse," preferring to leave the matter of interpretation to the courts.

The legal age of statutory sexual consent in the United States varies widely: age 7 in one state; age 10 in 3 states; age 12 in 9 states; age 13 to 16 in 23 states; age 17 in one state; and age 18 in 13 states. Penalties range from one year imprisonment to life imprisonment.

P. Mrazek, in "Definition and Recognition of Sexual Child Abuse: Historical and Cultural Perspectives" (*Sexually Abused Children and Their Families*, 1981) states that professionals who work with child sexual abuse develop their own "operational" definitions and goes on to give several "clinical" definitions including one that I feel is very important: "The prevailing cultural attitudes about sexuality in the community."

I certainly feel that in many communities if a judge failed to give a child molester the maximum sentence he would be a subject of a recall vote or a massive voter turnout to turn him out. Politics and community actions and reactions play important roles as judges, district attorneys and prosecutors desire to head for "bigger things." Conversely, a judge that was "soft" on this type of offender might find himself wondering where his next defendant was.

The doctors Kempe report: "Sexual abuse is defined as the involvement of dependent, developmentally immature children and adolescents in sexual activities that they do not fully comprehend and to which they are unable to give informed consent or that violate the social taboos of family roles" (Schechter & Toberge, 1976).

Another definition: "The sexual use of a child by an adult for his or her sexual gratification without consideration of the child's psychosocial sexual development" (Mrazek & Mrazek, 1981). This definition comes from experts who deal in retrospective surveys and fails to define "child"; perhaps they mean from birth through adolescence.

And another: "1. The battered child abuse injuries are primarily in the genital area; 2. The child who has experienced attempted or actual intercourse and/or other inappropriate genital contact with an adult; 3. The child who has been inappropriately involved with an adult in sexual activities not covered by 1 or 2." (Mrazek, et al., 1981).

Once again, "child" is not defined, and the use of the word "inappropriate" seems too vague.

J. Bulkley says, "There is a basic dilemma about whether child sexual abuse should be regarded as a crime, a form of mental illness, or—particularly in cases of incest—as a major symptom of broader family dysfunction." (*Child Sexual Abuse and the Law*, 1981.)

The Clearinghouse on Child Abuse and Neglect definition includes sexual molestation, incest and exploitation for prostitution or the production of pornographic materials.

The Clearinghouse also says that child abuse and neglect encompass a wide range of behaviors and patterns of family interaction. In general, these terms refer to harm or predictable harm to a child under the age of 18 caused by a parent, guardian, or other person responsible for a child's welfare (such as a residential child care worker or day care provider), resulting from either assault, willful inattention, or failure to provide the necessities of life.

Acts of sexual abuse committed by a stranger or a person not responsible for the full-time care of a child (such as a teacher or recreation leader) usually have *not* been covered under state child abuse and neglect laws for child protective purposes, but only under criminal laws.

Another definition, this from the National Committee for the Prevention of Child Abuse: The exploitation of a child for the sexual gratification of an adult, as in rape, incest, fondling of the genitals, exhibitionism, or pornography.

David Finkelhor (*Sexually Victimized Children*, 1979) considers taking all of the terms used by professionals, such as sexual assault, child rape, child molestation and incest, and concludes that these terms focus only on specific aspects of the problem. He suggests the term "sexual victimization." I think this term the most appropriate because it emphasizes that the children are victimized because of their age, naivete, and relationship with the suspect rather than being victimized by the aggressive intent of the abusive behavior.

Whatever the definition, or the reason for the victimization, this type of sexual activity does show disregard of the victim's emotional and developmental needs and often the victim's personal safety as well. Most definitions seem to agree that the abuse occurs for sexual gratification or other purposes of the adult offender like pornography or child prostitution.

Finally, let me quote what the National Center on Child Abuse and Neglect (*Child Sexual Abuse: Incest, Assault, and Sexual Exploitation,* August 1978) has adopted as a definition of child sexual abuse: "contacts or interactions between a child and an adult when the child is being used for the sexual stimulation of the perpetrator or another person. Sexual abuse may also be committed by a person under the age of eighteen when that person is either significantly older than the victim or when the perpetrator is in a position of power or control over another child."

I can't argue with that.

Other definitions of interest are the following categories of sexual abuse:

Child Molester: A significantly older person whose conscious sexual interests and overt sexual behavior are directed either partially or exclusively toward prepubertal children.

Child Pornography: Still, video, or film production involving minors in any sexual acts that include other children, adults or animals.

Child Prostitution: This involves children who perform sex acts for profit. Children may act on their own but most often an adult (pimp) and even parents manage the child and reap the profits.

Child Rape: Rape is most commonly associated with adolescent victims, although forcible sexual assaults are also reported involving young children. The sexual acts are usually forced oral, vaginal, or anal penetration. Injuries may result either from the act or the force used to secure the submission of the victim. Although child rape can occur within the family, the offender is usually not known to the victim. Typically, enticement or abduction is used to separate and isolate the child from family and friends.

Exhibitionism (Indecent exposure): This involves the exposure of the genitals by a male to girls, boys, and women. The suspect may masturbate as a part of this sexual excitement action but does not usually make approaches or any other overt action. Very young children may not even recognize the sexual intent of the act. They may think the adult is deformed or has an abnormal growth in his private area.

Hebephilia: Love of youth. I have not found a dictionary definition except of "Hebe," who in Greek mythology was the goddess of youth, but I recall Dr. Nicholas Groth (1980) used the term, and FBI Special Agent Kenneth Lanning quoted the expression in his excellent publication *Child Molesters: A Behavioral Analysis,* 1987. My definition is that a hebephile has a main sexual attraction for children just entering puberty through 14 or 15 years of age or so.

Incest: Any physical sexual activity between family members. Use "family" in the broad social connotation, as blood relationship is not required.

Stepfathers or stepmothers and nonrelated brothers and sisters as a result of previous marriages are included, as are relatives not living with the victim — uncles, aunts and grandparents, for example.

Molestation: This includes fondling, touching or kissing the victim on the breast or genital areas. It may include masturbation of the victim or urging the victim to fondle or masturbate the suspect. I should point out that molestation in itself is a rather vague term (Kempe, 1984) because you cannot really define the limits of the acts.

Pederasty: Sexual relations between men, especially between men and boys.

Pedophilia: Love of child. The preference of an adult for prepubertal children as the means of achieving sexual gratification or excitement. (Pedophilia is impressively described in Thomas Mann's short story "Death in Venice.")

Rape: Is defined as sexual intercourse, or attempted intercourse, without the consent of the victim.

Sexual Intercourse (Statutory Rape): This includes fellatio (oral-genital contact), sodomy (anal-genital contact), or penile-vaginal intercourse. All of these actions may occur without physical violence by the use of seduction, bribes, use of authority, persuasion or any other threat.

Sexual Sadism: Inflicting bodily injury on another as a way of obtaining sexual gratification or excitement.

We have seen the federal law (the Child Abuse Prevention and Treatment Act) and discussed general differences in state laws. What about the specifics of state laws? Naturally I cannot reproduce the laws of all 50 states in the limited space of this book, but perhaps it will be helpful to take a close look at the laws of one state, California, which are quoted at length below:

California Child Abuse Reporting Law

Penal Code, Article 2.5. Child Abuse Reporting. Section 11165. Definitions. As used in this article:
(a) "Child" means a person under the age of 18 years.
(b) "Sexual abuse" means sexual assault or sexual exploitation as defined by the following:
(1) "Sexual assault" means conduct in violation of one or more of the following sections of this code: Section 261 (rape), 264.1 (rape in concert), 285 (incest), 286 (sodomy, subdivision [a] or [b] of Section 288 [lewd or lascivious acts upon a child under 14 years of age]), 288a (oral copulation), 289 (penetration of a genital or anal opening by a foreign object), or 647a (child molestation).
(2) "Sexual exploitation" refers to any of the following:
(A) Conduct involving matter depicting a minor engaged in obscene acts in violation of Section 311.2 (preparing, selling, or distributing obscene matter)

or subdivision (a) of Section 311.4 (employment of minor to perform obscene acts).

(B) Any person who knowingly promotes, aids, or assists, employs, uses, persuades, induces, or coerces a child, or any parent or guardian of a child under his or her control who knowingly permits or encourages a child to engage in, or assist others to engage in, prostitution or to either pose or model alone or with others for purposes of preparing a film, photograph, negative, slide, or live performance, involving obscene sexual conduct for commercial purposes.

(C) Any person who depicts a child in, or who knowingly develops, duplicates, prints, or exchanges, any film, photograph, videotape, negative, or slide in which a child is engaged in an act of obscene sexual conduct, except for those activities by law enforcement and prosecution agencies and other persons described in subdivisions (c) and (e) of Section 311.3.

(c) "Neglect" means the negligent treatment or maltreatment of a child by a person responsible for the child's welfare under circumstances indicating harm or threatened harm to the child's health or welfare. The term includes both acts and omissions on the part of the responsible person.

(1) "Severe neglect" means the negligent failure of a person having the care or custody of a child to protect the child from severe malnutrition or medically diagnosed nonorganic failure to thrive. "Severe neglect" also means those situations of neglect where any person having the care or custody of a child willfully causes or permits the person or health of the child to be placed in a situation such that his or her person or health is endangered, as proscribed by subdivision (d), including the intentional failure to provide adequate food, clothing, shelter, or medical care.

(2) "General neglect" means the negligent failure of a person having the care or custody of a child to provide adequate food, clothing, shelter, medical care, or supervision where no physical injury to the child has occurred.

For the purposes of this chapter, a child receiving treatment by spiritual means as provided in Section 16509.1 of the Welfare and Institutions Code or not receiving specified medical treatment for religious reasons, shall not for that reason alone be considered a neglected child. An informed and appropriate medical decision made by parent or guardian after consultation with a physician or physicians who have examined the minor shall not constitute neglect.

(d) "Willful cruelty or unjustifiable punishment of a child" means a situation where any person willfully causes or permits any child to suffer, or inflicts thereon, unjustifiable physical pain or mental suffering, or having the care or custody of any child, willfully causes or permits the person or health of the child to be placed in a situation such that his or her person or health is endangered.

(e) "Corporal punishment or injury" means a situation where any person willfully inflicts upon any child any cruel or inhuman corporal punishment or injury resulting in a traumatic condition.

(f) "Abuse in out-of-home care" means a situation of physical injury on a child which is inflicted by other than accidental means, or of sexual abuse or neglect or the willful cruelty or unjustifiable punishment of a child, as defined in this article, where the person responsible for the child's welfare is a foster parent or the administrator or an employee of a public or private residential home, school, or other institution or agency.

(g) "Child abuse" means a physical injury which is inflicted by other than accidental means on a child by another person. "Child abuse" also means the sexual abuse of a child or any act or omission proscribed by Section 273a (willful cruelty or unjustifiable punishment of a child) or 273d (corporal punishment or injury). "Child abuse" also means the neglect of a child or abuse in out-of-home care, as defined in this article.

(h) "Child care custodian" means a teacher, administrative officer, supervisor of child welfare and attendance, or certificated pupil personnel employee of any public or private school; an administrator of a public or private day camp; a licensee, an administrator, or an employee of a community care facility licensed to care for children; headstart teacher; a licensing worker or licensing evaluator; public assistance worker; employee of a child care institution including, but not limited to, foster parents, group home personnel and personnel of residential care facilities; a social worker or a probation officer.

(i) "Medical practitioner" means a physician and surgeon, psychologist, dentist, resident, intern, podiatrist, chiropractor, licensed nurse, dental hygienist, or any other person who is currently licensed under Division 2 (commencing with Section 500) of the Business and Professions Code, any emergency medical technician I or II, paramedic, or other person certified pursuant to Division 2.5 (commencing with Section 1797) of the Health and Safety Code, or a psychological assistant registered pursuant to Section 2913 of the Business and Professions Code.

(j) "Nonmedical practitioner" means a state or county public health employee who treats a minor for venereal disease or any other condition; a coroner, a marriage, family, or child counselor; or a religious practitioner who diagnoses, examines, or treats children.

(k) "Child protective agency" means a police or sheriff's department, or a county welfare department.

(l) "Commercial film and photographic print processor" means any person who develops exposed photographic film into negatives, slides, or prints, or who makes prints from negatives or slides, for compensation. The term includes any employee of such a person; it does not include a person who develops film or makes prints for a public agency.

I'm going to add the following Sections as I believe that it is important that you know who *must* report child sexual abuse. Several men have stated they wished to discuss their problem with someone but were afraid they would be reported. I can find no requirement under California law that states a priest, rabbi, preacher or pastor must report a person because they discussed their sexual involvement with children. However, if you are thinking of talking to a member of the clergy I suggest you call first and find out how that person sees his duty on reporting or not reporting. I also suggest you look through the Resource Guide for names and addresses of agencies that might help you.

Section 11166. Report; duty; time

(a) Except as provided in subdivision (b), any child care custodian, medical practitioner, nonmedical practitioner, or employee of a child protective agency who has knowledge of or observes a child in his or her professional capacity or within the scope of his or her employment whom he or she knows or reasonably suspects has been the victim of child abuse shall report the known or suspected instance of child abuse to a child protective agency immediately or as soon as practically possible by telephone and shall prepare and send a written report thereof within 36 hours of receiving the information concerning the incident. For the purposes of this article, "reasonable suspicion" means that it is objectively reasonable for a person to entertain such a suspicion, based upon facts that could cause a reasonable person in a like position, drawing when appropriate on his or her training and experience, to suspect child abuse.

(b) Any child care custodian, medical practitioner, nonmedical practitioner, or employee of a child protective agency who has knowledge of or who reasonably suspects that mental suffering has been inflicted on a child or his or her emotional well-being is endangered in any other way, may report such known or suspected instance of child abuse to a child protective agency.

(c) Any commercial film and photographic print processor who has knowledge of or observes, within the scope of his or her professional capacity or employment, any film, photograph, video tape, negative or slide depicting a child under the age of 14 years engaged in an act of sexual conduct, shall report such instance of suspected child abuse to the law enforcement agency having jurisdiction over the case immediately or as soon as practically possible by telephone and shall prepare and send a written report of it with a copy of the film, photograph, video tape, negative or slide attached within 36 hours of receiving the information concerning the incident. As used in this subdivision, "sexual conduct" means any of the following:

(1) Sexual intercourse, including genital-genital, oral-genital, anal-genital, or oral-anal, whether between persons of the same or opposite sex or between humans and animals.

(2) Penetration of the vagina or rectum by any object.

(3) Masturbation, for the purpose of sexual stimulation of the viewer.

(4) Sadomasochistic abuse for the purpose of sexual stimulation of the viewer.

(5) Exhibition of the genitals, pubic or rectal areas of any person for the purpose of sexual stimulation of the viewer.

(d) Any other person who has knowledge of or observes a child whom he or she knows or reasonably suspects has been a victim of child abuse may report the known or suspected instance of child abuse to a child protective agency.

(e) When two or more persons who are required to report are present and jointly have knowledge of a known or suspected instance of child abuse, and when there is agreement among them, the telephone report may be made by a member of the team selected by mutual agreement and a single report may be made and signed by such selected member of the reporting team. Any member who has knowledge that the member designated to report has failed to do so, shall thereafter make the report.

(f) The reporting duties under this section are individual, and no supervisor or administrator may impede or inhibit the reporting duties and no person making such a report shall be subject to any sanction for making the report. However, internal procedures to facilitate reporting and apprise supervisors and administrators of reports may be established provided that they are not inconsistent with the provisions of this article.

(g) A county probation or welfare department shall immediately or as soon as practically possible report by telephone to the law enforcement agency having jurisdiction over the case, to the agency given the responsibility for investigation of cases under Section 300 of the Welfare and Institutions Code, and to the district attorney's office every known or suspected instance of child abuse as defined in Section 11165, except acts or omissions coming within the provisions of paragraph (2) of subdivision (c) of Section 11165, which shall only be reported to the county welfare department. A county probation or welfare department shall also send a written report thereof within 36 hours of receiving the information concerning the incident to any agency to which it is required to make a telephone report under this subdivision.

A law enforcement agency shall immediately or as soon as practically possible report by telephone to the county welfare department, the agency given responsibility for investigation of cases under Section 300 of the Welfare and Institutions Code, and to the district attorney's office every known or suspected instance of child abuse reported to it, except acts or omissions coming within the provisions of paragraph (2) of subdivision (c) of Section 11165, which shall only be reported to the county welfare department. A law enforcement agency shall also send a written report thereof within 36 hours of receiving the information concerning the incident to any agency to which it is required to make a telephone report under this subdivision.

Section 11166.5. Employment as child care custodian, medical or nonmedical practitioner or with child protective agency; knowledge of and compliance with 11166.

Any person who enters into employment on and after January 1, 1985, as a child care custodian, medical practitioner, or nonmedical practitioner, or with a child protective agency, prior to commencing his or her employment, and as a prerequisite to that employment, shall sign a statement on a form provided to him or her by his or her employer to the effect that he or she has knowledge of the provisions of section 11166 and will comply with its provisions.

The statement shall include the following provision:

Section 11166 of the Penal Code requires any child care custodian, medical practitioner, nonmedical practitioner, or employee of a child protective agency who has knowledge of or observes a child in his or her employment whom he or she knows or reasonably suspects has been the victim of child abuse to report the known or suspected instance of child abuse to a child protective agency immediately or as soon as practically possible by telephone and to prepare and send a written report thereof within 36 hours of receiving the information concerning the incident.

"Child care custodian" includes teachers, administrative officers, supervisors of child welfare and attendance, or certificated pupil personnel employees of any public or private school; administrators of a public or private day camp; licensed day care workers; administrators of community care facilities licensed to care for children; headstart teachers, licensing workers or licensing evaluators; public assistance workers; employees of a child care institution including, but not limited to, foster parents, group home personnel, and personnel of residential care facilities; and social workers or probation officers.

"Medical practitioner" includes physicians and surgeons, psychiatrists, psychologists, dentists, residents, interns, podiatrist, chiropractors, licensed nurses, dental hygienists, or any other person who is licensed under Division 2 (commencing with section 500) of the Business and Professions Code.

"Nonmedical practitioner" includes state or county public health employees who treat minors for venereal disease or any other condition; coroners; paramedics; marriage, family or child counselors; and religious practitioners who diagnose, examine, or treat children. The signed statements shall be retained by the employer. The cost of printing, distribution, and filing of these statements shall be borne by the employer.

Section 11167. Report; contents

(a) A telephone report of a known or suspected instance of child abuse shall include the name of the person making the report, the name of the child, the present location of the child, the nature and extent of the injury, and any other information, including information that led that person to suspect child abuse, requested by the child protective agency.

(b) Information relevant to the incident of child abuse may also be given to an investigator from a child protective agency who is investigating the known or suspected case of child abuse.

(c) The identity of all persons who report under this article shall be confidential and disclosed only between child protective agencies, or to counsel representing a child protective agency, or to the district attorney in a criminal prosecution or in an action initiated under section 602 of the Welfare and Institutions Code arising from alleged child abuse, or to counsel appointed pursuant to Section 318 of the Welfare and Institutions Code, or to the county counsel or district attorney in an action initiated under section 232 of the Civil Code or Section 300 of the Welfare and Institutions Code, or when those persons waive confidentiality, or by court order.

(d) Persons who may report pursuant to subdivision (d) of section 11166 are not required to include their names.

Section 11167.6. Confidentiality of reports; violations; disclosure

(a) The reports required by section 11166 shall be confidential and may be disclosed only as provided in subdivision (b). Any violation of the confidentiality provided by this article shall be a misdemeanor punishable by up to six months in jail or by a fine of five hundred dollars ($500) or by both.

(b) Reports of suspected child abuse and information contained therein may be disclosed only to the following:

(1) Persons or agencies to whom disclosure of the identity of the reporting party is permitted under section 11167.

(2) Persons or agencies to whom disclosure of information is permitted under subdivision (b) of section 11170.

(3) Persons or agencies with whom investigations of child abuse are coordinated under the regulations promulgated under section 11174.

(4) Multidisciplinary personnel teams as defined in subdivision (d) of section 18951 of the Welfare and Institutions Code.

(c) Nothing in this section shall be interpreted to require the Department of Justice to disclose information contained in records maintained under section 11169 or under the regulations promulgated pursuant to section 11174, except as otherwise provided in this article.

(d) This section shall not be interpreted to allow disclosure of any reports or records relevant to the reports of child abuse if the disclosure would be prohibited by any other provisions of state or federal law applicable to the reports or records relevant to the reports of child abuse.

Section 11168. Written reports; forms

The written reports required by Section 11166 shall be submitted on forms adopted by the Department of Justice after consultation with representatives of the various professional medical associations and hospital associations and county probation or welfare departments. Such forms shall be distributed by the child protective agencies.

Section 11169. Preliminary reports to Department of Justice; unfounded reports

A child protective agency shall forward to the Department of Justice a preliminary report in writing of every case of known or suspected child abuse which it investigates, other than cases coming within the provisions of paragraph (2) of subdivision (c) of Section 11165, whether or not any formal action is taken in the case. However, if after investigation the case proves to be unfounded no report shall be retained by the Department of Justice. If a report has previously been filed which has proved unfounded, the Department of Justice shall be notified of that fact. The report shall be in a form approved by the Department of Justice. A child protective agency receiving a written report from another child protective agency shall not send such report to the Department of Justice.

Section 11170. Notice to child protective agency of information maintained; indexed reports

(a) The Department of Justice shall maintain an index of all preliminary reports of child abuse submitted pursuant to Section 11169. The index shall be continually updated by the department and shall not contain any reports that are determined to be unfounded. The department may adopt rules governing recordkeeping and reporting pursuant to this article.

(b) The Department of Justice shall immediately notify a child protective agency which submits a report pursuant to Section 11169, or a district attorney who requests notification, of any information maintained pursuant to subdivision (a) which is relevant to the known or suspected instance of child abuse reported by the agency. A child protective agency shall make that information available to the reporting medical practitioner, child custodian, guardian ad litem appointed under Section 326, or counsel appointed under Section 318 of the Welfare and Institutions Code, if he or she is treating or investigating a case of known or suspected child abuse.

When a report is made pursuant to subdivision (a) of Section 11166, the investigating agency shall, upon completion of the investigation or after there has been a final disposition in the matter, inform the person required to report of the results of the investigation and of any action the agency is taking with regard to the child or family.

Section 11171. X-rays of child; exemption from privilege

(a) A physician and surgeon or dentist or their agents and by their direction may take skeletal X-rays of the child without the consent of the child's parent or guardian, but only for purposes of diagnosing the case as one of possible child abuse and determining the extent of such child abuse.

(b) Neither the physician-patient privilege nor the psychotherapist-patient privilege applies to information reported pursuant to this article in any court proceeding or administrative hearing.

Section 11172. Immunity from liability; attorney fees; failure to report; offense

(a) No child care custodian, medical practitioner, nonmedical practitioner, or

employee of a child protective agency who reports a known or suspected instance of child abuse shall be civilly or criminally liable for any report required or authorized by this article. Any other person reporting a known or suspected instance of child abuse shall not incur civil or criminal liability as a result of any report authorized by this article unless it can be proven that a false report was made and the person knew that the report was false. No person required to make a report pursuant to this article, nor any person taking photographs at his or her direction, shall incur any civil or criminal liability for taking photographs of a suspected victim of child abuse, or causing photographs to be taken of a suspected victim of child abuse, without parental consent, or for disseminating the photographs with the reports required by this article. However, the provisions of this section shall not be construed to grant immunity from such liability with respect to any other use of the photographs.
(b) Any child care custodian, medical practitioner, nonmedical practitioner, or employee of a child protective agency who, pursuant to a request from a child protective agency, provides the requesting agency with access to the victim of a known or suspected instance of child abuse shall not incur civil or criminal liability as a result of providing that access.
(c) The Legislature finds that even though it has provided immunity from liability to persons required to report child abuse, that immunity does not eliminate the possibility that actions may be brought against those persons based upon required reports of child abuse. In order to further limit the financial hardship that those persons may incur as a result of fulfilling their legal responsibilities, it is necessary that they not be unfairly burdened by legal fees incurred in defending those actions. Therefore, a child care custodian, medical practitioner, nonmedical practitioner, or an employee of a child protective agency may present a claim to the State Board of Control for reasonable attorneys' fees incurred in any action against that person on the basis of making a report required or authorized by this article if the court has dismissed the action upon a demurrer or motion for summary judgement made by that person, or if he or she prevails in the action. The State Board of Control shall allow that claim if the requirements of this subdivision are met, and the claim shall be paid from an appropriation to be made for that purpose. Attorneys' fees awarded pursuant to this section shall not exceed an hourly rate greater than the rate charged by the Attorney General of the State of California at the time the award is made and shall not exceed an aggregate amount of fifty thousand dollars ($50,000).

This subdivision shall not apply if a public entity has provided for the defense of the action pursuant to Section 995 of the Government Code.
(d) Any person who fails to report an instance of child abuse which he or she knows to exist or reasonably should know to exist, as required by this article, is guilty of a misdemeanor and is punishable by confinement in the county jail for a term not to exceed six months or by a fine of not more than one thousand dollars ($1,000) or by both.

Section 11174. Guidelines
The Department of Justice, in cooperation with the State Department of Social Services, shall prescribe by regulation guidelines for the investigation of child abuse, as defined in subdivision (f) of Section 11165, in group homes or institutions and shall ensure that the investigation is conducted in accordance with the regulations and guidelines.

As we continue to discuss legal aspects in this section of *MAN/child* I am adding the California laws pertaining to the taking of a minor into custody of the juvenile court or the temporary custody of a peace officer, probation officer, or social worker.

Welfare and Institutions Code section 300 describes those minors who may come within the jurisdiction of the juvenile court. Subdivision (a) includes those minors in need of proper and effective parental care or control who have no parent or guardian or whose parent or guardian is not willing to exercise or is not capable of exercising such care or control. Subdivision (b) includes a minor who is destitute or who is not provided with the necessities of life, or who is not provided with a home or suitable place of abode. Subdivision (c) includes a minor who is physically dangerous to the public because of a mental or physical deficiency, disorder or abnormality. Subdivision (d) includes those minors whose homes are unfit by reason of neglect, cruelty, depravity or physical abuse of either of their parents or of the guardian or other person in whose custody or care the minors are. Subdivision (e) includes a minor who has been freed for adoption from one or both parents for 12 months by either relinquishment or termination of parental rights and for whom an interlocutory decree has not been granted pursuant to section 224n of the Civil Code or an adoption petition has not been granted.

Under the provisions above, a peace officer or probation officer may, in order to protect a child under 18 from further abuse or neglect, take a child into temporary protective custody without a warrant; they do not exempt the officer from the requirements of the Fourth Amendment. (Welf. & Inst. Code, 305.) In 1984, the Legislature amended Welfare and Institutions Code section 306 to authorize social workers employed by county welfare departments to:

"Take into temporary custody and maintain temporary custody of a minor, without warrant, when the social worker has reasonable cause to believe that the minor is a person who is described in subdivision (a) or (b) of Section 300." (Welf. & Inst. Code, 306, subd. (c).)

The officer may transport the child to either a hospital, temporary shelter care or emergency foster care, or to an approved community service program for abused and neglected children (Welf. & Inst. Code, 307.5), with or without parental consent, if abuse is suspected. When a minor is taken into temporary custody, the officer must take immediate steps to notify the minor's parents, guardians or responsible relatives and inform them where the minor is unless it can be shown to the court that such notification would endanger the child or that the parents are likely to flee with the child. (Welf. & Inst. Code, 308, subd. (a).)

Immediately after taking a minor to a place of confinement and except where physically impossible, no later than one hour after the minor has been taken into custody, the minor has the right to make at least two telephone calls from the place where he or she is being held, one call completed to his or her parent or guardian, a responsible relative, or employer, and another call completed to an attorney. It is a misdemeanor for any public officer or employee to deprive a minor of the right to make these telephone calls. (Welf. & Inst. Code, 308, subd. (b).)

A minor being held in temporary custody by a peace officer, social worker, or probation officer must be released within 48 hours after being taken into custody, excluding nonjudicial days, unless within that time a petition to declare the minor a dependent child has been filed. (Welf. & Inst. Code, 313, subd. (a).)

The law also requires that the court shall appoint an attorney or the district attorney to represent the child. Counsel appointed by the court shall represent the minor at the detention hearing and subsequent proceedings. It also specifies that: (a) any counsel entering an appearance on behalf of a minor shall continue to represent that minor unless relieved by the court upon substitution of other counsel or for cause; (b) the duties and rights of the child's counsel, including the right and duty to file a civil action pursuant to Penal Code Section 11171; subdivision (b) against a person who has failed to make a mandated report, (c) the counsel's right of access to all records relevant to the case which are maintained by state or local public agencies, hosp:·als or by medical or nonmedical practitioners or by child care custodians, and relevant information in the Department of Justice Child Abuse Central Registry of child abuse reports. (Welf. & Inst. Code, 318.)

A minor taken into custody must be brought before a judge or referee of the juvenile court for a detention hearing before the expiration of the next judicial day after the filing of the dependency petition to determine whether the minor should be further detained pending the jurisdiction hearing. If the minor is not brought before the judge within this period, he or she must be released. (Welf. & Inst. Code, 315.)

The petition is usually filed by the county child welfare department or, in some counties, the probation department still performs this function. A copy of the petition is sent to the parents, guardian or other person having care or custody of the child. A dependency petition may also be filed without first taking the child into protective custody.

In all cases in which a criminal prosecution arising from neglect or abuse of the minor is initiated, the probation officer or a social worker who files the petition shall be the guardian ad litem to represent the interests of the minor in dependency proceedings, unless the court appoints another adult. The guardian ad litem shall not be the attorney responsible for presenting evidence alleging child abuse or neglect in judicial proceedings. (Welf. & Inst. Code, 326.)

A jurisdiction hearing in the juvenile court must then be held within 15 judicial days of the detention hearing or 30 days of filing the petition if the child is not in custody. A judge decides at that point if the child comes within the description of a dependent child of the court as set forth in Welfare and Institutions Code section 300. If the court finds that the minor is such a person, a disposition hearing is scheduled, usually within 15 days of the jurisdiction hearing. The court may then make "... any and all reasonable orders for the care, supervision, custody, maintenance and support of such minor including medical treatment, and may direct participation in counseling or parent education program including but not limited to parent education and parenting subject to further order of the court." (Welf. & Inst. Code, 362.)

If a child is declared to be a dependent of the juvenile court, the court may order the child to remain at home under the supervision of the child welfare services department (or probation department, depending on the county), or the court may take custody from the parents and order the child to be placed in "out-of-home" care.

Removal of the child requires a finding of any of the following:

- There is substantial danger to the physical health of the minor and there are no reasonable means to protect the child in the home.
- The parent or guardian is unwilling to have physical custody of the child.
- The minor is suffering severe emotional damage and there are no reasonable means to protect the child's emotional health.
- The minor has been sexually abused and there are no reasonable means to protect the child from further sexual abuse.
- The minor is under the age of three, and the court makes a finding of severe physical abuse.

The court must state the facts on which the decision to remove was based. The standard of proof for removal is "clear and convincing evidence." The court must also inform the parents that their parental rights may be terminated permanently if they do not resume custody within 12 months, or immediately if the court finds that return of a child under three, who has been found to be severely physically abused, would be detrimental to the minor.

In a case where a minor is removed from the parents, the court will order the social worker or probation officer to provide child welfare services to the family for the purpose of facilitating reunification for a maximum of 12 months. Services may be extended up to an additional six months if it can be shown that the objectives of the service plan can be achieved within the extended period.

Children found to be dependents of the court, who are not reunited with their parents, are usually placed with relatives, in foster homes, group homes or in other child residential treatment facilities.

The status of every dependent child in foster care must be reviewed periodically, but no less frequently than once every six months as calculated from the date of the original dispositional hearing, until the permanency planning hearing is completed. (Welf. & Inst. Code, 366, subd. (a).)

The court determines the continuing necessity for and appropriateness of the placement, the extent of compliance with the case plan, the extent of progress toward alleviating the causes necessitating placement and a likely date for return home. (Welf. & Inst. Code, 366, subd. (c).)

A permanency planning hearing is conducted no later than 12 months after the original placement. If the court has made a finding that it would be detrimental to return a severely physically abused child under three to his or her home, the permanency planning hearing will be held no later than six months after the original placement. (Welf. & Inst. Code, 366.25.)

At the permanency planning hearing, with the exception noted above, the court determines whether the minor should be returned to his or her parent. If not, the court determines whether there is a substantial probability that the minor will be returned within six months. If so, the court may set another permanency planning hearing for not more than six months.

If the court determines at the initial or extended permanency planning hearing that the child cannot be returned to the physical custody of his or her parent or guardian, the court is required to develop a permanent plan for the child. The court must consider placement in the following order:

- Adoption
- Legal guardianship
- Long-term foster care

Child abusers may be arrested, prosecuted, fined, imprisoned or instructed to take part in treatment programs. The following are summaries of California Penal Code sections pertaining to crimes against children:

Penal Code section 11165. Partially summarized
• is part of Article 2.5 — the Child Abuse Reporting Law. Section 11165 provides that a child is any person under 18 years of age, and "child abuse" is evidenced by:
1. physical injury which is inflicted by other than accidental means on a child by another person;
2. sexual abuse of a child;
3. willful cruelty or unjustifiable punishment (any act or omission proscribed by Pen. Code, 273a);
4. cruel or inhuman corporal punishment or injury (Pen. Code, 273d);
5. neglect of a child;
6. abuse in out-of-home care.

Neglect

Penal Code section 11165, subdivision (c). Neglect — summarized
"Neglect" means the negligent treatment or the maltreatment of a child by a caretaker under circumstances indicating harm or threatened harm to the child's health or welfare. The term includes both acts and omissions on the part of the responsible person.
"Severe neglect" means the negligent failure of a parent or caretaker to protect the child from severe malnutrition or medically diagnosed nonorganic failure to thrive. It also includes those situations of neglect where the parent or caretaker willfully causes or permits the person or health of the child to be placed in a situation such that his or her person or health is endangered. This includes the intentional failure to provide adequate food, clothing, shelter, or medical care.
"General neglect" means the negligent failure of a parent or caretaker to provide adequate food, clothing, shelter, medical care or supervision where no physical injury to the child has occurred.

Penal Code section 270. Failure to provide — summarized
If a parent of a minor child willfully omits, without lawful excuse, to furnish necessary clothing, food, shelter or medical attendance, or other remedial care for his or her child, he or she is guilty of a misdemeanor punishable by a fine not exceeding $2,000, or by imprisonment in the county jail not exceeding one year, or by both such fine and imprisonment.
If a parent has notice of a final adjudication in either a civil or criminal action and then willfully omits without lawful excuse to furnish necessary clothing, food, shelter, medical attendance or other remedial care for his or her child, this conduct is punishable by imprisonment in the county jail, not exceeding one year or in a state prison for a determinate term of one year and one day, or by a fine not exceeding $2,000 or by both fine and imprisonment. A parent who does not have legal custody of a child is not relieved from such criminal liability.

Physical Abuse/Emotional Maltreatment

Penal Code section 273a. Willful cruelty—summarized
1. Any person, who, under circumstances or conditions likely to produce great bodily harm or death, willfully causes or permits any child to suffer, or inflicts thereon unjustifiable physical pain or mental suffering, or having the care or custody of any child, willfully causes or permits the person or health of such child to be injured, or willfully causes or permits such child to be placed in such situation that its person or health is endangered, is punishable by imprisonment in the county jail not exceeding one year, or in state prison for two, four or six years.
2. Any person, who under circumstances or conditions other than those likely to produce great bodily harm or death, willfully causes or permits any child to suffer, or inflicts thereon unjustifiable physical pain or mental suffering, or having the care or custody of any child, willfully causes or permits the person or health of such child to be injured, or willfully causes or permits such child to be placed in such situation that its person or health may be endangered, is guilty of a misdemeanor.

Penal Code section 273d. Corporal punishment or injury—summarized
Any person who willfully inflicts upon any child any cruel or inhuman corporal punishment or injury resulting in a traumatic condition is guilty of a felony, and upon conviction thereof shall be punished by imprisonment in the state prison for two, four or six years, or in the county jail for not more than one year.

Sexual Assault

As defined by Penal Code section 11165, subdivision (b) (1), sexual assault includes conduct in violation of the following sections:
Penal Code section 261. Rape—summarized
• is defined and interpreted by the courts as an act of sexual intercourse with a victim who is not the spouse of the perpetrator where:
1. The victim is incapable of giving consent because of mental infirmity or because of physical disability and this is known by the perpetrator;
2. the victim is forced or overcome by fear of immediate and unlawful bodily injury on the victim or another;
3. the victim is prevented from resisting by any intoxicating, narcotic, or anaesthetic substance administered by or with the privity of the perpetrator;
4. the victim is at the time unconscious of the nature of the act, and this is known to the perpetrator;
5. the victim is deceived to believe that the perpetrator is his or her spouse;
6. the victim's resistance is overcome by threats of retaliation to kidnap, falsely imprison, or to inflict extreme pain, serious bodily injury or death against the victim or any other person, and there is a reasonable possibility that the perpetrator will execute the threat;
7. the victim is forced by the perpetrator's threats to use the authority of a public official to incarcerate, arrest, or deport the victim or another, and the victim has a reasonable belief that the perpetrator is a public official.
This felony is punishable by imprisonment in the state prison for three, six, or eight years. (Pen. Code, 264.)

Penal Code section 264.1. Rape in concert — summarized
• is defined as voluntarily acting in concert with another person, by force or
violence and against the will of the victim, to commit an act of rape or penetration of genital or anal openings by foreign object, either personally or by aiding
and abetting such other person. This felony is punishable by imprisonment in
the state prison for five, seven, or nine years.

Penal Code section 285. Incest — summarized
• is defined and interpreted by the courts as marriage or acts of intercourse between the following persons: Parents and children; ancestors and descendants
of every degree; brothers and sisters of half and whole blood; and uncles and
nieces or aunts and nephews. (Civ. Code, 4400.) This felony is punishable by
imprisonment in the state prison.

Penal Code section 286. Sodomy — summarized
• is defined and interpreted by the courts as sexual contact between the penis
of one person and the anus of another person and is punishable as a misdemeanor or felony as specified:
1. the victim is under 18 years of age — imprisonment in state prison or county
jail for a period not to exceed one year; however, if the victim is under 16 years
of age and the perpetrator is over 21 years — it is punishable as a felony;
2. the victim is under 14 years of age and the perpetrator is at least 10 years
older — imprisonment in state prison for three, six, or eight years;
3. the victim is overcome by means of force, violence, duress, menace or fear
of immediate and unlawful bodily injury on the victim or another person —
imprisonment in state prison for three, six, or eight years;
4. any person who voluntarily aids and abets another person in the act of
sodomy when the victim's will is overcome by means of force, or fear of immediate and unlawful bodily injury on the victim or another person —
imprisonment in state prison for five, seven, or nine years;
5. any person who participates in an act of sodomy with any person of any age
while confined in a state prison or in any local detention facility —
imprisonment in state prison or county jail for not more than one year;
6. any person who commits an act of sodomy, and the victim is at the time unconscious of the act — imprisonment in state prison or county jail for not more
than one year;
7. the victim is at the time incapable, due to mental infirmity or physical
disability, of giving legal consent and this is known or should be known by the
perpetrator — imprisonment in state prison or county jail for not more than one
year.
    Penal Code section 18 provides that: "Except in cases where a different
punishment is prescribed by any law of this state, every offense declared to be
a felony, or to be punishable by imprisonment in a state prison, is punishable
by imprisonment in any of the state prisons for 16 months, or two or three years;
provided, however, every offense which is prescribed by any laws of the state
to be a felony punishable by imprisonment in any of the state prisons or by a
fine, but without an alternate sentence to the county jail, may be punishable
by imprisonment in the county jail not exceeding one year or by a fine, or by
both."

Penal Code section 288. Lewd and lascivious acts with a child — summarized

• is defined and interpreted by the courts as causing any touching of a child under 14 years of age by the perpetrator or by the child at the direction of the perpetrator for the purpose of arousing, appealing to or gratifying the lust, or the passions, or the sexual desires of the person or the child. This felony is punishable by imprisonment in state prison for three, six, or eight years.

If the perpetrator uses force, violence, duress, menace, or threat of great bodily harm, the crime is punishable as a felony by imprisonment in state prison for three, six, or eight years.

The law also provides that in any arrest or prosecution under this section, the peace officer, district attorney and court shall consider the needs of the child victim and do whatever is necessary and constitutionally permissible to prevent psychological harm to the child victim.

Penal Code section 288a. Oral copulation—summarized
• is defined and interpreted by the courts as the act of copulating the mouth of one person with the sexual organ or anus of another person and is punishable as specified:
1. if the perpetrator is over 21 and the victim is under 18—imprisonment in the state prison or in a county jail for not more than one year;
2. if the perpetrator is over 21 and the victim is under 16—felony;
3. if the victim is under 14 and the perpetrator is at least 10 years older, or when the act is accomplished against the victim's will by means of force, violence, duress, menace, or fear of immediate and unlawful bodily injury on the victim or another person—punishable as a felony by imprisonment in state prison for three, six, or eight years;
4. any person voluntarily acts in concert with another person or aids in the commission of such an act and the act is accomplished against the person's will as described above—punishable as a felony by imprisonment in state prison for five, seven, or nine years;
5. any person who merely participates in such an act while confined in state prison or a local detention facility not devoted exclusively to the detention of minors, with any person of any age, regardless of whether or not accomplished by force or fear as described above—imprisonment in the state prison or county jail for not more than one year;
6. the victim is unconscious of the nature of the act and this is known to the perpetrator—imprisonment in state prison or county jail for not more than one year;
7. the victim is at the time incapable, due to mental infirmity or physical disability, of giving legal consent, and this is known to the perpetrator—imprisonment in state prison or county jail for not more than one year.

Penal Code section 289. Penetration of genital or anal opening by foreign objects—summarized
• is defined as the slightest penetration of a genital or an anal opening of another person using any foreign object, substance, instrument or device where such penetration is accomplished by force, violence, duress, or menace, or threat of immediate and unlawful bodily injury on the victim or on the person of another for the purpose of sexual arousal, gratification, or abuse—punishable as a felony by imprisonment in the state prison for three, six, or eight years.

If the same act is committed with the same intent on a victim who is incapable, through mental infirmity whether temporary or permanent, of giving legal consent, and this is known to the perpetrator—imprisonment in the state prison or county jail for not more than one year.

Foreign object, substance, instrument or device shall include any part of the body except a sexual organ.

Penal Code section 647a. Child molestation—summarized
• is defined and interpreted by the courts as any act motivated by unnatural or abnormal sexual interest in children, which act would reasonably be expected to disturb, irritate, trouble or offend the victim, whether or not the victim is so affected; no touching of the victim is necessary—imprisonment in the county jail for not more than six months or fine not exceeding $1,000 or by both.

Acts occurring after entering a dwelling are punishable by imprisonment in the state prison or county jail for a period not exceeding one year. For second and subsequent convictions of this section, the perpetrator is punishable by imprisonment in state prison. If previously convicted of 288, conviction for any 647a violation results in imprisonment in state prison.
Note: Although the child abuse reporting law does not specifically require reporting of other sexual offenses, such as assault with intent to commit rape and attempted rape, reports of these crimes may be required as child abuse generally, as are other crimes such as murder, mayhem or other assaults.

Sexual Exploitation

As defined by Penal Code section 11165, subdivision (b)(2), sexual exploitation includes conduct in violation of the following sections of the Penal Code:

Penal Code section 311.2. Pornography—summarized
• prohibits the following activities regarding any obscene matter:
1. importation, sale, or distribution;
2. possessions, preparation, publication, or printing with the intent to distribute or exhibit to others for commercial consideration;
3. offering to distribute to others;
4. exhibition to others for commercial consideration.
(These prohibited acts are punishable as misdemeanors.)
• prohibits engaging in such prohibited acts if it is known that such obscene matter depicts a minor under age 18 engaging in or simulating defined sexual conduct.
(Punishable as a felony by imprisonment in state prison for two, three, or four years or by a fine not exceeding $50,000 or both fine and imprisonment.)

In certain specified situations, this section is not applicable to motion picture operators, or projectionists acting within the scope of their employment.

Penal Code section 311.3. Minors and pornography—summarized
• with certain exceptions, prohibits the development, duplication, or exchange of any film, photograph, videotape, negative or slide depicting a child under 14 years of age engaged in defined sexual conduct.
(First offense, misdemeanor—imprisonment in the county jail for not more than one year or a fine of up to $2,000 or both.)
(Second offense, felony—imprisonment in state prison.)

Penal Code section 311.4. Employment; use; coercion; obscene acts—summarized
• prohibits the hire, employment or use of a minor to do or assist in specified sexual acts—misdemeanor;
• prohibits the promotion, employment, use, persuasion, inducement, or coercion of a minor under age 17 to engage in or assist others to engage in either posing or modeling alone or with others for the purposes of preparing a film, photograph, negative, slide, or live performance involving sexual conduct by a minor under 17 for commercial purposes—felony;
• also makes it a felony for any parent or guardian to permit a minor under age 17 and under his or her control to engage in such activity.
(These felony acts are punishable by imprisonment in the state prison for three, six, or eight years.)
   The following sections of the Labor Code are also related to investigation of sexual exploitation cases:

Labor Code sections 1309.5-1309.6. Sale or distribution of pornography—summarized
• requires persons engaged in various activities related to the sale or distribution of films, photographs, slides or magazines depicting minors under 16 years of age engaged in defined sexual conduct to keep, for three years, confidential records of the names and addresses of persons from whom such material is obtained (1309.5);
• failure to keep such records and make them available to law enforcement officers on request for a period of three years after obtaining or acquiring such material is a misdemeanor which could result in assessment of a civil penalty of up to $5,000 for each violation (1309.6).

Other Child Abuse Cases

   Although the foregoing codes were designed specifically for the protection of children, all crimes defined in the Penal Code are intended to protect children as well as adults.

   There are 3,041 counties in the United States ... and a district attorney in each one, and each district attorney enforces the law as he sees or interprets it, as does each judge in each county, and so forth.
   If you have ever had any confrontation with "the Law" I know you have experienced a lengthy, involved, and frequently unintelligible series of events. We are all aware that the legal process is arduous and traumatic. You can imagine what it is like for a child victim and his parents. All involved need strong emotional support to help them through this period of time.
   Family life has been disrupted. There is a loss of work and school time. The victim must be forced to relive the experience again and again and then face cross-examination by an attorney hired by the suspect. Add the presentation of police reports, medical records and various "experts" and/or witnesses ... it must be absolutely overwhelming for a youngster.
   About the only therapeutic value I can see about a court appearance is that it might be helpful to some child victims to be given a feeling of being a

"grown-up" and a person who matters—a person whose rights are to be defended.

Most inmates I talked to entered a plea of not guilty. They were advised by their attorneys of the legal inconsistencies in this particular type of crime and the possibility that the child, advised by his family, might withdraw completely because of the machinations of the legal process. I entered a plea of guilty when I took the option of plea-bargaining. I just could not have my victims go through the additional trauma of a court trial. It took me several weeks to finally decide to admit I was guilty and that I needed to change myself and get some treatment for this now obvious character flaw.

Anyway, progress is being made in some child sexual abuse areas and in some states. California, for example, now mandates that medical graduates must be tested for basic understanding in the field of child abuse including sexual abuse.

According to the doctors Kempe, in the late 1970s Colorado established a law that allowed for appointing a guardian ad litem for the victim of child abuse. Scottish, Israeli, Swedish and Danish laws use nonlawyers as well. Some states in the United States are substituting for an attorney because of the costs involved and because so much of the work involved is not legal in nature.

In the United States any case of sexual abuse is heard in juvenile or family court. It should be presented in criminal court when investigation determines a criminal act has been committed and can be proved beyond a "reasonable doubt."

As I have mentioned, it is very traumatic for a victim to appear as a witness and face cross-examination by a hostile defense attorney. Several states have attempted to avoid this trauma by making exceptions to proscriptions against hearsay evidence (that is, allowing the evidence presented by a third party when a victim of child sexual abuse complains to that third party about his/her violation); ruling that another person may testify on behalf of the victim's complaints, which means that the victim may not have to appear in court to again retell the victimization; and increasingly allowing video tapes of victim interviews as evidence in court. However, the constitutionality of these measures is hotly disputed. (See discussion of recent legislative changes under "What is the legal response to child sexual abuse?" in the Question and Answer section, pages 71–75.)

Changes to existing laws are continually being made as lawmakers are made aware of the necessity of doing so. Since 1975 more than 40 states have changed their rape laws, and 20 have rewritten their sex offense statutes, increasing penalties and imposing mandatory sentence requirements.

Incest offenders can take advantage of a legal criminal bypass procedure wherein the district attorney and child protective service workers have the suspect sign a contract which includes the requirement that he subscribe to at least two years of treatment. An incest guilty plea can be made in closed court, so that there is no publicity, and no loss of job or social standing. This procedure does keep the family intact while giving the victim maximum protection from future abuse.

The Incest Diversion Program developed by the El Paso County District Attorney's office and the Department of Social Services, Colorado Springs, Colorado, shows how different agencies can work together to provide varied treatments for cases of incest. The program aims to reduce the trauma for everyone involved by, among other policies, minimizing the number of criminal filings on incestuous fathers and eliminating the need to have children testifying about sexual assaults committed by their parents. It also allows the family to get immediate therapy rather than having to wait until procedural hurdles are cleared.

Many other areas have three-month treatment programs, which I think would be tantamount to the 90-day "observation" programs common to so many counties: worthless.

I wish to add this note about the juvenile sexual offender. The judicial system had better reflect on their present thinking regarding these youthful suspects. Age 18 is not "a new start on life" for these suspects if future tragedies are to be avoided.

See the bibliography for additional information: Bulkley, J., "Analysis of Civil Child Protection Statutes Dealing with Sexual Abuse," in Bulkley, J., ed., *Child Sexual Abuse and the Law; Innovations in the Prosecution of Child Sexual Abuse Cases;* Bulkley, J., reporter, *Recommendations for Improving Legal Intervention in Intrafamily Child Sexual Abuse Cases;* Bailey, T., and Bailey, W., *Criminal Or Social Intervention in Child Sexual Abuse;* Conte, J., and Berliner, L., "Sexual Abuse of Children: Implications for Practice"; Lerman, L., "State Legislation on Domestic Violence"; Melton, G., "Procedural Reforms to Protect Child Victim/Witnesses in Sex Offense Proceedings"; Melton, G., with Bulkley, J., and Wulkan, D., "Competency of Children as Witnesses"; Lloyd, D., "The Corroboration of Sexual Victimization of Children"; Whitcomb, D., "Assisting Child Victims in the Courts: The Practical Side of Legislative Reform"; and Cramer, R., "The District Attorney as a Mobilizer in a Community Approach to Child Sexual Abuse." (The above references also pertain to the "What is the legal response to child sexual abuse?" question in the Questions and Answers section, pages 71–75.)

Resource Guide:
Names and Addresses

This section is designed for those of you who desire assistance or further answers to questions about child abuse; runaway or missing children; non-custodial abductions; sexual exploitation of children; or any additional questions you may have.

Action for Child Protection. 428 Fourth St., Suite 5B, Annapolis MD 21403. 1-301-263-2509.

Adults Molested As Children United (AMACU). P.O. Box 952, San Jose CA 95108. 1-408-280-5055.

American Academy of Pediatrics. 141 Northwest Point Blvd., P.O. Box 927, Elk Grove Village IL 60009-0927. 1-800-433-9016.

American Association for Protecting Children. Children's Division of the American Humane Association, 9725 E. Hampden Ave., Denver CO. 1-303-695-0811.

American Bar Association. National Legal Resource Center for Child Advocacy and Protection, 1800 M St., N.W., Suite 200, Washington DC 20036. 1-202-331-2250. Professional and institutional inquiries only.

American Guidance Service (AGS). Publishers' Bldg., Circle Pines MN 55014. 1-800-328-2560 (toll-free outside Minnesota) and 1-612-786-4343 (inside Minnesota).

American Humane Association. American Association for Protecting Children, 9725 E. Hampden Ave., Denver CO 80231. 1-301-695-0811, 1-800-227-5242.

American Indian Law Center (AILC). 1117 Standard N.E., P.O. Box 4456-Station A, Albuquerque NM 87196. 1-505-277-5462.

American Journal of Orthopsychiatry. 1775 Broadway, New York NY 10019.

American Journal of Psychotherapy. 114 E. 78th St., New York NY 10021.

American Medical Association. Health and Human Behavior Department, 535 N. Dearborn, Chicago IL 60610. 1-312-645-5066.

American Public Welfare Association. 1125 15th St., N.W., Suite 300, Washington DC 20005. 1-202-293-7550.

American Youth Work Center (AYWC). 1346 Connecticut Ave., N.W., Suite 925, Washington DC 20036. 1-202-785-0764.

Association of Junior Leagues. 660 First Ave., New York NY 10016. 1-212-355-4380. Contact: For legislative information, the Public Policy Director; for individual Junior Legal Programs, Child Abuse and Neglect, the League Services Department.

Boys Clubs of America. Government Relations Office, 611 Rockville Pike, Suite 230, Rockville MD 20852. 1-301-251-6676.

Bubbylonian Productions, Inc. 7204 W. 80th St., Overland KS 66204.

Center for the Prevention and Control of

Rape. Department of Health, Education and Welfare, Washington DC 20013.

Child Find. P.O. Box 277, New Paltz NY 12561.

Child Welfare League of America. 440 First St., N.W., Suite 310, Washington DC 20001. 1-202-638-2952. Professional and institutional inquiries only.

Childhelp USA. 6463 Independence Ave., Woodland Hills CA 91367. Hotline: 1-800-4-A-CHILD or 1-800-422-4453. *For a detailed description of this organization see page 150*

Children of the Night. 1800 N. Highland, Suite 128, Hollywood CA 90028.

Coalition for Child Advocacy. P.O. Box 159, Bellingham WA 98227.

Effectiveness Training, Inc. 531 Stevens Ave., Solana Beach CA 92075. 1-619-481-8121.

EPPIC. Educate People-Protect Innocent Children, P.O. Box 3110, Camarillo CA 93010. 1-805-484-2404.

Family and Child Abuse Prevention Center. One Stranahan Square, Suite 134, Toledo OH 43604. 1-419-244-3053.

Family Communication, Inc. 4802 5th Ave., Pittsburgh PA 15213. 1-412-687-2990.

GCN. (Gay rights.) 62 Berkeley St., Boston MA 02116.

General Federation of Women's Clubs. 1734 N St., N.W., Washington DC 20036. 1-202-347-3163.

Institute for the Community as Extended Family. P.O. Box 952, San Jose CA 95108-0952.

Journal of the American Medical Association. 535 N. Dearborn St., Chicago IL 60610.

Just Us. (Gay rights legal aid.) Box 13673, El Paso TX 79913.

Maltreatment of Youth Project. Boys Town Center for Study of Youth Development, Boys Town NE 68010.

Military Family Resource Center (MFRC). Ballston Centre Tower Three, Ninth

Floor, 4015 Wilson Blvd., Arlington VA 22203. 1-202-696-4555.

Morality in Media. 475 Riverside Dr., New York NY 10115.

National Association of Counsel for Children (NACC). 1205 Oneida St., Denver CO 80220. 1-303-321-3963.

National Association of Former Foster Children, Inc. (NAFFC). P.O. Box 169, Bay Ridge Station, Brooklyn NY 11220. 1-718-853-6795.

National Association of Social Workers. 7981 Eastern Ave., Silver Spring MD 20910. 1-301-565-0333. Professional and institutional inquiries only.

National Black Child Development Institute, Inc. (NBCDI). 1463 Rhode Island Ave., N.W., Washington DC 20005. 1-202-387-1281.

National Center on Child Abuse and Neglect (NCCAN). Children's Bureau, Administration for Children, Youth and Families, U.S. Department of Health and Human Services (HHS), P.O. Box 1182, Washington DC 20013. 1-202-245-2856. *For a detailed description of this organization see pages 146–149.*

National Center for Missing and Exploited Children. 1835 K St., N.W., Suite 700, Washington DC 20006. 1-202-634-9821 or 1-800-843-5678. *For a detailed description of this organization see pages 150–151.*

National Child Abuse Coalition (NCAC). 1125 15th St., N.W., Suite 300, Washington DC 20005. 1-202-293-7550.

National Child Abuse Hotline (Referral service). 1-800-422-4453 (1-800-4-A CHILD).

National Coalition of Hispanic Mental Health and Human Services Organizations. 1030 15th St., N.W., Suite 1053, Washington DC 20005. 1-202-371-2100.

National Committee for Prevention of Child Abuse. 332 S. Michigan Ave., Chicago IL 60604. 1-312-663-3520. *For a detailed description of this organization see page 151.*

National Council of Juvenile and Family Court Judges. P.O. Box 8970, Reno NV 89507. 1-702-784-6012. Primarily professional and institutional inquiries.

National Council on Child Abuse and Family Violence. 1050 Connecticut Ave., N.W., Suite 300, Washington DC 20036. 1-800-222-2000.

National Crime Prevention Council. 733 15th St., N.W., Room 540, Washington DC 20005. 1-202-393-7141.

National Education Association (NEA). Human and Civil Rights Unit, 1201 16th St., N.W., Room 714, Washington DC 20036. 1-202-822-7711.

National Exchange Club Foundation for Prevention of Child Abuse. 3050 Central Ave., Toledo OH 43606. 1-419-535-3232.

National Law Enforcement Administration (Branch of the U.S. Department of Justice), Washington DC 20051.

National Lawyers' Guild: Gay Rights. 3501 S. Congress Ave., Lake Worth FL 33461.

National Network of Runaway and Youth Services (NNRYS). 905 6th St., S.W., Suite 411, Washington DC 20024. 1-202-488-0739.

National Organization for Victim Assistance (NOVA). 717 D St., N.W., Washington DC 20004. 1-202-393-NOVA.

National Runaway Switchboard. 2210 North Hansted, Chicago IL 60614. 1-800-621-4000. In Illinois: 1-800-972-6004.

Native American Coalition of Tulsa (NAC). 1740 W. 41st St., Tulsa OK 74107. 1-918-446-8432.

North American Man / Boy Love Association (NAMBLA). P.O. Box 48772, Los Angeles CA 90048. (213) 281-7103.

Paedophile Information Exchange (PIE). P.O. Box 318, London, England SE38QD.

Parents Anonymous. 7120 Franklin Ave., Los Angeles CA 90046. 1-800-421-0353 (toll-free), 1-213-410-9732 (business phone). Has 1200 chapters nationwide; a national program of professionally facilitated self-help groups. Each state has different program components.

Parents' Music Resource Center. 1500 Arlington Blvd., Arlington VA 22209.

Parents United / Daughters and Sons United / Adults Molested as Children United. P.O. Box 952, San Jose CA 95108. 1-408-280-5055. 150 chapters nationwide. Provides guided self-help for sexually abusive parents and child and adult victims of sexual abuse.

Parents Without Partners, Inc. (PWP). 7910 Woodmont Ave., Bethesda MD 20814. 1-301-654-8850; toll-free number 1-800-638-8078.

Prison, Parole and Probation. Gay Community Services Center, Box 38777, Los Angeles CA 90038.

Psychiatric Quarterly. 72 Fifth Ave., New York NY 10011.

RFD. (Gay rights.) P.O. Box 68, Liberty TN 37095.

Runaway Hotline. P.O. Box 52896, Houston TX 77052. 1-800-231-6946. In Texas: 1-800-392-3352.

San Francisco Child Abuse Council. 4093 24th St., San Francisco CA 94114.

Sexaholics Anonymous. (A 12-step recovery program.) P.O. Box 300, Simi Valley CA 93062.

SLAM. Society's League Against Molestation, P.O. Box 1267, Chino CA 91710. 1-714-865-2151.

Stepfamily Association of America (SAA). 28 Allegheny Ave., Suite 1307, Baltimore MD 21204. 1-301-823-7570.

Stepfamily Foundation, Inc. 333 W. End Ave., New York NY 10023. 1-212-877-3244.

United Way. Services Outreach Division, 801 N. Fairfax St., Alexandria VA 22314.

Victims of Child Abuse Laws (VOCAL). P.O. Box 1314, Orangevale CA 95662. 1-813-347-1197 (United States East Coast) 1-916-988-9482 (United States West Coast). Provides parents who are falsely accused of child abuse and neglect with support and referrals to legal counsel and expert witnesses.

Youth Services Clearinghouse. Contact Center, Inc., P.O. Box 81826, Lincoln NE 68501. 1-800-228-8813.

Information on Child Abuse and Neglect

National Center on Child Abuse and Neglect Clearinghouse. P.O. Box 1182, Washington DC 20013. 1-202-245-2840.

National Committee for Prevention of Child Abuse. 332 S. Michigan Ave., Suite 950, Chicago IL 60604-4357. 1-312-663-3520.

National Resource Centers for Child Welfare Services

The Department of Health and Human Services maintains nine national centers for assistance in maintaining child welfare services. Clearinghouses are operated by HHS and the Department of Justice as national distribution points for public educational materials, research literature, and specialized programmatic information. Following are listings of the national units.

National Resource Center for Family Based Services. School of Social Work, University of Iowa, N-240A Oakdale Hall, Iowa City IA 52242. 1-319-335-4123.

National Resource Center for Foster and Residential Care. P.O. Box 77364, Station C, Atlanta GA 30357. 1-404-876-1934.

National Legal Resource Center for Child Welfare Services. American Bar Association, 1800 M St., N.W., Suite S-200, Washington DC 20036. 1-202-331-2250.

National Resource Center for Child Welfare Program Management and Administration. University of Southern Maine, 246 Deering Ave., Portland ME 04102. 1-207-780-4430.

National Resource Center for Youth Services. University of Oklahoma, 440 South Houston, Suite 751, Tulsa OK 74127. 1-918-581-2986.

National Resource Center for Special Needs Adoption: Spaulding-Michigan, Spaulding for Children. 3660 Waltrous Rd., P.O. Box 337, Chelsea MI 48118. 1-313-475-8693.

National Resource Institute on Children with Handicaps (NRICH). University of Washington, Clinical Training Unit, Child Development and Mental Retardation Center, Seattle WA 98195, 1-206-545-1350.

National Child Abuse Clinical Resource Center. Kempe Center, University of Colorado, Health Sciences Center, 1205 Oneida St., Denver CO 80220. 1-303-321-3963.

National Resource Center for Child Abuse and Neglect. American Humane Association, American Association for Protecting Children, 9725 East Hampden Ave., Denver CO 80231. 1-303-695-0811.

The National Center on Child Abuse and Neglect*

The National Center on Child Abuse and Neglect (NCCAN) was first authorized by the U.S. Congress in 1974, with the mission of helping professionals improve services to children and families in turmoil and to draw public attention to the problem of child abuse and neglect. NCCAN is located in the Office of Human Development Services within the U.S. Department of Health and Human Services and is responsible for:

a. Conducting research on the causes of child abuse and neglect and its prevention and treatment

b. Compiling, publishing, and dis-

*Information quoted from NCCAN publications.

seminating recent and current research information

c. Providing technical assistance
d. Assessing the incidence of maltreatment of children
e. Developing a master plan for coordinating and focusing activities
f. Establishing and operating an information clearinghouse

CLEARINGHOUSE ON CHILD ABUSE AND NEGLECT INFORMATION

The Clearinghouse is a national information resource center for service providers; public and private agencies at the local, state, and national level; members of Congress; researchers; and concerned members of the general public. The Clearinghouse provides support services to assist NCCAN in the accomplishment of its objectives. The primary functions of the Clearinghouse include the identification, acquisition, development, and dissemination of child abuse and neglect information and materials.

At the core of the Clearinghouse is a computerized database. The publicly searchable database, DIALOG File 64, contains several types of information related to child abuse and neglect. These include:

a. Published Documents
b. Audiovisual Materials
c. State Laws
d. Court Case Decisions
e. Research Projects
f. Programs

Through extensive use of the database and many other resources, the Clearinghouse develops publications and services to fulfill user requests. The publications include NCCAN produced materials, bibliographies, compilations of research, compilations of state laws, and the directories of programs. The Clearinghouse also offers database searching for a fee as well as other limited research and reference services.

SPECIAL PRODUCTS AND SERVICES

Child Sexual Abuse Prevention: Tips to Parents. Available in bulk quantities. 20-01036.

Prevención del Abuso Sexual de los Ninos. Available in bulk quantities. 20-01042.

Child Abuse and Neglect: A Brief Overview. 1985. 15p. 20-01048.

Child Abuse and Neglect: An Informed Approach to a Shared Concern. 1985. 26p. 20-01016.

Child Abuse Prevention and Treatment Act. 1985. 14p. 85-30343.

Data Tape with Documentation. Nat'l incidence study, 1981/82. 20-01002.

Thesaurus. Child Abuse and Neglect Thesaurus with 1986 addendum. 1983. 150p. 22-01018.

MAJOR TOPICAL PUBLICATIONS

Adolescent Maltreatment: Issues and Program Models. 1984. 116p. 84-30339.

Analysis of Child Abuse and Neglect Programs. 1983. 55p. 20-01021.

Child Protection: Guidelines for Policy and Program. 1982. 178p. 20-01006.

Children's Trust Funds: Creative Financing for Child Abuse and Neglect Prevention. 1986. 132p. 21-01020.

Families in Stress. 1981. 20p. 80-30162.

Literature Review of Sexual Abuse. 1987. 56p. 87-30530.

National Study of the Incidence and Severity of Child Abuse and Neglect: Study Findings. 1981. 56p. 81-30325R.

National Study of the Incidence and Severity of Child Abuse and Neglect: Study Methodology. 1981. 325p. 81-30326.

National Study of the Incidence and Severity of Child Abuse and Neglect: Executive Summary. 1981. 17p. 81-30329.

Perspectives on Child Maltreatment in the Mid '80s. 1984. 72p. 84-30338.

Recruitment and Selection of Staff: A Guide for Managers of Preschool and Child Care Programs. 1985. 9p. 85-31191.

Representation for the Abused and

Neglected Child: The Guardian Ad Litem and Legal Counsel. 1980. 22p. 80-30272.

Review of Child Abuse and Neglect Research, 1985. 1986. 207p. 20-01068R.

Selected Readings on Adolescent Maltreatment. 1981. 118p. 81-30301.

Selected Readings on Child Neglect. 1980. 68p. 80-30253.

A Self Instructional Text for Head Start Personnel. 1978. 135p. 78-31103.

Special Report: Protection of Native American Children from Child Abuse and Neglect. 1986. 96p. 20-01069.

Volunteers in Child Abuse and Neglect Programs. 1980. 49p. 80-30151.

Leaders' Manual: A Curriculum on Child Abuse and Neglect. 1979. 348p. 79-30220.

Resource Materials: A Curriculum on Child Abuse and Neglect. 1979. 123p. 79-30221.

Specialized Training for Child Protective Service Workers: A Curriculum on Child Abuse and Neglect. 1979. 301p. 79-30222.

THE USER MANUAL SERIES

During 1979 and 1980, the National Center on Child Abuse and Neglect published a series of 20 documents known collectively as the User Manual Series. The manuals were based on the *Federal Standards for Child Abuse and Neglect Prevention and Treatment Programs and Prospects.* These manuals are a significant part of NCCAN's mission to assist professionals in improving services to children and families and to draw public attention to the child abuse and neglect problem.

Child Neglect: Mobilizing Services. 1980. 60p. 80-30257.

Child Protection in Military Communities. 1980. 90p. 80-30260.

Child Protection: Providing Ongoing Services. 1980. 92p. 80-30262.

Child Protection: The Role of the Courts. 1980. 73p. 80-30256.

Child Protective Services: A Guide for Workers. 1979. 95p. 79-30203.

A Community Approach: The Child Protection Coordination Committee. 1979. 84p. 79-30195.

Crisis Intervention: A Manual for Child Protective Workers. 1979. 45p. 79-30196.

Early Childhood Programs and the Prevention and Treatment of Child Abuse and Neglect. 1979. 84p. 79-30198.

The Educator's Role in the Prevention and Treatment of Child Abuse and Neglect. 1984. 80p. 84-30172R.

Family Violence: Intervention Strategies. 1980. 101p. 80-30258.

Guidelines for the Hospital and Clinic Management of Child Abuse and Neglect. 1980. 71p. 80-30167.

The Nurse's Role in the Prevention and Treatment of Child Abuse and Neglect. 1979. 80p. 79-30202.

Parent Aides in Child Abuse and Neglect Programs. 1979. 75p. 79-30200.

Preventing Child Abuse and Neglect: A Guide for Staff in Residential Institutions. 1980. 71p. 80-30255.

Reaching Out: The Volunteer in Child Abuse and Neglect Programs. 1979. 55p. 79-30174.

The Role of Law Enforcement in the Prevention and Treatment of Child Abuse and Neglect. 1984. 69p. 84-30193.

The Role of Mental Health Professionals in the Prevention and Treatment of Child Abuse and Neglect. 1979. 103p. 79-30194.

Supervising Child Protective Workers. 1979. 61p. 79-30197.

Training in the Prevention and Treatment of Child Abuse and Neglect. 1979. 85p. 79-30201.

Treatment for Abused and Neglected Children. 1979. 90p. 79-30199.

STATUTES

The Statutes series is a compilation of the child abuse and neglect state statutes signed into law as of December 31, 1985. It includes the legislative provisions of the 50 states, the District of Columbia, American Samoa, Guam, Puerto Rico, and the Virgin Islands. It is intended as a research tool for professionals and individuals concerned with the legal aspects of child maltreatment. This compilation is published in four volumes as well as individually by STATE and each of the 38 SUBJECT element areas.

The Comparative Analyses (State Child Abuse/Neglect Laws, 1984, 1985) provide a comparative analysis for each of the 38 SUBJECT areas, noting similarities and differences among the States.

PROGRAMS

Since 1975, the National Center on Child Abuse and Neglect (NCCAN) has been collecting information about child abuse and neglect service programs in the United States and its territories. The latest edition of the *Directory* contains 3,257 entries reflecting the results of a survey conducted in Winter/Spring 1985.

The *Directory* is available in two versions. The *Unabridged Edition* includes basic program identification information: accession number, administering organization's name and address, title of the program, program director(s), date the program began operation, and if provided, the program office phone number and/or hotline. An abstract concisely describing the program's services, clientele, staffing, organization, coordination, and funding is also provided. The *Abridged Edition* contains only the basic program identification information.

In addition to the two main editions, program information is also available for the individual states.

CLEARINGHOUSE BIBLIOGRAPHIES

The Clearinghouse is offering revised and updated bibliographies on frequently requested topics from its database. The most recent reviews are listed below.

Adults Sexually Abused as Children. 30p. 07-86001.

Characteristics of Abused Children. 36p. 07-86002.
Characteristics of Abusive Parents. 17p. 07-86003.
Child Exploitation. 51p. 07-86004.
Curricula. 47p. 07-86005.
Etiology of Abuse: Recent Additions. 108p. 07-86006.
Evaluation of Child Abuse and Neglect: Documents. 111p. 07-86007.
Handicapped and Child Abuse. 45p. 07-86017.
Interviews: Abuse and Incest. 51p. 07-86008.
Prediction, Detection, and High Risk Factors. 106p. 07-86009.
Primary Prevention. 46p. 07-86010.
Sexual Abuse Prevention. 62p. 07-86011.
Sexual Abuse Programs. 49p. 07-86016.
Sexual Abuse: Recent Additions. 101p. 07-86012.
Sexual Abuse Treatment. 82p. 07-86013.
Teachers and Child Abuse and Neglect. 60p. 07-86014.
Therapy and Treatment Programs for Child Abuse Victims. 60p. 07-86015.
Training: Child Protective Services. 25p. 07-86018.
Child Abuse and Neglect in Day Care. 35p. 20-01061.
Child Neglect: A Selected Annotated Bibliography. 43p. 20-01047.
Court Appointed Special Advocates (CASAs): A Selected Annotated Bibliography. 39p. 20-01062.
Parenting: An Annotated Bibliography. 1981. 34p. 81-30134.
Prevention of Sexual Abuse: A Selected Annotated Bibliography. 14p. 20-01063.
Selected Resources in Domestic Violence. 1987. 55p. 20-01071.
Teen Parenting: A Selected Annotated Bibliography. 20p. 20-01064.
Treatment of Sexual Abuse: A Selected Annotated Bibliography. 16p. 20-01065.

A complete catalog (20-01017) may be obtained by writing the Clearinghouse.

Childhelp USA*

The National Child Abuse Hotline, 1-800-4-A-CHILD (1-800-422-4453) was established [by Childhelp USA] in January, 1982, following a careful study of the child abuse and neglect problems nationwide. This study showed there existed a great need for a national toll-free crisis and referral service to help protect children from abuse.

Initially, service was provided only during the day. Staff consisted mostly of volunteers doing peer counseling. By the end of the first year of operation, the volume of calls to the Hotline and the level of distress of callers necessitated that service be extended to 24 hours a day, 7 days a week, and that professionally trained counselors be available at all times.

The Hotline operates from offices in Hollywood, California. Counselors provide information and referrals for child abuse reporting, make referrals to prevention and treatment services in the callers' geographic area and provide information and suggested reading material about child abuse and parenting.

The Hotline encourages callers to make reports of child abuse directly to appropriate state or local child protective service agencies. Should the caller be a child or it seems likely the suggested call will not be made, the caller is networked through to the appropriate agency. The Hotline counselor will remain on the line until the two parties are connected. Calls from teenagers and younger victims are routinely networked.

In addition to information and referral services, telephone crisis counseling is provided to child abuse victims, abusers and others closely involved in the situations. A substantial number of calls are received from distraught parents who feel they are on the verge of physically abusing their children and from parents who were sexually assaulted in their childhood who now wish to prevent something similar happening to their children....

The Hotline has developed its own resource directories. These are loose leaf books containing around 1500 pages of referral numbers covering information and referrals for every state. They are arranged by states alphabetically and provide the most frequently used referral information. Continual outreach is made to search for new referrals and to update and correct information.

The National Center for Missing and Exploited Children**

The National Center for Missing and Exploited Children was established in June of 1984. The Center is a nonprofit organization created through a cooperative agreement with the U.S. Department of Justice, Office of Juvenile Justice and Delinquency Prevention and is located in Washington, DC.

The National Center serves as a clearinghouse of information, provides technical assistance to citizens and law-enforcement, offers training programs to schools and law-enforcement, and publishes a wide variety of informational materials on the issues of missing or exploited children [including the *Missing and Exploited Children's Resource Guide*].

A toll-free telephone line is open for those who have information that could lead to the location and recovery of a missing child. That number is 1-800-843-5678. In response to the calls, Technical Advisors at the National Center assist citizens and law-enforcement agencies involved in cases of missing children,

*Information quoted from Childhelp USA information guide.
**Information quoted from Center publications.

child victimization, child pornography, and child prostitution.

Washington, DC, residents call a local number: 634-9836. The TDD hotline (for the deaf) is 1-800-826-7653. The 15 toll-free hotlines cover Canada as well as the United States.

In addition, the National Center distributes photos and descriptions of missing children nationwide; delivers education and prevention programs throughout the country; and provides information and advice on effective state legislation to assure the safety and protection of children.

A number of publications have been designed to alert and educate the public and the law-enforcement community about the issues of missing and exploited children.

The National Committee for Prevention of Child Abuse*

The National Committee for Prevention of Child Abuse (NCPCA) distributes and publishes educational materials that deal with a variety of topics, including parenting, child abuse, and child abuse prevention. The NCPCA catalog is available free upon request from NCPCA, Publishing Dept., 332 S. Michigan Ave., Suite 950, Chicago IL 60604-4357, (312) 663-3520.

Written in a conversational style, the publications are excellent for professionals, lay persons, students, and children. Selected publications are available in Spanish. Some NCPCA titles are:

Child Abuse — Emotional Maltreatment of Children; Physical Child Neglect; Maltreatment of Adolescents; Selected Child Abuse, Information and Resources Directory; Think You Know Something About Child Abuse?; Physical Child Abuse; A Look at Child Sexual Abuse.

Child Abuse Prevention — An Approach to Preventing Child Abuse; Self-Help and the Treatment of Child Abuse; Child Care and the Family; Strengthening Families Through the Workplace; Evaluating Child Abuse Prevention Programs; Talking About Child Sexual Abuse; My Brother Got Here Early; When School's Out and Nobody's Home; I Hear You; Making the World Safe for Jeffery; Who Stole Mrs. Wick's Self-Esteem?; Stress and the Single Parent; Physical Neglect; Annie Overcomes Isolation; Emotional Abuse: Words *Can* Hurt.

Children's Materials — Amazing Spider-Man and Power Pack (Child sexual abuse prevention); Amazing Spider-Man on Emotional Abuse; You're Not Alone (Kid's Book about Alcoholism and Child Abuse).

Parenting — Foster Parenting Abused Children; What Every Parent Should Know; Child Discipline: Guidelines for Parents; Growth and Development Through Parenting; Getting New Parents Off to a Good Start; Parent-Child Bonding: The Development of Intimacy.

Special Subjects — Educators, Schools, and Child Abuse; Catapulting Abusive Alcoholics to Successful Recovery; The Disabled Child and Child Abuse; Child Abuse and the Law (A Legal Primer for Social Workers).

State Child Protection Agencies

Because the responsibility for investigating reports of suspected child abuse and neglect rests at the state level, each state has established a child protective services reporting system. Listed below are the names and addresses of the child protective services agency in each state, followed by the procedures for reporting suspected child maltreatment. A number of states have toll-free (800) tele-

*Information quoted from Committee publications.

phone numbers that can be used for reporting.

Alabama: Alabama Department of Human Resources, Division of Family and Children's Services, Office of Protective Services, 64 N. Union St., Montgomery AL 36130-1801. During business hours, make reports to the County Department of Human Resources, Child Protective Services Unit. After business hours, make reports to local police.

Alaska: Department of Health and Social Services, Division of Family and Youth Services, Box H-05, Juneau AK 99811. To make reports in-state, ask the operator for Zenith 4444. Out-of-state, add area code 907. This telephone number is toll-free.

American Samoa: Government of American Samoa, Office of the Attorney General, Pago Pago, American Samoa 96799. Make reports to the Department of Human Resources at 1-684-633-4485.

Arizona: Department of Economic Security Administration for Children, Youth and Families, P.O. Box 6123, Site COE 940A, Phoenix AZ 85005. Make reports to Department of Economic Security local offices.

Arkansas: Arkansas Department of Human Services, Division of Children and Family Services, P.O. Box 1437, Little Rock AR 72203. Make reports in-state to 1-800-482-5964.

California: Office for Child Abuse Prevention, Department of Social Services, 714-744 P St., Rm. 950, Sacramento CA 95814. Make reports to County Department of Welfare and the Central Registry of Child Abuse 1-916-445-7546, maintained by the Department of Justice.

Colorado: Department of Social Services, Central Registry, P.O. Box 181000, Denver CO 80218-0899. Make reports to county departments of social services.

Connecticut: Connecticut Department of Children and Youth Services, Division of Children's and Protective Services, 170 Sigourney St., Hartford CT 06105. Make reports in-state to 1-800-

842-2288 or out-of-state to 1-203-344-2599.

Delaware: Delaware Department of Services for Children, Youth and Their Families, Division of Child Protective Services, 330 E. 30th St., Wilmington DE 19802. Make reports in-state to 1-800-292-9582.

District of Columbia: District of Columbia Department of Human Services, Commission on Social Services, Family Services Administration, Child and Family Services Division, 500 First St., N.W., Washington DC 20001. Make reports to 1-202-727-0995.

Florida: Florida Child Abuse Registry, 1317 Winewood Blvd., Tallahassee FL 32301. Make reports in-state to 1-800-342-9152 or out-of-state to 1-904-487-2625.

Georgia: Georgia Department of Human Resources, Division of Family and Children Services, 878 Peachtree St., N.W., Atlanta GA 30309. Make reports to county departments of family and children services.

Guam: Department of Public Health and Social Services, Child Welfare Services, Child Protective Services, P.O. Box 2816, Agana GU 96910. Reports made to the State Child Protective Services Agency at 1-671-646-8417.

Hawaii: Department of Social Services and Housing, Public Welfare Division, Family and Children's Services, P.O. Box 339, Honolulu HI 96809. Make reports to each island's Department of Social Services and Housing Child Protective Services Reporting hotline.

Idaho: Department of Health and Welfare, Field Operations Bureau of Social Services Child Protection, 450 West State, 10th Floor, Boise ID 83720. Make reports to Department of Health and Welfare regional offices.

Illinois: Illinois Department of Children and Family Services, Station 75, State Administrative Offices, 406 East Monroe St., Springfield IL 62701. Make reports in-state to 1-800-25-ABUSE or out-of-state to 1-217-785-4010.

Indiana: Indiana Department of Public Welfare-Child Abuse and Neglect, Division of Child Welfare-Social Services, 141 S. Meridian St., Sixth Floor, Indianapolis IN 46225. Make reports to county departments of public welfare.

Iowa: Iowa Department of Human Services, Division of Social Services, Central Child Abuse Registry, Hoover State Office Bldg., Fifth Floor, Des Moines IA 50319. Make reports in-state to 1-800-362-2178 or out-of-state (during business hours) to 1-515-281-5581.

Kansas: Kansas Department of Social and Rehabilitation Services, Division of Social Services, Child Protection and Family Services Section, Smith-Welson Bldg., 2700 W. Sixth St., Topeka KS 66606. Make reports to Department of Social and Rehabilitation Services area offices.

Kentucky: Kentucky Cabinet of Human Resources, Division of Family Services, Children and Youth Services Branch, 275 E. Main St., Frankfort KY 40621. Make reports to county offices in 14 state districts.

Louisiana: Louisiana Department of Health and Human Resources, Office of Human Development, Division of Children, Youth, and Family Services, P.O. Box 3318, Baton Rouge LA 70821. Make reports to parish Protective Service units.

Maine: Maine Department of Human Services, Child Protective Services, State House, Station 11, Augusta ME 04333. Make reports to Regional Office of Human Services; in-state to 1-800-452-1999 or out-of-state to 1-207-289-2983. Both operate 24 hours a day.

Maryland: Maryland Department of Human Resources, Social Services Administration, Saratoga State Center, 311 W. Saratoga St., Baltimore MD 21201. Make reports to county departments of social services or to local law enforcement agencies.

Massachusetts: Massachusetts Department of Social Services, Protective Services, 150 Causeway St., 11th Floor, Boston MA 02114. Make reports to area offices or Protective Screening Unit or in-state to 1-800-792-5200.

Michigan: Michigan Department of Social Services, Office of Children and Youth Services, Protective Services Division, 300 S. Capitol Ave., Ninth Floor, Lansing MI 48926. Make reports to county departments of social services.

Minnesota: Minnesota Department of Human Services, Protective Services Division, Centennial Office Bldg., St. Paul MN 55155. Make reports to county departments of human services.

Mississippi: Mississippi Department of Public Welfare, Bureau of Family and Children's Services, Protection Department, P.O. Box 352, Jackson MS 39205. Make reports in-state to 1-800-222-8000 or out-of-state (during business hours) to 1-601-354-0341.

Missouri: Missouri Child Abuse and Neglect Hotline, Department of Social Services, Division of Family Services, DFS, P.O. Box 88, Broadway Bldg., Jefferson City MO 65103. Make reports in-state to 1-800-392-3738 or out-of-state to 1-314-751-3448. Both operate 24 hours a day.

Montana: Department of Family Services, Child Protective Services, P.O. Box 8005, Helena MT 59604. Make reports to county departments of family services.

Nebraska: Nebraska Department of Social Services, Human Services Division, 301 Centennial Mall South, P.O. Box 95026, Lincoln NE 68509. Make reports to local law enforcement agencies or to local social service offices or in-state to 1-800-652-1999.

Nevada: Department of Human Resources, Welfare Division, 2527 N. Carson St., Carson City NV 89710. Make reports to Division of Welfare local offices.

New Hampshire: New Hampshire Department of Health and Welfare, Division for Children and Youth Services, 6 Hazen Dr., Concord NH 03301-6522. Make reports to Division for Children and Youth Services district offices or in-state to 1-800-852-3345, Ext. 4455.

New Jersey: New Jersey Division of Youth and Family Services, P.O. Box CN717, One S. Montgomery St., Trenton NJ 08625. Make reports in-state to 1-800-792-8610. District offices also provide 24-hour telephone services.

New Mexico: New Mexico Department of Human Services, Social Services Division, P.O. Box 2348, Santa Fe NM 87504. Make reports to county social services offices or in-state to 1-800-432-6217.

New York: New York State Department of Social Services, Division of Family and Children Services, State Central Register of Child Abuse and Maltreatment, 40 N. Pearl St., Albany NY 12243. Make reports in-state to 1-800-342-3720 or out-of-state to 1-518-474-9448.

North Carolina: North Carolina Department of Human Resources, Division of Social Services, Child Protective Services, 325 N. Salisbury St., Raleigh NC 27611. Make reports in-state to 1-800-662-7030.

North Dakota: North Dakota Department of Human Services, Division of Children and Family Services, Child Abuse and Neglect Program, State Capitol, Bismarck ND 58505. Make reports to county social services offices.

Ohio: Ohio Department of Human Services, Bureau of Children's Protective Services, 30 E. Broad St., Columbus OH 43266-0423. Make reports to county departments of human services.

Oklahoma: Oklahoma Department of Human Services, Division of Children and Youth Services Child Abuse/Neglect Section, P.O. Box 25352, Oklahoma City OK 73125. Make reports in-state to 1-800-522-3511.

Oregon: Department of Human Resources, Children's Services Division, Child Protective Services, 198 Commercial St., S.E., Salem OR 97310. Make reports to local Children's Services Division offices or to 1-503-378-4722.

Pennsylvania: Pennsylvania Department of Public Welfare, Office of Children, Youth and Families, Child Abuse Registry, Lanco Lodge, P.O. Box 2675, Harrisburg PA 17105. Make reports in-state to CHILDLINE 1-800-932-0313 or out-of-state to 1-713-783-8744.

Puerto Rico: Puerto Rico Department of Social Services, Services to Families with Children, P.O. Box 11398, Fernandez, Juncos Station, Santurez PR 00910. Make reports to 1-809-724-1313.

Rhode Island: Rhode Island Department for Children and Their Families, Division of Child Protective Services, 610 Mt. Pleasant Ave., Bldg. #9, Providence RI 02908. Make reports in-state to 1-800-RI-CHILD or 742-4453 or out-of-state to 1-401-457-4996.

South Carolina: South Carolina Department of Social Services, 1535 Confederate Ave., P.O. Box 1520, Columbia SC 29202-1520. Make reports to county departments of social services.

South Dakota: Department of Social Services, Child Protection Services, Richard F. Kneip Bldg., 700 Governors Dr., Pierre SD 57501. Make reports to local social services offices.

Tennessee: Tennessee Department of Human Services, Child Protective Services, Citizen Bank Plaza, 400 Deadrick St., Nashville TN 37219. Make reports to county departments of human services.

Texas: Texas Department of Human Services, Protective Services for Families and Children Branch, P.O. Box 2960, MC 537-W, Austin TX 78769. Make reports in-state to 1-800-252-5400 or out-of-state to 1-512-450-3360.

Utah: Department of Social Services, Division of Family Services, P.O. Box 45500, Salt Lake City UT 84110. Make reports to Division of Family Services district offices.

Vermont: Vermont Department of Social and Rehabilitative Services, Division of Social Services, 103 S. Main St., Waterbury VT 05676. Make reports to district offices or to 1-802-241-2131.

Virgin Islands: Virgin Islands Department of Human Services, Division of Social Services, P.O. Box 550, Charlotte Amalie, St. Thomas VI 00801. Make reports to Division of Social Services 1-809-774-9030.

Virginia: Commonwealth of Virginia, Department of Social Services, Bureau of Child Protective Services, Blair Bldg., 8007 Discovery Dr., Richmond VA 23229-8699. Make reports in-state to 1-800-552-7096 or out-of-state to 1-804-281-9081.

Washington: Department of Social and Health Services, Division of Children and Family Services, Child Protective Services, Mail Stop OB 41-D, Olympia WA 98504. Make reports in-state to 1-800-562-5624 or local Social and Health Services offices.

West Virginia: West Virginia Department of Human Services, Division of Social Services, Child Protective Services, State Office Bldg., 1900 Washington St., East, Charleston WV 25305. Make reports in-state to 1-800-352-6513.

Wisconsin: Wisconsin Department of Health and Social Services, Division of Community Services, Bureau for Children, Youth, and Families, 1 W. Wilson St., Madison WI 53707. Make reports to county social services offices.

Wyoming: Department of Health and Social Services, Division of Public Assistance and Social Services, Hathaway Bldg., Cheyenne WY 82002. Make reports to county departments of public assistance and social services.

Child Sexual Abuse Treatment Centers

These references include programs that were developed exclusively to treat child sexual abuse or that have special components and resources to deal with some aspect of this problem. If your state is not listed here, try contacting the state child protection agency listed in the previous section.

Alaska:

South Peninsula Women's Services, Box 2328, Homer AK 99603. Women in Safe Homes, P.O. Box 6552, Ketchikan AK 99901.

Rape Incest Program Judith Group, Inc., P.O. Box 2334, Soldotna AK 99669.

Arizona:

Behavior Associates, 330 E. 13th St., Tucson AZ 85701.

Arkansas:

SCAN (Suspected Child Abuse/Neglect) University of Arkansas School of Social Work, 33rd & University, Little Rock AR 72204.

California:

Incest Help, Inc., 719 Jackson St., Albany CA 94706.

Families in Crisis Program, Psychological Associates, 735 Duarte Rd., Arcadia CA 91006.

Child Sexual Abuse and Treatment Program, Solano County Department of Mental Health, 1408 Pennsylvania Ave., Fairfield CA 94533.

Family Crisis Center, Fresno County Department of Social Services, 4455 E. Wings Canyon, Fresno CA 93750.

Incest Awareness Project, Women's Resource Program, 1213 N. Highland, Hollywood CA 90038.

Lompoc Mental Health Services, Santa Barbara County Mental Health Services, 401 E. Cypress, Lompoc CA 93436.

Child Sexual Abuse Project, LA County Department of Social Services, 5427 Whittier Blvd., Los Angeles CA 90022.

Child Sexual Abuse Treatment Program — Child Protective Services, 401 Broadway, Oakland CA 94607.

Riverside Inter-Agency Sexual Abuse

Council, Riverside County Department of Public Social Services, 4260 Tequesquite Ave., Riverside CA 92501.

Child Sexual Abuse Program, Family Service Agency, 1669 E. Northeast St., San Bernardino CA 92405.

Child Sexual Abuse Treatment Program, San Diego County Department of Welfare, 6950 Levant St., San Diego CA 92111.

Child and Adolescent Sexual Abuse Resource Center, San Francisco General Hospital Medical Center, 1001 Potrero Ave., San Francisco CA 94110.

Santa Clara County Child Abuse Program, 840 Guadalupe Pkwy., San Jose CA 95011.

Child Sexual Abuse Treatment Program, Marin County Department of Health and Human Services, P.O. Box 4160 Civic Center Branch, San Rafael CA 94903.

Child Abuse Sexual Treatment Program, Family Resource Center, 500 Hilby, Seaside CA 93955.

Sexual Abuse Treatment Program, Forensic Psychology Associates, 5430 Van Nuys Blvd., Van Nuys CA 91401.

Colorado:

Sexual Abuse Program, Boulder County Department of Social Services, 3400 Broadway, Boulder CO 80306.

Child Protective Services, El Paso County Department of Social Services, P.O. Box 2692, 105 N. Spruce, Colorado Springs CO 80901.

Child Sexual Abuse Treatment Program, University of Colorado Medical Center, 4200 E. 9th Ave., Denver CO 80262.

National Center for the Prevention and Treatment of Child Abuse and Neglect, 1205 Oneida St., Denver CO 80220.

Connecticut:

Sex Crimes Unit, Connecticut State Police Department, Meriden CT 06540.

Sex Offender Program, Connecticut State Department of Corrections, P.O. Box 100, Somers CT 06701.

Waterbury Child Sexual Abuse Treatment Program, Waterbury Collaboration for the Prevention of Child Abuse and Neglect, 56 Franklin St., Waterbury CT 06702.

District of Columbia:

Child Sexual Victim Assistance Project, Child Protection Center, Children's Hospital, National Medical Center, 111 Michigan Ave., Washington DC 20010.

Sexual Abuse Prevention Program, DC Rape Crisis Center, P.O. Box 21005, Washington DC 20009.

Florida:

Advocates for Sexually Abused Children/Advocates for Victims, 1515 N.W. 7th St., Miami FL 33125.

Family Crisis Clinic, Jackson Memorial Hospital, 1611 N.W. 12th Ave., Miami FL 33136.

Victim—Court Liaison Services, State Attorney, 9th Judicial Circuit, P.O. Box 1673, Orlando FL 32801.

Child Development Center, Community Mental Health Center of Escambia County, 1201 W. Hernandez, Pensacola FL 32501.

Child Protection Team, Suite 212, 301 Broadway, Riviera Beach FL 33404.

Juvenile Welfare Board of Pinellas County, 4140 49th St., St. Petersburg FL 33709.

Child Sexual Abuse Treatment Program, Tampa Women's Health Center, Inc., 3004 Fletcher, Tampa FL 33612.

Georgia:

Rape Crisis Center, Grady Memorial Hospital, 80 Butler St., Atlanta GA 30303.

Hawaii:

Child Sexual Abuse Treatment Program, Catholic Social Service, 250 S. Vineyard St., Honolulu HI 96813.

Parents United, Daughters and Sons United, 1060 Bethel St., Honolulu HI 96813.
Sexual Abuse Treatment Program, Kapiolani Children's Hospital, 1319 Punahou St., Honolulu HI 96826.

Idaho:

Women's Crisis Center, Young Women's Christian Association, 720 W. Washington St., Boise ID 83702.
Incest Program, Idaho State Department of Health and Welfare, 431 Memorial Dr., Pocatello ID 83201.

Illinois:

Child Sexual Abuse Treatment and Training Center, 345 Manor Ct., Bolingbrook IL 60439.
Child Abuse Unit for Studies, Education and Services, 836 W. Wellington Ave., Chicago IL 60657.
Rape and Sexual Abuse Care Center, Box 154, Edwardsville IL 62026.
Council on Children at Risk, 1630 Fifth Ave., Moline IL 61265.

Indiana:

Youth Services Bureau, Samuel Strong Bldg., 330 W. Lexington St., Elkhart IN 46514.
Child Sexual Abuse Component, Marion County Department of Public Welfare, 143 S. Meridian St., Indianapolis IN 46225.

Iowa

Domestic Violence Program, Catholic Social Services, Council Bluffs IA 51501.
Department of Pediatrics/Adolescent Clinic, University Hospital, Iowa City IA 52242.
Counseling for Sexual Abuse, Catholic Charities Diocese of Sioux City, Sioux City IA 51104.

Kansas:

Kansas Committee for the Prevention of Child Abuse, 112 W. 6th St., Suite 305, Topeka KS 66603.

Maine:

Sexual Exploitation Project, Department of Mental Health and Corrections, Rm. 411, State Office Bldg., Augusta ME 04333.
Sexual Abuse Treatment Program, Community Counseling Center, 622 Congress St., Portland ME 04101.
Sexual Exploitation Project, Fairharbor Shelter, YWCA, Portland ME 04101.

Maryland:

Multidisciplinary Committee on Physical and Sexual Abuse and Neglect, Anne Arundel County Department of Social Services, Arundel Center, 44 Calvert St., Annapolis MD 21401.
Sex Offense Task Force, Baltimore City State's Attorney's Office, Criminal Courts Bldg., Rm. 221, Baltimore MD 21202.
Sexual Abuse Treatment Program, Baltimore City Department of Social Services, 312 E. Oliver St., Baltimore MD 21202.
Sexual Assault People Program, Baltimore City Hospitals, Department of Medical Social Work, 4940 Eastern Ave., Baltimore MD 21224.
Prince Georges Hospital Sexual Assault Center, Prince Georges General Hospital and Medical Center, Hospital Dr., Cheverly MD 20785.
Family Assessment and Treatment Program: Child Sexual Abuse, Montgomery County Department of Social Services, 5630 Fishers Lane, Rockville MD 20852.
National Center for the Prevention and Control of Rape, National Institute of Mental Health, 5600 Fishers Lane, Rockville MD 20852.
Sexual Abuse Treatment Program, Protective Services Unit, Baltimore

County Department of Social Services, 620 York Rd., Towson MD 21204.

Massachusetts:

Sexual Abuse Treatment Team, Children's Hospital Medical Center, 300 Longwood Ave., Boston MA 02115.

Victim Counseling Service, Boston City Hospital, Department of Nursing Services, 818 Harrison Ave., Boston MA 02118.

Center for Diagnosis and Treatment of Sexually Dangerous Persons, Massachusetts Department of Mental Health, Bridgewater MA 02324.

Protective Services Unit, Massachusetts Department of Welfare, 75 Commercial St., Brockton MA 02402.

Victims Support Group, 260 River Dr., Hadley MA 01035.

Incest Consultation Network, P.O. Box 625, Northhampton MA 01060.

Somerville Women's Mental Health Collective, 61 Roseland, Somerville MA 02143.

Incest Treatment Project, Baystate Medical Center, 759 Chestnut St., Springfield MA 01107.

Michigan:

Victims Support Group, P.O. Box 7883, Ann Arbor MI 48107.

Bay City Office—Lutheran Child and Family Service, P.O. Box B, Bay City MI 48707.

Special Family Problem Services, Children's Aid Society of Detroit, 7700 2nd St., Detroit MI 48202.

Genesee County Child Abuse Consortium, 6th Ave. & Begole, Flint MI 48502.

Minnesota:

Dakota Sexual Assault Services, Community Action Council, Inc., 13760 Nicollet Ave. S., Burnsville MN 55337.

Child Sexual Abuse Prevention Program, Illusion Theater & School, 528 Hennepin Ave., Rm. 309, Minneapolis MN 55403.

Christopher Street, Inc., Incest Program, 2344 Nicollet Ave., S. Minneapolis MN 55405.

Judson Family Center, 4101 Harriet Ave., S. Minneapolis MN 55409.

Sexual Assault Services—Hennepin County Attorney's Office, C-2000 Government Center, Minneapolis MN 55487.

Center for Parents & Children, 1015 7th Ave., Moorhead MN 56560.

Family Incest Program, Wilder Child Guidance Clinic, 919 Lafond Rd., St. Paul MN 55104.

Family Sexual Abuse Treatment and Training Program, Meta Recourse, 821 Ragmond Ave., St. Paul MN 55114.

Ramsey County Community Human Services, 529 Jackson St., St. Paul MN 55101.

Interagency Identification, Intervention, and Treatment of Incest, Winona County Department of Social Services, 157 Lafayette St., Winona MN 55987.

Missouri:

Child Sexual Abuse Management Program, St. Louis Children's Hospital, 500 S. Kingshighway Blvd., P.O. Box 14871, St. Louis MO 63178.

Child Sexual Abuse Treatment Program, Christian Family Life Center, 6636 Clayton Rd., St. Louis MO 63117.

Nebraska:

Cat and Mouse, Girls Club of Omaha, 3706 Lake St., Omaha NE 68111.

Parents United and Daughters and Sons United of Sarpy and Douglas Counties, 1210 Golden Gate Dr., Papillon NE 68046.

New Jersey:

Atlantic County Adolescent Maltreatment Program, Division of Youth and Family Services, 26 S. Pennsylvania Ave., Atlantic City NJ 08401.

Adult Diagnostic and Treatment Center, Rahway Prison (Offenders Program), P.O. Box 190, Avenel NJ 07001.

Family Service of Burlington County, Meadow Health Center, Woodlake Rd., Mount Holly NJ 08060.

Incest Counseling Unit, New Jersey State Division of Youth and Family Services, Mercer County District Office, 1901 N. Olden Ave., Trenton NJ 08618.

New York:

Otsego County Council on Child Abuse and Neglect, Bassett Hospital, P.O. Box 731, Cooperstown NY 13326.

Queensboro Society for the Prevention of Cruelty to Children, 161-20 89th Ave., Jamaica NY 11432.

New York Society for the Prevention of Cruelty to Children, 110 E. 71st St., New York NY 10021.

Sex Crimes Prosecution Unit, New York County Office of the District Attorney, 155 Leonard St., New York NY 10013.

Therapeutic Alternatives to Sexual Abuse, Family Services of Rochester, 30 N. Clinton Ave., Rochester NY 14606.

Alliance Child Abuse Coordination Program — Catholic Charities, Family Services Division, 1654 W. Onondaga St., Syracuse NY 13204.

Victims of Incest, Westchester Jewish Community Services, 172 S. Broadway, White Plains NY 10605.

North Carolina:

Sexual Abuse Prevention Project, Alamance-Caswell Area Mental Health-Mental Retardation Program, 407 S. Broad St., Burlington NC 27215.

North Carolina Sexual Abuse Identification and Treatment Project, Department of Social Services, 325 N. Salisbury St., Raleigh NC 27611.

North Dakota:

Sexual Assault Program, Rape and Abuse Crisis Center, Fargo ND 58107.

Rape Crisis Center, Grand Forks County Social Service Center, 118 N. 3rd St., Grand Forks ND 58201.

Jamestown Area Sexual Abuse Treatment Unit, Jamestown Area Social Services Center, Box 334, Jamestown ND 58401.

Ohio:

Cleveland Rape Crisis Center, 3201 Euclid Ave., Cleveland OH 44115.

Sexual Abuse Treatment/Training Project, Federation for Community Planning, 1001 Huren Rd., Cleveland OH 44115.

Child Assault Prevention Program, Women Against Rape, P.O. Box 02084, Columbus OH 43202.

Child Sexual Abuse Program, Child and Family Services, 535 Marmion Ave., Youngstown OH 44504.

Oklahoma:

Pediatric Psychology Service, Oklahoma Children's Memorial Hospital, Box 26901-900 N.E. 13th St., Oklahoma City OK 73104.

Public Health Guidance Center, Oklahoma State Department of Health, N.E. 10th and Stonewall Sts., Oklahoma City OK 73105.

At-Risk-Parent-Child Program, Hillcrest Medical Center and the University of Oklahoma College of Medicine, Utica on the Park, Tulsa OK 74104.

Oregon:

Adolescent Victims Counseling Groups, Oregon Department of Human Resources, Children's Service Division, 1102 Lincoln St., Eugene OR 97401.

Christian Family Institute, Counseling Services, 1501 Pearl St., Eugene OR 97401.

Incest Treatment Program, 1188 S.W. 4th St., Onterio OR 97914.

Child Abuse Sexual Treatment Program, Child Protective Services, 1031 E. Burnside, Portland OR 97215.

Child Incest Treatment Program, Parents United, Inc., 3905 S.E. Belmont, Suite 1, Portland OR 97214.

Mid-Valley Center Against Domestic and Sexual Violence, P.O. Box 851, Salem OR 97308.

Pennsylvania:

Incest Counseling Program and INNOCENSE (Rap Group for Women Victims), Women Organized Against Rape in Bucks County, P.O. Box 793, Langhorne PA 19047.

Incest and Sexual Abuse Program, Joseph J. Peters Institute, 112 S. 16th St., Philadelphia PA 19102.

Sexual Abuse Advocacy Program, Women Organized Against Rape, 1220 Sansom St., Philadelphia PA 19107.

Parents United, Parents Anonymous of Pittsburgh, 1718 Allegheny Bldg., 429 Forbes Ave., Pittsburgh PA 15219.

Tennessee:

Project Against Sexual Abuse of Appalachian Childen, Child and Family Services of Knox County, Inc., 114 Dameron Ave., Knoxville TN 37917.

Sex Abuse Help Line, Child and Family Services of Knox County, Inc., 114 Dameron Ave., Knoxville TN 37917.

Child Sex Abuse Technical Assistance Project, Tennessee Department of Human Services and Social Service Department, 410 State Office Bldg., Nashville TN 37219.

Texas:

Dallas Sexual Abuse Project, Texas Department of Human Resources, Social Services Branch, John H. Reagan Bldg., Austin TX 78701.

Sex Abuse Counseling Program, Family Service Association, 230 Pereida St., San Antonio TX 78210.

Virginia:

Parents United-Fredericksburg Chapter, Fifteenth District Court Service Unit, 601 Caroline St., Fredericksburg VA 22401.

Norfolk Family Sexual Trauma Team, Norfolk Police Department, P.O. Box 358, Norfolk VA 23501.

North West Center for Community Mental Health, 11420 Isaac Newton Square, Reston VA 22090.

Sexual Abuse Treatment Program, Virginia Department of Social Services, Municipal Center, Virginia Beach VA 23456.

Washington:

Lewis County Hotline, P.O. Box 337, Chehalis WA 98532.

Incest Treatment Program, Family Services of King County, 31003 18th Ave. S., Federal Way WA 98003.

Domestic Violence Program, Washington State Department of Social and Health Services, Olympia WA 98504.

Victims of Sexual Assault, Washington State Department of Social and Health Services, Olympia WA 98504.

Committee for Children, Seattle Institute for Child Advocacy, P.O. Box 15190, Seattle WA 98405.

Juvenile Sex Offender Treatment Program, Adolescent Clinic, University of Washington, Seattle WA 98195.

Sexual Assault Center, Harborview Medical Center, Seattle WA 98104.

Teenage Abuse Prevention Program, Center for the Prevention of Sexual and Domestic Violence, 4250 Somend, Seattle WA 98118.

Rape Crisis Network, Lutheran Social Service of Washington, Spokane WA 99201.

Child Sexual Abuse and Treatment Program, Tacoma School District, P.O. Box 1357, Tacoma WA 98401.

Incest: Community Treatment Model in Children's Protective Services, Washington State County Community Services, 420 E. 115th St., Tacoma WA 98402.

Incest Family Services, P.O. Box 44608, Tacoma WA 98444.

Pierce County Rape Relief, Allenmore Medical Center, S. 19th and Union Ave., Tacoma WA 98405.

Sexual Assault Program, Central Washington Comprehensive Mental Health, Yakima WA 98901.

West Virginia:

Sexual Abuse Treatment and Training, 3375 Rt. 60 E., P.O. Box 8069, Huntington WV 25705.

Wisconsin:

Parental Stress Center, Inc., 1506 Madison St., Madison WI 53711.

Rape Crisis Center, 312 E. Wilson St., Madison WI 53703.

Incest Treatment Service, Family Hospital, 2711 W. Wells St., Milwaukee WI 53208.

Parents Anonymous, Intrafamily Sexual Abuse Program, Parents Anonymous of Greater Milwaukee, P.O. Box 11415, Milwaukee WI 53211.

Bibliography
with Selected Annotations

The following references represent as much material as I could gather over the years of study. They are not categorized as to prevention, detection, dynamics, legal issues, treatment, effects or definitions. I have not read all of the listed material as it is difficult to obtain copies of articles specifically written for periodicals and journals and some books and pamphlets are just not available or out of print.

Many of the works I have been able to obtain are those designed for parents and children, and thus I am able to provide annotations for a number of these references. All works of special interest to parents, whether annotated or not, are preceded by an asterisk (*) for easy identification. Many of these are suitable for use with young children, such as read-aloud storybooks or coloring books that can be used as a basis for discussion.

The variety of materials represented in this listing may give the reader some idea of what is currently being done in the study of child sexual abuse. Several prevention curricula, some of them produced by local school boards, are included as examples of current directions in prevention education. Some curriculum materials have been packaged for wider distribution and are available from the publishers indicated; users of this bibliography may find such materials helpful in developing their own programs.

Many articles and papers listed here were written for professionals and for and by those pursuing specific areas of concern that may not be of interest to every user of this bibliography. For example, many of the books, articles, studies and papers I researched dealt with incest and physical child abuse. As I have no personal knowledge of these areas, I have primarily directed your attention to references on sexual child molestation outside the family unit. However, the fact remains that incest is another word for child molestation — just closer to home.

Abel, Gene G., et al. *The Treatment of Child Molesters.* 1984. New York: SVC-TM (722 West 168 Street, Box 17, 10032).

Abel, Gene G.; Becker, Judith; and Cunningham-Rathner, Jerry. "Complications, Consent, and Cognitions in Sex Between Children and Adults." *International Journal of Law and Psychiatry* 7, 1984.

————; ————; and ————. "How a Molester Perceives the World." *International Journal of Law and Psychiatry,* 1984.

Abel, Gene G.; Becker, Judith; Murphy, William D.; and Flanagan, Barry. "Identifying Dangerous Child Molesters." *Violent Behavior: Social Learning Approaches.*

Abel, Gene G., and Blanchard, E.B. "The Role of Fantasy in the Treatment of Sexual Deviation." *Archives of General Psychiatry* **30**, 1974.

Abel, Gene G.; Blanchard, Edward B.; and Becker, Judith. "An Integrated Program for Rapists." In R.T. Rada, ed., *Clinical Aspects of the Rapist*, 1978.

Abel, Gene G., and Cunningham-Rathner, Jerry. *The Self-Reported Molestations of Non-Incarcerated Child Molesters.* 1986.

Abel, Gene G.; Harlow, David H.; Blanchard, Edward; and Guild, Donald. "The Components of Rapists' Sexual Arousal." *Archives of General Psychiatry,* August 1977.

Abel, Gene G.; Mittelman, Mary S.; and Becker, Judith. *Sexual Offenders: Results of Assessment and Recommendations for Treatment.* Unpublished manuscript, Columbia University, New York, 1984.

Abel, Gene G.; Rouleau, J.L.; and Cunningham-Rathner, J. "Sexually Aggressive Behavior." In Curran, A., et al., eds., *Modern Legal Psychiatry and Psychology.* Philadelphia: Davis.

Adams, C. "Considering Children's Development Stages in Prevention Education." In Nelson, M., and Clark, K., eds., *The Educator's Guide to Preventing Child Sexual Abuse.* Santa Cruz CA: Network, 1986.

*Adams, Caren, and Fay, Jennifer. *No More Secrets: Protecting Your Child from Sexual Assault.* San Luis Obispo CA: Impact, 1981. Provides parents with information on how to talk to children about sexual abuse, prevention games to play, indicators of potentially dangerous situations, and how to help the child who has been victimized. Produced with the assistance of King County Rape Relief, Renton WA.

*_____, and _____. *Nobody Told Me It Was Rape.* Santa Cruz CA: Network, 1984. Acquaintance rape and how to avoid sexual exploitation. Designed for parents to help educate their adolescents.

*_____, and _____. "Parents as Primary Prevention Educators." In Nelson, M., and Clark, K., eds., *The Educator's Guide to Preventing Child Sexual Abuse.* Santa Cruz CA: Network, 1986. Discussion of parents' role in school-based child sexual abuse prevention programs. Emphasizes importance of parental involvement and suggests strategies for increasing that involvement.

*Adams, Caren; Fay, Jennifer; and Loreen-Martin, Jan. *No Is Not Enough.* San Luis Obispo CA: Impact, 1984. A well-written parental guide to help teenagers avoid sexual assault. Excellent suggestions like when to talk about sexual assaults, date rape, family stress.

Adams, Jay. "Molester Myths and Stereotypes: Understanding Child Sexual Abuse." *Forum,* May-June 1985.

Adams, M., and Neel, J. "Children of Incest." *Pediatrics,* July 1967.

Adams, M.; Davidson, R.; and Cornell, P. "Adoptive Risks of the Children of Incest: A Preliminary Report." *Child Welfare,* 1967.

Adams, P. *Carnal Aggression and Abuse: Intervention Strategies.* Louisville KY: 1978.

_____. *Dynamics of Some Attitudes Toward Children.* Louisville KY: 1981.

_____. *Language Patterns of Opponents to a Child Protection Program.* New York: 1981.

Adams-Tucker, C. *A Sociological Overview of 28 Sex-Abused Children.* Elmsford NY: 1981.

_____. "Defense Mechanisms Used by Sexually Abused Children." *Children Today,* January-February 1985.

_____. "Early Treatment of Child Incest Victims." *American Journal of Psycho-Therapy,* October 1984.

_____. "Proximate Effects of Sexual Abuse in Childhood: A Report on 28 Children." *American Journal of Psychiatry,* October 1982.

_____. *Sex Abused Children: Pathology and Clinical Traits.* Paper presented at the Annual Meeting of the American Psychiatric Association, San Francisco CA, May 1980.

_____. *Sexually Abused Children's Defense Mechanisms.* (Suite 3438, Medical Arts Building, 1169 Eastern Parkway, Louisville KY 40217.)

Adolescent Perpetrator Network's Cooperative Newsletter. *Adolescent Perpetrators.* Undated.

"Adult Seduction of the Child: Effects on the Child." *Medical Aspects of Human Sexuality,* March 1973.

*Ageton, Susanne. *Facts About Sexual Assault.* Rockville MD: National Institute of Mental Health, 1985. A report for adults who work with teenagers. The report is based on a national study of 1700 children aged 11–17. Includes discussion of date rape, a comparison of victims and nonvictims, notes on the aftermath of assault, and suggestions for reducing risks.

*_____. *Sexual Assault Among Adolescents.* Lexington MA: Heath, 1983. Data on adolescents who have been victims. Also information about possible suspects.

Aguilora, D.; Messisk, J.; and Farrel, M. *Crisis Intervention Theory and Practice.* St. Louis MO: Mosby, 1974.

*Aho, Jennifer. *Learning About Sex: A Guide for Children and Their Parents.* New York: Holt, Rinehart and Winston, 1978.

*Aho, Jennifer Sowle, and Petras, John W. *Learning About Sexual Abuse.* Hillside NJ: Enslow, 1985. Fictionalized episodes and an introductory discussion present the dangers of child molesting in its various forms and suggest ways of preventing and dealing with it. Emphasizes that children need confidence to take action against the suspect and need assurances that there are adults who can be trusted. The authors also stress that children need to know they are not to blame for anything. They are victims.

Al-Tifach, A. *Les delices des coeurs.* 1971.

Alder, Christine. "An Exploration of Self-Reported Sexually Aggressive Behavior." *Crime and Delinquency* 31, 1985.

Alderson, J.; Hennessy, D.; and Thompson, J. "Child Abuse and Neglect: Meeting the Challenge of Prevention." *Health Visitor,* February 1983.

Allen, C. *Textbook of Psychosexual Disorders.* London: Oxford University Press, 1962.

*Allen, Charlotte Vale. *Daddy's Girl.* New York: Wyndham, 1980. Autobiography discusses the author's abuse by her father from age 6.

Allen, D. "Young Male Prostitutes: A Psychosocial Study." *Archives of Sexual Behavior* 9, 1980.

*"The Amazing Spider Man and Power Pack." Chicago IL: National Committee for the Prevention of Child Abuse, 1984. A specially made comic book tells three stories of abuse and teaches children ages 5–12 how to protect themselves. Teacher's Guide also available from the committee (P.O. Box 2866, Chicago IL 60609).

American Bar Association. *Innovations in the Prosecution of Child Sexual Abuse Cases.* Washington DC: National Legal Resource Center for Child Advocacy and Protection, November 1981.

American Christian Voice Foundation. *A Convicted Molester's Testimony.* Washington DC: Child Protection Alert, 1985.

American Humane Association. *Highlights of Official Child Neglect and Abuse Reporting, 1984.* Denver: American Humane Association, 1986.

_____. "Reports of Child Maltreatment Increase Again." News Release, November 8, 1985.

*_____. *Stop! Don't Hurt Me!* Englewood CO: Undated. Written in a question-and-answer format for children. Discusses physical abuse and neglect as well as sexual abuse.

American Humane Association in Association with the Denver Research Institute. *National Analysis of Official Child Abuse and Neglect Reporting.* Denver: American Humane Association, September 1979, November 1979.

American Nurses Association. *A Report on the Hearings on the Unmet Health Needs of Children and Youth.* Kansas City MO: 1979.

*Amerson, R. *Hi! My Name Is Sissy: I Am 6 Years Old.* Sanford NC: Lee County Department of Social Services. Sponsored by DHHS, Washington DC, 1984. Coloring book tells the story of a six-year-old girl whose uncle touched her in a way she didn't like. Stresses that children should report abuse to a trusted adult.

*Ames, Louise Bates, and Ilg, Frances L. *Your 2[3, 4, 5, 6] Year Old.* New York: Delacorte, 1977–1979.

*Amstutz, B. *Touch Me Not!* Parkville MO: Precious Resources, 1984. Large type, easy for children to read. Pictures of boys' and girls' bodies show "touch-me-not" areas (breasts, genitals, anal area) and tells children to run from persons who want to touch them there.

Anderson, Cordelia. "Interview: A History of the Touch Continuum." In Nelson, M., and Clark, K., eds., *The Educator's Guide to Preventing Child Sexual Abuse.* Santa Cruz CA: Network, 1986. Anderson discusses her work in developing sexual abuse curricula and the future of prevention education.

*_____. *No Easy Answers Curriculum.* Minneapolis: Illusion Theater (304 Washington Ave., North Minneapolis MN, 55401).

*Anderson, D. *Margaret's Story: About Sexual Abuse and Going to Court.* Minneapolis MN: Dillon, 1986.

Anderson, J., and Benson, J. *Respond. Student Handbook.* Seattle WA: Special Child, 1985.

_____, and _____. *Respond: Teaching Child Self-Protection. Course Guide.* Seattle WA: Special Child, 1985. Provides instruction and exercises to teach children how to protect themselves from abuse and abduction. Ten lesson plans are included.

Anderson, L.M., and Shafer, G. "The Character-Disordered Family: A Community Treatment Model for Family Sexual Abuse." St. Paul MN: Ramsey County Mental Health Department, Ramsey County Child Abuse Team. *American Journal of Orthopsychiatry,* July 1979.

Anderson, Wayne P.; Kunce, Joseph T.; and Rich, Brice. "Sex Offenders: Three Personality Types." *Journal of Clinical Psychology,* July 1979.

Angelou, M. *I Know Why the Caged Bird Sings.* New York: Bantam, 1971.

Annis, Laurence V. "A Residential Treatment Program for Male Sex Offenders." *International Journal of Offender Therapy and Comparative Criminology* 26, 1982.

Annis, Laurence V.; Mathers, Leigh G.; and Baker, Christy A. "Victim Workers as Therapists for Incarcerated Sex Offenders." *Victimology: An International Journal* 9, 1984.

Annon, Jack S., and Robinson, Craig. *The Sexual Offender: Treatment and Prevention.* Paper presented at the International Symposia on Reproductive Health Care, Maui HI, October 1982.

Araji, S., and Finkelhor, D. "Explanations of Pedophilia: Review of Empirical Research." *Bulletin of the American Academy of Psychiatry and the Law* 13, 1985.

*Arenberg, Gerald. *Preventing Missing Children: A Parental Guide to Child Security.*

Hollywood FL: Compact, 1984. Arenberg, the former director of the National Association of Chiefs of Police, includes a chapter on the sexual exploitation of children and says that education is the best form of prevention. Good solid suggestions.

Arkis, H. *The Questions of Incest and the Properties of a Moral Argument.* Presented to the Conference on Childhood Sexual Abuse, Chicago, 1978.

Arony, J.P., and Kempf, R. *La penis et la demoralisation de l'occident.* 1978.

*Armstrong, L. *Kiss Daddy Goodnight.* New York: Hawthorn, 1978. Over 150 incest victims tell of their trauma.

Arthur, Lindsay. "The Abuse Problem." *Juvenile and Family Court Journal,* 1986.

Atcheson, J.D., and Williams, D.C. "A Study of Juvenile Sex Offenders." *American Journal of Psychiatry* 3, 1954.

Atcom, Inc. *Children's Sexuality: Abuse, Incest, Pedophilia. Special Report.* New York: Atcom, 1958. A collection of 36 articles on various forms of sexual exploitation of children.

_____. *Physical and Sexual Abuse.* New York: 1983.

"Attacking the Last Taboo: Researchers Are Lobbying Against the Ban on Incest." *Time Magazine,* April 14, 1980.

Attorney General's Task Force on Family Violence. *Final Report.* Washington DC: September 1984.

*Austin Child Guidance Center. *Sexual Abuse: Information for Pre-teens and Teenagers.* Austin TX: Texas Abuse Services Division, undated. Booklet gives an overview of sexual abuse of adolescents. Offers suggestions for prevention and for treating victims.

Avery-Clark, C.; O'Neil, J.A.; and Laws, D.R. *A Comparison of Intrafamilial Sexual and Physical Child Abuse.* California: Atascadero State Hospital, 1981.

Awad, G. "Father-Son Incest: A Case Report." *The Journal of Nervous and Mental Disease* 162, 1976.

Awad, George A.; Saunders, Elisabeth; and Levene, Judy. "A Clinical Study of Male Adolescent Sexual Offenders." *International Journal of Offender Therapy and Comparative Criminology,* 1984.

Bagley, C. "Incest Behavior and the Incest Taboo." *Social Problems* 16, 1969.

_____. "Mental Health and the In-Family Sexual Abuse of Children and Adolescents." Calgary University, Alberta, Canada. *Canada's Mental Health* 32, June 1984.

_____. "Varieties of Incest." *New Society,* 1969.

Bagley, Christopher, and McDonald, Margaret. "Adult Mental Health Sequels of Child Sexual Abuse: Physical Abuse and Neglect in Maternally Separated Children." *Canadian Journal of Community Mental Health,* Spring 1984.

*Bahr, A. *Your Body Is Your Own. A Book for Parents and Children to Read Together.* New York: Grosset and Dunlap, 1986.

Bailey, T.F., and Bailey, W.H. *Criminal or Social Intervention in Child Sexual Abuse: A Review and a Viewpoint.* Denver: American Humane Association, 1983.

Baisden, M.J. *The World of Roseaphrenia: The Sexual Psychology of the Female.* Sacramento CA: Allied Research Society, 1971.

Baizerman, Michael; Thompson, Jacquelyn; Stafford-White, Kimaka; and An Old Young Friend. "Adolescent Prostitution." *Children Today,* September-October 1979.

Baker, C.D. "Preying on Playgrounds: The Exploitation of Children in Pornography and Prostitution." *Pepperdine Law Review* 5, 1978.

Baker, S.K., and Chambers, J.C. *Sacramento Child Sexual Abuse Treatment Program.*

Resource Consortium Project. Final Report. Sacramento CA: Sacramento Child Sexual Abuse Treatment Program, undated.

Baker-Benfield, G. *The Spermatic Economy: A 19th Century View of Sexuality.* In Gordon, M., ed., *The American Family in Social-Historical Perspectives.* New York: St. Martin's, 1978.

*Bakker, Cornelias B., and Bakker-Rabdau, Marianne K. *No Trespassing: Explorations in Human Territoriality.* San Francisco: Chandler and Sharp, 1973.

Bandura, A. *Aggression: A Social Learning Analysis.* Englewood Cliffs NJ: Prentice-Hall, 1973.

Barbaree, H., et al. *Alcohol Intoxication and Inhibition of Sexual Arousal to Rape Cases.* Paper presented to the Annual Convention of the Ontario Psychological Association, Toronto, February 1980.

Barbaree, H.E.; Marshall, W.L.; and Lanthier, R.D. "Deviant Sexual Arousal in Rapists." *Behavior Research and Therapy* 17, 1979.

Bard, M. *Family Crisis Intervention: From Concept to Implementation.* Washington DC: National Institute of Law Enforcement and Criminal Justice, December 1973.

Bard, M., and Zacker, J. "The Prevention of Family Violence: Dilemmas of Community Intervention." *Journal of Marriage and the Family,* November 1971.

Barn House, R. "Sex Between Patient and Therapist." *Journal of the American Academy of Psychoanalysis* 6, 1978.

Barnard, C. "Alcoholism and Incest. Part 1: Similar Traits. Common Dynamics." *Focus on the Family* 27, no. 29, January-February 1984.

Barnard, C.P. *Families, Incest, and Therapy: A Special Issue of International Journal of Family Therapy.* Menomonie WI: Wisconsin-Stout University, Clinical Services Center. *International Journal of Family Therapy,* Summer 1983.

Barry, M., and Johnson, A. "The Incest Barrier." *Psychoanalytic Quarterly,* 1953.

Barry, R.J. "Incest: The Last Taboo (Conclusion)." Delinquency Control Institute, Los Angeles CA. *FBI Law Enforcement Bulletin,* February 1984.

Barton, B.R., and Marshall, A.S. "Pivotal Partings: Forced Termination with a Sexually Abused Boy." *Clinical Social Work Journal,* Summer 1986.

Basic Facts About Child Sexual Abuse. Chicago: National Center for the Prevention of Child Abuse (332 So. Michigan Ave. Suite 950, Chicago IL 60604-4357).

*Bass, Ellen. "I Like You to Make Jokes with Me, But I Don't Want You to Touch Me." In *Stories for Free Children.* New York: McGraw-Hill, 1982. Affirms a child's right to say no to uncomfortable touch.

Bass, Ellen, and Davis, Laura. *The Courage to Heal: A Guide for Survivors of Child Sexual Abuse.* 1988.

*Bass, Ellen, and Thornton, Louise, with Brister, J., et al., eds. *I Never Told Anyone: Writings by Women Survivors of Child Sexual Abuse.* New York: Harper and Row, 1983. Includes statistics on offenses and offenders, as well as personal stories of victims.

*Basset, K. *My Very Own Special Body Book.* 3rd edition. Redding CA: Hawthorne, April 1985. Picture book. Teaches children to respect their bodies and say "no" to inappropriate touching. Explains different forms of sexual abuse.

Bastani, J., Bowman, M.D., and Kentsmith, David K., M.D. "Psychotherapy with Wives of Sexual Deviants." *American Journal of Psychotherapy,* January 1980.

*Bateman, Py. *Acquaintance Rape: Awareness and Prevention for Teenagers.* Seattle WA: Alternatives to Fear, 1982. A workbook for adolescents explaining the concept of date rape. Suggestions for keeping control of potentially dangerous situations.

_____. "Male Socialization and Child Sexual Abuse: What's the Connection?" *Connections,* Winter 1986.

_____. *So What If You're Not an Expert—You Can Still Take Steps to Protect Yourself Against Sexual Assault.* Seattle WA: Alternatives to Fear, 1984. Advice in self-protection for teenagers. Assertive action is stressed.

*Bateman, Py, and Mahoney, Bill. *Macho? What Do Girls Really Want?* Seattle WA: Alternatives to Fear, 1985. A guide for boys in developing dating habits.

*Bateman, Py, and Stringer, Gayle. *Where Do I Start? A Parent's Guide for Talking to Teens About Acquaintance Rape.* Seattle WA: Alternatives to Fear, 1984.

*Bauer, M. *Foster Child.* Seabury, 1977.

Baugh, Jack, and Morgan, Jefferson. *Why Have They Taken Our Children? (The Chowchilla Case).* New York: Dell, 1979.

Bavolek, S.J. *Etiology of Sexual Abuse.* Wisconsin University at Eau Claire, Department of Special Education. Springfield IL: Thomas, 1985.

Baxter, D.J., et al. "Deviant Sexual Behavior: Differentiating Sex Offenders by Criminal and Personal History, Psychometric Measures and Sexual Response." *Criminal Justice and Behavior* 11, 1984.

*Beaudy, J., and Ketchem, L. *Carla Goes to Court.* New York: Human Sciences, 1983.

Becker, J.V., and Abel, G.G. *The Rights and Treatment of the Sexually Abused Client.* Columbia University, New York, College of Physicians and Surgeons, 1980.

Becker, J.V.; Cunningham-Rathner, J.; and Kaplan, M.S. *The Adolescent Sexual Perpetrator: Demographics, Criminal History, Victims, Sexual Behavior and Recommendations for Reducing Future Offenses.* New York Psychiatric Institute.

Becker, J.V.; Skinner, L.J.; and Abel, G.G. "Sequelae of Sexual Assault: The Survivor's Perspective." In Greer, J., and Stuart, I., eds., *The Sexual Aggressor: Current Perspectives on Treatment.* New York: Van Nostrand Reinhold, 1983.

Becker, J.V.; Skinner, L.J.; Abel, G.G.; Axelrod, R.; and Cichon, J. "Sexual Problems of Sexual Assault Survivors." Columbia University, New York, College of Physicians and Surgeons. *Women and Health,* Winter 1984.

Becker, J.V.; Skinner, L.J.; Abel, G.G.; Howell, J.; and Bruce, K. "The Effects of Sexual Assault on Rape and Attempted Rape Victims." *Victimology: An International Journal* 7, 1982.

Becker, J.V.; Skinner, L.J.; Abel, G.G.; and Treacy, E. "Incidence of Sexual Dysfunction in Rape and Incest Victims." *Journal of Sex and Marital Therapy* 8, 1982.

*Beland, Kathy, and Van Dyke, Gretchen. *Talking About Touching.* Seattle WA: Committee for Children, 1985. A storybook for children, kindergarten through fourth grade. Teaches personal safety skills. Available in supersize, compact and bilingual versions. A video entitled "Yes You Can Say No" is also available.

Belcastro, Philip A. "A Comparison of Latent Sexual Behavior Patterns Between Raped and Never Been Raped Females." *Victimology: An International Journal* 7, 1982.

Bell, Quentin. *Virginia Woolf: A Biography.* New York: 1972.

Bellinger, D. *The Judiciary and Sexual Assault. Minnesota Program for Victims of Sexual Assault.* St. Paul MN: December 1984.

Bender, D. *Human Sexuality.* St. Paul MN: Greenhaven, 1986.

Bender, L., and Grugett, A. "A Follow-Up Report on Children Who Had Atypical Sexual Experience." *American Journal of Orthopsychiatry* 22, 1952.

*Benedict, H. *Safe, Strong and Street Wise.* Boston: Atlantic Monthly Press, 1987.

Benward, J., and Densen-Gerber, J. "Incest as a Causative Factor in Anti-Social Behavior: An Exploratory Study." *Contemporary Drug Problems,* Fall 1975, and the American Academy of Forensic Sciences, 27th Annual Meeting, Chicago, February 1976.

Berdie, Jane; Baizerman, Michael; and Lourie, Ira. "Violence Toward Youth: Themes from a Workshop." *Children Today,* March-April 1977.

Berest, J. *Medical-Legal Aspects of Sex Research.* August 1968.

*Berg, Eric. *Stop It!* Santa Cruz CA: Network, 1985. A booklet that focuses on children's right to say no. Also includes information on touches, intuition, secrets, body rights and telling someone.

*_____. *Tell Someone!* Santa Cruz CA: Network, 1985. Stresses that child abuse is *not* the victim's fault. Also includes information on touch, intuition, body rights and saying no.

*_____. *Touch Talk.* Santa Cruz CA: Network, 1985. Booklet about touch designed for kindergarten through 2nd grade. Teaches kinds of touch: good, bad or confusing. Also stresses telling someone of secrets.

Bergart, A.M. "Isolation to Intimacy: Incest Survivors in Group Therapy." United Charities of Chicago. *Social Casework,* May 1986.

Berkeley Planning Associates. *The Exploitation of Client Characteristics. Service and Outcomes: Draft Final Report: Evaluation of the Clinical Demonstration of Child Abuse and Neglect.* Berkeley CA: August 1982.

Berkeley Planning Associates and Urban and Rural Systems Associates. *Historical Case Studies: Evaluation of the Clinical Demonstration of Child Abuse and Neglect.* Berkeley CA: January 22, 1982.

Berlin, Fred S. *Pedophilia: Diagnostic Concepts, Treatment and Ethical Considerations.* Baltimore MD: Department of Psychiatry and Behavioral Sciences, The Johns Hopkins University School of Medicine, undated.

Berlin, Fred S., and Melnecke, Carl F. "Treatment of Sex Offenders with Antiandrogenic Medication: Modalities and Preliminary Findings." *American Journal of Psychiatry,* May 1981.

Berliner, L. *Counseling and Follow-Up Interaction for the Sexually Abused Child.* Harborview Medical Center. Seattle WA: Sexual Assault Center, 1982.

_____. "Do Children Tell the Truth?" *Sexual Violence Quarterly,* Spring 1985.

_____. "Incest: Treatment and the Law." In *Proceedings of the First National Conference on Child Sexual Victimization.* Washington DC, November 29, 30, and December 1, 1979.

_____. "Some Issues for Prevention of Child Sexual Assault." Harborview Medical Center, Seattle WA. *Journal of Preventive Psychiatry,* Fall/Winter 1984. Berliner, a representative of the Harborview Center, discusses characteristics of sexual abuse cases reported to the center and their implications for professionals.

Berliner, L., and Stevens, D. *Advocating for Sexually Abused Children in the Criminal Justice System.* In Jones, Jenstrom, and MacFarlane, eds., *Sexual Abuse of Children: Selected Readings.* Washington DC: National Center on Child Abuse and Neglect, November 1980.

Bernard, F. *Degerolgen voor het Kind.* In van Eaten, P., ed., *Sex met Kinderen.* 1972.

Bernstien, G., and Ten Bensel, R. "Incest: Detection and Treatment by the Physician." *Minnesota Medical Journal,* 1977.

Berry, G. "Incest: Some Clinical Variations on a Classical Theme." *Journal of the American Academy of Psychoanalysis* 3, 1975.

*Berry, Joy. *Alerting Kids to the Danger of Sexual Abuse.* Waco TX: Word Educational Products, 1984. Designed for parents and teachers to read to children. Includes sections on private parts, sexual abusers, intercourse, guilt, and tricks that abusers use. Offers some good advice and deflates some popular myths.

*Berry, Joy, and McBride, Kathy. *A Parent's Guide to the Danger Zones.* Waco TX: Word, 1985.

Besharov, D. "Building a Community Response to Child Abuse and Maltreatment." *Children Today* 4, September-October 1975.

*Bessell, Harold; Bessell, Kelly; and Thomas, J. *The Parent Book: The Holistic Program for Raising the Emotionally Mature Child.* Sacramento CA: Jalmar, 1977.

Bettelheim, B. *The Uses of Enchantment.* New York: Vintage, 1977.

Bigras, J., et al. "On Disappointment and the Consequences of Incest in the Adolescent Girl." *Canadian Psychiatric Association Journal* 11, 1966.

Bigras, N. "The Biological Foundations of the Incest Taboo." *Social Science Information,* December 1972.

Blake-White, J., and Kline, C.M. "Treating the Dissociative Process in Adult Victims of Childhood Incest." Delta Mental Health Center, British Columbia. *Social Casework,* September 1985.

Blanchard, G. "Counseling the Sexually Addicted Incest Offender." *Protecting Children,* Fall 1985.

Bliss, J. *Prism: Andrea's World.* New York: Stein & Day, 1985.

Blose, J. *Sexual Abuse of Children in Massachusetts: Preliminary Study of System Response.* Boston: Statistical Analysis Center, 1979.

Bloxham, J. *The Chameleon.* London, England: 1884.

Blum, J., and Gray, S. *Strategies for Communicating with Young Children.* Presented at 16th Annual Child Abuse and Neglect Symposium, Keystone CO, 1987.

Blumberg, M. "Child Abuse: Ultimate in Maltreatment Syndromes." *New York Journal of Medicine,* March 1978.

Boatman, B.; Borkan, E.L.; and Schetky, D.H. "Treatment of Child Victims of Incest." Oregon University, Portland, Department of Psychiatry. *American Journal of Family Therapy,* Winter 1981.

*Boegehold, Betty. *You Can Say No.* Racine WI: Western, 1985. A storybook covering various potentially dangerous situations.

*Boocher, Dianna. *Rape: What Would You Do If. . .?* New York: 1981. Awareness and prevention for teenagers. Teaches how to avoid assault and how to survive if attacked.

Books, B. "Sexually Abused Children and Adolescent Identity Development." Jewish Board of Family and Children's Services. *New York American Journal of Psychotherapy,* July 1985.

Borgman, R. "Problems of Sexually Abused Girls and Their Treatment." Dobbs School, Kinston NC. *Social Casework: The Journal of Contemporary Social Work,* March 1984.

Borkin, J., and Frank, L. *Sexual Abuse Prevention for Preschoolers: A Pilot Program.* Cincinnati University, Ohio, School of Social Work, January/February 1986. Describes a project on primary prevention and early detection of child sexual abuse carried out in Cincinnati, 1983–1984.

Bosley, Jackson. "Treatment of Sex Offenders." *Sex Abuse Treatment Center Newsletter.* Honolulu HI: Kapiolani Children's Medical Center, 1982.

Boswell, John. *Christianity, Social Tolerance and Homosexuality.* 1980.

_____. *The Kindness of Strangers: The Abandonment of Children in Western Europe from Late Antiquity to the Renaissance.* New York: Pantheon.

Bradham, G.B. "The Establishment of a Treatment Center for Victims of Rape." South Carolina Medical University, Charleston Medical University Hospital. *Journal of the South Carolina Medical Association,* June 1981.

*Brady, K. *Father's Days.* New York: Seaview, 1979. A story of one victim of incest and how the act affected her life.

Brant, R. *Management of Families of Sexually Abused Children.* Harvard University, Department of Psychiatry, 1982.

Brant, R., and Tisza, V. "The Sexually Mis-Used Child." *American Journal of Ortho-psychiatry,* January 1977.

_____, and _____. "The Sexually Victimized Child." *RN* **43**, 1980.

Brassard, M., and Hart, S. *Emotional Abuse: Words Can't Hurt.* Chicago: National Committee for the Prevention of Child Abuse, 1987.

Brassard, M.R.; Tyler, A.H.; and Kehle, T.J. "School Programs to Prevent Intrafamilial Child Abuse." Utah University, Salt Lake City Department of Educational Psychology. *Child Abuse and Neglect,* 1983. Gives suggestions for starting programs for both children and parents. Discusses some programs that have been successful.

Brecker, E. *Treatment Programs for Sex Offenders.* National Institute for Law Enforcement and Criminal Justice System, Law Enforcement Assistance Administration, U.S. Department of Justice. Washington DC: Government Printing Office, January 1978.

Breer, William. *The Adolescent Molester.* 1987.

Brierel, John. *The Effects of Childhood Sexual Abuse on Late Psychological Functioning: Defining a Post-Sexual Abuse Syndrome.* Paper presented at the third National Conference on Sexual Victimization of Children, Children's Hospital, National Medical Center, Washington DC, April 1984.

*Briggs, Dorothy C. *Your Child's Self-Esteem.* Garden City NY: Doubleday, 1975. Author Briggs suggests that "it is the child's feeling about being loved or unloved that affects how he will develop" and that "helping children build high self-esteem is the key to successful parenthood."

British Association for the Study and Prevention of Child Abuse and Neglect. *Child Sexual Abuse.* Rochdale (England), July 1981.

Broadhurst, D.D. *The Educator's Role in the Prevention and Treatment of Child Abuse and Neglect.* Washington DC: Office of Human Development Services, September 1984. Manual for educators—one in a series based on the federal standards for child abuse and neglect prevention and treatment programs. Discusses reporting of cases; physical and behavioral indicators of abuse; and reasons for educators to become involved in prevention programs. Extensive bibliography.

Broadhurst, D.D.; Drews, R.; Ragan, C.K.; and Salus, M.R. *Family Violence Workshop.* Washington DC: Creative Associates, 1982.

Brongersma, Edward. "Aggression Against Pedophiles." *International Journal of Law and Psychiatry* **7**, 1984.

_____. *Homosexualiteit en Strafrecht.* 1971.

_____. *Sex en Straf.* 1976.

Brown, W. "Murder Rooted in Incest." In Masters, R.E.L., ed., *Patterns of Incest.* New York: Messner, 1963.

Browne, A., and Finkelhor, D. "The Impact of Child Sexual Abuse: A Review of the Research." *Psychological Bulletin* **99**, 1986.

Browning, D., and Boatman, B. "Incest: Children at Risk." *American Journal of Psychiatry* **134**, January 1977.

Brownmiller, S. *Against Our Will.* New York: Simon and Schuster, 1975.

Brunold, H. "Observations After Sexual Trauma Suffered in Childhood." *Excerpta Criminologia* **11**, 1964.

Buffiere, F. *Eros Adolescent.* 1980.

Bulkley, J. "Analysis of Civil Child Protection Statutes Dealing with Child Sexual Abuse." In Bulkley, J., ed., *Child Sexual Abuse and the Law.* Washington DC: American Bar Association, National Legal Resource Center for Child Advocacy and Protection, 1981.

_____. *Evidentiary and Procedural Trends in State Legislation and Other Emerging*

Legal Issues in Child Sexual Abuse Cases: A Paper Delivered to a Forum on Child Abuse of the National Council of Juvenile and Family Court Judges. Undated.

_____. "The Law and Child Sexual Abuse." In *Dealing with Child Sexual Abuse.* Chicago: National Committee for the Prevention of Child Abuse, 1982.

_____, ed. *Child Sexual Abuse and the Law.* Washington DC: American Bar Association. National Legal Resource Center for Child Advocacy and Protection, 1981.

_____, ed. *Innovations in the Prosecution of Child Sexual Abuse Cases.* Washington DC: American Bar Association, National Legal Resource Center for Child Advocacy and Protection, November 1981.

_____, ed. *Papers for a National Policy Conference on Legal Reforms in Child Sexual Abuse Cases.* Washington DC: American Bar Association, National Legal Resource Center on Child Advocacy and Protection, 1985.

_____, reporter. *Recommendations for Improving Legal Intervention in Intrafamily Child Sexual Abuse Cases.* Washington DC: American Bar Association, National Legal Resource Center for Child Advocacy and Protection, November 1981.

Bulkley, J., and Davidson, H. *Child Sexual Abuse—Legal Issues and Approaches.* Washington DC: American Bar Association, 1980.

*Bulkley, J.; Ensminger, J.; Fontana, V.J.; and Summit, R. *Dealing with Child Sexual Abuse.* Chicago: National Committee for Prevention of Child Abuse, 1982. Information about child sexual abuse from a number of different authors and perspectives, including legal, medical, social work, and psychotherapy issues.

Bullough, V., and Bullough, B. *Prostitution: An Illustrated Social History.* New York: Crown, 1978.

_____. *Sin, Sickness and Sanity.* New York: New American Library, 1977.

Burgess, A.W. "Intra-Familial Sexual Abuse." In Campbell, J., and Humphreys, J., eds., *Nursing Care of Victims of Family Violence.* Reston VA: Reston, 1984.

_____. *Research on the Use of Children in Pornography.* Paper presented at a Briefing on Child Pornography Projects funded by the National Center on Child Abuse and Neglect, Washington DC, December 18, 1982.

*_____. *The Sexual Victimization of Adolescents.* University of Pennsylvania, Philadelphia. Washington DC: Government Printing Office, 1985. Manual for helping professionals. Information on understanding adolescent sexual assault, identifying victims, preventing assault, and helping victims use support services. Good resource for school personnel, recreation directors, mental health workers.

_____, ed. *Child Pornography and Sex Rings.* Lexington MA: Lexington/ Heath, 1984.

Burgess, A.W., et al. *Comprehensive Examination for Child Sexual Assault: Diagnostic, Therapeutic and Child Protection Issues.* 1978.

*Burgess, A.W.; Groth, A.; Holmstrom, L.; and Sgroi, S. *Sexual Assault of Children and Adolescents.* Lexington MA: Lexington, 1978. Designed for professionals who work with victims or suspects.

Burgess, A.W., and Holmstrom, L. *Interviewing Young Victims, 1978. The Child and Family During Court Process, 1978.* (For additional information about the court process refer to *Child Protection: The Role of the Courts.* Department of Health and Human Services, Publication Number 80-30256, May 1980.)

_____, and _____. "Rape Trauma Syndrome." *American Journal of Psychiatry,* September 1974.

Burgess, A.W.; Holmstrom, L.L.; and McCausland, M.P. "Child Sexual Abuse by a Family Member: Decisions Following Disclosure." *Victimology: An International Journal* 2, Summer 1977.

_____; _____; and _____. *Counseling Young Victims and Their Families.* Chestnut Hill MA: Boston College, Department of Nursing, 1978. (Also contact St. Elizabeth's Hospital Psychodrama Department, Washington DC, for information about the training model and material developed for child protection workers.)

_____; _____; and _____. *Divided Loyalty in Incest Cases.* Chestnut Hill MA: Boston College, Department of Nursing, 1978.

Burgess, A.W., and McCausland, M. "Child Sex Initiation Rings." *American Journal of Orthopsychiatry* **51**, 1981.

Burgess, A.W.; McCausland, M.P.; and Wolbert, W.A. "Children's Drawings as Indicators of Sexual Trauma." Boston University, School of Nursing. *Perspectives in Psychiatric Care,* March-April 1981.

Burgoyne, M.A. "Treatment of Child Sexual Abuse." Southwest Psychotherapy Associates, Magnolia TX. Springfield IL: Thomas, 1985.

*Burn, H. *Better Than the Birds, Smarter Than the Bees: No-Nonsense Questions About Sex and Growing Up.* Arlington, 1969.

Burton, L. *Vulnerable Children.* London: Routledge and Kegan Paul, 1968.

Burton, R.F. *The Book of the Thousand Nights and a Night.* 1886.

*Buschman, J. *Strangers Don't Look Like the Big Bad Wolf.* Edmonds WA: Charles Franklin, 1985.

*Butler, S. *Conspiracy of Silence: The Trauma of Incest.* San Francisco: New Glide, 1978. Reports multiple cases of runaway children and male and female sexual abuse in San Francisco.

_____. "Thinking About Prevention: A Critical Look." In Nelson, M., and Clark, K., eds., *The Educator's Guide to Preventing Child Sexual Abuse.* Santa Cruz CA: Network, 1986.

Buxbaum, E. "Vulnerable Mothers, Vulnerable Babies." In Call, J.; Galenson, R.; and Tyson, R., eds., *Frontiers of Infant Psychiatry.* New York: Basic, 1983.

*Byerly, Carolyn. *The Mother's Book.* Dubuque IA: Kendall/Hunt, 1985. As the title suggests, this is a book for mothers whose children have been abused. Mainly concerned with father-daughter incest.

Calderone, M.S. "On the Possible Prevention of Sexual Problems in Adolescence." *Hospital and Community Psychiatry* **34**, 1983.

California Assembly Committee on Criminal Justice. *Child Molestation.* Pomona CA: November 12, 1980.

California Joint Committee for Revision of the Penal Code. *Hearing on Child Molestation.* Sacramento CA, December 16, 1980.

California State Department of Social Services. *Report to the Legislature. The Hidden Tragedy: A Report on the Santa Clara County Sexual Abuse Demonstration and Training Project.* Sacramento CA, August 1980.

Campbell, Robert. *Singularities Book I.* Amsterdam: Acolyte, 1989.

Canavan, J.W. *Sexual Child Abuse.* State University of New York, Buffalo, School of Medicine, 1980.

Canepa, G., and Bandini, T. "The Personality of Incest Victims." *International Criminal Police Review,* 1967.

Cantwell, H. "Sexual Abuse of Children in Denver, 1979: Reviewed with Implications for Pediatric Intervention and Possible Prevention." Denver General Hospital, Department of Pediatrics. *Child Abuse and Neglect* **5**, 1981.

_____. "Vaginal Inspection As It Relates to Child Sexual Abuse in Girls Under Thirteen." *Child Abuse and Neglect* **7**, 1983.

*Carlison, Dale. *Girls Are Equal Too.* New York: Atheneum, 1973.

Carlson, Allan C. "Family Abuse." *Reason,* May 1986.

Carnes, Patrick. *Out of the Shadows: Understanding Sexual Addiction.* Minneapolis: CompCare, 1983.

Carroll, C.A., and Gottlieb, B. *Sexual Abuse: Therapeutic and Systems Considerations for the Child and Family.* Colorado State Department of Social Services, Denver, Division of Family and Children Services, 1983.

Carter, H., and Glisk, P. *Marriage and Divorce.* Cambridge MA: Harvard University Press, 1976.

Caruso, P. "Pelvic Inflammatory Disease: Rare Sequels of Battered Child Syndrome." *New York Journal of Medicine,* 1975.

Cascade Child and Family S.T.E.P. Clinic. *Parents United: Child Incest Treatment Project: Final Report.* Portland OR, undated.

Cavallin, R. "Incestuous Fathers: A Clinical Report." *American Journal of Psychiatry* **122,** 1966.

Cavanaugh-Johnson, T. "Child Perpetrators: Children Who Molest Children." *Child Abuse and Neglect* **11,** 1987.

Cavara, M., and Ogren, C. "Protocol to Investigate Child Abuse in Foster Care." Hennepin County Community Services, Minneapolis MN. *Child Abuse and Neglect,* 1983.

*Cedar House Staff. *Aware Bears Activity Book.* Long Beach CA: Cedar House, 1984. Personal safety workbook for children. Three stories deal with abuse by strangers, uncomfortable touches from family members, and the importance of saying "no." Games and activities teach important concepts such as private areas of the body.

Chamberlin, Nan. *My Day at the Court House.* 1985.

Chandler, S. "Knowns and Unknowns in Sexual Abuse in Children." In Conte, J., and Shore, D., eds., *Social Work and Child Sexual Abuse/Journal of Social Work and Human Sexuality* **1,** January-February 1982.

Chapman, J., and Gates, M. *The Victimization of Women.* Beverly Hills CA: Sage, 1978.

Chase, D.H. "Caring for the Rape Victim." *Bulletin of the American Protestant Hospital Association,* 1977.

Chase, N. *A Child Is Being Beaten: Violence Against Children, An American Tragedy.* New York: Holt, Rinehart and Winston, 1975.

Check, W.A. "'Public Health Problem' of Violence Receives Epidemiologic Attention." *Journal of the American Medical Association,* August 16, 1985.

*Chetin, Helen. *Frances Ann Speaks Out: My Father Raped Me.* Stanford CA: New Seed, 1977. Written as a play. Tells the story of a victim abused by her stepfather from a very young age.

Child Abuse Prevention and Treatment Act (42 USC 5101) as amended by Public Law 98-457, 98th Congress, October 9, 1984.

Child Abuse Prevention Handbook. Sacramento: Crime Prevention Center, Office of the Attorney General of the State of California. General information on sexual and other physical abuse of children. Includes state penal codes on child abuse.

Child Abuse Research and Education Productions. *Trust Your Feelings.* 1984.

"Child Molesters and Rapists: Differences Highlighted." *Children and Teens in Crisis* **5,** no. 38 (April 1985).

"Child Pornography: Sickness for Sale." *Chicago Tribune,* May 15, 1977.

"Child Sex Victim: Social, Psychological and Legal Perspectives." *Child Welfare* **52,** 1973.

*Childhelp U.S.A. *No One Knew My Secret 'Til One Day.* Woodland Hills CA, 1983.

Childproof for Sexual Abuse. Yakima WA: Parent Education Center of Yakima,

1984. A book for parents. Gives suggestions for talking about sexual abuse at different age levels.

Children Helping Children. San Jose CA: Institute of the Community as Extended Family, San Jose CA, 1981. Booklet prepared by Daughters and Sons United, a self-help group for adults who were victims of sexual abuse in childhood.

"Children Who Are Victims of Sexual Assault and the Psychology of Offenders." *American Journal of Psychotherapy,* 1976.

*Children's Hospital National Medical Center. *A Message to Parents About: Child Sexual Abuse.* Washington DC: Child Sexual Abuse Victim Assistance Project, 1979. Advice and information for parents, covering definitions, behavioral changes in victims, suggestions for prevention, and what to expect from police, courts, and medical personnel.

_____. *Public Concern and Personal Action: Child Sexual Abuse.* Washington DC, 1980.

*Chlad, D. *Strangers.* Chicago: Childrens, 1984.

Christiansen, E., and Twohig, M. *Group Psychotherapy with Adolescent Incest Victims.* Sioux City IA: Catholic Charities, Nov. 17, 1979.

Chubb, R. *The Heavenly Cupid.* Newbury: Privately published, 1934.

Chutis, L. *Child Sexual Abuse Prevention Manual.* Chicago: Ravenwood Hospital Medical Center, undated. Written for the prevention program in Chicago schools. Includes lesson plans and teacher training suggestions. Information on abuse, such as definitions, myths, and characteristics, is included. Glossary of names of body parts and sexual processes.

Clark, A., and Bingham, J. "The Play Technique: Diagnosing the Sexually Abused Child." Child Protective Services, Fort Worth TX. *Tarrant County Physician,* August 1984.

Clark, K. *Sexual Abuse Prevention Education: An Annotated Bibliography.* Santa Cruz CA: Network, 1986.

Clements, Carl B., Ph.D. *Offender Needs Assessment.* College Park MD: Correctional Association (4321 Hartwick Rd., Suite L-208), 1986.

*Cleveland, D. *Incest: The Story of Three Women.* Lexington MA: Lexington, 1986. Describes the long-term effects of father-daughter incest in three victims' stories.

Cohan, M., and Friedman, S. "Nonsexual Motivations of Adolescent Sexual Behavior." *Medical Aspects of Human Sexuality,* September 1975.

Cohen, M., and Boucher, R. "Misunderstandings About Sex Criminals." *Sexual Behavior,* 1972.

Cohen, M., and Seghorn, T. "Sociometric Study of the Sex Offender." *Journal of Abnormal Psychology* 74, 1969.

Cohn, A.H. *Can We Prevent Child Abuse? Can We Prove We Prevent It?* Chicago: National Committee on Child Abuse, Summer 1984.

_____. *Testimony Presented by the National Committee for Prevention of Child Abuse.* Washington DC, 98th Congress, U.S. House of Representatives, Select Committee on Children, Youth and Families. Hearing, March 12, 1984.

Cohn, N. *Europe's Inner Demons.* New York: Basic, 1975.

Coigney, V. *Children Are People Too: How We Fail Our Children and How We Can Love Them.* New York: Morrow, 1975.

*Colao, Flora, and Hosansky, Tamar. *Your Children Should Know.* New York: Bobbs-Merrill, 1983. For parents and children. Emphasis on self-defense and ideas for spotting suspicious behavior and how to safely escape. An excellent "Children's Bill of Personal Safety Rights" is reproduced in the Question and Answer section. The authors suggest that if we present information correctly, in a nonalarming and practical way and on the child's intelligence level, children will be excited with this new knowledge.

Colby, C. "Mechanical Restraint of Masturbation in a Young Girl." *New York Medical Record* **52**, 1897. (Some advice: "Tie her arms to the bedposts.")

Coleman, P. *Incest: Family Treatment Model.* Tacoma WA: Child Protective Services, undated.

Collins, J.L.; Hamlin, W.T.; Minor, M.A.; and Knasel, A.L. "Incest and Child Sexual Abuse." Howard University Hospital, Washington DC. *Journal of the National Medical Association,* June 1982.

Colorado Department of Health. *The Epidemiology of Sexual Assault: A Review of the Literature.* Denver: 1983.

Colton, H. "How a Sex Counselor Brought Up Her Children." *The Osteopathy Physician,* May 1975.

Comfort, A. *The Anxiety Makers.* London: Nelson, 1967.

Comfort, R.L. "Sex, Strangers, and Safety." *Child Welfare,* September-October 1985. Article aimed at parents. Encourages them to provide early, developmentally appropriate instruction for their children regarding personal safety and sexual abuse prevention.

Committee for Children. *Personal Safety and Decision Making.* Seattle WA: Seattle Institute for Child Advocacy (172-20th Avenue, 98122), 1984.

_____. *Talking About Touching with Preschoolers.* Seattle WA: Seattle Institute for Child Advocacy. Companion to *Talking About Touching* (*see* Beland, K., and Van Dyke, G.).

Committee on Sexual Offences Against Children and Youths. *Sexual Offences Against Children. Volume 2.* Ottawa, Canada: Canadian Government Publishing Center, Supply and Services Canada, 1984.

Community Council of Greater New York. *Sexual Abuse of Children: Implications from the Sexual Trauma Treatment Program of Connecticut.* New York: April 1979.

Connecticut Division of Children and Protective Services. *Connecticut Children's Protection and Treatment Demonstration Programs. Final Report.* Hartford CT: undated. Supported by DHHS, Washington DC.

Connelly, M. *The Response to Prostitution in the Progressive Era.* Chapel Hill: University of North Carolina Press, 1980.

Constantine, L., and Martinson, F. *Children and Sex: New Findings, New Perspectives.* Boston: Little, Brown, 1981.

Conte, J. *The Effects of Sexual Abuse on the Child Victim and Its Treatment.* Presented at the Fourth Annual Symposium on Child Sexual Abuse. Huntsville AL, 1988.

_____. "The Effects of Sexual Victimization on Children: A Critique and Suggestions for Future Research." *Victimology: The International Journal,* 1984.

_____. "Evaluating Prevention Education Programs." In *The Educator's Guide to Preventing Child Sexual Abuse.* Santa Cruz CA: Network, 1986.

_____. *A Look at Child Sexual Abuse.* Chicago: National Committee for Prevention of Child Abuse. This booklet reviews and summarizes recent understanding of child abuse, including descriptions of an offender's motives and characteristics and a discussion of treatment and prevention efforts.

Conte, J.R., and Berliner, L. "The Impact of Sexual Abuse on Children: Empirical Findings." In *Handbook on Sexual Abuse of Children: Assessment and Treatment Issues.* New York: Springer, undated.

_____, and _____. "Prosecution of the Offenders in Cases of Sexual Assault Against Children." *Victimology: The International Journal* **6**, 1981.

_____, and _____. "Sexual Abuse of Children: Implications for Practice."

Chicago University, School of Social Services Administration. *Social Casework* **62**, December 1981.

Conte, J.R.; Rosen, C.; and Saperstein, L. *An Analysis of Programs to Prevent Victimization of Children*. Chicago: University of Chicago, School of Social Services Administration, Spring 1985.

Conte, J.R.; Rosen, C.; Saperstein, L.; and Shermack, R. "An Evaluation of a Program to Prevent the Sexual Victimization of Young Children." University of Chicago, School of Social Services Administration. *Child Abuse and Neglect* **9**, 1985. Examines the effects of sexual abuse prevention and children's ability to learn prevention techniques.

Conte, J.R., and Shore, D., eds. *Social Work and Child Sexual Abuse/Journal of Social Work and Human Sexuality* **1**, January-February 1982. For professionals who work with sexually abused children and their families.

Cook, M., and Howells, K. *Adult Sexual Interest in Children*. University College, Swansea (England). New York: Academic, 1981.

*Cooney, J. *Coping with Sexual Abuse*. New York: Rosen, 1987.

Cooper, I.K. "Decriminalization of Incest—New Legal-Clinical Responses." In Eekeaar, J.M., and Katz, S., eds., *Family Violence: An International and Interdisciplinary Study*. Toronto: Butterworths, 1978.

Cooper, S.; Lutter, Y.; and Phelps, C. *Strategies for Free Children—A Leader's Guide to Child Assault Prevention*. Women Against Rape. Columbus OH: Child Assault Prevention Project, 1983.

Cormier, B.; Kennedy, J.; and Sangowiez, J. "Psycho-Dynamics of Father-Daughter Incest." *Canadian Psychiatric Association Journal* **7**, 1962.

Corstjens, J.M.H. *Opvoeding en Pedofilie*. Netherlands, 1975.

Costell, R.M. *The Nature and Treatment of Male Sex Offenders*. Washington DC: George Washington University, School of Medicine, November 1980.

————. "The Nature and Treatment of Male Sex Offenders." In Jones, Jenstrom, and MacFarlane, eds., *Sexual Abuse of Children: Selected Readings*. Washington DC: National Center on Child Abuse and Neglect, November 1980.

Coult, A. "Causality and Cross-Sexual Prohibitions." *American Anthropologist*, 1963.

Council for Prevention of Child Abuse and Neglect. *Intra-Family Child Sexual Abuse Team. Final Report*. Lansing MI: December 26, 1983.

Courtois, C.A., and Watts, D. *Women Who Experienced Childhood Incest: Research Findings and Therapeutic Strategies*. College Park MD: Maryland University, September 1980.

Cramer, Robert E. "The District Attorney as a Mobilizer in a Community Approach to Child Sexual Abuse." In *Papers from a National Policy Conference on Legal Reforms in Child Sexual Abuse Cases*. Washington DC: National Legal Resource Center on Child Advocacy and Protection, 1985.

Crawford, David A., and Allen, Judith V. "A Social Skills Training Program with Sex Offenders." In Cook, M., and Wilson, G., eds., *Love and Attraction: An International Conference*. Oxford, England: Pergamon, 1979.

Creative Associates. *Navy Family Advocacy. Training Project: Final Report*. Washington DC: December 1982.

"Crime in California." *Time* Magazine, March 2, 1953.

Crisci, G.A. *Personal Safety Curriculum: Prevention of Child Sexual Abuse. Pre-School Through Grade 6*. North Hampton MA: Franklin Hampshire Community Health Center, 1983. Curriculum produced from a study of prevention education among rural and Hispanic children. Grade-appropriate lesson materials from pre-school through grade 6 are included, as are pre- and post-tests. Lists names, addresses, and phones of six prevention projects in the United States. Spanish-language version available.

Crisci, G.A.; Kent, C.A.; Plummer, C.; and Olsen, M. *Prevention of Sexual Abuse by Working with Children.* Workshop presented at the Sixth Annual National Conference on Child Abuse and Neglect, Baltimore MD: September 25–28, 1983.

Crisci, G.A., and Torres, M.I. "Child Sexual Abuse Prevention Project in an Hispanic Community." In *The Educator's Guide to Preventing Child Sexual Abuse.* Santa Cruz CA: Network, 1986. This project used a "train-the-trainer" approach in a school-based prevention project for Hispanic children of migrant workers in western Massachusetts. Cultural differences, particularly Hispanic values relating to the family and to privacy, were given careful attention in the research design.

*Cross, Laurella. *Jenny's New Game: A Guide for Parents to Protect Your Children Against Kidnapping.*

*Cultural Information Service. *TV Alert—Something About Amelia.* Bulletin prepared by the Cultural Information Service, P.O. Box 786, Madison Square Station, New York NY 10159, January 9, 1984.

Currier, R. "Debunking the Double Think on Juvenile Sexuality." *Human Behavior,* September 1977.

Dabney, M. *Incest Annotated Bibliography: Offenders, Victims, Families, Treatment Programs.* Eugene: Oregon University, 1982.

Dailey, D.M. *Services to Sexual Abuse Families: Restructuring Attitudes and Perspectives.* Kansas University, Lawrence, School of Social Welfare. Ann Arbor MI: Undated.

Dale, P.; Waters, J.; Davies, M.; Roberts, W.; and Morrison, T. "The Towers of Silence: Creative and Destructive Issues for Therapeutic Teams Dealing with Sexual Abuse." Jacob Brights' Children's Center, Rochdale, England, N.S.P.C.C. Child Protection Team. *Journal of Family Therapy,* February 1986.

Daley, M. "Burnout—Smoldering Problem in Protective Services." *Social Services,* September 1979.

Daro, D. *Confronting Child Abuse: Theory, Policy and Program.* New York: Free Press, 1988.

Dasberg, L. *Grootbrengen door Kleinhouden.* 1975.

Daugherty, Lynn B. *Why Me? Help for Victims of Child Sexual Abuse.* Racine WI: Mother Courage, 1984.

Daughters and Sons United. *Children Helping Children: Daughters and Sons United. Help for Sexually Abused Children and Their Families.* San Jose CA: April 1, 1981.

Davidson, H. *Child Sexual Exploitation Background and Legal Analysis: A Monograph.* Washington DC: American Bar Association, National Legal Resource Center for Child Advocacy and Child Protection, undated.

_____. *Protection of Children Through Criminal History Record Screening: Well-Meaning Promises and Legal Pitfalls.* Washington DC: American Bar Association, National Legal Resource Center for Child Advocacy and Protection, Spring 1985.

Davidson, H., and Bulkley, J. *Child Sexual Abuse—Legal Issues and Approaches.* Washington DC: American Bar Association, National Legal Resource Center for Child Advocacy and Protection, October 1980.

Davies, R. "Incest and Vulnerable Children." *Science News* 116, 1978.

Davis, I.L. "The Role of the Teacher in Preventing Child Sexual Abuse." In Nelson, M., and Clark, K., eds., *The Educator's Guide to Preventing Child Sexual Abuse.* Santa Cruz CA: Network, 1986.

Dawson, R. "Therapeutic Intervention with Sexually Abused Children." *Journal of Child Care,* 1984.

*Dayee, F.S. *Private Zone. A Book Teaching Children Sexual Assault Prevention Tools.* Edmonds WA: Charles Franklin, 1982. A "read-aloud" story book covering the concept of a child's right to say "no" and teaching the child how to get help. Does not deal with developing intuitive skills. Appropriate for ages 3–9.

*DeAlcorn, Susan. *Source Book for Educators: Sexual Assault Prevention for Adolescents.* Tacoma WA: Pierce Co. Rape Relief (Allenmore Medical Center, 19th and Union, 98405).

Dean, K.S., and Gentry, C.E. *Project Against Sexual Abuse of Appalachian Children: Final Report.* Washington DC: National Center on Child Abuse and Neglect, June 1, 1983.

Deaton, F.A., and Sandlin, D.L. "Sexual Victimology Within the Home: A Treatment Approach." Portsmouth (VA) Psychiatric Center. *Victimology,* 1980.

De Beauvoir, S. *The Second Sex.* New York: Bantam, 1953.

DeCourcy, P. *A Silent Tragedy: Child Abuse in the Community.* Alfred, 1973.

DeFrancis, V. "Protecting the Child Victim of Sex Crimes." *Children Today,* July-August 1976.

_____. *Protecting the Child Victim of Sex Crimes.* Denver: American Humane Association, Children's Division, 1965.

_____. *Protecting the Child Victim of Sex Crimes Committed by Adults: Final Report.* Denver: American Humane Association, Children's Division, 1969.

_____. *Protective Services and Community Expectations.* Denver: American Humane Association, Children's Division.

DeHohn, Allen R. "Letter to the Editor." *Child Abuse & Neglect* 9, 1985.

Deighton, J., and McPeek, P. "Group Treatment: Adult Victims of Childhood Sexual Abuse." Children's Aid Society, Detroit MI, Emergency Foster Care. *Social Casework,* September 1985.

Deisher, R.W.; Wenet, G.A.; Paperny, D.M.; Clark, T.F.; and Fehrenback, P.A. "Adolescent Sexual Offense Behavior: The Role of the Physician." *Journal of Adolescent Health Care* 2, 1982.

DeJong, A.R. "Epidemiologic Factors in Sexual Abuse of Boys." *American Journal of Diseases of Children* 136, November 1982.

_____. *Predictors of Depression in Sexually Abused Children.* Paper presented before the Society for Developmental and Behavioral Pediatrics First Annual Meeting, Washington DC, May 4, 1983.

_____. "Sexual Abuse of Children." *American Journal of Diseases of Children* 36, February 1982.

Delson, N., and Clark, M. "Group Therapy with Sexually Molested Children." Children's Home Society of California, Eureka. *Child Welfare,* March 1981.

DeMause, L. *The History of Childhood.* New York: Psychohistory, 1974.

_____. "Our Forebearers Made Childhood a Nightmare." *Psychology Today,* April 1975.

DeMontesquieu. *De L'esprit des Lois.* 1748.

DeMott, B. "The Pro-Incest Lobby." *Psychology Today* 13, 1980.

DePanfilis, Diane. *Literature Review of Sexual Abuse.* Washington DC: Clearinghouse on Child Abuse and Neglect Information, August 1986. Excellent overview.

Devereaux, G. *The Social and Cultural Implications of Incest Among the Mojave Indians."* Psychoanalytic Quarterly, 1939.

DeVine, R.A. *Incest: A Review of the Literature.* Children's Hospital National Medical Center, Washington DC, Department of Ambulatory Medicine, November 1980.

_____. "Sexual Abuse of Children: An Overview of the Problem." In Jones,

Jenstrom, and MacFarlane, eds., *Sexual Abuse of Children: Selected Readings.* Washington DC: National Center on Child Abuse and Neglect, November 1980.

_____. *Sexual Abuse — Who Cares?* Children's Hospital National Medical Center, Washington DC, Department of Pediatrics, 1977. Discusses common myths and assumptions about sexual abuse, and offers suggestions for reducing the incidence of abuse.

de Young, M. "Case Reports: The Sexual Exploitation of Incest Victims by Helping Professionals." *Victimology,* 1982.

_____. *Child Molestation: An Annotated Bibliography.* Jefferson NC and London: McFarland, 1987.

_____. *Incest: An Annotated Bibliography.* Jefferson NC and London: McFarland, 1985.

_____. "Incest: The Broken Taboo." *Wonderland,* March 9, 1980.

_____. "Incest Victims and Offenders: Myths and Realities." *Journal of Psychosocial Nursing and Mental Health Services* **19,** 1981.

_____. "Innocent Seducer or Innocently Seduced? The Role of the Child Incest Victim." *Journal of Clinical Child Psychology* **11,** 1982.

_____. "Promises, Threats and Lies: Keeping Incest Secret." *Journal of Humanics* **9,** 1981.

_____. "Self-Injurious Behavior in Incest Victims: A Research Note." *Child Welfare* **61,** November-December 1982.

*_____. *The Sexual Victimization of Children.* Jefferson NC and London: McFarland, 1982. Discusses incest and pedophilia, using studies of victims, suspects, and non-participating family members. Excellent and highly recommended.

_____. "Siblings of Oedipus: Brothers and Sisters of Incest Victims." *Child Welfare* **60,** 1981.

Diagnostic and Statistical Manual of Mental Disorders. 3rd edition. Washington DC: American Psychiatric Association, 1980.

Dietz, C., and Craft, J. "Family Dynamics of Incest: A New Perspective." *Social Casework* **61,** 1980.

Dietz, Park Elliot. "Sex Offenses: Behavioral Aspects." In Kadish, S.H., et al., eds., *Encyclopedia of Crime and Justice.* New York: Free Press, 1983.

_____. "Victim Consequences and Their Control." *Victimology: An International Journal* **7,** 1982.

Dill, D.L. *Victim Advocacy as Therapy.* Copper County Mental Health Center, Hancock MI. Lexington MA: Lexington/Heath, 1984.

Dillingham, J.W., and Melmed, E.C. *Child Pornography: A Study of the Social Sexual Abuse of Children.* Paper presented at a briefing on child pornography projects in Washington DC, December 18, 1982.

Dixon, K., et al. "Father-Son Incest: Under-Reported Psychiatric Problem?" *American Journal of Psychiatry* **135,** 1978.

Dolan, E. *Child Abuse.* New York: Watts, 1980.

Donaldson, M.A. *Incest, Years After: Putting the Pain to Rest.* Fargo ND: Village Family Service Center, 1983.

Donaldson, M.A., and Gardner, R. "Diagnosis and Treatment of Traumatic Stress Among Women After Childhood Incest." In Figley, C.R., ed., *Trauma and Its Wake: The Study and Treatment of Post-Traumatic Stress Disorders.* New York: Bruhner/Mazel, 1985.

Donnely, Robert T. "Teaching Basic Morality to Juveniles." In *Juvenile and Family Court Journal,* February 1983.

Donovan, H., and Beran. "Sexual Child Abuse: The Psychotherapist and the Team

Concept." In *Dealing with Sexual Child Abuse*. Chicago: National Committee for the Prevention of Child Abuse, 1978.

Dover, K.J. *Greek Homosexuality*. 1976.

Downer, A. "Training Teachers to Be Partners in Prevention." In Nelson, M., and Clark, K., eds., *The Educator's Guide to Preventing Child Sexual Abuse*. Santa Cruz CA: Network, 1986. Discusses problems in implementing school-based prevention programs and offers suggestions for overcoming them. Includes suggestions for effective teacher training.

*_____. *Personal Safety and Decision Making*. Seattle WA: Committee for Children (P.O. Box 51049, 98115).

*Drake, E., and Gilroy, A. *Getting Together, Helping You to Help Yourself*. Gainesville FL: Child Care (P.O. Box 12024, University Station, 32604), 1983. Booklet answering questions for girls (4th grade and older) who have been sexually abused.

Drake, Elizabeth D., and Gilroy, Anne, with Raone, Thomas H. *Working Together: A Team Effort*. 1986.

Dreikurs, R. *Coping with Children's Misbehavior*. New York: Hawthorn, 1972.

Drews, K., and Hall, I. *Workers Burnout in Child Protective Services*. National Professional Resource Center for Child Abuse and Neglect.

Dudar, H. "America Discovers Pornography." *MS* Magazine, August 1977.

Dutile, Fernand; Forest, Cleon H.; and Webster, D., eds., *Early Childhood Intervention and Juvenile Delinquency*. 1982.

Eaddy, V., and Gentry, C. "Use of Play in Interviewing Abused/Neglected Children." *Public Welfare*, 1981.

Ebel, H. "The Evolution of Childhood Reconsidered." *Journal of Psychohistory* 5, 1977.

Eberle, Paul, and Eberle, Shirley. *The Politics of Child Abuse*. Secaucus NJ: Lyle Stuart, 1986.

Edwards, L. *Dealing with Parent and Child in Serious Abuse Cases*. Institute for the Community as Extended Family, undated.

Eist, H.I., and Mandel, A.U. "Family Treatment of Ongoing Incest Behavior." Minnesota University, Minneapolis, Department of Psychiatry. *Family Process* 7, 1968.

Elias, A., and Brangale, R. *The Psychology of Sex Offenders*. Springfield IL: Thomas, 1956.

Elias, J., and Gebhard, P. "Sexuality and Sexual Learning in Childhood." *Phi Delta Kappan*, 1969. Also in D. Taylor, ed., *Human Sexual Development*. Philadelphia: Davis, 1970.

Ellerstein, N.S., and Canavan, J.W. "Sexual Abuse of Boys." *American Journal of Diseases of Children* 134, 1980.

Ellis, A. *The Encyclopedia of Sexual Behavior*. New York: Hawthorn, 1961.

Elmer, E. *Children in Jeopardy: A Study of Abused Minors and Their Families*. Pittsburgh: University of Pittsburgh Press, 1967.

_____. *Fragile Families, Troubled Children: The Aftermath of Infant Trauma*. Pittsburgh: University of Pittsburgh Press, 1977.

Emmerman, L. "Children Abusing Children: Victims Becoming Victimizers." *Chicago Tribune*, "Tempo," January 27, 1985.

Emslie, G., and Rosenfeld, A. "Incest Reported by Children and Adolescents Hospitalized for Severe Psychiatric Problems." *American Journal of Psychiatry* 140, June 1983.

Ensminger, J. *Sexual Child Abuse and the Social Worker*. Philadelphia: Joseph J. Peters Institute, 1982.

The Epidemiology of Sexual Assault: A Review of the Literature. Denver: Colorado Department of Health, 1983. A study examining the extent of sexual abuse. Includes some characteristics of the victim and the suspect and some indications of the short and long-term results of assault.

Erickson, E.L.; McEvoy, A.W.; and Colucci, N.D. *Child Abuse and Neglect: A Guidebook for Educators and Community Leaders.* 2nd edition. Holmes Beach FL: Learning, 1984. Encourages school involvement in prevention education and the provision of protective services. Recommendations for school policies on reporting are included, along with guidelines for identifying possible victims of abuse. Prevention-oriented activities are described.

Eskin, M. *Child Abuse and Neglect: A Literature Review and Selected Bibliography.* Washington DC: U.S. Department of Justice, National Institute of Justice, 1980.

Evans, S.; Schaffer, S.; and Sterne, M. *Sexual Victimization Patterns of Recovering Chemically Dependent Women.* Paper presented at International Institute on Prevention and Treatment of Alcoholism, Athens, Greece, May 1984.

*Ezrine, Linda. *Anna's Secret.* Baltimore MD: Spector, 1985. Story shows family's reaction when Anna tells that a young male babysitter has been abusing her.

Faehl, L., and Hughes, D. *Short-Term Groups as an Intervention with Sexually Abused Adolescents.* Rap Hours/Oasis House, Nashville TN. Practice Application, St. Louis MO. Center for Adolescent Mental Health. Winter 1984.

Fagan, J. "New Evidence Links Multiple Personalities to Child Abuse." *Children and Teens in Crisis* 4, June 1984.

Faller, K.C. *Evaluation of a Sexual Abuse Treatment Program.* University of Michigan, Ann Arbor, School of Social Work. June 1979.

Farber, Edward D.; Showers, Jacy; Johnson, Charles F.; Joseph, Jack A.; and Oshins, Linda. "The Sexual Abuse of Children: A Comparison of Male and Female Victims." *Journal of Clinical Child Psychology* 13, 1984.

Faria, G., and Belochavek, N. *Treating Female Adult Survivors of Childhood Incest.* Kansas University, Lawrence, School of Social Welfare Casework, October 1984.

Farson, R. *Birthrights: A Bill of Rights for Children.* New York: Free Press, 1974.

Fast, I., and Cain, A. "The Stepparent Role: Potential for Disturbances in Family Functioning." *American Journal of Orthopsychiatry* 36, 1960.

Fay, J. "Guidelines for Selecting Prevention Education Resources." In Nelson, M., and Clark, K., eds., *The Educator's Guide to Preventing Child Sexual Abuse.* Santa Cruz CA: Network, 1986.

*_____. *He Told Me Not to Tell.* Renton WA: King County Rape Relief (305 South 43rd, 98055), 1979. Suggestions for parents or teachers on how to talk to children about sexual abuse, how to instill survival skills, and what to do if it is learned that a child has been abused.

*Fay, J.J., and Flerchinger, B.J. *Top Secret. Sexual Assault for Teenagers Only.* Renton WA: King County Rape Relief, 1982. Provides information about all forms of sexual assault, including incest and "date rape." Questions and answers, stories and a varied format. Appropriate for junior high and high school students. Teachers' discussion guide is also available; see Flerchinger, B.J., and Fay, J.J.

Fein, E., and Lyon, E. *Child Sexual Abuse.* Hartford CT: Child and Family Services, September 1983.

Fein, E.; Bander, K.; and Bishop, G. *Child Sex Abuse Treatment: The Intricacies of Program Operation.* Hartford CT: Child and Family Services, Research Department, April 21–25, 1981.

Feldman, E. "Prostitution, the Alien Woman and the Progressive Imagination: 1910–1915." *American Quarterly* 19, 1967.

Fellman, R., and Fellman, M. "The Role of Moderation in Late 19th Century American Sexual Ideology." *Journal of Sex Research* 17, 1981.

Field, L.H., and Williams, Mark. "A Note on the Scientific Assessment and Treatment of the Sexual Offender." *Medicine, Science and the Law*, October 1971.

Finch, S. "Sexual Abuse by Mothers." *Medical Aspects of Human Sexuality* 7, 1973.

_____. "Sexual Activity of Children with Other Children and Adults." *Clinical Pediatrics*, 1967.

Finkelhor, D. "Abusers: Special Topics." University of New Hampshire, Durham, Family Violence Research Program. In Finkelhor, D., et al., *A Sourcebook on Child Sexual Abusers*. Beverly Hills CA: Sage, 1986.

*_____. *Child Sexual Abuse: New Theory and Research*. New York: Free Press, 1984. Also suggests possibilities for future studies.

_____. *Child Sexual Abuse in a Sample of Boston Families*. Unpublished report. April 19, 1982. Available from Family Violence Research Program, University of New Hampshire, Durham, 03824.

_____. *Designing Studies on the Impact and Treatment of Child Sexual Abuse*. Unpublished paper, 1984.

_____. "How Widespread Is Child Sexual Abuse?" *Perspectives on Child Maltreatment in the Mid 80's*. Washington DC: National Center on Child Abuse and Neglect, 1984.

_____. "Implications for Theory, Research and Practice." In Nelson, M., and Clark, K., eds., *The Educator's Guide to Preventing Child Sexual Abuse*. Santa Cruz CA: Network, 1986.

_____. "Initial and Long-Term Effects: A Review of the Research." In Finkelhor, D., et al., *A Sourcebook on Child Sexual Abuse*. Beverly Hills CA: Sage, 1986.

_____. "Prevention: A Review of Programs and Research." University of New Hampshire, Durham, Family Violence Research Program. In Finkelhor, D., et al., *A Sourcebook on Child Sexual Abuse*. Beverly Hills CA: Sage, 1986.

_____. "Removing the Child—Prosecuting the Offender in Cases of Sexual Abuse: Evidence from the National Reporting System for Child Abuse and Neglect." University of New Hampshire, Durham, Family Violence Research Program. *Child Abuse and Neglect* 7, 1983.

_____. "Risk Factors in the Sexual Victimization of Children." In Finkelhor, D., *Sexually Victimized Children*. New York: Free Press, 1979.

_____. "Risk Factors in the Sexual Victimization of Children." *Child Abuse and Neglect*, 1980.

_____. "Sex Among Siblings: A Survey on Prevalence, Variety and Effects." *Archives of Sexual Behavior* 9, 1980.

_____. "Sexual Abuse and Physical Abuse: Some Critical Differences." University of New Hampshire, Durham, Family Research Laboratory. In Newberger, E.H., and Bourns, R., eds., *Unhappy Families*. Littleton MA: PSG, 1985.

*_____. *Sexually Victimized Children*. New York: Free Press, 1979.

_____. "What's Wrong with Sex Between Adults and Children: Ethics and the Problem of Sexual Abuse." *American Journal of Orthopsychiatry*, October 1979.

Finkelhor, D., et al. *The Dark Side of Families: Current Family Violent Research*. Beverly Hills CA: Sage, 1983.

Finkelhor, D., and Araji, S. *The Prevention of Child Sexual Abuse: A Review of Current Approaches*. Unpublished paper. Prepared for the National Center for Prevention and Control of Rape, December 1983.

_____, and _____. "Explanations of Pedophilia: Review of Empirical Research." *Bulletin of the American Academy of Psychiatry and the Law*, 1985.

Finkelhor, D.; Araji, S.; Baron, L.; Brounce, A.; and Peters, S.D. *A Sourcebook on Child Sexual Abuse*. Beverly Hills CA: Sage, 1986.

Finkelhor, D., and Browne, A. "The Traumatic Impact of Child Sexual Abuse: A Conceptualization." *American Journal of Orthopsychiatry* **55**, October 1985.

Finkelhor, D., and Carson, B. "The Scope of Contemporary Social and Domestic Violence." In Warner, C., and Braen, G.R., eds., *Management of the Physically and Emotionally Abused.* Norwalk CT: Appleton-Century-Crofts, 1982.

Finkelhor, D., and Hotaling, G. "Sexual Abuse in the National Incidence Study of Child Abuse and Neglect: An Appraisal." *Child Abuse and Neglect* **8**, 1984.

Fisher, B.; Berdie, J.; Cook, J.; and Day, N. *Adolescent Abuse and Neglect— Intervention Strategies.* San Francisco: Urban and Rural Systems Associates, January 1980.

Fisher, G. "Psychological Needs of Heterosexual Pedophiliacs." *Diseases of the Nervous System* **30**, 1969.

Fleck, S., et al. "The Interfamilial Environment of the Schizophrenic Patient." In Masserman, J., ed., *Science and Psychoanalysis. Vol. 2.* New York: Grune and Stratton, 1959.

Fleming, K., and Fleming, A. *The First Time.* New York: Simon and Schuster, 1975.

Flerchinger, B.J., and Fay, J.J. *Top Secret: A Discussion Guide.* King County Rape Relief, Renton WA. Santa Cruz CA: Network, 1985. Teachers' guide to using *Top Secret (see* Fay, J.J., and Flerchinger, B.J.) in the classroom. Includes discussion points and classroom exercises.

Fontana, V. *Maltreated Child: The Maltreatment Syndrome in Children.* Springfield IL: Thomas, 1964, 1971.

————. "Sexual Abuse of Children." In *Dealing with Child Sexual Abuse.* Chicago: National Committee for the Prevention of Child Abuse, 1982.

————. "Sexual Child Abuse and the Medical Professional." In *Dealing with Sexual Child Abuse.* Chicago: National Committee for the Prevention of Child Abuse, 1982.

————. *Somewhere a Child Is Crying: Maltreatment: Causes and Prevention.* New York: New American Library, 1983.

————. "When Systems Fail: Protecting the Victim of Child Sexual Abuse." *Children Today,* July-August 1984.

Fontana, V., and Besharov, D. *The Maltreated Child: The Maltreatment Syndrome in Children—A Medical, Legal and Social Guide.* 4th edition. Springfield IL: Thomas, 1979.

Ford, C. *Child Sexual Abuse.* October 1985.

Ford, C., and Beach, F. *Patterns of Sexual Behavior.* New York: Harper and Row, 1951.

Forgione, R. "The Use of Mannequins in the Behavioral Assessment of Child Molesters: Two Case Reports." *Behavior Therapy* **7**, 1976.

Forseth, L.B., and Brown, A. "A Survey of Intrafamilial Sexual Abuse Treatment Centers: Implications for Intervention." Family Support Center, Salt Lake City UT. *Child Abuse and Neglect,* 1981.

*Fortune, M.M. *Sexual Abuse Prevention: A Study for Teenagers.* Center for the Prevention of Sexual and Domestic Violence, Seattle WA. New York: United Church Press, 1984. Five-session course teaches prevention techniques. Films accompany sessions 2 and 5.

*————. *Sexual Violence: The Unmentionable Sin.* Mount Dera FL: Kidsrights, 1983. For pastors and congregations. Discusses social and religious perspectives on sexual abuse and offers suggestions for counseling and supporting victims.

Fortune, R. *Incest.* In Seligman, E., ed., *Encyclopedia of Social Sciences. Vol. 7.* London, England: MacMillan, 1952.

*Forward, S., and Buch, C. *Betrayal of Innocence: Incest and Its Devastation.* Van

Nuys Psychiatric Hospital CA. Los Angeles CA: Tarcher, 1978. Uses case histories and discusses the many different types of incestuous relationships.

Foster, H.H., and Freed, J.J. "A Bill of Rights for Children." *Family Law Quarterly* **6**, 1972.

Fowler, C.; Burns, S.R.; and Roehl, J.E. "Counseling the Incest Offender." Center Against Sexual Assault, Phoenix AZ. *International Journal of Family Therapy*, Summer 1983.

————, ————, and ————. "The Role of Group Therapy in Incest Counseling." Center Against Sexual Assault, Phoenix AZ. *International Journal of Family Therapy*, Summer 1983.

Fox, J. "Sibling Incest." *British Journal of Sociology* **13**, 1962.

Fradkin, A. "Incest in Middle Class Differs from That Processed by Police." *Clinical Psychiatric Newsletter*, 1974.

Fraiburg, S.; Adelson, E.; and Shapiro, V. "Ghosts in the Nursery: Psychoanalytic Approach to the Problems of Impaired Infant-Mother Relationships." In Fraiburg, S.C., ed., *Clinical Studies in Infant Mental Health: The First Year of Life.* New York: Basic, 1980.

Frances, V., and Frances, A. "The Incest Taboo and Family Structure." *Family Process*, 1976.

Fraser, M. "The Child." In Taylor, B., ed., *Perspectives on Paedophilia.* London: Batsford Academic and Educational, 1981.

Frederich, W.N.; Urquiza, A.J.; and Beilke, R. "Behavioral Problems in Sexually Abused Young Children." *Journal of Pediatric Psychology*, 1986.

*Freeman, L. *It's My Body.* Seattle WA: Parenting, 1982. A book for helping the very young child be aware of the right to say "no" to uncomfortable touches. Appropriate for pre-schoolers. For a parents' companion book, see Hart-Rossi, J.

Freeman, Lucy, with Laura White. "Shattered Innocents: Incest — The Mother's Story." *Penthouse,* December 1989.

Friedman, Kenneth; Bischoff, Helen; Davis, Robert; and Person, Andresa. *Victims and Helpers: Reactions to Crimes.* Washington DC: U.S. Department of Justice, National Institute of Justice, May 1982.

Friedman, Virginia, and Morgan, Marcia. *Interviewing Sexual Abuse Victims Using Anatomical Dolls.* Eugene OR: Migima Designs, 1985.

Friedman, Z.; O'Donnell, J.; Secret, T.; and Erne, D. *Discussion Guide for Interviewing the Incestuous Family.* Curriculum developed for the New York State Department of Social Services Statewide Training for Law Enforcement and Children's Protective Services. Undated.

Freud, E.; Freud, L.; and Grubrich-Simitis. *Sigmund Freud: His Life in Pictures and Words.* New York and London: 1978.

Freud, S. *The Origins of Psycho-Analysis: Letters to Wilholm Fliess: Drafts and Notes 1887–1902.* New York: 1954.

————. *Three Essays on the Theory of Sexuality.* New York: Basic, 1962.

————. *Totem and Taboo.* London: Routledge and Kegan Paul, 1924.

Freund, K., et al. "Males Disposed to Commit Rape." *Archives of Sexual Behavior* **15**, 1986.

Fuchs, E. *Illustrierte Sittengeschichte — Renaissance.* 1909.

Furniss, T. "Mutual Influence and Interlocking Professional — Family Process in the Treatment of Child Sexual Abuse and Incest." Hospital for Sick Children, London, Department of Psychological Medicine. *Child Abuse and Neglect*, 1983.

Gagnon, J. "Female Child Victims of Sexual Offences." *Social Problems*, Fall 1965.

————. *Human Sexualities.* Glenview IL: Scott, Foresman, 1977.

_____. "Sexuality and Sexual Learning in the Child." *Psychiatry* **28**, no. 3, 1965.

Gagnon, J., and Simon, W. *Sexual Conduct: The Social Sources of Human Sexualities.* Chicago: Aldine, 1973.

Galambos, N., and Dixon, R. "Adolescent Abuse and the Development of Personal Sense of Control." *Child Abuse and Neglect* **8**, 1984.

Gale, N. *Child Sexual Abuse in Native American Communities.* National American Indian Court Judges Association, Washington DC. Boulder CO: National Indian Law Library, August 1985. Includes discussion of family and social factors contributing to the risk of abuse, and takes into consideration the special problems and resources of the American Indian community.

Gallagher, V. *Speaking Out, Fighting Back: Personal Experiences of Women Who Survived Childhood Sexual Abuse in the Home.* Seattle WA: Madrona, 1985.

Garberino, A., and Garberino, J. *Emotional Maltreatment of Children.* Chicago: National Committee for Prevention of Child Abuse, 1980.

Garberino, J., and Stocking, S., with Collins, A., et al. *Protecting Children from Abuse and Neglect: Developing and Maintaining Effective Support Systems for Families.* San Francisco: Jossey-Bass, 1980.

Garrett, T., and Wright, R. "Wives of Rapists and Incest Offenders." *Journal of Sex Research,* May 1975.

The Gay Commission. International Marxist Group. *Our Line on Paedophilia.* Internal discussion document, 1979.

Gaylin, W. "The Competency of Children: No Longer All or None." *The Hennings Center Report* **12**, 1982.

Gebhard, O.; Gagnon, J.; Pomeroy, W.; and Christenson, C. *Sex Offenders: An Analysis of Types.* New York: Harper, 1965.

Geiser, R. *Children Victims.* Boston: Beacon, 1979.

*_____. *Hidden Victims: The Sexual Abuse of Children.* Nazareth Child Care Center, Boston, Department of Psychology. Boston: Beacon, 1979. Includes discussion of incest, pornography, obscenity, and prostitution. Specifically covers both male and female abuse.

Geiser, R., and Norberta, Sister M. "Sexual Disturbance in Young Children." *American Journal of Child Nursing,* May-June 1976.

Gelinas, Denise J. "The Persisting Negative Effects of Incest." *Psychiatry,* November 1983.

Gentry, C.E. "Child Abuse: How Can We Stop It?" Tennessee Department of Human Services. *The Record,* March 1977.

_____. "Incestuous Abuse of Children: The Need for an Objective View." Child and Family Services, Knoxville TN. *Child Welfare,* June 1978. Reviews responses of the victim, the offender, and the family. Stresses that societal attitudes toward incest hinder effective prevention and treatment, and urges that such attitudes be changed.

Gerbner, G., et al. *Child Abuse: An Agenda for Action.* New York: Oxford University Press, 1980.

Giarretto, H. "A Comprehensive Child Sexual Abuse Treatment Program." Institute for the Community as Extended Family, San Jose CA. *Child Abuse and Neglect,* 1982.

_____. "A Comprehensive Child Sexual Abuse Treatment Program." In Mrazek, P.B., and Kempe, C.H., eds., *Sexually Abused Children and Their Families.* New York: Pergamon, 1981.

_____. "Humanistic Treatment of Father-Daughter Incest." In Helfer, R.E., and Kempe, C.H., eds., *Child Abuse and Neglect: The Family and the Community.* Cambridge MA: Ballinger, 1976.

_____. *Humanistic Treatment of Father-Daughter Incest.* San Jose CA: Santa Clara County Department of Juvenile Probation, Child Sexual Abuse Treatment Program, 1976.

_____. *Integral Psychology in the Treatment of Father-Daughter Incest.* California Institute of Asian Studies, San Francisco. Doctoral Dissertation. Ann Arbor MI: University Microfilms, 1978.

_____. *Integrated Treatment of Child Sexual Abuse: A Treatment and Training Manual.* Palo Alto CA: Science and Behavior, 1982.

_____. *Treating Sexual Abuse — Working Together.* San Jose CA: Santa Clara County Juvenile Probation Department, Child Sexual Abuse and Neglect Program, 1977.

_____. "The Treatment of Father-Daughter Incest: A Psychosocial Approach." Santa Clara County Juvenile Probation Department, San Jose CA, Child Sexual Abuse Treatment Program. *Children Today,* July-August 1976.

Giarretto, H.; Giarretto, A.; and Sgroi, S.M. *Coordinated Community Treatment of Incest.* San Jose CA: Child Sexual Abuse Treatment Program of Santa Clara County, 1978.

Giarrusse, Roseann; Johnson, Paula; Goodchilds, Jacqueline; and Zellman, Gail. *Adolescents' Cues and Signals: Sex and Assault.* Paper presented at the Western Psychological Association Meeting, 1979.

Gibbens, T.C.N.; Soothill, K.L., and Way, C.K. "Sex Offences Against Young Girls: A Longterm Record Study." *Psychological Medicine* **11**, 1981.

_____; _____; and _____. "Sibling and Parent-Child Incest Offenders." *British Journal of Criminology,* January 1978.

_____; _____; and _____. "Behavioral Types of Rape." *British Journal of Psychiatry* **130**, 1977.

Gigeroff, A., et al. "Sex Offenders on Probation: Heterosexual Pedophiles." *Federal Probation* **32**, 1968.

Gil, E. *Institutional Abuse of Children in Out-of-Home Care.* San Francisco: San Francisco Child Abuse Council, 1982. Demonstrates that children are often abused by caretakers who are supposed to be providing them with a safe, rehabilitative environment. Urges investigation, collection of data, and study of problem.

Gil, E. *Outgrowing the Pain: A Book for and About Adults Abused as Children.* 1983.

_____. *Treatment of Adult Survivors of Childhood Abuse.*

Gilbert, A. "Conceptions of Homosexuality and Sodomy in Western History." *Journal of Homosexuality* **6**, 1981.

Gilbert, N., and Daro, D. *Child Sexual Abuse Prevention: Development of Educational Materials Geared to Preschool Children.* University of California, Berkeley, Family Welfare Research Group (1950 Addison St. Suite 104, Berkeley CA 94704), October 1985–September 1987. A highly complex study involving the attitudes and knowledge of children and parents concerning abusive behavior.

Gilchrist, R. *Report to the Board of School Trustees, School District 3 (Kimberly) on the C.A.R.E. Program: A Program on Personal Safety.* Child Abuse Research and Education, Production Association of British Columbia, 1984.

Gilder, S.A. *Safety, Touch and Me.* Bethesda MD: Sexual Assault Service, 1983. Curriculum for assault prevention for grades 4–6. Includes classroom activities, pre- and post-tests, and games children can play at home to enhance their learning experience.

Gilgun, J.F. *A Non-Coercive Method of Helping Children Discuss Their Own Sexual Abuse. Part II: An Example of Intervention by Multiple Qualitative Case Studies.* Minnesota University, Minnesota School of Social Work, 1984.

Gill, D. *Child Abuse and Violence*. American Orthopsychiatric Association. New York: AMS, 1979.

_____. *Violence Against Children*. Cambridge MA: Harvard University Press, 1973.

Gill, John. *Stolen Children: How and Why Parents Kidnap Their Kids—and What to Do About It*. New York: Seaview, 1981.

Giovannoni, J., and Becerra, R. *Defining Child Abuse*. New York: Free Press, 1979.

*Girard, L. *My Body Is Private*. Niles IL: Whitman, 1984.

*_____. *Who Is a Stranger and What Should I Do?* Niles IL: Whitman, 1985.

Gligor, A. *Incest and Sexual Delinquency*. Dissertation Abstracts, Case Western Reserve University, 1966.

Gochrus, H.L. "Social Work and the Sexual Oppression of Youth." *Journal of Social Work and Human Sexuality*, 1982.

Goffman, Jerry M. *The MAN Program: Self Help Counseling for Men Who Molest Children*. San Francisco: B.A., 1986.

*Goldman, R. *Silent Shame: The Sexual Abuse of Children and Youth*. Interstate, 1986.

Goldstein, A. "New Directions in Aggression Reduction." In Hinde, R., and Groebel, J., eds., *Aggression and War: Biological and Social Basis*. Cambridge: Cambridge University Press, 1987.

Goldstein, J.; Freud, A.; and Solnit, A. *Beyond the Best Interest of the Child*. New York: Free Press, 1973.

Goldstein, M. "Exposure to Erotic Stimuli and Sexual Deviance." *Journal of Social Issues* **29**, 1973.

Goldstein, S. "Sexual Exploitation of Children: Ignorance vs. Innocence." Berkeley Police Department, Berkeley CA. *Journal of California Law Enforcement*, January 1980. For law enforcement personnel. Includes information on incidence and descriptions of a variety of abusive behaviors. Outlines investigative techniques for complete case assessment.

_____. *Sexual Exploitation of Children: Practical Guide to Assessment, Investigation and Intervention*. Available from Childhelp USA, 966 North Lake Avenue, Pasadena CA 91104.

_____. *The Sexual Exploitation of Children*. New York: Elsevier, 1987.

Gomes-Schwartz, R.; Horowitz, J.M.; and Sauzier, M. "Severity of Emotional Distress Among Sexually Abused Preschool, School-Age and Adolescent Children." *Hospital and Community Psychiatry* **36**, May 1985.

Goodwin, J. *Helping the Child Who Reports Incest: A Case Review*. Albuquerque: University of New Mexico, School of Medicine, 1982.

_____. "Helping the Child Who Reports Incest: A Case Review." In Goodwin, J., ed., *Sexual Abuse: Incest Victims and Their Families*. Boston: Wright, 1982.

_____. *Incest from Infancy to Adulthood: A Developmental Approach to Victims and Families*. Albuquerque: University of New Mexico, Department of Psychiatry, 1982.

_____. "Suicide Attempts: A Preventable Complication of Incest." Albuquerque: University of New Mexico, School of Medicine. In Goodwin, J., ed., *Sexual Abuse: Incest Victims and Their Families*. Boston: Wright, 1982.

_____. "The Use of Drawings in Incest Cases." Albuquerque: University of New Mexico, School of Medicine, 1982.

_____, ed. *Sexual Abuse: Incest Victims and Their Families*. Boston: Wright, 1982.

Goodwin, J.; Sahd, D.; and Rada, R. "Incest Hoax: False Accusations, False Denials." *Crime and Sexuality*, 1976.

Goodwin, Jean; Simms, Mary; and Bergman, Robert. "Hysterical Seizures: A Sequel to Incest." *American Journal of Orthopsychiatry*, October 1979.

Gordon, L. "Incest as a Revenge Against the Pre-Oedipal Mother." *Psychoanalytic Review* **42**, 1955.

*Gordon, S., and Gordon, J. *A Better Safe Than Sorry Story Book.* Fayetteville NY: Ed-U, 1984. For children ages 3–9. "Read-aloud" format offers basic information about sexual abuse. Parents' guide also available, with suggestions for enhancing child's awareness of abuse prevention techniques.

Gordy, P.L. "Group Work That Supports Adult Victims of Childhood Incest." LeHigh County Family and Children's Services, Allentown PA. *Social Casework,* May 1983.

Gottlieb, B., and Dean, J. "The Co-Therapy Relationship in Group Treatment of Sexually Mistreated Adolescent Girls." In Mrazek, P.B., and Kempe, C.H., eds., *Sexually Abused Children and Their Families.* New York: Pergamon, 1981.

Gough, Jamie. "Childhood Sexuality and Pedophilia." *Gay Left,* Summer 1979.

Graham, D.T., and Smithwick, W.K. *Working with Sexually Abused Girls in Residential Group Care.* Salem VA: Virginia Baptist Children's Home and Family Services, Spring 1985.

Graham McWhorter Research Corporation. *Program Evaluation Final Report: Sexual Abuse Education Demonstration Projects.* Final report prepared for the National Center on Child Abuse and Neglect, December 1982.

Greaves, T. "Explaining Incest Rules." *Cornell Journal of Social Relations,* 1966.

Green, Christopher. "Filicidal Impulses as an Anniversary Reaction to Childhood Incest." *American Journal of Psychotherapy,* April 1982.

Greenberg, H.H. "Incest: Treatment and the Law." In *Proceedings of the First National Conference on Child Sexual Victimization.* Washington DC: Children's Hospital National Medical Center, November 29, 30 and December 1, 1979.

Greenberg, W.C. "The Multiple Personality." *Perspectives of Psychiatric Care* **20**, July-September 1982.

Greene, N. "A View of Family Pathology Involving Child Molest—from a Juvenile Probation Perspective." *Juvenile Justice,* February 1977.

Greenland, C. "Incest." *British Journal of Delinquency* **9**, 1958.

Greenland, Cyril. "Psychiatry and the Dangerous Sexual Offender." *Canada Psychiatry Association Journal* **22**, 1977.

Greenwald, H. *The Call Girl.* New York: Ballantine, 1958.

Greer, Joanne G., and Stuart, Irving R. *The Sexual Aggressor: Current Perspectives on Treatment.* New York: Van Nostrand Reinhold, 1983.

Gregorio, P.; Keer, N.; Fay, J.; and Robbins, D. *Curricula for the Prevention of Sexual Abuse of Children and Youth.* Seattle WA: Northwest Resource Center for Children, Youth and Families, November 1983.

Griffen, S. *Pornography and Silence: Culture's Revolt Against Nature.* New York: 1982.

Groth, A. *An Interview: Child Molesting.* Medical Aspects of Human Sexuality, May 1985.

_____. *Anatomical Drawings for the Use in the Investigation and Intervention of Child Sexual Abuse.* Newton Center MA: Forensic Mental Health Associates, 1984.

_____. *Guidelines for Assessment and Management of the Offender.* In Burgess, et al., eds., *Sexual Assault of Children and Adolescents.* Lexington MA: Lexington Books, 1978.

_____. *Guidelines for the Assessment and Management of the Offender.* Harrinton Memorial Hospital, Southbridge MA. Forensic Mental Health Department, 1978.

_____. "Patterns of Sexual Assault Against Children and Adolescents." In Burgess, et al., *Sexual Assault of Children and Adolescents.* Lexington MA: Lexington, 1978.

_____. "Sexual Trauma in the Life Histories of Rapists and Child Molesters." *Victimology: An International Journal* **4**, 1979.

_____. "The Adolescent Sexual Offender and His Prey." *Journal of Offender Therapy and Comparative Criminology* **21**, 1977.

Groth, A.N., et al. "A Study of Child Molesters: Myths and Realities." *Law Journal of the American Criminal Justice Association* **41**, 1978.

Groth, A.N., and Birnham, H.J. "Adult Sexual Orientation and Attraction to Underage Persons." *Archives of Sexual Behavior,* May 1978.

_____, and _____. "Adult Sexual Orientation and Attraction to Underage Persons." In Jones, Jenstrom, and MacFarlane, eds., *Sexual Abuse of Children: Selected Readings.* Washington DC: National Center on Child Abuse and Neglect, November 1980.

Groth, A.N., and Burgess, A.W. "Male Rape: Offenders and Victims." *American Journal of Psychiatry* **137**, 1980.

_____, and _____. "Motivation Intent in the Sexual Assault of Children." *Criminal Justice and Behavior* **4**, 1977.

Groth, A.N.; Burgess, A.W.; Birnbaum, H. Jean; and Gary, Thomas S. "A Study of the Child Molester: Myth and Realities." *Journal of the American Criminal Justice Association* **41**, 1978.

Groth, A.N.; and Freeman-Longo, R. *Men Who Rape: The Psychology of the Offender.* New York: Plenum, 1979.

Groth, A.N., and Hobson, William F. "Child Abuse." *Medical Aspects of Human Sexuality* **19**, 1985.

Groth, A.N.; Hobson, W.F.; and Gray, T.S. "The Child Molester: Clinical Observations." *Journal of Social Work and Human Sexuality,* January-February 1982.

_____; _____; and _____. "The Child Molester: Clinical Observations." In Conte and Shore, *Social Work and Child Sexual Abuse/Journal of Social Work and Human Sexuality* **1**, January-February 1982.

Groth, A.N.; Hobson, W.F.; Lucey, K.P.; and St. Pierre, J. "Juvenile Sexual Offenders: Guidelines for Treatment." *International Journal of Offender Therapy and Comparative Criminology* **25**, 1981.

Groth, A.N.; Longo, R.E.; and McFadin, J.B. "Undetected Recidivism Among Rapists and Child Molesters." *Crime and Delinquency* **128**, 1982.

Groth, A.N., and Loredo, C.M. "Juvenile Sexual Offenders: Guidelines for Assessment." *International Journal of Offender Therapy and Comparative Criminology* **25**, 1981.

Gruber, K. "The Child Victim's Role in Sexual Assault by Adults." *Child Welfare* **40**, 1981.

Guillory, D. *Children's Trauma Center: Final Report.* Oakland CA: Children's Hospital Medical Center of Northern California, May 1982.

Gundlach, R. "Sexual Molestation and Rape Reported by Homosexual and Heterosexual Women." *Journal of Homosexuality* **2**, 1977.

Gundlach, R., and Riess, B. "Birth Order and Sex Siblings: In a Sample of Lesbians and Non-Lesbians." *Psychological Reports* **20**, 1967.

Gutheil, T.G., and Avery, N.C. "Multiple Overt Incest as Family Defense Against Loss." Harvard Medical School, Boston. *Family Process,* March 1977.

*Haddad, Jill, and Martin, Lloyd. *What If I Say No.* This 1981 book is written in workbook form. Describes good and bad touches by strangers or friends and relatives. Appropriate for elementary age children.

*Haden, D., ed. *Out of Harm's Way: Readings on Child Sexual Abuse, Its Prevention and Treatment.* Phoenix AZ: Oryx, 1986.

Hail, C. *A Primer of Freudian Psychology.* New York: World, 1954.

*Hall, R.P., and Kassees, J.M. *All in My Family.* Wilmington DE: Parents Anonymous of Delaware, 1985. Two fictional accounts of adolescent offenders are accompanied by discussion of how to prevent and treat the problem. In one story, a teenage boy abuses his sister; in the other, a teenage boy is arrested and treated for molesting the child he babysits.

Halleck, S. "Victims of Sex Offenses." *Journal of the American Medical Association* **180**, 1962.

Halliday, L. *The Silent Screen: The Reality of Sexual Abuse.* 1981.

Halperin, M. *Helping Maltreated Children: School and Community Involvement.* St. Louis MO: Mosby, 1979.

Hammer, E. "A Comparison of H.T.P.'s of Rapists and Pedophiles: III. The Dead Tree as an Index of Psychopathology." *Journal of Clinical Psychology* **11**, 1955.

Hammer, E., and Gleuck, B. "Psychodynamic Patterns in Sex Offenders." *Psychiatric Quarterly* **31**, 1957.

Hanson, N.E. *Sexual Abuse Prevention Program: Pilot Project Evaluation.* Master's Thesis. British Columbia University, Vancouver, Canada. September 1982.

Harbert, T.; Hersen, J.; Barlow, D.; and Austin, J. "Measurement and Modification of Incestuous Behavior: A Case Study." *Psychological Reports,* February 1974 to February 1976.

Harcourt, M. *Child Sexual Abuse.* Marion County Child Protective Services, Indianapolis. Springfield IL: Thomas, 1986.

Harms, R., and James, D. *Talking About Touching: A Personal Safety Curriculum.* Seattle WA: Seattle Institute for Child Advocacy, Committee for Children, 1984. For grades K–6. Teaches awareness and prevention techniques through photos, stories, activities. Each lesson includes objectives and discussion questions. Resource guide also included.

Harris, P.V., and Sneed, R.H. *A Commitment to Children: Strengthening Families, Communities and Services. Conference Proceedings. Sixth Annual Conference on Child Abuse and Neglect.* Sponsored by National Center on Child Abuse and Neglect (DHHS), Washington DC, September 25–28, 1983.

*Hart-Rossi, J. *Protect Your Child from Sexual Abuse: A Parent's Guide.* Planned Parenthood of Snohomish County WA. Seattle WA: Parenting, 1984. Companion book to *It's My Body* (*see* Freeman, L.). Gives parents suggestions on how to approach concepts necessary to help children protect themselves. Also offers a page-by-page guide for reading *It's My Body* with a child. Especially helpful for parents of pre-school children.

Hartly, A. "Reporting Child Abuse." *Texas Medicine,* 1975.

Hartman, A., and Nicolay, R. "Sexually Deviant Behavior in Expectant Fathers." *Journal of Abnormal Psychology* **71**, 1966.

Hartman, Carol R., et al. "Typology of Collectors." In Burgess, A.W., ed., *Child Pornography and Sex Rings.* Lexington MA: Lexington, 1984.

Haskins, J. *The Child Abuse Book.* Reading MA: Addison-Wesley, 1982.

Hauptman, W. *Gewaltlose Unzucht mit Kindern.* 1975.

Hawkins, D. "An Open Letter to Child Sexual Abusers." Arcadia CA: Focus on the Family (Box 500, 91006), 1986.

Hawkins, P. *Children at Risk: My Fight Against Child Abuse — A Personal Story and a Public Plea.* Bethesda MD: Adler and Adler, 1986.

Hawkins, P.A. "Appendix D: Fighting Adult Entertainment Centers at the Grassroots Level." Marion County Victim Advocate Program, Indianapolis IN. In Burgess, A.W., ed., *Child Pornography and Sex Rings.* Lexington MA: Lexington/Heath, 1984.

Hayden, T. *One Child.* New York: Putnam, 1980.

Haynes-Seman, C. *Impact of Sexualized Attention on the Preverbal Child.* Presented at 16th Annual Child Abuse and Neglect Symposium, Keystone CO, 1987.

_____. *Review of the Literature on Child Abuse and Neglect.* Presentation at the 14th Annual Child Abuse and Neglect Symposium, Keystone CO, May 1985.

Haynes-Seman, C., and Hart, J. "Doll Play of Failure to Thrive Toddlers: Clues to Infant Experience." C. Henry Kempe National Center for the Prevention and Treatment of Child Abuse and Neglect, April 1987.

_____, and _____. "Interactional Assessment: Evaluation of Relationships in Abuse and Neglect." In Bross, D., et al., eds., *Child Protection Team Handbook,* Revised edition, 1987.

*Hechinger, Grace. *How to Raise a Street Smart Child.* New York: Hechinger, 1984. A general guide for parents about safety. Offers practical information about muggers, thieves, gangs, bullies, and child molesters.

Hechler, David. *The Battle and the Backlash: The Child Sexual Abuse War.* 1988.

Heider, K.G. "Anthropological Models of Incest Laws in the United States." *American Anthropologist* **71,** 1969.

Heims, L., and Kaufman, I. "Variations on a Theme of Incest." *American Journal of Orthopsychiatry* **33,** 1963.

Hekman, R. *The Sexual Offender: Punishment vs. Treatment.* Paper delivered to a forum on Child Abuse of the National Council at Juvenile and Family Court Judges, undated.

Helbruck, C. *Breaking the Cycle of Child Abuse.* Minneapolis: Winston, 1979.

Helfer, R., and Kempe, C., eds. *Child Abuse and Neglect: Community Approach to Family Treatment.* Cambridge MA: Ballinger, 1976.

_____, and _____, eds. *Child Abuse and Neglect: The Family and Community.* Cambridge MA: Ballinger, 1976.

_____, and _____. *The Battered Child.* Chicago: University of Chicago Press, 1974.

Henderson, J. "Incest: A Synthesis of Data." *Canadian Psychiatric Association Journal* **17,** August 1972.

Henn, F., et al. "Forensic Psychiatry: Profiles of Two Types of Sex Offenders." *American Journal of Psychiatry* **133,** 1976.

Hennepin County Attorney's Office. *Sexual Assault: A Manual for Law Enforcement.* Minneapolis: Medical Social Service, Volunteer and Prosecutorial Personnel and Agencies, Nov. 1978.

Herjanic, B., and Wibois, R. "Sexual Abuse of Children: Detection and Management." *Journal of the American Medical Association,* January 23, 1978.

*Herman, J. *Father-Daughter Incest.* Cambridge MA: Harvard University Press, 1981. An analysis of the phenomenon; a clinical study; social responses. Also deals with remedies and prevention.

_____. "Recognition and Treatment of Incestuous Families." *International Journal of Family Therapy* **5,** Summer 1983.

Herman, J., and Hirschman, L. "Father-Daughter Incest." *Journal of Women in Culture and Society,* 1977.

_____, and _____. "Father-Daughter Incest." *Signs,* 1977.

_____, and _____. "Incest and Family Disorders." *British Medical Journal,* May 13, 1972.

Herman, J., and Schatzow, E. "Time-Limited Group Therapy for Women with a History of Incest." Harvard Medical School, Cambridge MA. *International Journal of Group Psychotherapy,* October 1984.

Herner and Co. *Child Sexual Abuse: Incest, Assault, and Sexual Exploitation.* Arlington VA: Issued 1979, revised 1981.

_____. *Evaluation of Child Abuse and Neglect Clinical Demonstration Project — Data Tape Documentation.* Child Abuse and Neglect Clearinghouse Project. Arlington VA: November 1983.

Hersko, M., et al. "Incest: A Three-Way Process." *Journal of Social Therapy,* 1961.

*Hettlinger, R. *Growing Up with Sex: A Guide for the Early Teens.* New York: Continuum, 1980.

Hill, E. *The Family Secret.* Santa Barbara CA: Capra, 1985.

*Hindman, J. *A Very Touching Book . . . for Little People and for Big People.* Durkee OR: McClure Hindman, 1983. Much more explicit than most prevention books. Deals with names of body parts, good and bad touches, secret touching, and how to get help. Appropriate for elementary age children.

Hindman, M. "Child Abuse and Neglect: The Alcohol Connection." Hood College, Frederick MN. *Lifelines,* Winter 1977.

Hiroto, D. "Focus of Control and Learned Helplessness." *Journal of Experimental Psychology* **1022,** 1974.

Holder, W. "Crisis Intervention in the Family in the Initial Work with the Sexually Abusing Family." In Holder, W., ed., *Sexual Abuse of Children: Implications for Treatment.* Denver: American Humane Association, 1980.

Holder, W., ed. *Sexual Abuse of Children: Implications for Treatment.* Denver: American Humane Association, 1980.

Hollingsworth, C. "Recognition and Treatment of Child Sexual Abuse." In *Providing for the Emotional Health of the Pediatric Patient.* New York: Spectrum, 1983.

Hollingsworth, J. *Unspeakable Acts.* New York: Congdon and Weed, 1986.

Holmes, R.M. "Annotated Bibliography on Sex Crimes Against Children." In *The Sex Offender and the Criminal Justice System,* 1983.

The Home Front: Notes from the Family War Zone. New York: McGraw-Hill, 1983.

Horowitz, Robert. *The Legal Rights of Children.* Monterey CA: Shepard's/McGraw-Hill, 1984. For lawyers who represent and work with children.

Horton, Anne L., and Williamson, Judith, eds., *Abuse and Religion: When Playing Isn't Enough.* 1988.

Horwitz, A.N. "Guidelines for Treating Father-Daughter Incest." *Social Casework* **64,** November 1983.

Howells, K. "Adult Sexual Interest in Children: Considerations Relevant to Theories of Etiology." In Cook, M., and Howells, K., eds., *Adult Sexual Interest in Children.* New York: Academic, 1981.

Howells, Kevin. "Some Meanings of Children for Pedophiles." In Cook, M., and Wilson, G., eds., *Love and Attraction: An International Conference.* Oxford, England: Pergamon, 1979.

Howard, H. "Incest: The Revenge Motive." *Delaware State Medical Journal* **31,** 1959.

HQ Pacific Air Forces Command. *Child Abuse and Neglect: Selected Readings.* Gucjan AFB HI: Library Branch Operation Division, September 1983.

*Hubbard, Kate, and Berlynn, Evelyn. *Help Yourself to Safety.* Edmonds WA: Charles Franklin, 1985. A guide to avoiding dangerous situations.

Huber, M. *A Community Approach to Preventing Sexual Abuse of Children.* Albany: New York State Council on Children and Families, New York State Self-Help Clearinghouse, Summer 1984.

*Huchton, L. *Protect Your Child: A Parent's Safeguard Against Child Abduction and Sexual Abuse.* Englewood Cliffs NJ: Prentice-Hall, 1985.

Hunt, M. *Sexual Behavior in the 1970s.* Chicago: Playboy Press, 1974.

Husain, A., and Ahmad, A. *Sexual Abuse of Children: Diagnosis and Treatment.* Columbia: University of Missouri, Medical Sciences Center, June 1982.

Husain, A., and Chapel, J.L. "History of Incest in Girls Admitted to a Psychiatric Hospital." *American Journal of Psychiatry* **140**, May 1983.

*Hutchinson, Barbara, and Chevalier, Anne. *My Personal Safety Coloring Book.* Fridley MN: Police Department, 1982. For use in conjunction with a personal safety program for elementary schools.

*Hyde, M. *Missing Children.* New York: Watts, 1985.

_____. *My Friend Has Four Parents.* New York: McGraw-Hill, 1981.

_____. *My Friend Wants to Run Away.* New York: McGraw-Hill, 1979.

_____. *Sexual Abuse: Cry Softly, the Story of Child Abuse.* Philadelphia: Westminster, 1980.

*_____. *Sexual Abuse: Let's Talk About It.* Philadelphia: Westminster, 1984. One of the best books I have read on this subject. Author Hyde says that "sexual abuse of children is the best kept secret in the world. People don't want to talk about it or even think about it. Yet if the same number of children suffered from a disease, alarms would sound against the epidemic." Emphasizes that education must begin early (most abuse begins before a child is 12) and that even very small children can learn how to avoid inappropriate adult behavior and to realize they are not to blame. Talks about good and bad touching; "what if" games; dispells myths and offers suggestions to be aware of "tricks" used by suspects. The use of case histories really gives the reader an insight into this problem. Margaret Hyde has also written: *Cry Softly, the Story of Child Abuse,* 1980; *My Friend Has Four Parents,* 1981; and *My Friend Wants to Run Away,* 1979.

Hymer, Sharon. "The Self in Victimization: Conflict and Developmental Perspectives." *Victimology: An International Journal* **9**, 1984.

"I Married My Sister." *Newsweek* **94**, 1979.

Ikeda, Y. "A Short Introduction to Child Abuse in Japan." Japanese Institute of Mental Health, Ichikawa. *Child Abuse and Neglect,* 1982.

Ilg, F.L., and Ames, L.B. *Child Behavior: Normal Stages of Sex Play.* (Available from Childhelp USA, 966 North Lake Ave., Pasadena CA 91104.)

"Incest and Family Disorder." *British Medical Journal,* May 13, 1972.

Ingebritson, M., and McBride, M. *Family Sexual Abuse Treatment Demonstration Project: Final Report.* Minneapolis: Fairview-Southdale Hospital, Family Sexual Abuse Treatment Program, October 31, 1982.

Inglis, R. *Sins of the Fathers: A Study of the Physical and Emotional Abuse of Children.* New York: St. Martin's, 1978.

Ingram, D.L.; White, S.T.; Durfee, M.F.; and Pearson, A.W. "Sexual Contact in Children with Gonorrhea." *American Journal of Diseases of Children* **136**, November 1982.

Ingram, M. "Reaction to Paedophile Acts." *Libertarian Education* **2**, 1977.

_____. "The Participating Victim: A Study of Sexual Offences Against Pre-Pubertal Boys." In Cook, M., and Wilson, G., eds., *Love and Attraction: An International Conference.* Oxford, England: Pergamon, 1979.

Institute for the Community as Extended Family. *Child Sexual Abuse Treatment Training Institute: Final Program Progress Report.* San Jose CA: September 30, 1979–September 30, 1983.

_____. *Children Helping Children.* San Jose CA: Daughters and Sons United, 1981.

International Children's Center. *Child Abuse and Neglect: A Document for Nurses, Midwives, Social Workers, Teachers and Parents.* Paris, France: 1980. Overview covering difficulties with definitions; incidence; traumatic and nontraumatic pathology; situational factors; rejection; high-risk parents; and related subjects.

International Society for the Prevention of Child Abuse and Neglect. *Preventing Child Abuse: A Community Responsibility.* Abstracts from the International Congress on Child Abuse and Neglect, Montreal, September 16–19, 1984.

Issac, C. *Identification and Interruption of Sexually Offending Behavior in Pre-Pubescent Children.* Presented at 16th Annual Child Abuse and Neglect Symposium, Keystone CO, 1987.

*J.M.H./U.M. Medical Center. *Child Sexual Abuse: An Ounce of Prevention....* Miami FL: University of Miami Medical Center Rape Treatment Center, Spring 1987. Brochure for parents and teachers. Offers suggestions on what and how to tell children about sexual abuse.

Jackson, I. *A Preliminary Survey of Adolescent Sex Offenses in New York: Remedies and Recommendations.* Syracuse NY: Safer Society, 1983.

Jacobson, J.J. *Psychiatric Sequelae of Child Abuse.* Springfield IL: Thomas, 1986.

Jaffe, A.; Dynneson, L.; and TenBensel, R. "Sexual Abuse of Children: An Epidemiologic Study." *American Journal of Diseases of Children* 129, June 1975.

James, B., and Nasjleti, M. *Treating Sexually Abused Children and Their Families.* Palo Alto CA: Consulting Psychologists, 1983.

James, J. "Physician Reporting of Sexual Abuse of Children." *Journal of the American Medical Association,* September 1978.

James, J., and Meyerding, J. "Early Sexual Experience and Prostitution." *American Journal of Psychiatry* 134, December 1977.

————, and ————. "Early Sexual Experience Is a Factor in Prostitution." *Archives of Sexual Behavior* 7, 1978.

James, K. "Incest: The Teenager's Perspective." *Psychotherapy* 19, 1977.

*Jance, J. *It's Not Your Fault.* Edmonds WA: Charles Franklin, 1985. Teaches that abuse or attempted assault is not the fault of the victim, and that the offender is usually someone the child knows.

Janus, S. *The Death of Innocence.* New York: Morrow, 1981.

*Jenkins, Jeanne K., and McDonald, Pam. *Growing Up Equal: Activities and Resources for Parents and Teachers of Young Children.* Englewood Cliffs NJ: Prentice-Hall, 1979.

Jessor, S., and Jessor, R. "Transition from Virginity to Non-Virginity Among Youths: A Social Psychological Study Over Time." *Developmental Psychology* 11, 1975.

Johnson, C.L. *Child Sexual Abuse Case Handling in Tennessee.* Athens GA: Regional Institute of Social Welfare Research, July 1979.

————. *Child Sexual Abuse Handling Through Public Agencies in the Southeast.* Athens GA: Regional Institute of Social Welfare Research, March 1980.

*Johnson, Karen, and Forssell, Linda. *The Trouble with Secrets.* Seattle WA: Parenting, 1986. Helps young children understand the difference between secrets to be kept and those they need to tell to a trusted adult.

Johnson, R.L., and Shrier, D.K. "Sexual Victimization of Boys: Experience at an Adolescent Medical Clinic." *Journal of Adolescent Health Care* 6, 1985.

Johnson, Shawn A., and Anderson, Raymond. "Development of Scales to Measure Sexual Aggressives." *International Journal of Offender Therapy and Criminology* 29, 1985.

Jones, B.; Jenstrom, L.; and MacFarlane, K., eds. *Sexual Abuse of Children: Selected Readings.* Washington DC: National Center on Child Abuse and Neglect, November 1980.

Jones, B.M., and Thomas, J.N. *Sexual Victimization of Children: Trauma, Trial, and*

Treatment. Proceedings of the Conference. Washington DC: Children's Hospital National Medical Center, Child Protection Center, November 29, 30 and December 1, 1979.

Jones, David P.H., and McQuiston, Mary. *Interviewing the Sexually Abused Child.* 2nd edition. 1986.

Jorne, P.S. "Treating Sexually Abused Children." Children's Center, Detroit MI. *Child Abuse and Neglect* 3, 1979.

Josephson, Gordon W., M.D. "The Male Rape Victim: Evaluation and Treatment." *JACEP,* January 1979.

Justice, B. *The Abusing Family.* New York: Human Sciences, 1976.

*Justice, B., and Justice, R. *The Broken Taboo: Sex in the Family.* Texas University, Houston, School of Public Health. New York: Human Sciences, 1979. Study of incest includes suggestions for dealing with intrafamily abuse.

Kadushin, A., and Martin, J. *Child Abuse: An Interactional Event.* New York: Columbia University Press, 1981.

Kalisch, B. *Child Abuse and Neglect: An Annotated Bibliography.* Westport CT: Greenwood, 1978.

Kane, G.D. *The Word That Must Be Spoken.* Denver: American Humane Association, December 1977.

Kanin, E., and Parcell, S. "Sexual Aggression: A Second Look at the Offended Female." *Archives of Social Behavior* 6, 1977.

Kantan, A. "Children Who Were Raped." *Psychoanalytic Study of the Child* 28, 1973.

Kaplan, S.J.; Salzinger, S.; Montero, G.; and Pelcovitz, D. *Psychopathology of Parents in Father-Daughter Child Sexual Abuse.* Manhasset NY: North Shore University Hospital, Family Crisis Program, 1980–1986.

Karlen, A. *Sexuality and Homosexuality.* New York: Norton, 1971.

Karsch-Haack, F. *Das Leichgeschlechtliche Leben der Naturvolker.* 1911.

_____. *Das Leichgeschlechtliche Leben der Ostasiaten.* 1906.

Katzman, M. "Early Sexual Trauma." *Sexual Behavior,* February 1972.

Kaufman, I.; Peck, A.; and Tagiuri, C. "The Family Constellation and Overt Incestuous Relations Between Father and Daughter." *American Journal of Orthopsychiatry* 24, 1954.

*Keating, K. *The Hug Therapy Book.* Minneapolis: CompCare, 1983.

Kellogg, J. *Plain Facts About Sexual Life.* Battle Creek MI: Office of the Health Reformer, 1887.

Kelley, S.J. "The Use of Art Therapy with Sexually Abused Children." Boston College MA, Maternal-Child Health Graduate Program. *Psychosocial Nursing,* December 1984.

Kelly, Ronald D. "Protecting Your Children from Sexual Abuse." *Plain Truth* Magazine, September 1988.

Kempe, C.H. *Helping the Battered Child and His Family.* Philadelphia: Lippincott, 1972.

_____. *Incest and Other Forms of Sexual Abuse.* Denver: Colorado University, Department of Pediatrics, 1980.

Kempe, C.H., and Helfer, R. *The Battered Child.* 3rd edition. Chicago: University of Chicago Press, 1980.

Kempe, C.H.; Silverman, F.; Steele, B.; Droegemueller, W.; and Silver, H. "The Battered Syndrome." *Journal of the American Medical Association,* 1962.

*Kempe, R.S., and Kempe, C.H. *Child Abuse.* Colorado University, Denver, Medical Center. Cambridge MA: Harvard University Press, 1978.

198 Bibliography

Kempe, R.S., and Kempe, C.H. *The Common Secret: Sexual Abuse of Children and Adolescents.* Colorado University, Denver, School of Medicine. New York: Freeman, 1984. Historical references and information regarding incest. The doctors Kempe have profound insight into the field of child abuse. One of their suggestions in this book is that some professionals have "shied away" from dealing with sexual abuse because they are unable to deal with their personal feelings about it.

Kendrick, M.M. "What We've Learned from Community Responses to Intrafamily Child Sexual Abuse." In *Perspectives on Child Maltreatment in the Mid 80's.* Washington DC: National Center on Child Abuse and Neglect, 1984.

Kennedy, M., and Cormier, B. "Father-Daughter Incest—Treatment of the Family." *Laual Medical Journal,* November 1969.

*Kent, Cordelia. *Child Sexual Abuse Prevention Project: An Educational Program for Children.* Minneapolis: Hennepin County Attorney's Office, Child Sexual Abuse Project (C-2100 Government Center, 55487), 1979. Curriculum focusing on a "touch continuum" (from good to bad touches).

Kent, M. "Remarriage: A Family System Approach." *Social Casework* 61, 1980.

Kercher, G. *Responding to Child Sexual Abuse: A Report to the 67th Session of the Texas Legislature.* Huntsville TX: Sam Houston University, 1980.

Kerns, D. "Medical Assessment of Child Sexual Abuse." In Mrazek, P.B., and Kempe, C.H., eds., *Sexually Abused Children and Their Families.* New York: Pergamon, 1981.

Kett, J. "Adolescence and Youth in 19th Century America." *Journal of Interdisciplinary History* 11, 1971.

Kiersh, E. "Can Families Survive Incest?" *Corrections* Magazine, April 1980.

Kilmann, Peter R.; Sablis, Robert F.; Gearing, Milton L. II; Bukstel, Lee H.; and Scovern, Albert W. "The Treatment of Sexual Paraphilias: A Review of the Outcome Research." *The Journal of Sex Research,* August 1982.

Kilroy, J.M. *Incest: A Beginning Look at Assessment and Treatment.* Rhinebeck NY: Astor Home for Children, April 1978.

Kinsey, A., et al. *Sexual Behavior in the Human Female.* Philadelphia: Saunders, 1953.

_____. *Sexual Behavior in the Human Male.* Philadelphia: Saunders, 1948.

Kirstein, L. "Sexual Involvement with Patients." *Journal of Clinical Psychiatry* 39, 1978.

Kleven, S.L. *Project Evaluation—Feelings and Your Body: A Pre-School Curriculum for the Prevention of Child Sexual Abuse.* Bellingham WA: Coalition for Child Advocacy, undated.

*_____. *Sexual Abuse Prevention: A Lesson Plan.* Bellingham WA: Coalition for Child Advocacy, 1984. Uses the film "Who Do You Tell?" as basis for discussion. Includes (for teachers) a list of criteria for evaluating sexual abuse prevention curricula.

*_____. *Touching.* Bellingham WA: Coalition for Child Advocacy, 1985. Storybook for pre-school and elementary children teaches how to distinguish "good" and "bad" touching, and how to avoid the latter.

*Kleven, S.L., and Krebill, J. *The Touching Problem.* Bellingham WA: Coalition for Child Advocacy, 1981. A one-hour program for children in elementary schools.

Kline, D.F. *Long Term Impact of Child Maltreatment on the Victims as Reflected in Further Contact with the Utah Juvenile Court and the Utah Department of Adult Corrections.* Logan: Utah State University, 1987.

Knopp, F.H. "Early Intervention and Treatment for Young Sex Offenders." In *Justice for Children, Vol. 1,* 1985.

_____. *Remedial Intervention in Adolescent Sex Offenders: Nine Program Descrip-*

tions. Syracuse NY: Safer Society, 1982. For professionals. Includes interviews with adolescent offenders, suggestions for early intervention, study of treatment programs and resources.

_____. *Retraining Adult Sex Offenders: Methods and Models.* Syracuse NY: Safer Society, 1984. For professionals and lay persons. Gives an overview of methods used to treat adult offenders.

_____. *The Youthful Sex Offender: The Rationale and Goals of Early Intervention and Treatment.* Syracuse NY: Safer Society, 1985. For judges, attorneys, and prosecutors. Provides a rationale for therapeutic intervention with young offenders.

Knopp, F.H.; Rosenberg, Jean; and Stevenson, William. *Report on Nationwide Survey of Juvenile and Adult Sex-Offender Treatment Programs and Providers.* Prison Research Education Action Projects, 1986.

Kocen, L.; Bulkley, J. "Analysis of Criminal Sex Offenses Statutes." In Bulkley, J., ed., *Child Sexual Abuse and the Law.* Washington DC: American Bar Association, National Legal Resource Center for Child Advocacy and Protection, 1981.

Koch, M. *Sexual Abuse in Children.* St. Paul MN: St. Paul Ramsey Hospital, Department of Psychiatry, Fall 1980.

Kopp, S. "The Character Structure of Sex Offenders." *American Journal of Psychiatry* 16, 1962.

Korbin, J.E. *Child Abuse and Neglect: Cross-Cultured Perspectives.* Berkeley: University of California Press, 1981.

Kosof, A. *Incest: Families in Crisis.* New York: Watts, 1985.

Kourany, R.F.C.; Maretin, J.E.; and Armstrong, S.H. "Sexual Experimentation by Adolescents While Babysitting." *Adolescence* 14, 1979.

Kraemer, W., et al. *The Forbidden Love.* Sheldon, 1976.

Kraft-Ebing, R. *Psychopathia Sexualis.* New York: Physicians and Surgeons, 1935.

*Kraizer, S.K. *The Safe Child Book.* New York: Delacorte, 1985. Specific suggestions for parents on how to help children avoid abduction and abuse. Uses the "what if" game as a basis for discussion with children. Also gives information on how to report sexual abuse and how to tell when the victim needs psychological therapy.

Kratcoski, Peter C., and Kratcoski, Lucille D. "The Relationship of Victimization Through Child Abuse to Aggressive Delinquent Behavior." *Victimology* 7, 1982.

*Krause, Elaine. *For Pete's Sake, Tell!,* Oregon City OR: Krause House (P.O. Box 880, 97045), 1983. For youngsters ages 7–12. Teaches parents to teach children to be aware, alert and assertive about sexual abuse.

*_____. *Speak Up, Say No!* Oregon City OR: Krause House, 1983. A cartoon character, "Penelope Peabody," helps parents to teach children to distinguish between "Okay" and "Not Okay" touches. A booklet version of a filmstrip featuring mice teaching prevention. Preschoolers through third grade.

Krener, P. "Clinical Experiences After Incest: Secondary Prevention?" University of California, Davis, School of Medicine, Department of Psychiatry. *Journal of the American Academy of Child Psychiatry,* March 1985.

Krenk, C.J. "Training Residence Staff for Child Abuse Treatment." CPC Cedar Hills Hospital, Portland OR. *Child Welfare,* March-April 1984.

Krieger, M., et al. "Problems with the Psychotherapy of Children with Histories of Incest." *American Journal of Psychotherapy* 34, 1980.

Kroll, J. "The Concept of Childhood in the Middle Ages." *Journal of the History of Behavioral Sciences* 13, 1977.

Kronhausen, E., and Kronhausen, P. "The Psychology of Pornography." In Ellis, A., *The Encyclopedia of Sexual Behavior.* New York: Hawthorn, 1961.

Kroth, A.J. *Child Sexual Abuse: Analysis of a Family Therapy Approach.* Springfield IL: Thomas, 1979.

_____. "Family Therapy Impact on Intrafamilial Child Sexual Abuse." *Child Abuse and Neglect* **3,** 1979.

Kroth, A.J.; Manheim, T.; Higgenbotham, J.; and Steele, S. *Evaluation of the Child Sexual Abuse Demonstration and Treatment Project.* Sacramento: California State Department of Health, Office of Child Abuse Prevention, June 30, 1978.

Krugman, R.D. "The Multidisciplinary Treatment of Abusive and Neglectful Families." Colorado University, Denver, School of Medicine. *Pediatric Annals,* October 1984.

Krupinski, Eve, and Wiekel, Dana. *Death from Child Abuse . . . and No One Heard.* Undated.

Kubo, S. "Researches and Studies on Incest in Japan." *Hiroshima Journal of Medical Sciences* **8,** 1959.

Kurtz, Howard A. "The Effects of Victimization of the Acceptance of Aggression and the Expectations of Assertive Traits in Children as Measured by the General Social Survey." *Victimology: An International Journal* **9,** 1984.

Kutchinsky, B. "The Effect of Easy Availability of Pornography on the Incidence of Sex Crimes: The Danish Experience." *Journal of Social Issues* **29,** 1973.

*Kyte, K. *In Charge: A Complete Handbook for Kids with Working Parents.* New York: Knopf, 1983.

*_____. *Play It S.A.F.E.: The Kids' Guide to Personal Safety and Crime Prevention.* New York: Knopf, 1983. A book about crime, including sexual abuse. How children can be vulnerable to crime and how they can protect themselves.

LaBarbera, Joseph D., and Dozier, Clemmett. "Hysterical Seizures: The Role of Sexual Exploitation." *Psychosomatics,* November 1980.

Lamb, S. "Treating Sexually Abused Children: Issues of Blame and Responsibility." Massachusetts General Hospital, Boston, Department of Child Psychiatry. *American Journal of Orthopsychiatry,* April 1986.

Landau, E. *Child Abuse: An American Epidemic.* New York: Messner, 1984.

*Landau, Lynne. *Color Me Safe.* Portland OR: Community Advocates (4183 SE Division, 97202). Coloring book based on children's rights to be safe, strong, and free.

Landers, A. *Sisters Discover Dad Molested All Five of Them.* Chicago: Field Newspaper Syndicate, May 21, 1980.

Landis, J. "Experiences of 500 Children with Adult Sexual Deviants." *Psychiatric Quarterly Supplement* **30,** 1956.

Lane, S., and Zamora, P. "A Method for Treating the Adolescent Sex Offender." In Mathias, R.A., ed., *Sourcebook for Treatment of the Violent Juvenile Offender.* National Council on Crime and Delinquency, 1985.

Langelier, P. *Child Sexual Abuse: Community Guidelines.* Paper delivered to the 1985 Summer College of the National Council of Juvenile and Family Court Judges, undated.

_____. *Interviewing the Child Witness.* Paper delivered to a forum on Child Abuse of the National Council of Juvenile and Family Court Judges, undated.

Langevin, R.; Paitich, D.; Ramsay, G.; Anderson, C.; Kamrad, J.; Pope, S.; Geller, G.; Pearl, L.; and Newman, S. "Experimental Studies of the Etiology of General Exhibitionism." *Archives of Sexual Behavior* **8,** 1979.

Langsley, D.; Schwartz, M.; and Fairbairn, R. "Father-Son Incest." *Comprehensive Psychiatry,* May 1968.

Lanning, K. *Child Molesters: A Behavioral Analysis.* Washington DC: National Center for Missing and Exploited Children, April 1987.

Lanning, K., and Burgess, A.W. "Child Pornography and Sex Rings." *Federal Bureau of Investigation Law Enforcement Bulletin* **53,** 1984.

Laroche, G. *La Puberté.* 1938.

Larson, N.R. *An Analysis of the Effectiveness of a State-Sponsored Program Designed to Teach Intervention Skills in the Treatment of Family Sexual Abuse.* Minneapolis: University of Minnesota, Doctoral Dissertation. Ann Arbor MI: University Microfilms, 1980.

_____. *Family Sexual Abuse Training Program.* Minneapolis: University of Minnesota, Department of Family Practice and Community Health, 1979.

LaTorre, R.A. *An Evaluation of the Personal Safety Project: A Preventative Approach to Child Sexual Misuse.* Vancouver (B.C.) School Board, Evaluation and Research Services, July 1982.

Law, S. *Clinical Notes from Client Interviews.* Denver: Lookout Mountain School, Department of Youth Services, 1987.

Layman, W. "Pseudo-Incest." *Comprehensive Psychiatry,* July-August, 1972.

Leaman, K.M. *Sexual Abuse: The Reactions of Child and Family.* Washington DC: Crisis Intervention Service of the Psychiatric Institute, November 1980.

_____. "Sexual Abuse: The Reactions of Child and Family." In Jones, Jenstrom and MacFarlane, eds., *Sexual Abuse of Children: Selected Readings.* Washington DC: National Center on Child Abuse and Neglect, November 1980.

Lederer, Laura, ed. *Take Back the Night.* New York: Morrow, 1980.

Lempp, R. *See Lische Schadigung von Kindern als Opfer von gewantlosen Sittlich Keitsdelekten.* Germany, 1968.

*Lenett, R. *It's O.K. to Say No: A Parent/Child Manual for the Protection of Children.* New York: Tor, 1985.

*Lenett, Robin, and Barthelme, Dana. *Kids Have Rights Too!* New York: Playmore, 1985. Part of a four-book series (*see* remaining titles below). Discusses the right to tell secrets, the right to say "no," wanted and unwanted touches.

*_____, and _____. *My Body Is My Own.* New York: Playmore, 1985. Coloring book. Discusses private parts, good and bad touches. Part of a four-book series (*see* other Lenett-Barthelme titles in this bibliography).

*_____, and _____. *Sometimes It's OK to Tell Secrets.* New York: Playmore, 1985. Coloring book showing the difference between surprises and secrets that need to be told. Part of a four-book series (*see* other Lennet-Barthelme titles in this bibliography).

*_____, and _____. *What Should You Do When. . . .* New York: Playmore, 1985. Coloring book teaching assertive skills. Part of a four-book series (*see* other Lennet-Barthelme titles in this bibliography).

Lenman, K. "The Sexually Abused Child." *Nursing,* May 1977.

Leo, J. "Cradle to Grave Intimacy." *Time,* September 7, 1981.

Lerman, L. "State Legislation on Domestic Violence." *Response* **3,** August-September 1980.

*LeShan, E. *Sex and Your Teen-Ager: A Guide for Parents.* New York: McKay, 1969.

Lester, D. "Incest." *Journal of Sex Research* **8,** 1972.

Levi-Strauss, C. *The Elementary Structure of Kinship.* Oxford, England: Alden, 1970.

Lew, Michael. *Victims No Longer.*

Lewis, D.O. "Diagnostic Evaluation of the Juvenile Offender: Toward the Classification of Often Overlooked Psychopathology." *Child Psychiatry and Human Development* **6,** 1976.

Lewis, D.O.; Shankok, S.; and Pincus, J.H. "Juvenile Male Sex Offenders." *American Journal of Psychiatry* **136,** 1979.

_____; _____; and _____. "Juvenile Male Sexual Assaulters: Psychiatric, Neurological, Psychoeducational, and Abuse Factors." In *Vulnerabilities to Delinquency.* Undated.

Lewis, Melvin, and Sarrel, Philip M., M.D. *Some Psychological Aspects of Seduction, Incest and Rape in Childhood.* Paper presented at A.A.P.C.C. Annual Meeting, New York, November 1968.

Licht, H. *Sittengaschichte Griechealands.* 1926.

*Lieff, S., and Parker, S. *Sexual Abuse: A Guide for Your Children's Safety.* Burlington NC: Sexual Abuse Prevention Project, August 1981. Pamphlet for parents. Defines child sexual abuse and offers instruction in recognizing symptoms, reporting abuse, and teaching children to protect themselves. "Checklist" format.

Liles, R.E., and Wahliquist, D.L. "An Interagency Program for the Treatment of Intrafamilial Child Sexual Abuse." *Social Work Papers,* Spring 1981.

Lindecker, C. *Children in Chains.* New York: Everest House, 1981.

Lindemann, E. "Symptomatology and Management of Acute Grief." *American Journal of Psychiatry,* September 1944.

Lindsey, G. "Some Remarks Concerning Incest, the Incest Taboo, and Psychoanalytic Theory." *American Psychologist,* December 1967.

List, S. *Forgiving.* New York: Dutton, 1982.

Litin, E.; Griffin, M.; and Johnson, A. "Parental Influence on Unusual Sexual Behavior in Children." *Psychoanalytic Quarterly* 25, 1956.

Lloyd, D. "The Corroboration of Sexual Victimization of Children." In Bulkley, J., ed., *Child Sexual Abuse and the Law.* Washington DC: American Bar Association, National Legal Resource Center for Child Advocacy and Protection, 1981.

Lloyd, R. *For Money or Love: Boy Prostitution in America.* New York: Vanguard, 1976.

Longo, R.E. "Child Molestation: The Offender and the Assault." In *Proceedings of the 112th Annual Congress, American Correctional Association.* Toronto: 1982.

_____. "The Impact of Sexual Victimization on Males." *Child Abuse and Neglect* 10, 1986.

_____. "Sexual Learning and Experience Among Adolescent Sexual Offenders." *International Journal of Offender Therapy and Comparative Criminology* 26, 1982.

Longo, R.E., and Groth, A.N. "Juvenile Sexual Offenses in the Histories of Adult Rapists and Child Molesters." *International Journal of Offender Therapy and Comparative Criminology* 27, 1983.

Longo, R.E., and McFadin, B. "Sexually Inappropriate Behavior: Development of the Sexual Offender." *Law and Order,* December 1981.

Lorand, S. *Perversions, Psychodynamics and Therapy.* Gramercy, 1956.

Lorulot, A. *La veritable education sexuelle.* 1928.

Lubell, D., and Soong, W.T. "Group Therapy with Sexually Abused Adolescents." British Columbia University, Vancouver, Department of Psychiatry. *Canadian Journal of Psychiatry,* June 1982.

Lubore, R. "The Progressives and the Prostitute." *The Historian* 14, 1962.

Lukianowicz, N. "Incest I." *British Journal of Psychiatry* 120, 1972.

_____. *Paternal Incest: II: Other Types of Incest.* Undated.

Lukton, R. "Crisis Theory: Review and Critique." *Social Service Review,* September 1974.

Lustig, N.; Dresser, J.; Spellman, S.; and Murray, T. "Incest: A Family Group Survival Pattern." *Archives of General Psychiatry* 14, 1966.

Luther, S.L., and Price, J.H. "Child Sexual Abuse: A Review." *Journal of School Health* 50, March 1980.

Lutier, J. "The Role of Cultural Factors of a Psycho-Social Nature in Rural Incestuous Families." *Annual Medical-Legal Journal,* 1961.

Lynch, Margaret, and Roberts, Jacqueline. *Consequences of Child Abuse.* 1982.

McCaghy, C. "Child Molesters: A Study of Their Careers as Deviants." In M. Clinard and R. Quinney, eds., *Criminal Behavior Systems: A Typology.* New York: Holt-Rinehart, 1967.

_____. "Child Molesting." *Sexual Behavior* 1, 1971.

_____. "Drinking and Deviance Dis-Avowal: The Case of Child Molesters." *Journal of Social Problems* 16, 1968.

McCausland, M.P. "Sexual Development and Sexual Abuse: Emergencies in Adolescents." Boston City Hospital MA, Department of Health and Hospitals. *Pediatrics Clinics of North America,* November 1979.

McConville, S. *What Fit Punishment?* Brighton, England: Sussex University, Department of Social Administration, 1981.

McCown, D.E. "Father-Daughter Incest: A Family Problem." University of Oregon, Portland, Health Sciences Center. *Pediatric Nursing,* July-August 1981.

MacCulloch, M.; Snowden, P.R.; Wood, P.J.W.; and Mills, H.E. "Sadistic Fantasy, Sadistic Behavior and Offending." *British Journal of Psychiatry* 143, 1983.

MacDonald, J. *Indecent Exposure.* Springfield IL: Thomas, 1973.

McFadden, E.J.; Ziefert, M.; and Stovall, B. *Preventing Abuse in Foster Care. Instructor's Manual.* Ypsilanti: Eastern Michigan University, Institute for the Study of Children and Families, 1984.

McFadden, S. *Feelings and Your Body: A Prevention Curriculum for Pre-Schoolers.* Bellingham WA: Coalition for Child Advocacy, 1982. Five-day curriculum to teach 4- and 5-year-olds how to avoid sexual abuse. Discusses the child's right to his feelings and right to say "no." Includes a film, "Twist and Turn."

MacFarlane, K. "Program Considerations in the Treatment of Incest Offenders." In Greer, J.G., and Stuart, I.R., eds., *The Sexual Aggressor.* New York: Van Nostrand, 1983.

_____. "Sexual Abuse of Children." In Chapman, J., and Gates, M., eds., *The Victimization of Women.* Beverly Hills CA: Sage, 1976.

MacFarlane, K., and Bulkley, J. "Treating Child Sexual Abuse: An Overview of Current Program Models." In Conte, J.R., and Shore, D., eds., *Social Work and Child Sexual Abuse/Journal of Social Work and Human Sexuality* 1, January-February 1982.

MacFarlane, K.; Jenstrom, L.; and Jones, B.M. *Conclusion: Aspects of Prevention.* In Jones, Jenstrom and MacFarlane, eds., *Sexual Abuse of Children: Selected Readings.* Washington DC: National Center on Child Abuse and Neglect, November 1980.

MacFarlane, K., and Korbin, J. "Confronting the Incest Secret Long After the Fact: A Family Study of Multiple Victimization with Strategies for Intervention." Children's Institute International, Los Angeles CA. *Child Abuse and Neglect,* 1983.

MacFarlane, K., and Sgroi, S. "Child Sexual Assault: Some Guidelines for Intervention and Assessment." In Burgess, A.W., et al., *Sexual Assault of Children and Adolescents.* Lexington MA: Lexington, 1978.

MacFarlane, K., and Waterman, Jill; with Conerly, Shawn; Damon, Linda; Durfee, Michale; and Long, Suzanne. *Sexual Abuse of Young Children.* New York: Guilford, 1986.

McGeorge, J. "Sexual Assaults on Children." *Medicine, Science and the Law* 4, October 1984.

*McGovern, Kevin. *Alice Doesn't Babysit Anymore.* Portland OR: McGovern and Mulbacker, 1985. Story about a babysitter who abused the children in her care. Stresses that children should tell other adults if sexual abuse happens.

_____. *Alternatives to Sexual Abuse.* P.O. Box 25537, Portland OR 97225.

McGuire, R.; Carlisle, J.; and Young, B. "Sexual Deviations as Conditioned Behavior: A Hypothesis." *Behavior Research and Therapy* 2, 1965.

Machota, P.; Pittman, F.; and Flomenhaft, K. "Incest as a Family Affair." *Family Process* 6, 1967.

McIvor, D.L., and Adolf, E.E. "Working with Incest Victims." *Canadian Journal of Psychiatric Nursing,* January-March 1983.

McIvor, D.L., and Evans, D. "Incest Victims: The Adults." *Canadian Journal of Psychiatric Nursing,* January-March 1983.

McKerrow, W.D. "Protecting the Sexually Abused Child." In *Second National Symposium on Child Abuse.* Denver: American Humane Association, 1973.

*Mackey, Gene, and Swan, Helen. *Dear Elizabeth.* Leawood KS: Children's Institute of Kansas City (9412 High Dr., 66206), 1983. Written in a diary format, this fictional story of a 14-year-old incest victim describes her feelings at disclosure, treatment, and long-term therapy.

*_____, and _____. *The Wonder What Owl.* Leawood KS: Children's Institute, 1984. A book to read to children (ages 3–7) about sexual abuse. Opportunities to discuss touch, secrets, telling an adult, and private body parts.

McLawhorn, Richard. *Summary of the Final Report of the Attorney General's Commission on Pornography.* Cincinnati OH: National Coalition Against Pornography (800 Compton Rd., Suite 9248), July 1986.

Maclay, D.T. "Boys Who Commit Sexual Misdemeanors." *British Medical Journal* 11, 1960.

McMenmon, M. *Personal Communication.* 1979.

McMillon-Hall, N. *The Focus of Group Treatment with Sexually Abused Children.* Chevery MN: Prince George's County Sexual Assault Center, 1977.

MacNamara, D. and Sagarin, E. *Sex Crime and the Law,* 1977.

Madlicott, R. *Parent-Child Incest.* Australia and New Zealand Journal of Psychiatry 1, 1967.

Magal, V., and Winnick, H. "Role of Incest in Family Structure." *The Israel Annals of Psychiatry and Related Disciplines,* December 1968.

Maisch, H. *Incest.* New York: Stein and Day, 1972.

Mann, E., and McDermott, J. "Play Therapy for Victims of Child Abuse and Neglect." In Schaefer, C., and O'Connor, K., eds., *Handbook of Play Therapy.* New York: Wiley, 1983.

Mann, Peggy. "How Shock Rock Harms Our Kids." *Reader's Digest,* July 1988.

Mann, Thomas. *Death in Venice.*

Marcuse, M. "Incest." *American Journal of Urology and Sexology* 16, 1923.

Margolin, Leslie. "Group Therapy as a Means of Learning About the Sexually Assaultive Adolescent." *International Journal of Offender Therapy and Comparative Criminology* 28, 1984.

_____. "A Treatment Model for the Adolescent Sex Offender." *Journal of Offender Counseling, Services and Rehabilitation* 8, 1983.

Markley, Oscar B. "A Study of Aggressive Sex Misbehavior in Adolescents Brought to Juvenile Court." *American Journal of Orthopsychiatry,* 1950.

Marois, M.R.; Perreault, L.A.; and Messier, C. *Incest: Three or More Is a Crowd— "Learning to Help Them...".* Quebec Ministere de la Justice, Comite de la protection de la jeunesse, 1984.

*Marsano, W. *The Street Smart Book.* New York: Messner, 1985.

Marshall, W. "Growth and Sexual Maturation in Normal Puberty." *Clinics in Endocrinology and Metabolism* 4, 1975.

Marshall, W., and Christie, M. "Pedophilia and Aggression." *Criminal Justice and Behavior* **8**, 1981.

*Marshner, Connie. *Decent Exposure: How to Teach Your Children About Sex.* Pomona CA: Focus on the Family, August 1988.

*Martens, J.H. *WHO (We Help Ourselves).* Dallas TX: Mental Health Association of Dallas, 1983. Curriculum guide to the *WHO* program, which teaches children to protect themselves from many harmful situations including potential sexual abuse. Includes materials for starting a *WHO* program in one's own community.

Martin, Harold P., ed. *The Abused Child: A Multidisciplinary Approach to Developmental Issues and Treatment.* 1976.

Martin, J. "A Psychological Investigation of Convicted Incest Offenders by Means of Projective Techniques." *Dissertation Abstracts,* 1960.

Martinson, F. *Infant and Child Sexuality.* St. Peter MN: Book Mark, 1973.

Maslow, A. *Toward a Psychology of Being.* New York: Van Nostrand, 1964.

Masson, J. *The Assault on Truth: Freud's Suppression of the Seduction Theory.* New York: Farrar, Straus and Giroux, 1984.

Masters, R.E.L. *Eros and Evil.*

_____. *Forbidden Sexual Behavior and Morality.*

_____. *The Homosexual Revolution.*

_____. *Patterns of Incest.* New York: Julian, 1963.

Masters, R.E.L., with Edwardes, Allen. *The Cradle of Erotica.*

Masters, R.E.L., and Lea, Eduard. *Perverse Crimes in History.* New York: Julian, 1963.

Masters, R.E.L., and Webster, Donald, eds. *Violation of Taboo: An Anthology.*

Masters, W., and Johnson, V. *Human Sexual Inadequacy.* Boston: Little, Brown, 1970.

_____, and _____. "Incest: The Ultimate Sexual Taboo." *Redbook* Magazine, April 1976.

Mathis, J. *Clear Thinking About Sexual Deviations.* Undated.

Maudsley, H. "Illustrations of a Variety of Insanity." *The Journal of Mental Disease,* 1963.

*May, G. *Understanding Sexual Child Abuse.* Chicago: National Committee for the Prevention of Child Abuse. An early overview of child sexual abuse.

Mayer, A. *Incest: A Treatment Manual for Therapy with Victims, Spouses and Offenders.* Holmes Beach FL: Learning, 1983.

_____. *Sexual Abuse Causes, Consequences, and Treatment of Incestuous and Pedophilia Acts.* Holmes Beach FL: Learning, 1985.

Mayhall, P., and Norgard, K. *Child Abuse and Neglect; Sharing Responsibility.* New York: Wiley, 1983.

Mead, M. *Coming of Age in Samoa.* New York: Morrow, 1928.

_____. *Sex and Temperament in Primitive Societies.* New York: Dell, 1968.

Meharry Community Mental Health Center. *Meharry Child Sexual Abuse Project: Final Progress Report.* Nashville TN: Meharry Medical College, 1986.

Meikamp, K.D. *Treatment of Child Sexual Abuse: A Selected Annotated Bibliography.* Washington DC: Office of Human Development Services, November 1986.

Meiselman, K. *Incest: A Psychological Study of Causes and Effects with Treatment Recommendations.* San Francisco: Jossey-Bass, 1978. Information about the effects of childhood incest in later years. Aimed largely at mental health professionals.

Meister, Robert. *Fathers: Daughters: Sons, Fathers, Reveal Their Deepest Feelings.* New York: Marek/St. Martin's, 1981.

Melton, G. "Procedural Reforms to Protect Child Victim/Witnesses in Sex Offense Pro-
ceedings." In Bulkley, J., ed., *Child Sexual Abuse and the Law*. Washington DC:
American Bar Association, National Legal Resource Center for Child Advocacy and
Protection, 1981.

Melton, G.; Bulkley, J.; and Wulkan, D. "Competency of Children as Witnesses." In
Bulkley, J., ed., *Child Sexual Abuse and the Law*. Washington DC: American Bar
Association, National Legal Resource Center for Child Advocacy and Protection,
1981.

*Meyer, L. *Safety Zone: A Book Teaching Child Abduction Prevention Skills*. Edmonds WA: Charles Franklin, 1984. Teaches preventive measures for children
through the use of read-aloud hypothetical situations. Gives adults suggestions for
ways to teach their children to be cautious. Attempts to teach problem-solving skills
and to create an atmosphere for open discussion of a serious subject.

Michigan State Department of Social Services. *Final Report Project: Live Theater for
the Prevention of Child Abuse*. Hart MI. Supported by National Center on Child
Abuse and Neglect. Washington DC, December 17, 1985.

Middleton, R. "Brother-Sister and Father-Daughter Marriages in Ancient Egypt."
American Sociological Review 27, 1962.

*Miklowitz, G. *Did You Hear What Happened to Andrea?* New York: Dell, 1979.

Milinowski, B. *Sex and Regression in Savage Society*. London: Routledge and Kegan
Paul, 1927.

*Miller, Alice. *Thou Shalt Not Be Aware: Society's Betrayal of the Child*. New York:
Farrar, Straus, and Giroux, 1984. Sensitive, logical understanding of children and
their feelings.

*Miller, D., and Brinkley, E.S. *Mothers and Others Beware: My Daughter from Baby
Dolls to Daddy's Doll*. Burbank CA: Restauration, 1985. Examines the author's personal experiences with father-daughter incest. Appendices include myths and facts
about incest.

Miller, Gail, and Tompkins, Sandra. *Kidnapped at Chowchilla*. Logos, 1977.

Miller, J., et al. "Recidivism Among Sex Assault Victims." *American Journal of
Psychiatry* 135, 1978.

Miller, P. *Blaming the Victim of Child Molestation: An Empirical Analysis*. Doctoral
Dissertation, Northwestern University, 1976.

Miller, V., and Mansfield, E. "Family Therapy for the Multiple Incest Family." Sacred
Heart Hospital, Eau Claire WI. *Journal of Psychiatric Nursing and Mental Health
Services*, April 1981.

Miner, L. "Sexual Molestation of Children: A Medico-Legal Problem." *Acta Medinale
Legalis et Socialis* 19, April-June 1966.

*Minnesota State Department of Public Welfare. *Protective Parenting: The Art of
Teaching Children About Sexual Abuse*. St. Paul MN: Criminal Justice Program, undated. Guidelines for parents, both in teaching prevention skills and in dealing with
sexual abuse if it happens. Describes Minnesota laws against child sexual abuse.

Minte, Dan, ed. "Criminal Justice and Child Molesters: A Dialogue." *Connections*,
Winter 1986.

Minuchin, S. *Families and Family Therapy*. Cambridge MA: Harvard University Press,
1974.

Mittleman, Mary; Abel, Gene G.; Becker, Judith V.; and Cunningham-Rathner, Jerry.
Predicting Treatment Outcome for Child Molesters. Paper presented at the NIMH
Sponsored Conference on Sex Offenders at Florida Mental Health Institute, 1986.

Missing and Exploited Children's Resource Guide. Washington DC: National Center
for Missing and Exploited Children.

Mohr, J. "The Pedophilias: Their Clinical, Social and Legal Implications." *Canadian Psychiatric Association Journal* 7, 1962.

Mohr, J.; Turner, R.; and Jerry, M. *Pedophilia and Exhibitionism.* Toronto: University of Toronto, 1964.

Molnar, G., and Cameron, P. "Incest Syndromes: Observations in a General Hospital Psychiatric Unit." *Canadian Psychiatric Association Journal* 20, August 1975.

Money, J., and Tucker, P. *Sexual Signatures.* Boston: Little, Brown, 1975.

Money, John. "Erotic Sex and Imaging in Sexual Hangups." In Bullough, Vern L., ed., *The Frontiers of Sex Research.* 1979.

*Montgomery, B., and Grimm, C. *Red Flag, Green Flag People — Program Guide.* Fargo ND: Rape and Abuse Crisis Center of Fargo-Moorhead, 1983. Curriculum guide to the "Red Flag — Green Flag" Program used in some Minnesota schools to teach children about sexual abuse. Includes films, discussion guidelines, coloring book activities, review exercises.

*Montgomery, Becky; Grimm, Carol; and Schwandt, Peg. *Once I Was a Little Bit Frightened.* Fargo ND: Rape and Abuse Crisis Center of Fargo-Moorhead, 1983. Designed for parents and teachers of children in grades K–3. Helps these adults to discover and deal with possible sexual abuse.

Morgan, E. "The Puritans and Sex." *The New England Quarterly* 15, 1942.

*Morgan, M.K. *My Feelings.* Eugene OR: Migima Designs, 1984. Coloring book. Teaches children to listen to their own feelings of warning or discomfort and to tell an adult about situations that make them feel this way.

_____. *Preventing Sexual Abuse of Children: A Curriculum for K–6 and 7–12 Grades.* Juneau AK: Council on Domestic Violence and Sexual Assault, 1983. Curriculum from the Alaska public schools. Offers background information on sexual abuse, facts about Alaska laws, and a special lesson plan on the effects of alcohol on decision-making. Many activities included; each lesson features a videotape.

*Morgan, Marcia K. *Safe Touch.* 1985. Curriculum for grades K–5. Background information, teacher training, complete 5-day lesson plans.

Morris, M. *If I Should Die Before I Wake.* Boston: Tarcher, 1982.

Moulton, J.; Greenberg, N.; et al. *Child Sexual Abuse: Four Case Studies.* Film on a workshop held in December 1976.

Mouzakitis, C.M., and Varghese, R. *Social Work Treatment with Abused and Neglected Children.* University of Maryland, Baltimore, School of Social Work and Community Planning. Springfield IL: Thomas, 1985.

Mrazek, D.A. "The Child Psychiatric Examination of the Sexually Abused Child." Colorado University, Denver, Health Sciences Center. *Child Abuse and Neglect,* 1980.

Mrazek, P.B. "Annotation: Sexual Abuse of Children." *Journal of Child Psychology/ Psychiatry* 21, 1980.

_____. "Definition and Recognition of Sexual Child Abuse: Historical and Cultural Perspectives." In Mrazek, P., and Kempe, C.H., *Sexually Abused Children and Their Families.* New York: Pergamon, 1981.

_____. *Group Psychotherapy with Sexually Abused Children.* Denver: Colorado University, Health and Sciences Center, 1981.

_____. "Sexual Abuse of Children." University of Colorado Medical Center, Denver, and the National Center for the Prevention and Treatment of Child Abuse and Neglect. *Journal of Psychology and Psychiatry,* 1980.

_____. "Special Problems in the Treatment of Child Sexual Abuse." In Mrazek, P.B., and Kempe, C.H., eds., *Sexually Abused Children and Their Families.* New York: Pergamon, 1981.

Mrazek, P.B., and Kempe, C.H., eds. *Sexually Abused Children and Their Families.* Colorado University, Denver, Health Sciences Center. New York: Pergamon, 1981. A very comprehensive book for professionals.

Mrazek, P.B., and Mrazek, D.A. "The Effects of Child Sexual Abuse: Methodological Considerations." In Mrazek, P.B., and Kempe, C.H., eds., *Sexually Abused Children and Their Families.* New York: Pergamon, 1981.

Muenchow, A., and Slater, E. "Rebuilding Families After Sexual Abuse of the Children." University of Washington, Seattle, School of Social Work. *Practice Magazine*, September 1978.

Muldoon, L. *Incest: Confronting the Silent Crime.* St. Paul: Minnesota Program for Victims of Sexual Assault, Documents Division (117 University Ave., 55155), 1979.

Murasaki (Lady) (Murasaki-Shikibu). *The Tale of Genji.* 1926.

Murdock, G. *Social Structure.* New York: Macmillan, 1949.

Murray, F. *Rondeaux of Boyhood.* London: Privately published, 1923.

Myerhoff, B. *Incest in Myth and Fact.* Masters Thesis, University of Chicago, 1963.

Myers, B. "Incest: If You Think the Word Is Ugly — Take a Look at Its Effects." In Jones, Jenstrom, and MacFarlane, eds., *Sexual Abuse of Children: Selected Readings.* Washington DC: National Center on Child Abuse and Neglect, November 1980.

Nabokov, V. *Lolita.* New York: Putnam, 1955.

Nair, N. *Narayana.* 1968.

Nakashima, I.I., and Zakus, G. *Incest: Review and Clinical Experience Pediatrics for Clinicians.* 1977.

————, and ————. "Incestuous Families." Colorado University, Denver, Medical School. *Pediatrics Annuals,* May 1979.

Nash, D. "Legal Issues Related to Child Pornography," *Legal Response: Child Advocacy and Protection* 2, 1981.

Nasjleti, M. "Suffering in Silence: The Male Incest Victim." *Child Welfare* 49, 1970.

National Center for the Prevention and Control of Rape. *Public and Private Sources of Funding for Sexual Assault Treatment Programs.* Rockville MN: August 1981.

National Center on Child Abuse and Neglect. *Child Sexual Abuse: Incest, Assault and Sexual Exploitation.* Washington DC: U.S. Department of Health, Education and Welfare, August 1978.

*————. *Child Sexual Abuse Prevention Tips to Parents.* Washington DC: U.S. Department of Health and Human Services, 1984.

————. *A Marketplace of Community Programs.* Washington DC: National Conference on Child Abuse and Neglect, Baltimore MD, September 25–28, 1983.

————. *Perspectives on Child Maltreatment in the Mid 80's.* Washington DC: 1984.

————. *Study Findings: National Study of the Incidence and Severity of Child Abuse and Neglect.* Washington DC: Department of Health and Human Services, 1981.

*National Child Safety Council. *All About Touching.* Jackson MI.

*————. *Beware and Be Aware of Dangerous Strangers.* Jackson MI.

*National Committee for the Prevention of Child Abuse. *Basic Facts About Child Sexual Abuse.* This pamphlet answers 27 basic questions about the incidence, nature, and legal aspects of sexual child abuse. Included in the pamphlet are a discussion of factors that contribute to incestuous behavior and descriptions of some physical, behavioral, and conversational symptoms a sexually abused child might present.

————. *Child Sexual Abuse Prevention Resources.* Chicago: 1984.

*————. *Guidelines for Child Sexual Abuse Prevention Programs.* Chicago: 1986. This pamphlet will help you to ensure the quality and effectiveness of child sexual

abuse prevention programs. Contains recommendations for the selection, effective use, and evaluation of such programs. Discusses the needs of special groups, the selection and training of program presenters, and other critical issues.

*_____. *Stop Child Sexual Abuse.* Comprehensive pamphlets concerning child sexual abuse: *Talking About Child Sexual Abuse; Guidelines for Child Sexual Abuse Prevention Programs; A Look at Child Sexual Abuse; Basic Facts About Child Sexual Abuse; You Don't Have to Molest That Child;* and *Spider-Man and Power Pack,* a sexual abuse prevention comic book, along with the *Teachers Guide* that accompanies the comic.

*National Education Association of the United States. *What Parents Should Know About Child Sexual Abuse.* West Haven CT: 1984.

National Legal Resource Center for Child Advocacy and Protection. *Innovations in the Protection of Child Sexual Abuse Cases.* Washington DC: American Bar Association, 1982.

_____. *Recommendations for Improving Legal Intervention in Intra-Family Child Sexual Abuse Cases.* Washington DC: American Bar Association, 1982.

Navarre, E.L. *Sexually Abused Children Prevention, Protection, and Care: A Handbook for Residential Child Care Facilities.* Indiana University-Purdue University at Indianapolis School of Social Work, 1983.

Navy Family Advocacy. Training Project: Final Report. Washington DC: December 1982.

*Nelson, B. *Making an Issue of Child Abuse: Political Agenda Setting for Social Problems.* Chicago: University of Chicago Press, 1984. The history of the various child abuse policies and how the government, legislation and the media play roles. Also includes incest, rape and child pornography.

Nelson, J.A. *The Impact of Incest: Factors in Self-Evaluation.* In Constantine, L., and Martinson, F., eds., *Children and Sex.* Boston: Little, Brown, 1981.

Nelson, M., and Clark, K., eds. *The Educator's Guide to Preventing Child Sexual Abuse.* Santa Cruz CA: Network, 1986. For professionals, including teachers, social workers, and law enforcement personnel. Describes 19 innovative prevention and education programs.

Nesbitt, W. *The Trail to Boyhood and Other Poems.* Indianapolis: Bobbs-Merrill, 1924.

Neuman, R. "Masturbation, Madness and the Modern Concepts of Childhood and Adolescence." *Journal of Social History* **8**, 1975.

Newberger, E. *Child Abuse.* Boston MA: Little, Brown, 1982.

Newberger, E.H., and Bourne, R. *Unhappy Families: Clinical and Research Perspectives on Family Violence.* Harvard Medical School, Cambridge MA. Littleton MA: PSG, 1985.

Newberger, E.H., and Newberger, C.M. *Sex with Children: Toward Policy.* Paper presented at the National Conference on the Sexual Abuse of Children, Washington DC, April 26, 1984.

New Jersey Department of Human Services. *Adolescent Maltreatment: First Statewide Conference, Smithville-Quail Hill Inn, Smithville, NJ.* Atlantic City NJ: Atlantic County Adolescent Maltreatment Project, October 22, 1981.

Newman, G. *The Punishment Response.* Philadelphia: Lippincott, 1978.

*Newman, S. *Never Say Yes to a Stranger: What Your Child Must Know to Stay Safe.* New York: Putnam, 1985. Stories illustrated with photographs depicting different situations in which children are approached by strangers and explaining the dangers of such encounters. Easy to read. Supporting questions and statements make up a review at the end of each chapter.

New Mexico Human Services Department. *Final Report: Sexual Abuse Team, Family Resource Center.* Albuquerque NM: Family Resource Center, Sexual Abuse Team, March 31, 1982.

Nicholson, J. *Love in Earnest: Sonnets, Ballads and Lyrics.* London: Eliot Stock, 1892.

Nobile, P. *Incest: The Last Taboo. Penthouse* Magazine, December 1977.

Nursing Clinics of North America. *Sexual Trauma of Children and Adolescents: Pressure, Sex and Secrecy.* September 1975.

Oaks, R. "Defining Sodomy in 17th Century Massachusetts." *Journal of Homosexuality* 6, 1980–81.

_____. "Things Fearful to Name: Sodomy and Buggery in 17th Century New England." *Journal of Social History* 12, 1978.

O'Brien, M. "Adolescent Sexual Offenders: A Community Faces Reality." *Change: A Juvenile Justice Quarterly* 5, 1983.

O'Brien, Shirley. *Child Abuse: A Crying Shame.* Provo UT: Brigham Young University Press, 1980.

_____. *Child Abuse and Neglect: Everyone's Problem.* Association for Childhood Education International, 1984.

_____. *Child Pornography.* Dubuque IA: Kendall Hunt, 1983.

O'Carroll, Tom. *Paedophilia—A Response.* Paedophile Information Exchange (PIE, P.O. Box 318 London, SE 3 8QD).

_____. *Paedophilia: The Radical Case.* London: Owen, 1980.

O'Day, B. *Preventing Sexual Abuse of Persons with Disabilities: A Curriculum for Hearing Impaired, Physically Disabled, Blind, and Mentally Retarded Students.* Minnesota State Department Adolescents Project. Santa Cruz CA: Network, June 1983. Examines the special vulnerability of disabled adolescents. Acquaintance rape, incest, myths and facts, victim reactions, personal safety and assertiveness are covered.

Oellerich, T., and Melvin, M. *Child Sexual Abuse Forum Resource Booklet.* Milwaukee: University of Wisconsin, Region V Child Abuse and Neglect Resource Center, April 6, 1981.

*Olesky, W. *The ABC's of Growing Up Safely.* New York: Modern, 1985. For children. Alphabet format includes two full-page drawings (suitable for coloring) for each letter, illustrating safety instructions. Includes colorful poster that can be hung in a child's room.

Olson, Marlys. *Personal Safety: Curriculum for Prevention of Child Sexual Abuse.* Tacoma WA: Tacoma School District Administration Building (P.O. Box 1357, 98401). Comprehensive curriculum includes bibliographic information and complete lesson plans for Headstart, K–2, 3–4, 5–6, junior high, and senior high levels. Teacher's manual included.

O'Neal, P.; Schaefer, J.; Bergmann, J.; and Robins, L. "A Psychiatric Evaluation of Adults Who Had Sexual Problems as Children: A Thirty-Five Year Follow-Up Study." *Human Organization,* Spring 1960.

Oppenheimer, R.; Howells K.; Palmer, R.L.; and Challner, D.A. *Adverse Sexual Experience and Clinical Eating Disorders: A Preliminary Description.* Unpublished paper. University Department of Psychiatry and Psychology, University of Leicester, United Kingdom, 1985.

Oremland, E., and Oremland, J. *The Sexual and Gender Development of Young Children: The Role of Education.* Cambridge MA: Ballinger, 1977.

Ortiz y Pino, J., and Goodwin, J. *What Families Say: The Dialogue of Incest.* Albuquerque NM: Family Resource Center, 1982.

*Pall, M. *Let's Talk About It! The Book for Children About Child Abuse.* Saratoga CA: Raul E., 1983.

*Palmer, P. *Liking Myself.* San Luis Obispo CA: Impact, 1977. Teaches young children how to trust and act on their own feelings.

Panton, J. "MMPI Profile Configurations Associated with Incestuous and Non-Incestuous Child Molesters." *Psychological Reports* 45, 1979.

Paperny, D.M., and Deisher, R.W. "Maltreatment of Adolescents: The Relationship to a Predisposition Toward Violent Behavior and Delinquency." *Adolescence* 18, 1983.

Parad, H., ed. *Crisis Intervention.* New York: Family Service Association of America, 1965.

Parent Education Center of Yakima. *Childproof for Sexual Abuse.* Yakima WA: 1984.

Parents United and the Child Sexual Abuse Treatment Project. *Help for Sexually Abused Children and Their Families.* Child Sexual Abuse Treatment Program Package, 1978.

Parker, G. "Incest." *The Medical Journal of Australia,* March 30, 1974.

Parker, S. "The Precultural Basis of the Incest Taboo: Toward a Biological Theory." *American Anthropologist,* 1976.

Parsons, T. "Social Structure of the Family." In Anghen, R., ed., *The Family: Its Function and Destiny.* New York: Harper, 1949.

Pasewark, R., and Albers, D. "Crisis Intervention: Theory in Search of a Program." *Social Work* 17, 1972.

Paulson, M., and Blake, P. "The Physically Abused Child: A Focus on Prevention." *Child Welfare* 48, 1969.

Payne, S.L., and Elgrich, M. *Community Resource Network Project.* Austin TX: Austin Child Guidance Evaluation Center, December 28, 1983.

Pelton, L. *The Social Context of Child Abuse and Neglect.* New York: Human Sciences, 1981.

*Peters, D.B. *Betrayal of Innocence: What Everyone Should Know About Child Sexual Abuse.* Waco TX: Word, 1986. Christian emphasis. Discusses basic information with special emphasis on caring assistance to victim and family. Teaching aids are described.

Peters, J. "Child Rape: Defusing a Psychological Time Bomb." *Hospital Physician* 9, February 1973.

_____. "Children Who Are Victims of Sexual Assault and the Psychology of Offenders." *American Journal of Psychotherapy* 30, 1976.

_____. Commentary in C. McCaghy, "Child Molesting." *Sexual Behavior* 1, 1971.

Peters, Joseph J., Institute. *Final Report of the Intrafamilial Child Sexual Abuse Treatment-Training Institute for Federal Regions I, II & III.* Philadelphia; September 30, 1983.

Peters, S.D.; Wyatt, G.E.; Finkelhor, D. "Prevalence: A Review of the Research." In Finkelhor, D., ed., *A Sourcebook on Child Sexual Abuse.* Beverly Hills CA: Sage, 1986.

Phillips, D. *The Federal Model Child Care Standards Act of '85: Step in the Right Direction or Hollow Gesture?* Washington DC: National Association for the Education of Young Children, January 1986.

*Phillips, Paul, and Cordell, Franklin. *Am I O.K.??* Niles IL: Franklin-Argus, 1975.

Pickett, J. *Child Sexual Abuse.* British Association for the Study and Prevention of Child Abuse and Neglect, 1981.

Pierce, R.L. *Child Pornography: A Hidden Dimension of Child Abuse.* St. Louis MO: Washington University, George Warren Brown School of Social Work, 1984. A very complete paper profiling children involved in pornography. Includes estimates of the number of children involved nationwide, discussion of the presumed effects of that involvement, a look at legal issues, and a recommendation for treatment and prevention.

Pierce, R.L., and Pierce, L.H. "Analysis of Sexual Abuse Hotline Reports." Washington University, St. Louis MO, George Warren Brown School of Social Work. *Child Abuse and Neglect,* 1985.

————, and ————. "The Sexually Abused Child: A Comparison of Male and Female Vicims." *Child Abuse and Neglect* **9,** 1985.

Pierce County Rape Relief. *Sourcebook for Educators: Sexual Assault Prevention for Adolescents.* Tacoma WA: Allenmore Medical Center (Bldg. B, Suite 2002, 9th and Union, 98405). Teacher's guide with comprehensive curriculum activities. Lesson plans ranging from one day to one week.

Piers, M. *Infanticide.* New York: Norton, 1978.

Pincus, L., and Dare, C. *Secrets in the Family.* London: Faber & Faber, 1978.

Pittman, F. "Counseling Incestuous Families." *Medical Aspects of Human Sexuality* **10,** April 1976.

Pizzey, E. *Scream Quietly or the Neighbors Will Hear.* Short Hills NJ: Enslow, 1977.

Plummer, C.A. "Child Sexual Abuse Prevention: Keys to Program Success." In Nelson, M., and Clark, K., eds., *The Educator's Guide to Preventing Child Sexual Abuse.* Santa Cruz CA: Network, 1986.

*————. *Preventing Sexual Abuse: Activities and Strategies for Those Working with Children and Adolescents. Curriculum Guide for: K–6, 7–12, and Special Populations.* Holmes Beach FL: Learning, 1984. Developmentally disabled children are included in these lesson plans. Teacher training and parental involvement are factors in this prevention program. Appendices include a sexual abuse fact sheet, definitions, a "touch continuum" (good to bad touches), a discussion of prevention skills, a list of incest indicators, reporting procedures, and a chart showing what happens when a report is made.

————. "Prevention Education in Perspective." In Nelson, M., and Clark, K., eds., *The Educator's Guide to Preventing Child Sexual Abuse.* Santa Cruz CA: Network, 1986.

Plummer, C.A., and Crisci, G.A. *Sexual Abuse Prevention: Sustaining and Expanding Programs.* Kalamazoo MI: Prevention Training Associates and Personal Safety Program (P.O. Box 421, 49005), February 1985 to August 1986.

Plummer, C.A., and Fields, J. *Personal Safety Protection Program.* Austin TX: Texas Congress of Parents and Teachers (408 West 11th St., 78701), September 1985–January 1987.

Plummer, K. *"The Paedophile's" Progress: A View from Below.* Colchester, England: Essex University, Department of Sociology, 1981.

Polansky, N. *Roots of Futility.* San Francisco: Jossey-Bass, 1972.

Polansky, N., et al. *Damaged Parents: An Anatomy of Child Neglect.* Chicago: University of Chicago Press, 1981.

*Polese, Carolyn. *Promise Not to Tell.* New York: Human Sciences, 1985. A fictional book about a child who is sexually abused. For parents, teachers, psychologists, and child welfare personnel to use in both prevention and treatment.

Polk County Intra-Family Sexual Abuse of Children Program. Project Evaluation. Des Moines IA: August 1984.

Pomeroy, W. *Your Child and Sex.* New York: Delacorte, 1974.

————. "A New Look at Incest." *The Best of Forum.* 1978.

*Porteaus, Trace. *Let's Talk About Sexual Abuse.* Victoria, Canada: Women's Sexual

Assault Centre, 1984. For young women. What sexual abuse is, why it happens, what to do, how to reduce the risks.

Porter, E. *Treating the Young Male Victim of Sexual Assault: Issues and Intervention Strategies.* Syracuse NY: Safer Society, 1986.

Porter, R. *Child Sexual Abuse Within the Family.* Ciba Foundation, London. New York: Tavistock, 1984.

Post, N. "Criminal and Civil Court Coordination." In *Papers from a National Policy Conference on Legal Reforms in Child Sexual Abuse Cases.* Washington DC: National Legal Resource Center on Child Advocacy and Protection, 1985.

Power, A.K., and D'Amico, M. *Meeting the Emotional Needs of Sexual Assault Victims.* Harrisburg PA: Harrisburg Area Rape Crisis Center, 1979.

Powers, J., and Chain, S. "The Adolescent Perpetrator in Child Sexual Abuse." *Colorado's Children,* 1982–1983.

Pozanski, E., and Blos, P. "Incest." *Medical Aspects of Human Sexuality,* October 1975.

Prince, J. "Father-Daughter Incest: An Attempt to Maintain the Family and to Meet Human Needs?" *Family and Community Health,* August 1981.

*Project Two. *Ice Cream Isn't Always Good!* New York: 1971. Fictional story of a girl who agrees to go with a stranger for an ice-cream cone, is abducted, and is eventually able to call the police and be rescued. Designed to teach children not to accept offers from strangers. Includes questions at the end to test the child's understanding of the story.

"Psychotherapeutic and Legal Approaches to the Sexually Victimized Child." *International Journal of Child Psychotherapy,* 1972.

Queen's Bench Foundation. *Sexual Abuse of Children.* San Francisco: 1976.

Quinn, P. *Cry Out!!* Nashville: Abingdon, 1984.

Quinsey, Vernon. "Men Who Have Sex with Children." In Weasstub, David N., ed., *Law and Mental Health: International Perspectives.* New York: Pergamon, 1986.

_____. "The Assessment and Treatment of Child Molesters: A Review." *Canadian Psychological Review,* July 1977.

Quinsey, Vernon L.; Bergersen, Sidney G.; and Steinman, Cary M. *Changes in Physiological and Verbal Responses of Child Molesters During Aversion Therapy.* 1976.

Quinsey, Vernon L.; Chaplin, Terry C.; and Carrigan, Wayne F. "Sexual Preferences Among Incestuous and Non-Incestuous Child Molesters." *Behavior Therapy* **10,** 1979.

Quinsey, Vernon L.; Steinman, Cary M.; Bergersen, Sidney G.; and Holmes, Timothy F. "Penile Circumference, Skin Conductance, and Ranking Responses of Child Molesters and 'Normals' to Sexual and Non-Sexual Visual Stimuli." *Behavior Therapy* **6,** 1975.

*Quiri, Patricia, and Powell, Suzanne. *Stranger Danger.* New York: Messner, 1985. This safety guide for children has several well-written stories about possible situations where a child could be assaulted. Also features a list of good, common sense safety tips.

Rada, Richard T. "Alcoholism and the Child Molester." *Annual of the New York Academy of Sciences,* May 28, 1979.

Ramsey, G.V. "The Sexual Development of Boys." *American Journal of Psychiatry* **56,** 1943.

Ramsey, J. "Dealing with the Last Taboo." *Siecus Report* **7,** 1979.

_____. "My Husband Broke the Ultimate Taboo." *Family Circle* Magazine, March 8, 1977.

Randolph, V. *Pissing in the Snow and Other Ozark Folktales*. Urbana: University of Illinois, 1976.

Raphling, D.; Carpenter, B.; and Davis, A. "Incest: A Genealogical Study." *Archives of General Psychiatry* **16**, April 1967.

Rapoport, L. "The State of Crisis: Some Theoretical Considerations." *Social Service Review* **36**, 1962.

Rascovsky, A., and Rascovsky, M. "The Prohibition of Incest, Filicide and the Socio-Cultural Process." *International Journal of Psychoanalysis,* 1972.

Rascovsky, M., and Rascovsky, A. "On Consummated Incest." *International Journal of Psychoanalysis* **31**, 1950.

Rasmussen, Augusta. *Die Bedeutung sexueller Attentäte auf Kinder unter 14 Jahren für die Entwicklung von Geisteskrankheiten und charakteranomalien.* Norway, 1934.

Raybin, J. "Homosexual Incest: Report of a Case of Homosexual Incest Involving Three Generations of a Family." *Journal of Nervous and Mental Disease,* February 1969.

"Readers Discuss Family Sex." *Forum*, July 1977.

Reed, C.J. *Multi-Intervention Strategies for Child Sexual Abuse Victims*. Los Angeles: California Department of Children's Services, Child Sexual Abuse Program, Summer 1985.

Regestein, Quentin R., M.D., and Reich, Peter, M.D. "Pedophilia Occurring After Onset of Cognitive Impairment." *Journal of Nervous and Mental Disease* **166**, 1978.

Reich, J.W., and Gutierres, S.E. "Escape/Aggression Incidence in Sexually Abused Juvenile Delinquents." *Criminal Justice Behavior* **6**, 1979.

Reich, W. *The Sexual Revolution*. Vision, 1972.

Reiss, A.J. "Sex Offenses: The Marginal Status of the Adolescent." *Law and Contemporary Problems* **25**.

Renshaw, D.C. *Incest: Understanding and Treatment*. Boston: Little, Brown, 1982. With the aim of increasing the sensitivity of helping professionals toward victims of incest and their families, this book discusses incest from anthropological, historical, legal, religious, moral, and psychosocial perspectives.

_____. Sex Talk for a Safe Child. Chicago: Loyola University and the American Medical Association, 1984. Designed to help parents teach their children to distinguish between normal and harmful sexual and affectionate behavior. Illustrations and explanations of genitalia are included, with an emphasis on their privacy.

Renton (WA) School District. *Sexual Abuse Prevention—A Unit in Safety*. Washington Department of Instruction, 1981.

Renvoize, J. *Incest: A Family Pattern*. London: Routledge and Kegan Paul, 1982.

Reposa, R.E., and Zuelzer, M.B. "Family Therapy with Incest." Community Guidance Center, San Antonio TX. *International Journal of Family Therapy*, Summer 1983.

Resnick, H.L.P., and Peters, Joseph J. *Outpatient Group Therapy with Convicted Pedophiles*. No publisher or date.

Resnick, H.L.P., M.D., and Wolfgang, Marvin E., Ph.D. *Sexual Behaviors: Social, Clinical, and Legal Aspects*. Boston: Little, Brown, 1972.

Resnick, P. "Child Murder by Parents: A Psychiatric Review of Filicide." *American Journal of Psychiatry*, September 1969.

Revitich, E., and Weiss, R. "The Pedophiliac Offender." *Diseases of the Nervous System* **23**, 1962.

Rhinehart, J. "Genesis of Overt Incest." *Comprehensive Psychiatry* **2**, 1961.

Ricks, C. *Carol's Story*. Wheaton IL: Tyndale House, 1985.

Riemer, S. "A Research Note on Incest." *American Journal of Sociology* **45**, 1939–1940.

Righton, P. "The Adult." In Taylor, B., ed., *Perspectives on Paedophilia*. London Batsford Academic and Educational, 1981.

Rist, K. "Incest: Theoretical and Clinical Views." *American Journal of Orthopsychiatry*, October 1979.

Rizma, M., and Niggeman, E. "Medical Evaluation of Sexually Abused Children: A Review of 311 Cases." *Pediatrics* **69**, 1982.

Roberts, D. "Incest, Inbreeding and Mental Abilities." *British Medical Journal*, 1967.

Rogers, C.M., and Terry, T. "Clinical Intervention with Boy Victims of Sexual Abuse." In Stuart, I.R., and Greer, J.G., eds., *Victims of Sexual Aggression: Men, Women, and Children*. New York: Van Nostrand Reinhold, 1984.

Rogers, C.M., and Thomas, J.N. "Sexual Victimization of Children in the U.S.A.: Patterns and Trends." Washington DC: Children's Hospital National Medical Center, Division of Child Protection. *Clinical Proceedings* **40**, July-August 1984. Analysis of 402 cases occurring March 1978–January 1981.

Rogers, D. *Hear the Children Crying*. Old Tappen NJ: Revell, 1978.

Rogers, E., and Weiss, J. "Study of Sex Crimes Against Children." In *California Sexual Deviation Research*. CA: Langly Porter, 1953.

Rooth, Graham. "Exhibitionism, Sexual Violence and Paedophilia." *British Journal of Psychiatry* **122**, 1973.

Rosen, D. *Lesbianism: A Study of Female Homosexuality*. Springfield IL: Thomas, 1974.

Rosenberg, C. "Sexuality, Class and Role in 19th Century America." *American Quarterly* **25**, 1973.

Rosenfeld, A.A. "Case Report LVIII—A Case of Sexual Misuse." Children's Hospital Medical Center, Boston MA. *Psychiatric Opinion*, April 1976.

_____. "Endogamic Incest and the Victim-Perpetrator Model." Stanford University CA, School of Medicine. *American Journal of Diseases of Children*, April 1979.

_____. "Sexual Misuse and the Family." *Victimology*, Summer 1977.

_____. *Sexual Misuse of Children*. Unpublished paper, Stanford University, 1978.

Rosenfeld, A.A.; Krieger, M.J.; Nadelson, C.D.; and Backman, J.H. "The Sexual Misuse of Children—A Brief Survey." Children's Hospital Medical Center, Boston MA. *Psychiatric Opinion*, April 1976.

Rosenfeld, A.A.; Nadelson, C.; and Krieger, M. "Fantasy and Reality in Patients' Reports of Incest." *Journal of Clinical Psychiatry*, April 1979.

Rosenzweig-Smith, J. *Human Sexuality Concerns in the Treatment of Child Sexual Abuse and Incest*. 1982.

*Ross, V., and Marlowe, J. *The Forbidden Apple: Sex in the Schools*. Palm Springs CA: ETC, 1985. For teachers, students, parents, and administrators who want insight and guidelines for dealing with sexual exploitation and harassment. Case studies of incidents occurring in North American schools include a custodian who exposed himself to girls he lured into the boiler room; a coach who seduced girls regularly; and a student who asked for help because a financial aid officer wanted sexual favors in exchange for a scholarship.

Rossman, P. *Sexual Experience Between Men and Boys*. New York: Associated Press, 1976.

Rottenberg, R. "Child Abuse: Handling Its Challenges." *Patient Care*, June 15, 1983.

*Rush, F. *The Best Kept Secret: Sexual Abuse of Children*. Englewood Cliffs NJ:

Prentice-Hall, 1980. Excellent, insightful, comprehensive. History of child abuse, discussing why it is so pervasive in our society.

_____. *The Freudian Cover-Up*. Chrysalis, 1977.

_____. "The Sexual Abuse of Children: A Feminist Point of View." In Connell, N., and Wilson, C., eds., *Rape: The First Sourcebook for Women*. New York: NAL/ Plume, 1974.

Russell, A., and Trainor, C. *Trends in Child Abuse and Neglect: A National Perspective*. Denver CO: American Humane Association, 1984.

*Russell, D. *Sexual Exploitation: Rape, Child Sexual Abuse and Workplace Harassment*. Beverly Hills CA: Sage. Includes the author's survey of 930 San Francisco women.

_____. "The Prevalence and Seriousness of Incestuous Abuse: Stepfathers vs. Biological Fathers." *Child Abuse and Neglect* 8, 1984.

*_____. *The Secret Trauma: Incest in the Lives of Girls and Women*. New York: Basic, 1986. Based on Russell's study of 930 San Francisco women.

Russell, Diana. "The Incidence and Prevalence of Intrafamilial and Extrafamilial Sexual Abuse of Female Children." *Child Abuse and Neglect* 7, 1983.

*Russell, P. *Do You Have a Secret??* Minneapolis: CompCare, 1986.

Ryan, G. "Annotated Bibliography: Adolescent Perpetrators of Sexual Molestation of Children." *Child Abuse and Neglect* 19, 1986.

_____. "The Child Abuse Connection." *Interchange*, January 1984.

_____. *Victim to Victimizer: Re-Thinking Victim Treatment*. Denver: Kempe National Center for Prevention and Treatment of Child Abuse and Neglect. Revised May 1988. (Submitted for publication in *Journal of Interpersonal Violence*.)

Ryan, G.; Lane, S.; Davis, J.; and Isaac, C. "Juvenile Sexual Offenders: Development and Correction." *Child Abuse and Neglect* 11, 1987.

Ryan, Gail, with Walers, Elsie, and Alexander, Helen. *The Lay Person's Role in the Prevention of Child Abuse and Neglect*. 1981.

Ryan, M.D. *Sexually Abusing Families*. Families West Branch IA: 1981.

Ryan, T.S. "Problems, Errors and Opportunities in the Treatment of Father-Daughter Incest." Child Sexual Abuse Treatment and Training Center of Illinois. *Journal of Interpersonal Violence*, March 1986.

Sack, W., and Mason, R. "Child Abuse and Conviction of Sexual Crimes." *Laward Human Behavior* 4, 1980.

Sadoff, D. "Treatment of Violent Sex Offenders." *International Journal of Offender Therapy and Comparative Criminology* 19, 1975.

Saffer, J., et al. "The Awesome Burden Upon the Child Who Must Keep a Family Secret." *Child Psychiatry and Human Development* 10, 1979.

Sagarin, E. *Deviants: Voluntary Actors in a Hostile World*. New York: General Learning, 1977.

_____. "Incest: Problems of Definition and Frequency." *Journal of Sex Research*, May 1977.

Sahd, Doris. "Psychological Assessment of Sexually Abusing Families and Treatment Implications." In Holder, W., ed., *Sexual Abuse of Children: Implications for Treatment*. Denver: American Humane Association, 1980.

Saikaku. *The Temple of Pederasty*. 1970.

Sale, J.S. *Child Care and Child Abuse: What Is the Connection?* University of California, Los Angeles, Child Care Services. Testimony Presented to the Select Committee on Children, Youth and Families (House), Hearing on Child Care, San Francisco CA, June 1, 1984.

Sandall, H.; Bell, C.M.; and Cady, K. *Treating Incest in Rural Families*. Virginia MN: Range Family Sexual Abuse Treatment Program, 1983.

*Sanford, L.T. *Come Tell Me Right Away: A Positive Approach.* Lebanon NH: New Victoria Printing Collective, 1982. Booklet explaining why children are vulnerable to sexual abuse. Provides suggestions to parents on how to improve children's self-esteem and intuitive skills to decrease vulnerability. This booklet is a condensed version of *The Silent Children* (*see* below).

_____. "Pervasive Fears in Victims of Sexual Abuse: A Clinician's Observations." In *Preventing Sexual Abuse.* National Family Life Education Network, 1987.

*_____. *The Silent Children: A Parents' Guide to the Prevention of Child Sexual Abuse.* Garden City NY: Anchor/Doubleday, 1980. The author states that "the child's best defense against sexual abuse is a sense of his own power; knowledge of what constitutes sexual abuse; and resources available for support and protection." Contains a section devoted to the special needs of minority parents, single parents, and parents of disabled children. An excellent book.

Sanger, Roger G., and Bross, Donald C., eds. *Clinical Management of Child Abuse and Neglect.* 1984.

Santiago, Jose M.; McCall-Perez, Fred; Gorcey, Michele; Beigel, Allen. "Long-Term Psychological Effects of Rape in 35 Rape Victims." *American Journal of Psychiatry,* November 1985.

Sarafino, E. "An Estimate of Nationwide Incidence of Sexual Offenses Against Children." *Child Welfare,* February 1979.

Sarles, R. "Incest." *Pediatric Clinics of North America* **33,** 1975.

Satullo, Jane A.W.; Russell, Roberta; and Bradway, Pat A. *It Happens to Boys Too.* 1987.

Sawyer, S.G. "Lifting the Veil on the Last Taboo." *Family Health,* June 1980.

Schafer, C.E.; Briesmeister, J.M.; and Fitton, M.E. *Family Therapy Techniques for Problem Behaviors of Children and Teenagers.* San Francisco: Jossey-Bass, 1984.

*Schatzman, M. *The Story of Ruth.* New York: Putnam, 1980.

Schechter, M., and Toberge, L. "Sexual Exploitation." In Helfer, R., and Kempe, C., eds., *Child Abuse and Neglect: The Family and the Community.* Cambridge MA: Ballinger, 1976.

Schelsky, H. *Manual for Kinship Analysis.* New York: Rinehart and Winston, 1955.

Scherer, E. *Emile Perverti.* 1974.

Scherzer, L.N., and Lala, P. "Sexual Offenses Committed Against Children." *Clinical Pediatrics* **19,** October 1980.

Schesinger, B. *Sexual Abuse of Children: A Resource Guide and Annotated Bibliography.* Toronto: University of Toronto Press, 1982.

Schmidt, R. *Beiträge zur indischen Erotils.* 1922.

Schoettle, W. "Child Exploitation." *American Academy of Child Psychiatry* **19,** 1980.

Schomerus, D.H. "Der Pädophile undsein Opfer." In Von Stockhert, F.G., *Das Sexuell Gefährdate Kind.* 1965.

Schorsch, E. *Liberalitat reicht nicht. Betrifft: Erziehung* **4,** 1974.

Schrier, C., and Ensminger, J. *Evidence Collection/Preparation for Court in Sexual Abuse Cases.* Paper delivered at the Hershey Conference on Sexual Abuse of Children. Undated.

*Schroeder, C. *The Sexual Abuse of Children: Preventing It.* Chapel Hill: University of North Carolina, Biological Sciences Research Center, Fall 1985. Suggestions for parents on preventing abuse by educating their children about sexuality, their bodies, and their right to privacy. Also discusses how to screen substitute caregivers and what to tell the child about caregivers who ask them to do uncomfortable things.

Schroeder, D. "Basic Principles of Staff Development and Their Implementation." In Wagner, G.W., and Briggs, T.C., eds., *Staff Development in Mental Health Services.* New York: NASW, 1966.

Schull, W., and Neel, J. *The Effects of Inbreeding on Japanese Children*. New York: Harper and Row, 1965.

*Schultz, D. "The Terror of Child Molestation." *Parents* Magazine, February 1977. Guidelines for parents on helping children avoid molestation. Also discusses how to deal with actual or attempted molestation if it happens. Includes a safety quiz for young school-age children.

Schultz, L. *Diagnosis and Treatment—Introduction*. Morgantown: West Virginia University, School of Social Work, 1980.

_____. "The Child as Sex Victim: Socio-Legal Perspectives." In Schultz, L., *Rape Victimology*. Springfield IL: Thomas, 1975.

_____. "The Child Sex Victim: Social, Psychological, and Legal Perspectives." *Child Welfare* **52**, March 1973.

_____. "Interviewing the Sex Offender's Victim." *Journal of Criminology, Criminal Law and Police Science*, 1960.

_____. *Rape Victimology*. Springfield IL: Thomas, 1975.

_____. "The Sexual Abuse of Children and Minors: A Bibliography." West Virginia University, Morgantown, School of Social Work. *Child Welfare*, March 1979.

_____. "Sexual Victims." In Gachros, H., and Gachros, G., eds., *The Sexually Oppressed*. New York: Association, 1977.

_____. *The Sexual Victimology of Youth*. West Virginia University, Morgantown, School of Social Work. Springfield IL: Thomas, 1980. Review of characteristics of child victims of sexual abuse. Other topics: incidence and frequency; legal issues; the relationship between babysitting and sexual risk; male victims; incest; research problems.

_____. "The Sexual Victimology of Youth." In *Proceedings of the First National Conference on Child Sexual Victimization*, Washington DC, November 29–December 1, 1979. Children's Hospital National Medical Center, 1981.

Schwab, G. *Gods and Heroes: Myths and Epics of Ancient Greece*. New York: Random House, 1974.

Schwartzman, J. "The Individual, Incest and Exogamy." *Psychiatry*, May 1974.

Seaberg, J. *Physical Child Abuse: An Expanded Analysis*. Saratosa: Century Twenty-One, 1980.

Seattle Rape Relief, Washington Developmental Disabilities Project. *Curriculum for Developing an Awareness of Sexual Exploitation and Teaching Self-Protection Techniques. Level II*. Seattle WA: Comprehensive Health Education Foundation, 1979.

Seemanova, E. "A Study of Children of Incestuous Matings." *Human Heredity* **21**, 1971.

Segner, L., and Collins, A. *Cross Cultural Study of Incest Myths*. Unpublished manuscript, 1967.

Seligman, B. "The Problem of Incest and Exogamy: A Restatement." *American Anthropologist*, July-September 1950.

Senaeve, P. *Incest in Belgian Criminal Law*. Katholieke University, Leuven, Belgium: Institute voor Familierecht, 1978.

Serenson, W., and Grimes, B. "Characteristics of Sex Offenders Admitted to a State Hospital for Pre-Sentence Psychiatric Investigation." *Psychiatric Quarterly*, 1958.

Sexual Assault Center, Harborview Medical Center. *Interviewing Child Victims: Guidelines for Criminal Justice System Personnel*. Seattle WA: Sexual Assault Center, Harborview Medical Center, May 1978.

"Sexual Molestation of Children—The Last Frontier in Child Abuse." *Children Today*, May-June 1975.

"The Sexually Exploited Child." *Southern Medical Journal* **69** (1976).

Sgroi, S.M. "Child Sexual Assault: Some Guidelines for Intervention and Assessment." In Burgess, A.W., et al., *Sexual Assault of Children and Adolescents.* Lexington MA: Lexington, 1978.

————. "Comprehensive Examination for Child Sexual Assault: Diagnostic, Therapeutic, and Child Protection Issues." In Burgess, A.W., et al., *Sexual Assault of Children and Adolescents.* Lexington MA: Lexington, 1978.

————. "Family Treatment of Child Sexual Abuse." In Conte, J., and Shore, D., eds., "Social Work and Child Sexual Abuse." *Journal of Social Work and Human Sexuality,* January-February 1982.

————. *Handbook of Clinical Interventions in Child Sexual Abuse.* Lexington MA: Lexington, 1982.

————. "The Sexual Assault of Children." In Community Council of Greater New York, ed., *Sexual Abuse of Children.* New York: The Council, 1979.

————. "Treatment Approaches for Victims of Child Sexual Abuse." *A Commitment to Children: Strengthening Families, Communities and Services.* Conference Proceedings, Sixth National Conference on Child Abuse and Neglect. Baltimore MD, September 25–28, 1983.

Sgroi, S.M., and Dana, N.T. "Individual and Group Treatment of Mothers of Incest Victims." In Sgroi, S.M., ed., *Handbook of Clinical Intervention in Child Sexual Abuse.* Lexington MA: Lexington, 1982.

Shaman, E.J. "Prevention Programs for Children with Disabilities." In Nelson, M., and Clark, K., eds., *The Educator's Guide to Preventing Child Sexual Abuse.* Santa Cruz CA: Network, 1986. Curriculum developed by the Seattle (WA) Disabilities Project. Designed to increase the child's self-esteem as well as to educate in appropriate preventive behavior.

Shapiro, D. *Parents and Protectors: A Study in Child Abuse and Neglect.* Research Center, Child Welfare League of America, 1979.

Sharron, H. "Angie's Story." *Social Work Today,* February 15, 1983. Case history of a victim of child abuse (now an adult). "Angie" describes how attitudes about parent's rights allowed social workers to return her and her six siblings to their home, and their parents' abuse, over and over again. "Angie" believes social workers should have more, not less, power to remove threatened children.

Shelton, W. "A Study of Incest." *Offender Therapy and Comparative Criminology* **19**, 1975.

Shengold, L. "Child Abuse and Deprivation: Soul Murder." *Journal of American Psychoanalytic Association,* 1979.

————. "The Parent as a Sphinx." *Journal of American Psychoanalytic Association,* 1963.

Shepher, J. "Mate Selection Among Second Generation Kibbutz Adolescents and Adults—Incest Avoidance and Negative Imprinting." *Archives of Sexual Behavior* **1**, 1971.

Sholevar, G. "A Family Therapist Looks at Incest." *Bulletin of the American Academy of Psychiatry and Law,* 1975.

Shoor, M.; Speed, M.H.; and Bartlet, C. "Syndrome of the Adolescent Child Molester." *American Journal of Psychiatry* **122**, 1962.

Shore, D.A. "Sexual Abuse and Sexual Education in Child-Caring Institutions." Joint Commission on Accreditation of Hospitals, Chicago. *Journal of Social Work and Human Sexuality,* 1982.

Showers, J., et al. "The Sexual Victimization of Boys: A Three Year Survey." *Health Values: Achieving High Level Wellness* **7**, July-August 1983.

Siegel, K. *Group Treatment for Adolescent Girls in Incestuous Families.* Pungo Medical Center, Virginia Beach. American Psychological Association 88th Annual Convention, Montreal, Quebec, September 1–5, 1980.

Sifneos, P. *Short-Term Psychotherapy and Emotional Crisis.* Cambridge MA: Harvard University Press, 1972.

Silber, T.J. "Clinical Spectrum of Pharyngeal Gonorrhea in Children and Adolescents: A Report of Sixteen Patients." Children's Hospital National Medical Center, Washington DC, Adolescent Medicine Outpatient Department. *Journal of Adolescent Health Care,* March 1983.

Silbert, M.H.; Pines, A.M.; and Lynch, T. "Substance Abuse and Prostitution." *Journal of Psychoactive Drugs* 14, July-September 1982.

Silver, Steven. "Setting Treatment Priorities for the Sexual Offender." *Sexual Violence Quarterly,* Spring 1985.

Simmel, G. "Secrecy." In Wolff, ed., *The Sociology of George Simmel.* New York: Free Press, 1964.

Simmons, James E.; Richter, Arthur; and Moore, Gregory W. "The Teenage Exhibitionist and Voyeur." *Medical Aspects of Human Sexuality* 16, 1982.

Slater, M. "Encological Factors in the Origin of Incest." *American Anthropologist,* 1959.

Sloan, I. *Child Abuse: Governing Law and Legislation.* Dobbs Ferry NY: Oceana, 1983.

Sloane, P., and Karpinski, E. "The Effects of Incest on the Participants." *American Journal of Orthopsychiatry* 12, 1942.

Sloane, P., and Zapharis, A.G. "Dynamics of Incestuous Families." *Response to Intra-Family Crime and Sexual Assault,* 1976.

Smidt, H.J. *Geschiedenis van het Wetboell van Strafrecht.* 1891.

Smith, L. *Juveniles in Prostitution: Fact Versus Fiction.* R & E, 1984.

*Smith, T. *You Don't Have to Molest That Child.* Chicago: National Committee for the Prevention of Child Abuse. This booklet speaks directly to the offender or potential offender, with advice on how to break out of the cycle of molestation. Includes a section for family and friends of offenders with suggestions for encouraging an offender to seek help.

Smith, Timothy M., ed. "Developing a Theoretical Framework for Evaluating Offenders." *Sexual Violence Quarterly,* Spring 1985.

Solhiem, Joan Senzek, with Johnson, Ernest L. *When a Child Needs You: Emergency Intervention for the Law Enforcement Officer.* 1983.

Sommerville, C. "English Puritans and Children: A Social-Cultural Explanation." *Journal of Psychohistory* 6, 1978.

Soothill, K.L., and Gibbens, T.N.C. "Recidivism of Sexual Offenders: A Re-Appraisal." *British Journal of Criminology,* July 1978.

Sorrenti-Little, Llisa; Bagley, Christopher; and Robertson, Sharon. "An Operational Definition of the Long-Term Harmfulness of Sexual Relations with Peers and Adults by Young Children." *Canadian Children* 9, 1984.

Spainer, G. *Sexual Socialization and Premarital Sexual Behavior.* Doctoral Dissertation, Northwestern University (Dissertation Abstracts International, 1979, University Microfilms—No. 73-30, 729), 1973.

Spaulding, W. *Interviewing Child Victims of Sexual Exploitation.* Washington DC: National Center for Missing and Exploited Children, 1987.

*Spelman, C. *Talking About Child Sexual Abuse.* Chicago: National Committee for Prevention of Child Abuse, 1985. Pamphlet for parents and for adults abused as children. Question-and-answer format gives basic information. Includes advice for talking to children about abuse, for evaluating caregivers, and for recognizing symptoms of abuse.

Spencer, J. "Father-Daughter Incest: A Clinical View from the Corrections Field." *Child Welfare* **57**, November 1978.

_____. *Father-Daughter Incest: Clinical View from the Corrections Field.* Cleveland OH: Case Western Reserve University, School of Applied Social Sciences, November 1978.

*Spiegel, L. *A Question of Innocence: A True Story of False Accusation.* Parsippany NJ: Unicorn, 1986.

Spivak, B. *Incest Histories Among Alcoholic Women.* Paper presented at the Michigan Alcohol and Addiction Association Conference, Bellaire MI, October 14, 1980.

Spring, D. "Symbolic Language of Sexually Abused, Chemically Dependent Women." Ventura (CA) Health Care Services. *American Journal of Art Therapy,* August 1985.

Squires, Sally. "Who Would Sexually Abuse a Child?" In *Washington Post Health,* June 18, 1986.

Stall, S. *What a Young Boy Ought to Know.* Philadelphia: Virginia, 1897.

*STAR Program and Family Outreach. *Stay Happy and Safe/Sé Feliz Seguro.* San Antonio TX: Family Outreach of San Antonio, 1985. Spanish-English coloring book. Parents can use it to discuss personal safety and sexual abuse prevention with their children.

Steele, B. *Abuse and Neglect in the Earliest Years: Groupwork for Vulnerability.* Denver: National Center for Prevention and Treatment of Child Abuse and Neglect.

_____. "The Effect of Abuse and Neglect on Psychological Development." In Call, J.; Galenson, E.; and Tyson, R., eds., *Frontiers of Infant Psychiatry.* New York: Basic, 1983.

_____. *Notes on the Lasting Effects of Early Child Abuse Throughout the Life Cycle.* Paper presented at the Kempe National Center's 14th Annual Symposium on Child Abuse and Neglect, Keystone CO, May 1985.

_____. "Notes on the Lasting Effects of Early Child Abuse Throughout the Life Cycle." *Child Abuse and Neglect* **10**, 1986.

_____. "Psychodynamic Factors in Child Abuse." In Kempe, C., and Holfer, B., eds., *Battered Child.* 3rd edition. Chicago: University of Chicago Press, 1980.

Steele, B.F., and Alexander, H. "Long-Term Effects of Sexual Abuse in Childhood." In Mrazek, P.B., and Kempe, C.H., *Sexually Abused Children and Their Families.* New York: Pergamon, 1981.

Steinbacher, John A. *Child Seducers.* Educator, 1971.

Steinem, Gloria. "Pornography—Not Sex but the Obscene Use of Pornography." *MS* Magazine, August 1977.

Steinmetz, S., and Straus, M., eds. *Violence in the Family.* New York: Harper and Row, 1974.

Stekel, Wilhelm. *Psychosexueller Infantilismus.* 1922.

Stember, C.J. *Art Therapy: A New Use in the Diagnosis and Treatment of Sexually Abused Children.* Garden City NY: Adelphi University, November 1980.

_____. "Art Therapy: A New Use in the Diagnosis and Treatment of Sexually Abused Children." In Jones, Jenstrom and MacFarlane, eds., *Sexual Abuse of Children: Selected Readings.* Washington DC: National Center on Child Abuse and Neglect, November 1980.

Stern, M., and Meyer, L. *Father-Daughter Incest: Family and Couple Interactional Patterns.* Philadelphia: Center for Rape Concern, February 1980.

Stevens, D., and Berliner, L. "Harborview Social Workers Advocate Special Techniques for Child Witness." *Response* 1, December 1976.

Stickrod, Alison; Hamer, Jim; and Janes, Bruce. *Informational Guide on the Juvenile Sex Offender: Three Oregon Program Descriptions and Workbook.* Hillsboro: Oregon Adolescent Sex Offender Treatment Network (1221 N.E. 51st St., #105, 97123), 1984.

Stinnott, N., and Walters, J. *Relationship in Marriage and Family.* New York: Macmillan, 1977.

Stoenner, H. *Plain Talk About Child Abuse.* Denver: American Humane Association, January 1973.

Stoller, R. *Perversion: The Erotic Form of Hatred.* New York: Pantheon, 1975.

Stone, A. "The Legal Implications of Sexual Activity Between Psychiatrist and Patient." *American Journal of Psychiatry* 133, 1976.

Stone, M.E. "New Myths About Child Sexual Abuse." In Nelson, M., and Clark, K., eds., *The Educator's Guide to Preventing Child Sexual Abuse.* Santa Cruz CA: Network, 1986. Refutes the recent idea that sexual abuse prevention education causes fabricated reports, fear of touch and closeness, suspicion. Discusses how such "new myths" demonstrate that sexual abuse is still a problem in our culture.

Stovall, B. *Child Sexual Abuse: Prevention and Treatment.* Continuing Education Manual. Ypsilanti: Eastern Michigan University, Department of Social Work. Supported by Administration for Children, Youth and Families (DHHS), Washington DC. Undated.

Stovall, B.M., and Williams, L.L. *Facing Up to the Sexual Abuse of Children.* Children's Aid Society, Detroit MI, Special Family Problems Services (Incest), 1977.

*Stowell, Joe, and Dietzel, Mary. *My Very Own Book About Me.* Spokane WA: Rape Crisis Resource Library, Lutheran Social Services of Washington (N. 1226 Howard, 99201), 1982. Coloring book covering the concepts of kids' rights, being aware of feelings, comfortable and uncomfortable touches, how to get help for abuse, other useful information. Several types of sexual abuse are described, including both boys and girls as victims and family and non-family members as offenders. Appropriate for ages 4–10. Parents' guide, teachers' guide, therapists' guide also available.

Straus, M.; Galles, R.; and Steinmetz, S. *Behind Closed Doors: Violence in the American Family.* Garden City NY: Doubleday, 1979.

Strong, B. "Toward a History of the Experiential Family: Sex and Incest in the 19th Century Family." *Journal of Marriage and the Family* 36, 1973.

Stuart, J., and Allen, L. *Incest: "You Too?!"* Long Beach CA: Sexual Abuse Anonymous, 1984.

Stucker, J. *I Tried to Fantasize That All Fathers Had Intercourse with Their Daughters.* *MS* Magazine, April 1977.

Sturkie, K. "Structured Group Treatment for Sexually Abused Children." Arkansas University, Little Rock, Graduate School of Social Work. *Health and Social Work,* 1983.

Summary of the Final Report of the Attorney General's Commission on Pornography. National Coalition Against Pornography (800 Compton Rd., Suite 9248, Cincinnati OH 45231), July 1986.

Summit, R. *Causes, Consequences, Treatment, and Prevention of Sexual Assault Against Children.* Los Angeles: University of California, School of Medicine, 1985.

_____. "The Child Sexual Abuse Accommodation Syndrome." *Child Abuse and Neglect* 7, 1983.

_____. "Father-Daughter Incest." *American Journal of Orthopsychiatry,* 1982.

_____. "Sexual Abuse: A Frustration of Love." *Frontiers, the Parents Anonymous Newsletter,* Mid-Summer 1975.

_____. *Sexual Child Abuse, the Psychotherapist, and the Team Concept.* In *Dealing with Sexual Child Abuse.* Chicago: National Committee for Prevention of Child Abuse, 1978.

Summit, R., and Kryso, J. "Sexual Abuse of Children: A Clinical Spectrum." *American Journal of Orthopsychiatry* **48,** 1978.

Swan, H.L.; Press, A.N.; and Briggs, S.L. "Child Sexual Abuse Prevention: Does It Work?" Children's Institute of Kansas. *Child Welfare* **64,** July-August 1985. Evaluation of a prevention program for children. Tested children's knowledge before and after the program and recorded the reactions of children, parents, and professionals to the program.

Swan, R.W. "The Child as Active Participant in Sexual Abuse." Tulane University, New Orleans LA, School of Social Work. *Clinical Social Work Journal,* Spring 1985.

Swanson, D. "Adult Sexual Abuse of Children." *Diseases of the Nervous System* **29,** 1968.

Swanson, L., and Biaggio, M.K. "Therapeutic Perspectives on Father-Daughter Incest." Washington State University, Pullman, Department of Psychology. *American Journal of Psychiatry,* June 1985.

*Sweet, P.E. *Something Happened to Me.* Racine WI: Mother Courage, 1981. A book for abused children, stressing the rewards for talking about abuse to a trusted and caring adult.

Swift, C. "Sexual Victimization of Children: An Urban Mental Health Center Survey." *Victimology* **2,** 1977.

_____. "The Prevention of Sexual Child Abuse: Focus on the Perpetrator." Wyandot Mental Health Center, Kansas City KS. *Journal of Clinical Child Psychology,* 1979. Examines two hypotheses about the development of molestation behavior in males: (1) that many males who sexually abuse children were themselves abused in childhood, and (2) that many such abusers are sexually ignorant and socially immature. This article shows how evidence supports these hypotheses and offers recommendations for prevention in accordance with this finding.

Swigert, V., et al. "Sexual Homicide: Social, Psychological, and Legal Aspects." *Archives of Sexual Behavior* **5,** 1976.

Szabo, D. "Problems of Socialization and Sociocultural Integration: A Contribution to the Etiology of Incest." *Canadian Psychiatric Association Journal,* 1962.

Taylor, B. "Motives for Guilt-Free Pederasty: Some Literary Considerations." *The Sociological Review* **24,** 1976.

_____, ed. *Perspectives on Pedophilia.* London: Batsford Academic and Educational, 1981.

Taylor, B.J., and Wagner, N. "Sex Between Therapists and Clients." *Professional Psychology* **7,** 1976.

Taylor, Leslie, and Maurer, Adah. *Think Twice: The Medical Effects of Physical Punishment.* 1985.

Taylor, P. "Denied the Power to Choose the Good: Sexuality and Mental Defect in American Medical Practice, 1850–1920." *Journal of Social History* **10,** 1977.

Taylor, R.L. "Marital Therapy in the Treatment of Incest." *Social Casework,* April 1984.

Teer, L.C. "Chowchilla Re-Visited: The Effects of Psychic Trauma Four Years After a

School Bus Kidnapping." *American Journal of Psychiatry,* 1983. Reprinted in Chess, S., and Thomas, A., eds., *Annual Progress in Child Psychiatry and Child Development.* New York: Brunner/Mazel, 1984.

————. "Play Therapy and Psychic Trauma: A Preliminary Report." In Schaefer, C., and O'Connor, K., eds., *Handbook of Play Therapy.* New York: Wiley, 1983.

*Terkel, S.N., and Rench, J.E. *Feeling Safe, Feeling Strong: How to Avoid Sexual Abuse and What to Do If It Happens to You.* Minneapolis: Lerner, 1984. Book for children on personal safety and personal rights. Includes six first-person stories about different kinds of sexual abuse. Each story is followed by information on the type of abuse and how to avoid it.

Terrell, M. "Identifying the Sexually Abused Child in a Medical Setting." *Health and Social Work,* November 1977.

Third International Congress on Child Abuse and Neglect. *Sexual Abuse: A Sociological Perspective.* Paper presented in Amsterdam, 1981.

Thomas, J. "Yes, You Can Help a Sexually Abused Child." *RN* **43,** 1980.

Thomas, J.N. "Juvenile Sex Offenders: Physician and Parent Communication." *Pediatric Annals* **11,** 1982.

Thomas, J.W., and Rogers, C.M. *A Treatment Program for Intrafamily Juvenile Sex Offenders.* Washington DC: Children's Hospital, Child Protection Center, 1983.

————, and ————. "A Treatment Program for Intrafamily Juvenile Sexual Offenders." In Greer, J.G., and Stewart, I.R., eds., *The Sexual Aggressor.* New York: Van Nostrand Reinhold, 1983.

Thompson, G., and Whann, W. "The Step-Daughter Paraphilia Neurosis." *Journal of Forensic Sciences,* 1957.

*Thorman, G. *Incestuous Families.* Springfield IL: Thomas, 1983.

Tiernan, S. *Sometimes Pretending Doesn't Help: An Honest Talk About Sexual Abuse.* Supported by National Center on Child Abuse and Neglect (DHHS), Washington DC. Undated.

Tilelli, J., et al. "Sexual Abuse of Children." *New England Journal of Medicine* **302,** 1980.

Tindall, R.H. "The Male Adolescent Involved with a Pederast Becomes an Adult." *Journal of Homosexuality* **3,** 1978.

Tissot, DeLonanisme. *Dissertation sur les maladies produites par la masturbation.* 1758.

*Tobin, P.; Levinson, S.; Russell, T.; and Valdez, M. *Children's Self-Help Project: A Manual for Presenters.* San Francisco: Children's Self-Help Project, 1983. Background information on child sexual abuse with emphasis on the dynamics and effects of sexual abuse and incest on the victim. How-to instruction for school personnel and parent workshops.

Tompkins, J. "Penis Envy and Incest: A Case Report." *Psychoanalytic Review* **27,** 1940.

Topper, A.B. "Options in 'Big Brother's' Involvement with Incest." Denver University. *Child Abuse and Neglect,* 1979.

Tormas, Y. *Child Victims of Incest.* Denver: American Humane Association, Children's Division, 1977.

*Towser, C.C. *Child Abuse and Neglect: A Teacher's Handbook for Detection, Reporting, and Classroom Management.* Washington DC: National Education Association, 1984.

*————, ed. *Questions Teachers Ask About Legal Aspects of Reporting Child Abuse and Neglect.* National Education Association, Chicago. Santa Cruz CA: Network, 1984.

*Towser, C.C., and McCauley, S.R. *What Parents Should Know About Child Abuse.* West Haven CT: National Education Association of the U.S.A., 1984. Informational brochure defines child sexual abuse; outlines situations that can lead to abuse; suggests information for parents to convey to their children; and outlines steps for parents to follow should abuse occur.

*Townley, R. *Safe and Sound: A Parent's Guide to Child Protection.* New York: Simon and Schuster, 1985.

Truesdell, D.L.; McNeil, J.S.; and Descher, J.P. "Incidence of Wife Abuse in Incestuous Families." Dallas County Child Welfare, Dallas TX. *Social Work,* March-April 1986.

Tsai, M., et al. "Childhood Molestation: Variables Related to Differential Impacts on Psychosexual Functioning in Adult Women." *Journal of Abnormal Psychology* 88, 1979.

Tsai, M., and Wagner, N. "Therapy Groups for Women Sexually Molested as Children." *Archives of Sexual Behavior* 7, 1978.

Tsang, Daniel, ed. *The Age Taboo.* Boston: Alyson, 1981.

Tuchman, B. *A Distant Mirror.* New York: Ballantine, 1978.

Tufts New England Medical Center. *Sexually Exploited Children: Service and Research Project.* Final Report of the Division of Child Psychiatry, Boston MA, to the Office of Juvenile Justice and Delinquency Prevention, Washington DC, March 1984.

Turecki, S. "Elective Brief Psychotherapy with Children." Beth Israel Medical Center, New York, Psychiatry Department. *American Journal of Psychotherapy,* October 1982.

*Turkel, D.; Cohen, G.M.; Macdonald, C.; Pearson, B.F.; and Trager, A. *Good Touches/Bad Touches: A Child Sexual Abuse Prevention Program for Fourth, Fifth and Sixth Graders.* White Plains NY: Mental Health Association of Westchester County, 1984. Program manual for teachers of grades 4-6. Includes objectives, facts about abuse, summary of relevant New York and Westchester County laws, discussion of teaching procedures, teacher's script for classroom discussion of two related films, student questionnaire, list of helping agencies.

Turner, G. "The Daughters of the Poor." *McClure's* Magazine 34, 1909.

Tyler, A.H., and Brassard, M.R. "Abuse in the Investigation and Treatment of Intrafamilial Child Sexual Abuse." Family Support Center, Salt Lake City UT. *Child Abuse and Neglect,* 1984.

Ungaretti, J. "Pederasty, Heroism and the Family in Classical Greece." *Journal of Homosexuality* 3, 1978.

_____. Committee on the Judiciary. Subcommittee on Juvenile Justice. *A Hearing to Consider the Effects of Pornography on Children and Women.* September 12, 1984.

U.S. Congress. House. Committee on Ways and Means. Subcommittee on Oversight. *Child Abuse and Day Care.* September 17, 1984.

U.S. Congress. Senate. Committee on Governmental Affairs. Permanent Subcommittee on Investigation. *Testimony Before the Subcommittee,* November 29, 1984.

U.S. Department of Education. *Child Abuse in the Classroom: Excerpts from Official Transcript of Proceedings Before the U.S. Department of Education in the Matter of Proposed Regulations to Implement ... the Hatch Amendment.* 2nd edition. Pere Marquette, 1984.

*U.S. Department of Health and Human Services. *Child Sexual Abuse Prevention: Tips to Parents.* Supported by National Center on Child Abuse and Neglect, Washington DC.

_____. *Preventing Sexual Abuse in Day Care Programs. National Program Inspec-

tion. Region X, Office of Inspector General, January 1985. Results of a national inspection undertaken by DHHS, involving interviews with 300 persons in 49 states. Those interviewed unanimously agreed that education is the most effective tool in preventing abuse.

U.S. Department of Justice. *Assisting Child Victims of Sexual Abuse: The Sexual Assault Center, Seattle Washington.* The Child Protection Center—Special Unit. Washington DC: National Institute of Justice, July 1981.

_____. *Attorney General's Task Force on Family Violence: Final Report.* Washington DC: Office of the Attorney General, September 1984.

_____. *How to Protect Yourself Against Sexual Assault: Take a Bite Out of Crime.* Washington DC: Office of Justice Assistance, Research, and Statistics, 1979.

_____. *Protecting Our Children: The Fight Against Molestation. A Resource Handbook.* Washington DC. Materials from a national symposium on child molestation (held October 1–October 14, 1984). Includes discussion of incidence, offender characteristics, effects of abuse on victim, and medicolegal aspects. Also covered are sex rings, child pornography, and the difficulties of prosecuting cases with child witnesses.

U.S. Federal Bureau of Investigation. "Sexual Trauma Team: The Norfolk Experience." Norfolk VA. *FBI Law Enforcement Bulletin,* February 1984.

University of Wisconsin Law School. *Punish the Offender, Protect the Victim, Treat the Family: A Guide for Communities Interested in Breaking the Cycle of Child Sexual Abuse.* Madison: 1986.

University YWCA Rape Relief, Seattle WA. *A Curriculum for Developing an Awareness of Sexual Exploitation and Teaching Self-Protection Techniques. Level I.* Seattle WA: Comprehensive Health Education Foundation, 1979.

Urban and Rural Systems Associates. *Clinical Demonstration Programs of the Treatment of Child Abuse and Neglect.* Semi-Annual Report, October 1, 1979–March 31, 1980. San Francisco CA: National Center on Child Abuse and Neglect, June 10, 1980.

Urzi, M. *Cooperative Approaches to Child Protection: A Community Guide.* St. Paul: Minnesota Department of Public Welfare.

Vachss, Andrew. *Strega.* New York: Signet, 1987.

van den Berg, J.H. *Metabletica.* 1956.

van der Kwast, S. *Seksuele Criminoliteit.* 1968.

VanDeventer, A.D., and Laws, D.R. "Orgasmic Reconditioning to Re-Direct Sexual Arousal in Pedophiles." *Behavior Therapy* **9,** 1978.

Van Gigseghem, H. "Father-Daughter Incest." *Vie Medicale au Canada Francaise,* March 1975.

Van Stolk, M. *The Sexually Abused Child.* Paper presented at the Meeting of the Second World Conference of the International Society on Family Law, Montreal, June 1977.

van Ussel, J.M.W. *Geschiedenis van het Seksuele Probleem.* 1968.

Veltkamp, L.J.; Alexander, P.J.; and Lankster, F. *The Identification, Assessment, and Treatment of Abused and Neglected Children, Adolescents, and Their Families: A Manual.* Lexington KY: University of Kentucky, Department of Psychiatry, 1982.

Verdun-Jones, Simon H., and Keltner, Alfred A. *Sexual Aggression and the Law.* Selected papers from a seminar on Sexual Aggression and the Law, Vancouver, Canada, 1981.

Virkkunen, M. "The Child As Participating Victim." Helsinski, Finland, University Central Hospital. *Psychiatric Clinic,* 1981. Discussion of the child's role in initiating and maintaining an abusive situation. Stresses that in incest, all family members have a role in precipitating the situation, and that investigation of family interactions (particularly the behavior of the mother) can prevent such crimes.

_____. "Incest Offences and Alcoholism." *Medicine, Science and the Law* 14, April 1974.

_____. "Incest Offences in Copenhagen — A Medico-Legal Study." *Forensic Science,* 1972.

Vischer, E., and Vischer, J. *Step-Families: A Guide to Working with Stepparents and Stepchildren.* New York: Brunner/Mazel, 1979.

Vitaliano, P.P.; James, J.; and Boyer, D. "Sexuality of Deviant Females: Adolescent and Adult Correlates." Seattle: University of Washington, Department of Psychiatry and Behavioral Sciences, November 1981.

*Vogel, Carole, and Goldner, Kathryn. *The Dangers of Strangers.* Minneapolis: Dillon, 1983. Preschool and primary grade level children are taught how to deal with advances made by strangers and how to avoid situations in which they might be harmed by a stranger. Excellent illustrations by Lynette Schmidt.

VOICE, Inc. *How to Organize Your Survivor Group.* Grand Junction CO: Undated.

Wachtel, A., and Lawton-Speert, S. *Child Sexual Abuse: Descriptions of Nine Program Approaches to Treatment.* United Way of Lower Mainland, Vancouver (British Columbia), Child Sexual Abuse Project. September 1983.

*Wachter, Oralee. *No More Secrets for Me.* Boston: Little, Brown, 1983. Includes four stories about children facing situations involving potential abuse, including babysitter, camp counselor, video parlor patron and stepfather. In each story the child models avoidance and telling someone. Appropriate for elementary age children.

Waggoner, R.W. "Juvenile Aberrant Sexual Behavior." *American Journal of Orthopsychiatry* 11, 1941.

Wakcher, B. *Child Abuse: Is It Happening to You?* Canoga Park CA: Teknek, 1984. Designed to help find the abused child in our society. Basic facts about child abuse are discussed with specific examples, e.g. tell a trusted adult when you are touched on your private parts; when someone takes pictures of you; if you are locked in a closet or beaten; left alone in a house or car; hungry; etc.

Walters, D.R. *Physical and Sexual Abuse of Children: Causes and Treatment.* Indiana University, Bloomington, Department of Forensic Studies. Bloomington: Indiana University Press, 1975.

Walters, R. *Child Pornography.* New Mexico State University, Las Cruces NM, January 1986. Includes description of offenders, victims, and types of child pornography; types of collectors; effects on child participants; history of laws against child pornography; and recommendations for prevention.

Ward, E. *Father-Daughter Rape.* New York: Grove, 1985.

Warner, C. *Rape and Sexual Assault.* Germantown MD: Aspen, 1980.

Washington State Department of Social and Health Services. *Child Sexual Abuse.* Olympia WA: Undated.

Watts, D. *Psychological Interventions in Cases of Incest: Treatment Issues.* Indiana University, Terre Haute, 1978.

Weber, E. "Incest — Sexual Abuse Begins at Home." *MS* Magazine, April 1977.

Weeks, R. "Counseling Parents of Sexually Abused Children." *Medical Aspects of Human Sexuality,* August 1976.

Weich, M. "The Terms 'Mother' and 'Father' as a Defense Against Incest." *Journal of the American Psychoanalytic Association* 16, 1968.

Weinberg, S. *Incest Behavior.* New York: Citadel, 1955.

Weiner, I.B. "A Clinical Perspective on Incest." Case Western Reserve University, Cleveland OH. *American Journal of Diseases of Children,* February 1978.
_____. "Father-Daughter Incest: A Clinical Report." *Psychiatric Quarterly* **36**, 1962.
_____. "On Incest: A Survey." *Excerpta Criminologia* 4, 1964.
Weisberg, D. Kelly. *Children of the Night.* Lexington MA: Lexington, 1985.
Weiss, J.; Rogers, E.; Darwin, M.; and Dutton, C. "A Study of Girl Sex Victims." *Psychiatric Quarterly* **29**, 1955.
Weitzel, W.D.; Powell, B.J.; and Penick, E.C. "Clinical Management of Father-Daughter Incest: A Critical Re-Examination." *American Journal of Diseases of Children,* February 1978.
*Wells, H. *The Sensuous Child: Your Child's Birthright to Healthy Sexual Development. (A Guideline for Parents).* New York: Scarborough, Stein and Day, 1976.
Wells, L.A. "Family Pathology and Father-Daughter Incest: Restricted Psychopathy." Mayo Clinic, Rochester MN. *Journal of Clinical Psychiatry,* May 1981.
West, D.J. *Homosexuality.* Pelican, 1960.
_____. *Homosexuality Re-Examined.* 1977.
Westermarck, E. *The History of Human Marriage.* New York: Allerton, 1889, 1922.
WGBH Educational Foundation. *Men Who Molest.* Boston (125 Western Avenue, 02134): 1985.
Whalley, L.J., and McGuire, R.J. "Measuring Sexual Attitudes." *Acta Psychiatric Scand.* **58**, 1978.
Whitcomb, D. "Assisting Child Victims in the Courts: The Practical Side of Legislative Reform." In *Papers from a National Policy Conference on Legal Reforms in Child Sexual Abuse Cases.* Washington DC: National Legal Resource Center on Child Advocacy and Protection, 1985.
_____. *Assisting Child Victims of Sexual Abuse: How Two Communities Developed Programs for the Special Needs of Child Victims.* Rockville MD: Aspen Systems, 1982.
_____. *Exemplary Projects: Assisting Child Victims of Sexual Assault.* The S/A Center, Seattle WA, Special Unit. Washington DC: U.S. Department of Justice, Office of Development, Testing and Dissemination, 1982.
_____. *Prosecution of Child Sexual Abuse: Innovation in Practice.* Testimony before the Sub-Committee on Children, Family, Drugs, and Alcoholism. Committee on Labor and Human Services, U.S. Senate, May 2, 1985.
White, L. "The Definition and Prohibition of Incest." *American Anthropologist,* July-September 1948.
_____. *The Evolution of Culture.* New York: McGraw-Hill, 1959.
*White, Laurie, and Spencer, Steven. *Take Care with Yourself: A Young Person's Guide to Understanding, Preventing, and Healing from the Hurts of Child Abuse.* Michigan: DayStar, 1983. Explains basic concepts of sexual abuse prevention. Emphasizes that sexual abuse is never the fault of the victim.
Wilbur, C.B. *The Effects of Child Abuse on the Psyche.* Paper presented at Symposium on Childhood Antecedents of Multiple Personalities, May 7, 1984.
Williams, G.J., and Money, J. *Traumatic Abuse and Neglect of Children at Home.* Baltimore MD: Johns Hopkins University Press, 1980.
Williams, J. "The Neglect of Incest—A Criminologist's View." *Medicine, Science, and Law,* January 1974.
Willock, Brent. "Play Therapy with the Aggressive Acting-Out Child." In Schaefer, C., and O'Connor, K., eds., *Handbook of Play Therapy.* New York: Wiley, 1983.
Wilson, C. *Origins of the Sexual Impulse.* Arthur Barkur, 1963.

Wilson, J. "Violence, Pornography and Social Science." *The Public Interest,* Winter 1971.

Winberg. *Incest Behavior.*

Wolf, A. "Adopt a Daughter-in-Law, Marry a Sister: A Chinese Solution to the Problems of the Incest Taboo." *American Anthropologist,* 1968.

————. "Childhood Association and Sexual Attraction: A Further Test of the Westermarck Hypothesis." *American Anthropologist,* 1970.

Wolf, Steven C.; Conte, Jon; and Engle-Menig, Mary. "Community Treatment of Adults Who Have Sex with Children." In Walker, Lenore E.A., ed., *Handbook on Sexual Abuse of Children: Assessment and Treatment Issues.* New York: Springer.

Wolfe, D.A.; MacPherson, T.; Blount, R.; and Wolfe, V.V. "Evaluation of a Brief Intervention for Educating School Children in Awareness of Physical and Sexual Abuse." *Child Abuse and Neglect* **10,** 1986.

————; ————; ————; and ————. *Evaluation of a Brief Intervention for Educating School Children in Awareness of Physical and Sexual Abuse.* London, Canada: University of Western Ontario, 1986.

*Wooden, Kenneth. *Child Lures: A Guide for the Prevention of Molestation and Abduction.* Shelburne VT: Wooden, 1984. Guide for parents and teachers. Emphasizes importance of personal body privacy, saying "no," and reporting uncomfortable situations to trusted adults. Outlines strategies used by abductors and molesters and how child can resist each strategy. Includes quiz on "lures."

————. "How Sex Offenders Lure Our Children." *Reader's Digest,* June 1988.

Woodling, Bruce A., and Kossoris, Peter D. "Sexual Misuse: Rape, Molestation and Incest." *Pediatric Clinics of North America,* May 1981.

*Wrage, K. *Children: Choice Or Chance.* Philadelphia: Fortress, 1969.

Yaffe, M. *The Assessment and Treatment of Paedophilia.* London: Guys Hospital Medical School, York Clinic, 1981.

————. "The Assessment and Treatment of Paedophilia." In Taylor, B., ed., *Perspectives on Paedophilia.* London: Batsford Academic and Educational, 1981.

Yates. A. *Sex Without Shame: Encouraging the Child's Healthy Sexual Development.* New York: Morrow, 1978.

Yates, A., and Beutler, L.E. "Drawings by Child Victims of Incest." University of Arizona, Tucson, Department of Psychiatry. *Child Abuse and Neglect,* 1985.

Yeary, J. "Incest and Chemical Dependency." *Journal of Psychoactive Drugs,* January-June 1982.

*YMCA Domestic Violence/Sexual Assault Service. *You Belong to You: A Coloring Book.* (310 East Third St., Flint MI 48502.) March 1982. Teaches prevention skills and positive identity. Child can color or doodle on pictures to express his feelings, or provide his own drawings.

Yorukoglu, A., and Kemph, J. "Children Not Severely Damaged by Incest with the Parent." *Journal of the American Academy of Child Psychiatry* **5,** 1966.

Yost, D., and Schertz, E. "The Role of Theater in Child Sexual Abuse Prevention." In Nelson, M., and Clark, K., eds., *The Educator's Guide to Preventing Child Sexual Abuse.* Santa Cruz CA: Network, 1986.

Young, J. "Incest." *Playgirl* Magazine, January 1978.

*You're in Charge! South Deerfield MA: Channing L. Bete, 1986. Coloring and activity book teaches children to distinguish between private and nonprivate body areas, good and bad touching.

Zaphiris, A.G. *Assessment and Treatment for Sexually Abused Families.* Workshop presented at the Meeting of the National Conference on Child Abuse and Neglect, April 1978.

_____. "Father-Daughter Incest." In Holder, W., ed., *Sexual Abuse of Children: Implications for Treatment.* Denver: American Humane Association, 1980.

_____. *Father-Daughter Incest: Definitional Parameters of the Relationship and Its Assessment and Treatment Dimensions.* Houston TX: University of Houston, School of Social Work, 1980.

_____. *Incest: The Family with Two Known Victims.* Houston TX: University of Houston, School of Social Work. Englewood CO: American Humane Association, 1978.

_____. *Methods and Skills for a Differential Assessment and Treatment in Incest, Sexual Abuse, and Sexual Exploitation of Children.* University of Houston, Houston TX, School of Social Work. Denver: American Humane Association, 1983.

_____. *Notes from a Child Abuse Conference.* Chico CA: November 10, 1979.

Zefran, J.; Riley, H.F.; Anderson, W.O.; Curtis, J.H.; and Jackson, L.M. "Management and Treatment of Child Sexual Abuse Cases in a Juvenile Court Setting." *Journal of Social Work and Human Sexuality,* 1982.

Zellman, Gail L., et al. *Adolescent Expectations for Dating Relationships.* Paper presented at the Meetings of the American Psychological Association, New York, 1979.

Zellman, Gail L.; Goodchilds, Jacqueline D.; Johnson, Paula B.; and Giarusso, Roseann. *Teenagers' Application of the Label "Rape" to Nonconsensual Sex Between Acquaintances.* Paper presented at the Meeting of the American Psychological Association, 1981.

Zilbach, J., and Grunebaum, M. "Pregenital Components in Incest as Manifested in Two Girls in Activity Group Therapy." *International Journal of Group Psychotherapy,* 1964.

Zuelzer, M.B., and Reposa, R.E. "Mothers in Incestuous Families." Texas University Health Science Center, San Antonio TX, Department of Psychiatry. *International Journal of Family Therapy,* Summer 1983.

Audiovisuals About Child Sexual Abuse

Aware and Not Afraid. Council on Domestic and Sexual Assault, Department of Public Safety, Pouch N, Juneau AK 99811. In this 20-minute 1983 video, five teenagers discuss frightening situations and how they successfully escape them. Available in ¾" and ½" formats.

Better Safe Than Sorry. FilmFair Communications, 10900 Ventura Blvd., Studio City CA 91604, (818) 985-0244. For children age nine to fourteen, this 14½-minute 1978 film presents potential dangers, including sexual abuse, and ways to avoid them. Spanish version also available. Captioned version available in videocassette only, any format.

Better Safe Than Sorry II. FilmFair Communications, 10900 Ventura Blvd., Studio City CA 91604, (818) 985-0244. This 14½-minute 1982 film presents the kindergartner or primary student with three simple rules to follow in preventing or dealing with sexual abuse. Captioned version available in videocassette only, any format.

Better Safe Than Sorry III. FilmFair Communciations, 10900 Ventura Blvd., Studio City CA 91604, (818) 985-0244. Aimed at junior/senior high level, this 1985 film covers sexual abuse, acquaintance rape, incest, personal safety and increasing teenage freedoms. 19 minutes.

Boys Beware. See *Girls Beware.*

Child Molestation: A Crime Against Children. AIMS Instructional Media, Inc., 626 Justin Ave., Glendale CA 91201, (213) 240-9300. This 11-minute film depicts elementary- and secondary-aged children discussing with a social worker their feelings about being molested and what to do if it should happen. 16mm film.

Child Molestation: When to Say No. (16mm/color/13 minutes). AIMS Instructional Media Service, Inc., 625 Justin Ave., Glendale CA 91201. Suggested for children over 8 years of age. Deals directly with sexual abuse.

Child Sexual Abuse: A Solution. James Stanfield and Company, P.O. Box 1983, Santa Monica CA 90406. Six comprehensive filmstrips include: 2 teacher's guides, 1 parent filmstrip, K–1, 2–4, and 5–6 grade levels. Primary grade format includes animal characters and children. Fifth to sixth level shows kids talking to kids. 1985.

Child Sexual Abuse: The Untold Secret. (Videocassette/color/30 minutes.) The University of Calgary, 2500 University Dr., N.W., Calgary Alberta, Canada T2N IN4. This video deals with incest and is recommended for junior or senior high school or community education groups.

Child Sexual Abuse: What Your Children Should Know. Indiana University Audio-Visual Center, Bloomington IN 47405, (812) 335-8087. This five-part series includes programs for adults (90 minutes), K–3 (30 minutes), 4–7 (30 minutes), 7–10 graders, and senior high students. It was shown on public television in September 1984. Videos.

Don't Get Stuck There. Communication Division, Boys Town Center, Boys Town NE 68010. This 14-minute film shows interviews with teenagers who have been victims of physical, sexual or emotional abuse. Good for initiating discussion on symptoms and effects of abuse and the need for getting help.

Double Jeopardy. (16mm/color/40 minutes.) MTI Teleprograms, Inc., 3710 Commercial Ave., Northbrook IL 60062. Focuses on the insensitivity shown sexual abuse victims during uncoordinated investigation. Also shows sensitive and gentle attention.

Girls Beware. (16mm/color/12 minutes.) *Boys Beware.* (16mm/color/14 minutes.) DACOM Communications Media, Inc., 626 Justin Ave., Glendale CA 91201. Both films are designed for adolescents. In one segment of *Boys Beware* the victim is approached by his trusted baseball coach and neighbor. In *Girls Beware* it is suggested that normal adult men are not interested in junior high school–age girls. The film also looks at incest.

Incest: The Hidden Crime. (16mm/color/16 minutes.) The Media Guild, c/o Association Film, 7838 San Fernando Rd., Sun Valley CA 91352. Produced by CBS New Magazine Series. Involves a 12-year-old girl and her father.

Incest: The Victim Nobody Believes. (Video or 16mm/color/21 minutes.) MTI Teleprograms, Inc., 3710 Commercial Ave., Northbrook IL 60062. Three women, all sexually abused as children, discuss their experiences.

Interviewing the Child Abuse Victim. (16mm/color/25 minutes.) MTI Teleprograms, Inc., 3710 Commercial Ave., Northbrook IL 60062. An interview by a social worker of a small boy left home much of the day, and a teacher's sensitive intervention into the life of a sexually abused girl.

It's OK to Say No! Council on Domestic and Sexual Assault, Department of Public Safety, Pouch N, Juneau AK 99811. In this 14½-minute video, four children discuss situations that involved appropriate touching. Available in ¾" and ½" formats. Not presently available.

No More Secrets. (16mm/color/13 minutes.) ODN Productions, Inc., 74 Varick St., Suite 304, New York NY 10013. (212) 431-8923. Suggested for a grade-school audience, this 1982 film shows schoolmates discussing abuse. (Also available in all video formats.)

Sexual Abuse: The Family. (16mm/color/25 minutes.) National Audio-Visual

Center, Order Section, Washington DC 20409. Incest discussed. A role-play example shows potential reactions of the family.

Shatter the Silence. (16mm or Video/color/29 minutes.) S-L Film Productions, P.O. Box 41108, Los Angeles CA 90041. An incest victim deals with anxiety and confusion.

Some Secrets Should Be Told. MTI Teleprograms, Inc., 3710 Commercial Ave., Northbrook IL 60062, 1-800-323-5343. Susan Linn and her puppets help children understand what sexual abuse is and how to get help. Available in 16mm and video. Grades 3–6; 12 minutes. Teacher's Guide included.

Speak Up, Say No. (Filmstrip/color/6 minutes.) Krause House, P.O. Box 880, Oregon City OR 97045. For younger children, ages 3–6. A cartoon format using animals explains child sexual abuse.

A Time for Caring: The School's Response to the Sexually Abused Child. (16mm/color/28 minutes.) Lawren Productions, Inc. c/o G.B. Media, 333 North Flores St., Los Angeles CA 90048. Depicts the role and responsibility of school personnel and shows indicators.

Touch. Illustion Theater, 528 Hennepin Ave., Suite 205, Minneapolis MN 55403, (612) 339-4944. Film adaptation of the theatrical presentation *Touch* for children kindergarten through sixth grade. The film presents a balanced approach to touch and sexual abuse while helping viewers think of appropriate actions to take if touch becomes abusive or exploitive. 16mm; 32 minutes.

W.H.O. (We Help Ourselves). Mental Health Association, 2500 Maple St., Dallas TX 75201-1998, (214) 871-2420. Videos (and written materials) for K–3, 4–6, 7–9 and 10–12th grades covering various potentially dangerous situations. Made for classroom use, to be stopped and discussed periodically.

What Taboo. MTI Teleprograms, Inc., 3710 Commercial Ave., Northbrook IL 60062, 1-800-323-5343. In this 1985, 18-minute film, viewers learn to protect themselves from hurt and danger from bullies, strangers, or people they know.

Who Do You Tell? MTI Teleprograms, Inc., 3710 Commercial Ave., Northbrook IL 60062, 1-800-323-5343. Through animation and live footage, this 11-minute 1981 videocassette or film for grades 1–6 presents suitable responses to problems children may be confronted with such as being lost, being in a fire, or being physically or sexually abused. Complete with leader's guide for discussion questions.

Yes, You Can Say No. Committee for Children. Seattle Institute for Child Advocacy, 172 20th Ave., Seattle WA 98122, (206) 322-5050. This 19-minute VHS or BETA video portrays a boy molested by his uncle. Skillfully addresses blame, telling, and general assertiveness.

Some of the previously mentioned material is also available from the C. Henry Kempe Center, 1205 Oneida St., Denver CO 80220. The Kempe Center has an Audio-Visual Catalog of 99 annotated items on 14 subjects, including sexual abuse, and has an index of suggested audiences, e.g. students, child welfare professionals, medical professionals, day care providers, foster parents, etc.

Index